WILLIAM L. DAWSON

AND THE LIMITS OF

BLACK ELECTORAL

LEADERSHIP

WILLIAM L. DAWSON
AND THE LIMITS OF
BLACK ELECTORAL
LEADERSHIP

Christopher Manning

NORTHERN ILLINOIS UNIVERSITY PRESS • DEKALB

© 2009 by Northern Illinois University Press

Published by the Northern Illinois University Press, DeKalb, Illinois 60115

Manufactured in the United States using postconsumer-recycled, acid-free paper.

All Rights Reserved

Design by Julia Fauci

Library of Congress Cataloging-in-Publication Data

Manning, Christopher.

William L. Dawson and the limits of Black electoral leadership / Christopher Manning.

   p.   cm.

Includes bibliographical references and index.

ISBN 978-0-87580-395-1 (clothbound : alk. paper)

1. Dawson, William L. (William Levi), 1886–1970. 2. African American legislators—Biography. 3. United States. Congress. House—Biography. 4. African Americans—Politics and government—20th century. 5. African American leadership—History—20th century. 6. African Americans—Civil rights—History—20th century. 7. Political parties—United States—History—20th century. 8. United States—Politics and government—1945–1989. 9. African Americans—Illinois—Chicago—Politics and government—20th century. 10. Chicago (Ill.)—Politics and government—20th century. I. Title.

E748.D24M36 2009

328.73092—dc22

[B]   2008049992

Pictures in this book from the Doris Evans Saunders Papers and material from the Ben Burns Papers are courtesy of the Vivian G. Harsh Research Collection of Afro-American History and Literature, Chicago Public Library

FRONTISPIECE—Doris Evans Saunders Papers, folder 208. Photographer: Harris & Ewing.

CONTENTS

Acknowledgments   vii

Introduction   "Don't Get Mad! Get Smart. Vote!"   3

1 "A Greater Understanding of Humanity"   12

2 Big Bill, the Ironmaster, and the Old Roman   50

3 "Second Ward for the Second Warders"   66

4 A New Era in the Political Life of the Nation—*Black America and the National Democratic Coalition, 1944–1952*   92

5 A Dream Deferred—*Party-building from the Late 1940s through the 1950s*   119

6 "Where Is the Invisible Man?"   140

Conclusion   "Times Are Different Now"   160

Appendix—Civil Rights, Resolutions, Remarks and Legislation, and Committee Legislation and Remarks, 1941–1950   169

Notes   171

Bibliography   225

Index   235

ACKNOWLEDGMENTS

The prospect of developing a book seems so far away as to almost exist in some kind of alternate reality when you begin. Yet with perseverance and good luck that day can arrive, and surprisingly you find yourself needing to thank all of the people who helped you along the way. Clearly, my deepest and most profound thanks go to my parents Curtis and Jean Manning. Despite being African American and growing up in Mississippi and Georgia well before the days of the civil rights movement, they secured an education, advanced their careers, traveled the world, and raised a family. As long as I can remember, both repeated the axiom, "If you're going to do something do it right." They have lived their lives by it, and, often to my dismay, they made me live my life by it. They are my heroes, and I simply do not know how I could have done it without them.

As I moved into my undergraduate career I had the good fortune of excellent mentorship from the superb faculty at the University of Alabama in Huntsville (UAH). When I entered UAH I assumed that my history major was merely the first step on my way to a law degree. Yet classes by professors such as Andrew Dunar, Richard Gerberding, Stephen Waring, Lee Williams II, and Carolyn White generated excitement within me regarding history in its own right. By my sophomore year Johanna Shields became my advisor, but, more important, she became my mentor and friend. For whatever reason, she saw potential in my development and began molding me into a historian even before I had decided to become one. I still remember the little cheer she let out when I told her that I had decided to pursue a doctorate in history instead of going to law school. Her advice on surviving and negotiating my way through graduate school proved invaluable, and she remains a role model of teaching and scholarship.

Of critical importance in those early days were a couple of programs designed to help minority students become aware of the opportunities available in academe. In 1993 I earned a spot in the University of Florida's Collegiate Scholars in History Program (CSHP), directed at the time by professors Julian Pleasants and Robert Hatch. This program provided my first sense of the profound effect that history can have on how we understand ourselves as a people as well as the realization that I could actually become a historian. From colleagues in the CSHP, I learned of the Committee on Institutional Cooperation's Summer Research Opportunities

Program (SROP), which offered research grants for underrepresented students at CIC host schools. Suffice it to say that my summer in the University of Chicago's program, run by Yvette Adeosun, set the course for my professional career. Nearly fifteen years later, I still run into former SROP kids who are now leaders in the arts, academia, and business, and we all recognize the debt we owe to the program for investing in minority undergraduates.

Commencing graduate studies at an institution with the reputation of Northwestern University could have proved an overwhelming experience were it not for the abundance of great people there. The university's coordinator of minority affairs, Penny Warren, made sure that we all felt supported from the day we set foot on campus. Meanwhile, I could not have asked for more invigorating classroom experiences than those provided by Sarah Maza, Edward Muir, and T. H. Breen. I also am very grateful that I had the opportunity to work closely with Robert Wiebe just before his retirement. His sharp critiques and vast historical knowledge humbled me and taught me to approach my chosen craft with an exacting discipline. Following Professor Wiebe's retirement, Adam Green became my guide into the African American experience in Chicago. I still stand in awe of Adam's ability to weave seemingly disparate concepts into dazzling analytical frameworks. Moreover, his insistence on recognizing African Americans as agents, rather than as victims, greatly influenced my examination of black politics in Chicago. Professors Nancy Maclean and Henry Binford rounded out the dissertation team, providing excellent insights throughout the process.

Every historian needs archivists, and I had the pleasure of working with some of the best. Without Archie Motley, the Chicago Historical Society's vast holdings would have been nearly impenetrable. Early in my archival research he pointed me toward several paper collections that revealed much about Dawson's early years in Chicago politics. Dennis Bilger, of the Harry S. Truman Library, provided equally important guidance to a wealth of correspondence between Congressman Dawson and members of the Truman administration. Finally, Michael Flug, curator of the Vivian G. Harsh Research Collection of Afro-American History and Literature at the Chicago Public Library, became an invaluable resource. Michael deftly combines an intricate knowledge of his institution's holdings and his own personal engagement with a significant portion of black history in the twentieth century. I easily learned as much about black Chicago between the 1940s and 1970s from several long conversations with Michael as I did from the Harsh collection's extensive materials.

Indeed, Michael introduced me to Doris Saunders, whose eclectic career had put her right in the middle of some of the most important currents of black Chicago history. After opening a bookstore and working for the Chicago Public Library, Doris was hired by a young "Johnny" Johnson, who wanted her to create a research library for the Johnson Publishing Company. During the late sixties, she knew many of Dawson's inner circle, including his daughter, Barbara Dawson, and his executive assistant, Fred Wall. When Dawson announced his retirement, Saunders took the initiative and collected his papers. She also interviewed his closest colleagues and his wife, Nellie. Doris then received a position in the communications department in Jackson State University, where her work to create a new program in print journalism prevented her from finishing her project on the congressman. Near the end of my research, she granted me access to her interviews and papers, which gave me a deeper understanding of Dawson's early adulthood and the relationships that sustained him throughout his political career. I am very grateful for her rigorous research and generous spirit.

Outside of the research process, I benefited from the sustaining friendships of some truly wonderful people. Chernoh Sessay, Neeraja Aravamudan, Sarah Fenton, and Lorelle Semley often challenged me and just made life more fun as we all pushed through our respective graduate careers. Even further from academe, Seth Patner and Aviva Brill joined me in my excursions into Chicago's dance community, while Lisa Meneses pushed me to find my identity as a dancer. I have been astonished to find that my calling as a dance teacher and choreographer has informed my vocation as a history professor and writer, and today Latin music still remains the soundtrack to my life.

I cannot really say enough about Loyola University. Anthony Cardoza and John Pelisserro took a risk on a very green sixth-year graduate student when they offered me a joint appointment as a visiting assistant professor in history and political science. From the start I was impressed by the encouraging attitude of Loyola's faculty and the deep commitment to social justice exhibited by our students. I am very happy to have as my academic home the history department at Loyola, which is a model of research excellence, committed teaching, and collegiality. I do not know how often I popped across the hall to Robert Bucholz's office for advice on anything from teaching to writing a book proposal. While junior faculty members shared their experiences of completing their first book, my department chairs, Susan Hirsch and then Barbara Rosenwein, kept tabs on my progress and offered sage advice on how to move forward. Timothy Gilfoyle provided a close reading of the entire manuscript and a detailed set of suggestions for improvement when I felt lost in a sea of criticisms. Meanwhile, Lewis Erenberg's infectious curiosity often reignited my own excitement in the book.

As the project moved closer to publication, I received superlative instruction from my editor at the Northern Illinois University Press, Melody Herr. Ever understanding and pragmatic, Melody guided me through the steps necessary to turn the dissertation into a book and provided constructive suggestions for accommodating the readers' feedback. Melody has since moved on to another press, and Sara Hoerdeman has ably stepped into her role.

Finally, there is my wife, Flori Manning. Words cannot begin to express the debts that I owe to her. From completing the dissertation, through my struggles as a novice professor to finishing the final manuscript, she comforted me through all of my fears and gave me the strength to keep going. I don't know that it is even possible to repay such love and kindness, but I am thankful that I have a lifetime to try.

WILLIAM L. DAWSON

AND THE LIMITS OF

BLACK ELECTORAL

LEADERSHIP

Introduction

"DON'T GET MAD!
GET SMART.
VOTE!"

We are a challenge to America and it will never realize its place as a world leader as long as we remain second-class citizens.[1]—*William L. Dawson*

On a warm spring day in May 1952, seven thousand black Mississippians gathered in Mound Bayou for an extraordinary event, the first annual convention of the Regional Council of Negro Leadership (RCNL).[2] Serving as a temporary safe haven in a state notorious for its murderous repression of civil rights leaders, the convention pursued a broad agenda that ranged from ending police brutality to obtaining equal restroom facilities in gas stations.[3] Indeed, with its encouragement of black Mississippians' increased militancy and political awareness, the RCNL anticipated the life-and-death voting rights struggles of the Mississippi Freedom Vote project of the early 1960s that culminated in the establishment of the Mississippi Freedom Democratic Party (MFDP) in 1964.[4]

Members of the RCNL believed, however, that the goals for that day could not be completed without the participation of the nation's most powerful black politician, Chicago congressman William L. Dawson. Part revival, part civics lesson, and part political rally, the convention sought to inspire all of its guests. An article from the *Jackson Advocate* noted that delegates drafted an ambitious program for promoting equal education, improving personal finance, and increasing black political participation. Between sessions, participants enjoyed entertainment by gospel singer Mahalia Jackson and a down-home barbeque.[5] Plus the RCNL's founder, Dr. T.R.M. Howard, delivered a stirring address in which he "emphasized the power of the ballot and the dollar."[6] Yet according to the *Advocate,* the highlight of the meeting involved a noteworthy guest:

> The outstanding feature of the meeting, which had been proclaimed "Dawson Day" in his honor, was the address of Congressman William L. Dawson of Illinois, Vice-Chairman of the Democratic National Committee, Secretary of the Democratic Congressional Election Committee, and Chairman of the House Committee on Expenditures in the Executive Departments of the Government who was the principal of the day.[7]

Dawson, who had fled the South in 1905 after an altercation with a white man, came back to Dixie to "round after round" of applause as he urged black Mississippians to become involved with politics at the "local, county, and state levels."[8]

Why did the RCNL select Dawson as the keynote speaker of its inaugural convention? The RCNL typified a growing political consciousness among southern blacks in the early 1950s, and no African American more strongly personified electoral politics than Dawson. The Illinois congressman came to this position along a somewhat tortuous path. A Georgia migrant, Dawson responded to the racial injustices that he saw as a combat officer in World War I by committing himself to an early version of what I call "the party-building philosophy": a dedication to electoral politics as a means to promote black equality. Thus in the 1920s he sought the tutelage of the pioneers of black politics in Chicago, Ed Wright and Oscar DePriest, who taught the young veteran the power of political organization, the limits of radicalism, and the importance of building strong relationships.

As he became increasingly independent of his mentors, Dawson pursued a community development agenda with a distinct tinge of racial militancy in the late 1920s. Placing emphasis on his military service, Dawson launched an independent campaign against First Congressional District representative Martin Madden, charging that Madden's race made him unfit to run the politics of the increasingly black South Side. Although the campaign failed, it established Dawson as a rising star and led to his election as alderman of the Second Ward in 1933, where he pushed for community development, fought for increased public housing, and mentored the fledgling Negro Labor Relations League—a group of young activists who led protest efforts for equal employment opportunities.[9]

Dawson soon found himself struggling for his political survival as the Depression and Democratic ascendancy forced black Republicans to feud among each other for a declining number of contestable offices. Meanwhile, community-based protest campaigns continued to yield underwhelming results. Thus, in 1939, Dawson joined Corneal Davis and Christopher Wimbish in their quest to create an independent black organization within the Democratic Party, and Dawson developed the final version of his party-building philosophy. By sanctifying the New Deal's implied egalitarianism, using new models of political organization, and connecting black South Siders to New Deal largess, the three World War I veterans successfully undermined Chicago blacks' historic connection to the party of Lincoln. Dawson, Wimbish, and Davis formed the core of what would become the nation's strongest black political organization, with Dawson as its head as congressman of the First Congressional District.[10] By this time, the apparent promise of electoral politics and New Deal idealism had led Dawson away from the radicalism of his youth to the matured version of the party-building philosophy: the effort to heighten black political organization in the Democratic Party to redress racial inequality.

As part of his new strategy, Dawson prioritized attending events by insurgent black political organizations like the RCNL, particularly in the late 1940s and early 1950s. Even after 1948, when he became the first black vice-chairman of the Democratic Party and the first black representative to chair a standing committee in the House, he still spent his own money to travel to various southern states, including Mississippi, Virginia, Texas, and North Carolina, to give the messages of hope and racial development through politics. In each of these places he made sure to deliver his characteristic line to his politically hungry listeners: "Don't get mad! Get smart. Vote." It was a message that routinely drew cheering audiences to their feet.[11]

Although the crowd's reaction at the RCNL probably did not surprise the Illinois representative, it is safe to say that Dawson's voter registration efforts in the Deep South would stun today's scholars of the modern black experience. Focusing on the years between 1956 and 1970, these scholars have largely ignored Dawson or dismissed him as a flunky of the Chicago Democratic organization,[12] but their analyses are short-sighted because they miss two-thirds of Dawson's political career as well as his activities in Congress and in the national party leadership. This period in fact marks the last fourteen years of a political career that stretched back to 1919 and demarcates the nadir of Dawson's ability to negotiate with Chicago's white Democratic leadership, as it came after Mayor Richard J. Daley undercut his influence and rendered Dawson merely the titular leader of local black politics.[13] Omitting the entirety of Dawson's career from the scholarship has thus created a gap in the historiography of black politics and the black civil rights struggle, for Dawson operated at many levels as a link between the insurgent black community of the postwar period and the United States government.

Indeed, the diverse array of opinions expressed by Dawson's contemporaries in civil rights, politics, and journalism belie modern scholars' evaluations. Some gave decidedly negative appraisals. *New York Post* writer Pete Hamill, for example, expressed the attitude of Dawson's harshest critics in a 1966 article that called the congressman Mayor Daley's "80-year old water boy." Like other pundits, Hamill uncritically accepted the accusation, originally fashioned by Dawson's political opponents, that Dawson's leadership had created practically all of black Chicago's negative circumstances. As Hamill put it, "Dawson in power has obtained for his faithful constituents the worst housing conditions in the city, a soaring crime rate, an increase in heroin addiction and the spread of teenage gangs who flock together in vicious packs, preying on strangers, extorting money from businessmen, and killing each other out of boredom."[14] Though polemical, Hamill and likeminded writers echoed the frustration of many black Chicagoans, particularly young activists, who wanted "The Man," as Dawson was called in Chicago, to fight the racially restrictive policies of the local Democratic Party.[15]

In contrast, at his death in December of 1970 many observers offered celebratory assessments of the congressman's career. Roy Wilkins, of the National Association for the Advancement of Colored People (NAACP), noted that Dawson had been a dependable supporter of civil rights in the House of Representatives and called Dawson the "embodiment of black power in the political arena."[16] One of Chicago's few independent black politicians, state senator Charles Chew, indicated that Dawson inspired him to enter politics and that the congressman had given him advice in his first campaign even though Chew ran against the regular Democratic organization.[17]

Other contemporaries praised his dedication to registering black voters. Edward Clayton noted this in his seminal work *Negro Politics* when he quoted Dawson as saying, "We must make our way to the polls. We will crack Mississippi. We will be back in there putting them on the books by the thousands. Our right of the ballot has been paid for in blood."[18] Statements such as this led Louis Martin to report that Dawson fought for "black power in the political mainstream before some of the young black power advocates of today were born."[19]

Although these divergent examples indicate the range of opinion regarding the South Side's representative, a set of balanced critiques revealed Dawson's complexity as a historical figure. These works set themselves apart by their consideration of Dawson's entire political career—a career traversing a diverse political landscape that included the local Republican Party, the Chicago city council, the national leadership of the Democratic Party, and the United States House of Representatives.

Pointing to Dawson's early career in the 1920s and 1930s, several journalists and intellectuals argued that Dawson forced the white political establishment, both locally and nationally, to take black political power seriously. James Q. Wilson, a prominent political scientist, wrote that Dawson created and sustained the first independent black political organization. *Defender* reporter Warner Saunders recollected one of the earliest battles in this effort when Dawson launched his campaign for representative of the First Congressional District in 1928. After giving a lengthy negative appraisal of Dawson's career, Chuck Stone, pundit and former editor of the *Chicago Defender,* quoted one South Sider who said, "He was a bitch" and, Stone conceded, Dawson "could hold his own in smoke-filled back rooms when the real decisions were usually made by white men."[20] Alderman Ralph Metcalfe echoed Stone when he said that Dawson "has been an inspiration. . . . [He] brought to the American public a new image of the black man. He was instrumental when redistricting occurred. I saw him wage a fight to get a black committeeman. He forced the County Central Committee. It was not easy. Then the fight that he waged which was much harder was [*sic*] to get the white man out. He had to lay his own committeemanship on the line."[21] Moreover, wrote *Jet* reporter Simeon Booker, Dawson sought to prove urban blacks' political viability despite the various social problems they faced.[22]

Dawson's tendency toward pragmatism when balancing civil rights and political concerns drew the most controversy of all of his political traits. Stone, for instance, asserted that Dawson had done nothing for civil rights since 1955, when he played a key role in ousting Mayor Martin Kennelly, whose crime policies undermined jitney cabs and the policy (or numbers) racket—two of the most lucrative and pervasive elements of the black South Side's underground economy.[23] Even then, Stone contends, Dawson toppled Kennelly to protect his own interests as much as he did to defend the black community.[24] Alden Whitman, to the contrary, claimed that the congressman's pragmatic style within the Democratic Party leadership and in the House got "things done without ballyhoo, without outblacking others." For instance, rather than publicizing his civil rights record and making strident speeches in favor of black equality as he had done in his youth, an older Dawson quietly convinced southern congressmen to leave the floor when it came time to vote on key civil rights legislation and secretly donated funds to southern civil rights campaigns. This strategy, wrote another reporter, represented the "last, best hope of successful black struggle."[25]

Several authors recognized that this quiet style alienated younger, more aggressive civil rights leaders. The new activists cared little for a political program that did not openly and vociferously challenge racism. Indeed, Dawson's distance from and refusal to nurture what the press dubbed as the "new breed" of black leadership, wrote Warner Saunders, proved one of Dawson's most tragic flaws.[26]

The pundits reserved their strongest criticism for Dawson's unwillingness to recognize the constraints of electoral politics and his inability to consider protest as an option. Saunders, for instance, lamented Dawson's apparent loyalty to the Chicago Democratic organization despite Mayor Daley's prioritization of white ethnics' prerogatives that included restricting black opportunities in housing and education. This emphasis on politics, argued the NAACP's Henry Lee Moon, led Dawson away from modern black sentiments and toward maintaining his own powerbase.[27]

This book continues the complex interrogation of Dawson's career begun by the pundits, intellectuals, and activists discussed above. Like those writers, it asks, To what extent did electoral politics at the urban and national levels prove a viable tool for bettering the condition of American blacks in Chicago and the nation as revealed by the career of William L. Dawson? Unlike recent scholars who have focused on isolated segments of Dawson's career, this book contextualizes Dawson's development through time and the multiple environments that shaped his worldview.

This broad examination reveals that Dawson's political efforts resulted from his adherence to the party-building philosophy: the effort to heighten black electoral political organization to redress racial inequality. Originating in Dawson's southern upbringing and his experiences as a young lieutenant in World War I, the party-building philosophy motivated Dawson's work for black uplift as a Republican in the 1920s and determined his switch to the Democratic Party in 1938. It guided his efforts to reshape the Democratic Party's racial priorities between 1942 and 1960 yet led him to support the Mississippi Freedom Democratic Party's challenge to the Mississippi congressional delegation in 1956, despite his distaste for the tactics of the civil rights movement.

As a strategy, however, party building proved significantly limited as a tool for racial uplift. Black electoral organization provided considerable opportunities for advancing a racially progressive agenda that included extending welfare benefits to black Americans, increasing blacks' presence in elective offices, and pushing the Democratic Party toward racial inclusiveness. Nevertheless, party participation demanded that Dawson consistently accommodate his program for black uplift with the Chicago Democratic organization and the national Democratic Party's racist imperatives.

Chapter 1, "A Greater Understanding of Humanity," reveals the origins of the party-building philosophy. Although Dawson spoke little of his childhood and time in the war, the available evidence points to both as laying the foundation for his ideology. Dawson's upbringing and education fostered within him a strong dedication to racial uplift, and the humiliations he experienced as a young officer in World War I forged his initial commitment to work for black equality through politics.

The remainder of the book traces Dawson's execution of the party-building philosophy throughout his political career. Chapter 2, "Big Bill, The Ironmaster, and the Old Roman," excavates Dawson's earliest forays into Chicago politics as a protégé of Ed Wright and Oscar DePriest in the 1920s. During these years Dawson fought on the front lines of Wright and DePriest's pioneering campaigns to leverage the South Side's growing black vote and to exploit divisions within the city's factionalized white political leadership. Nevertheless, the decentralized nature of Chicago politics forced Wright and DePriest to attach their political organizations to various white patrons while competing with other black political leaders for influence. Consequently, both leaders eventually fell prey to the very factionalism they sought to manipulate. Dawson's observations of his mentors' inability to maintain their political organizations fueled his desire to create a self-sustained organization that would unify black politics and thus command respect from the city's white political leadership.

Following these defeats, Dawson began to forge his own political identity by combining his mentors' tactics with the burgeoning community and civil rights activism of the late 1920s and early 1930s. This approach won Dawson a city council seat in 1933. Nevertheless, I argue in chapter 3, the new strategy brought few tangible victories for the black community and offered Dawson little political security. As a result, he moved toward a more strictly political model, joining fellow veterans Christopher Wimbish and Corneal Davis's insurgent effort to build a black political organization within the ascendant Democratic

Party. With Davis and Wimbish securing seats in the state legislature and Dawson winning a spot in Congress, the three men established the nation's strongest black political organization and Dawson came to the fully formed version of the party-building philosophy: the effort to heighten black political organization in the Democratic Party to redress racial inequality.

In chapter 4, I examine Dawson's continued application of the party-building strategy in Chicago and also study his efforts to execute his program in the leadership of the national Democratic Party and in the House of Representatives. The congressman's experiences during the 1940s and 1950s point to a tenuous and contingent relationship between the Democratic Party and black voters.[28] Although many black pundits, journalists, and intellectuals advised political nonalignment, Dawson had come to believe that New Deal liberalism offered the greatest prospects for racial advancement.[29] He thus played major roles in the struggle to isolate the party's segregationist southern contingent, to transform the party's position on civil rights, and to move blacks solidly into the Democratic column. I contend that his greatest victories came in the 1940s when he urged black voters toward the party, while successfully moving the party's national leadership toward a more accommodative position on black equality. In Congress, however, the party-building offensive produced mixed results: although it could not drive civil rights legislation past the phalanx of segregationist southern Democrats and conservative northern Republicans, it could parry some of their more overtly racist offensives. Back in Chicago Dawson's organization fostered increased black representation in office holding and patronage but could not address more deeply rooted racism in housing and education.

Indeed, as I argue in chapter 5, Dawson's inability to affect issues of structural inequality in Chicago pointed to severe weaknesses in the party-building strategy that became more pronounced at all levels throughout the 1950s. Crafted in the decentralized political environment of the 1920s and 1930s, the strategy could not counteract Mayor Daley's unprecedented appropriation of political and governmental power in the mid-1950s. Although Dawson faced increasing criticism from civil rights activists for his unwillingness to fight the Daley regime, he possessed few options because the mayor had conspired with younger black politicians to ruthlessly undercut Dawson's local influence. Meanwhile in Congress and the national party, southern Democrats responded to the burgeoning civil rights movement with a campaign of "massive resistance." Though avowedly opposed to the Democratic segregationist cohort, the congressman went along with the party leadership's attempt to placate its southern wing. Black voters, however, saw no value in such commitment and turned to the GOP in the 1956 presidential election.

After these failures Dawson retook the initiative in 1960 but found himself marginalized by a new wave of liberalism in the national leadership of the Democratic Party and a surge of racial militancy among black civil rights leaders. Eschewing the moderation that characterized Adlai Stevenson's campaign, Dawson played critical roles in supporting John F. Kennedy and in writing the strongest civil rights plank in Democratic Party history. Ironically, Kennedy's election brought a new level of executive commitment to African American equality that rendered Dawson's role as a party-based broker for black rights obsolete while doing little to move a civil rights agenda through Congress. Frustrated with the political establishment's slow progress on civil rights, the Chicago Freedom movement responded with a protest agenda to push for equality in public education and housing. The aging congressman, however, remained committed to the now decades-old party-building agenda. Espousing gradualist, government-based community development programs characteristic of the Great Society, Dawson rapidly found himself estranged and ridiculed by the young activist cohort. Thus, in chapter 6, we see that by the end of the 1960s Dawson was marginalized in both Chicago and Washington by the very forces he hoped to bring about.[30]

Dismissed by the young intellectuals and activists of the 1960s and 1970s, Dawson has occasionally resurfaced in modern historical accounts, most often as an accommodationist stooge of the Daley organization, the complexities of his long career largely forgotten. Perhaps the congressman himself is to blame for this state of affairs, for he maintained a wall of silence between his internal monologue and his outward actions. He also left little record of his life outside of politics. He gave practically no interviews, for example, that delved into any aspect of his personal history. In writing about him, I had considerable difficulty in assessing the motivations behind Dawson's political actions. Discussing his experiences observing Dawson for his influential work *Negro Politics,* James Q. Wilson indicated that the congressman told him that he never put anything important on paper—a veritable curse for historians. Dawson's secretive nature significantly hindered my attempt to paint even a "biographical portrait" of the congressman.[31] Nonetheless, as Dawson grappled with the terrible ordeals inherent in executing a social agenda within the confines of electoral politics, his triumphs, setbacks, and failures left an indelible impression on Chicago, American politics, and African American history, one that no historian can ignore.

Chapter One
"A GREATER UNDERSTANDING OF HUMANITY"

O father God, if you will just take me back home, I will give my life to teach my fellow man to use the ballot so that these kinds of things, these atrocities will not happen again. If you will, I promise you, God, I'll die teaching them how to use the ballot.[1]
—William L. Dawson.

When nineteen-year-old William L. Dawson engaged in a public confrontation with a white man in downtown Albany, Georgia, in 1905, some observers must have wondered whether the youngster would live to see his twentieth birthday. Moreover, the suggestion that this brash young Negro would one day be a leading figure in the Democratic Party, the party of segregationists, would have been met with guffaws and chuckles from blacks and whites alike.[2] Yet this moment, which could have very easily ended with a lynching, revealed that part of the foundation for Dawson's eventual commitment to obtaining black civil rights through politics had already been laid. In this chapter, I argue that the roots of the party-building philosophy originated in Dawson's experiences as a youth. His strong, nurturing family fostered a resolve to uplift the race and an unwillingness to blithely accommodate racial inequality, and Dawson's time at Fisk University only strengthened these tendencies. After Fisk, Dawson enlisted with the American Expeditionary Force in World War I, and his experiences of inequality in the war quickened his desire to improve the plight of black Americans into a zealous dedication to racial uplift through politics.

Born the second of seven children to Rebecca and Levi Dawson II on April 26, 1886, in Albany, Georgia, William Dawson entered a world in which whites had recently hardened the lines of racial segregation in southern life through violence and intimidation.[3] Indeed, Rebecca and Levi Dawson's childhoods spanned Reconstruction and Redemption, and William's childhood in Georgia bore witness to blacks' final removal from state politics and the legal establishment of Jim Crow. These events shaped Rebecca and Levi's worldview and greatly influenced how they would raise their children. Despite the odds against freed blacks in southwestern Georgia, the Dawson family steadfastly emphasized education and economic self-sufficiency to instill a strong sense of self-worth in all of their children.[4]

Levi Dawson and Rebecca Kendrick possessed pride in their diverse ancestry, which they passed on to their children and that factored in their successes as a black family in Albany. A painting of Rebecca reveals an unsmiling, squared-jawed woman who parted her hair at the center with a bun just above her shoulders. Of African, Native American, and European descent, Rebecca possessed a multiracial background, but her white father played an important role in the family's relatively good fortunes.[5] Family correspondence suggests that Dawson's maternal grandmother, Patsy Gill, had several children with her former owner, a local judge named Kendrick.[6] Patsy never let Rebecca forget that the Kendrick family held high status in Virginia and played a role as one of the earliest families to settle in Albany.[7] Because she was born in February 1865, however, Rebecca never knew Judge Kendrick as her master. He remained a part of her life mostly by occasionally giving presents and money to Patsy, who combined his gifts with her earnings as a nurse to buy the family home.[8]

Like his wife, Levi Dawson took pride in his heritage, which possessed both Native American and European ancestry.[9] His father, Levi Dawson I, began his life as a slave but eventually became a free man.[10] Understanding that the vicissitudes of southern racism could easily separate and destroy black families, he took the precaution of retaining multiple aspects of the family name in the names of his male children, and he asked his sons to do the same. As a result, the younger Dawson held the name of his father, and his brother George William Dawson received the name of his maternal grandfather, William Starkey. As the next generation of Dawsons arrived, the tradition continued with Levi Dawson II naming his sons Julian Levi Dawson and William Levi Dawson. Meanwhile, George William Dawson also named his son, William Levi Dawson.[11]

The instability of life in southwestern Georgia during the Levi Dawson II's childhood more than justified his father's apprehensions. Indeed, Levi and his future wife Rebecca grew up during a tumultuous period in which freed blacks fought valiantly to assert their newfound rights as American citizens, only to have them shredded by systematic terrorism on the part of white conservatives committed to eradicating any semblance of black political or economic independence.

In part, Albany and Dougherty County's great wealth set the stakes of this life-and-death struggle. In 1837 Albany was little more than a trading village with a tropical climate and rich soil, but by 1860 Albany and the surrounding Dougherty County had approximately 150 large plantations with a $3 million slave labor force numbering nearly 6,000. In addition to its copious cotton production, Dougherty County had become the heartland of Georgia agriculture with an abundance of slave produced secondary crops and food products, leading Albany's founder, Nelson Tift, to boast that it was the richest county in the world.[12]

The Civil War battles that scarred northern Georgia missed Albany. Nevertheless, it became a focal point in the struggle between the freed people and Georgia's planter class.[13] Albany blacks' ambitions initially aligned with those of the newly established Freedmen's Bureau, and they used the space afforded by this alliance to promote their independence: establishing a communally owned plantation; opening their own school, creating a local branch of the Georgia Equal Rights Association (GERA), and forging political relationships with the Republican Union League movement.[14]

This state of affairs would not last long, though, for conservative whites would soon retake the offensive. Reacting to the implementation of congressional Reconstruction in 1868, which sought to inhibit the re-establishment of planter power in the South, conservative whites executed a program of state-sanctioned terror and voter fraud to undermine the motley coalition of blacks, yeomen whites, and northern Republicans that timorously governed the state.[15] Their efforts brought conservatives control of the state's politics in 1870 with a Democratic sweep of the state legislature, and the following year they forced the resignation of the state's Republican governor.[16] The conservative Democratic leadership ratified their political order with a new constitution in 1877 that virtually nullified the black vote, united large planters and urban merchants, and left yeomen whites bitter toward their economic superiors and freed blacks.[17] Black political ambitions briefly resurfaced when class divisions emerged among Georgia whites during the Populist movement of the 1890s, but this flash of egalitarianism only sparked another vigorous effort to reinforce Georgia's caste system through Jim Crow laws that governed every facet of Georgia life.[18]

As Albany whites redeemed the state through segregation, they also struggled to reconcile the effects of an economic depression with their perception of Albany as a sophisticated and liberal community.[19] When visiting Albany at the turn of the century, W.E.B. DuBois noted the area's numerous declining plantations, its debt-ridden, impoverished plantation families, and depleted soil.[20] Although many of its stronger planters managed to survive the downturn, the Albany of Dawson 's childhood clearly did not approximate the Albany of Nelson Tift's heyday.[21]

Despite white Albany residents' staunch sense of their own gentility and cosmopolitanism, they still employed economic oppression and the threat of violence to support white supremacy.[22] Members of the town's business community described Albany as having one of the South's "most liberal" school systems, with good facilities for black and white students.[23] Indeed, it seems that white Albany residents believed that they had always had fair and positive relationships with the black community.[24] In *History and Reminiscences of Dougherty County, Georgia,* Emma R. Sutton claimed that Albany had never had a lynching, but she then recounts a far-fetched tale of a local African American man who had been convicted of rape in a "fair and impartial" trial. The story became even more implausible when she claimed that local blacks expressed disappointment when the court scheduled the hanging for a date later than expected.[25] In light of the public spectacle of lynchings in the new South, as well as the use of rape as an excuse for killing black men who posed challenges to the racial order, one cannot help but question the validity of this story.[26]

In fact, white Albany residents' sense of their own cultural diversity and liberality masked an intense racial economic oppression backed by the threat of violence. Blacks clearly fared poorly in postwar Albany.[27] Most lived in the countryside where they scraped out modest existences as they reeled from the effects of the cotton depression. Blacks in Dougherty County suffered rates of overcrowding comparable with the worst northern ghettos.[28] Eighty-six percent of Albany's blacks labored as farmers, farm hands, servants, or washerwomen. Moreover, with two-thirds of the black population illiterate, education offered escape for only a few.[29]

As "children of Reconstruction," Rebecca and Levi Dawson fought to empower and protect their family in this new Albany by providing a stable family life that stressed taking pride in labor, obtaining an education, and elevating the race. All of the family's adults worked. Levi owned and operated the town barbershop that catered to white customers. Rebecca cooked and washed clothes for local whites, and her mother, Patsy Gill, worked as a nurse.[30]

As of 1900, the family had seven children—three boys and four girls. William was the second eldest.[31] The children lived disciplined lives. All woke early and tended to chores before going to school. After school Dawson's sisters Lee and Janie headed back home to help their grandmother with tasks around the home. Meanwhile William, his older brother Wallace, and his younger brother Julian headed to the barbershop, where they tried to be seen but not heard as they tended to their father's white customers.[32]

The barbershop not only provided the boys with first-hand lessons about whites but also gave them a political education. When the customers left, politics dominated the conversation between Levi and his brother also who worked in the shop. The 1890s marked the rise of Populism and black Georgians' brief reentry into the political arena,[33] and this period also witnessed the final removal of blacks from state politics, culminating in the institution of the white primary near the end of the decade.[34] If children learn anything from listening to the adults around them, the Dawson boys could not have missed the centrality of politics to the lives of black Georgians.[35]

The boys' education did not stop there, though, for Rebecca and Levi, both literate, instilled in their children the value of reading and obtaining a formal education.[36] At home, the parents provided the children with the Bible, and works by Paul Lawrence Dunbar, Omar Khayyam, and Shakespeare.[37] Rather than trust the children's education to the public school for black children, which operated only three months each year, Levi, Rebecca, and Patsy scraped their earnings together to send the children to a Methodist school founded by the American Missionary Association. With a reputation for having faith in the intellectual potential of their young charges, the missionaries offered a regular nine-month school year and courses in grammar, agriculture, and music.[38]

Although Dawson appreciated the rigorous education he received at the hands of the missionaries, he never really took to Methodism.[39] Many decades away from his time at Albany Normal, Dawson told this story of his religious instruction:

> When I was a youngster back at Normal College in Albany, Georgia, I became a member of the Methodist faith. It was one of those schools that stressed religion, and every so often they would hold revival services and the students would have to come up to the mourner's bench. On one of those days I found myself on the mourner's bench while some of my classmates were outdoors playing ball. I could see them through the window

and it was my most earnest desire to get outside and join them. All around me, people were getting up and shouting that they "felt something" when they would join the church. But the longer I sat there, I not only did not "feel" anything, but my desire to get out and play ball grew stronger and stronger. Finally, I jumped up and shouted: "I got it!" and ran out of there so I could get to the ball playing.[40]

Despite Dawson's resistance to evangelism, the school's religious message meshed with Rebecca and Levi's staunchly moralistic ideals and dedication to racial improvement. Levi taught Sunday school and had a reputation for studying the Bible, and Rebecca often sang hymns with the children. She particularly enjoyed "Walk Together Children and Don't Get Weary, there's a great camp meeting in the Promised Land." In keeping with the spirit of this hymn Rebecca and Levi taught their children that they owed it to their race to help the less fortunate. Levi took this message seriously. In 1901, when a local African American man faced the threat of a potential lynch mob, Levi, along with fifteen-year-old William and thirteen-year-old brother Julian to stood guard at the man's home.[41]

Although Levi wanted his boys to understand that black men should defend themselves physically from armed whites, he edified them in the philosophies of Booker T. Washington. One of a handful of black entrepreneurs in Albany, Levi belonged to Booker T. Washington's National Negro Business League and believed that black America's future lay in business and agriculture. In July 1903, Levi took William to Boston to hear Washington speak and they witnessed the infamous "Boston Riot," in which William Monroe Trotter's supporters interrupted Washington's lecture to protest his accommodationist stance. Washington's dignity in the face of the brash Trotterites impressed Dawson to the end of his days.[42]

Upon returning from Boston, Dawson looked forward to attending a new school, but a family tragedy swept away the excitement of obtaining more education. Previously, Albany did not have anything like a secondary school for blacks. This changed when Joseph Winthrop Holley, a Brainard Institute graduate and former Andover student, came to town in 1902 to found the Albany Bible and Manual Institute (ABMI).[43] As they had with the children's primary education, Rebecca, Levi, and Patsy struggled to send the children to ABMI. Not long after seventeen-year-old William and fifteen-year-old Julian started school, however, their mother became mortally ill. On her deathbed, she gathered her children and told them, "I have no money to leave you. I have only the principles I taught you. Don't forsake your principles." She spoke to William in particular and made him promise to help all of his siblings get through school. Finally, she led the children in singing, "Walk together children and don't get weary" and passed on.[44]

Levi eventually remarried, but Patsy ran the household for the remainder of her life. Although Rebecca had been stern and principled, Patsy was almost Spartan. She permitted no self-indulgent behavior such as smoking, drinking, or gambling. Dawson's first biographer, Doris Saunders, said it best when she wrote of Patsy, "Under her code, pain was to be borne; tears to be unshed, pity was for the weak; emotions and temper were controlled without letting anyone know what was on the mind."[45]

Patsy's guidance apparently suited the children, for Julian, William, and Blanche quickly shot past ABMI's intellectual confines. The energetic youngsters enjoyed challenging each other to memorize entire books. Julian, despite being two years younger than William, sat only one grade behind him in school. Blanche rapidly followed behind them. It soon became clear that the two eldest boys would need to move on to complete their educations. Holley thought that Atlanta University would provide the best education, but because Atlanta struggled with financial difficulties, he suggested Fisk University, in Nashville, instead.[46] This suggestion became a necessity after a nineteen-year-old William shoved his way past the boundaries for black men under Jim Crow.

Racial violence always lurked in the background, posing a danger for blacks in Albany who did not stay in their place. As if Jim Crow did not suffice, lynch mobs infested the South at the turn of the century.[47] With 439 black lynchings between 1880 and 1930, Georgia ranked as one of the leading states in this repugnant practice. Furthermore, the state's Black Belt region, which included Albany, held the record for the most lynchings in Georgia. Most counties averaged three lynchings per year between 1880 and 1930, and in some counties lynchings numbered as high as ten per year.[48]

One can observe how black parents attempted to protect their children from white violence in the axiom Rebecca, Levi, and Patsy repeatedly taught their children from birth, "Don't ever let the other fellow know what you're thinking. Get straight on your own thought and keep your thought [to yourself]."[49] Rebecca and Levi's warnings were not enough though, for Dawson reached adulthood with a well-developed sense of what Charles Payne calls "individual efficacy." Payne contends that key native black leaders in Mississippi's version of the civil rights movement came from families whose parents refused to readily accept racism and who nurtured each other through the worst of times.[50] The Dawson family clearly fit this model. Thus, it should come as little surprise that William would eventually bump heads with old Jim Crow.

That day came in 1905 and resulted in Dawson leaving Albany. After graduating, Dawson continued to work in his father's barbershop polishing shoes. One afternoon he accidentally hurt a white customer's foot. When the irate man threatened him, Dawson brazenly dared the customer to take a swing at him. Fortunately, the customer did not answer William's challenge, but in an era in which whites killed blacks for lesser grievances it could have easily become a deadly affair. Realizing that his son's attitude could get him killed, Levi decided that it would be best to send him off to Fisk to continue his education.[51]

If Albany Normal instilled in Dawson a sense of self-confidence, Fisk University broadened his sense of the world, developed his leadership abilities, and reinforced his commitment to advancing the race. In so doing, Fisk more than suited Dawson and carried out the same mission as Bill Cosby's fictional historically black institution Hillman College in the popular early 1990s sitcom *A Different World*. The show gave U.S. television viewers a window into the world of historically black colleges with their dual missions of education and uplift. *A Different World* traced the transformation of an ensemble cast of young African Americans from youth to adulthood as they as they struggled through a rigorous education, navigated the turbulence of college life, and wrestled with many of the major political issues of the time.[52] Despite the ninety-year gap, Fisk University during Dawson's tenure could have served as the model for the television show. In the early twentieth century, Fisk sought to bring its pupils into a different world through an intense curriculum that matched the nation's best liberal arts colleges and attempted to create a new world by nurturing a cadre of future black leaders to help their communities. This environment suited Dawson (who, for reasons I could not ascertain, was nicknamed Villain) perfectly, and he would excel as a scholar, athlete, and student leader throughout his years in the university.[53]

Scholars have given mixed assessments of missionary institutions such as Fisk.[54] James Anderson typifies more recent historians who criticize the industrial education model and praise Fisk for its emphasis on a liberal curriculum. Founded by the American Missionary Association (AMA) in 1866, Fisk University always had the mission of educating African Americans. The AMA believed that the salvation of the nation lay in achieving equality before the law for American blacks. Motivated by their religious ideology and patriotism, they sought the creation of a moral, industrious, and educated black citizenry. Contrary to

Anderson, scholars such as Ronald E. Butchart have criticized the missionaries for their conservative and paternalistic tendencies. Many missionaries believed that slavery had left blacks ignorant and superstitious. Typically missionary educators drew their inspiration, not from a commitment to racial equality but a desire for saving souls through the civilizing force of education. As a result, the curricula they designed for black students rarely placed of issues race and power at the center of intellectual inquiry.[55]

Nevertheless, argues Henry Bullock, the tensions between paternalism and a belief in blacks' intellectual abilities proved fruitful. The AMA established a number of black colleges, each with a different emphasis: from Fisk and Atlanta Universities (now Clark-Atlanta University) with their emphases on liberal education, to Hampton Institute (now Hampton University) with its focus on industrial education, to Tougaloo and Talladega Colleges, which incorporated both educational styles.[56]

When Dawson reached Fisk in 1905, the institution was on its way to becoming one of the nation's premier black colleges. Resisting a nationwide push for greater emphasis upon industrial education, Fisk maintained a strict and wide-ranging liberal arts program. A brief look at its core curriculum will demonstrate its rigor. All students seeking admittance to the college needed to complete Fisk's college preparatory course or the equivalent elsewhere and the college demanded that all applicants demonstrate a strong grasp of English. Freshmen took courses in Latin (Cicero), Greek *(The Iliad)*, mathematics (higher algebra), English, elocution, trigonometry, and biblical history. Sophomore year saw continued coursework in math, elocution, Latin (Horace), English, and biblical history, as well as classes in physiology and botany. In their junior year, Fisk students added a language requirement in either German or French, as well as physics and astronomy. Finally, in their senior year the students tackled an almost entirely new set of subjects, including psychology, political economy, ethics, geology, chemistry, and sociology.[57] Evaluating this curriculum, the Federal Bureau of Education deemed Fisk comparable to most contemporary white schools.[58]

Albany Normal and his family's love of reading prepared Dawson well for this environment, for he excelled as a student scholar with grades second only to Fisk's most illustrious graduate, W.E.B. DuBois.[59] One of Dawson 's classmates, James E. Stamps (1907–1911), recounted that by the time he came to Fisk, Dawson "had already made his mark as an outstanding scholar."[60] Stamps's classmates apparently shared this opinion, deeming Dawson's chief characteristic in "Statistics of the College of '09" as "brilliancy."[61]

Stamps commented that Dawson made his mark in more than just academics. He also stood out as a participant in several of the school's more intellectually inclined extracurricular activities. Stamps claimed that while Dawson served as captain of the debating team they never lost a contest. Intercollegiate debates held prominent places in the academic year, and Dawson and his co-captains so consistently beat Atlanta and Wilberforce universities that Stamps went out and joined the team in his "sophomore, junior and senior years." Dawson and Stamps lived in Livingston Hall, which had three literary clubs that doubled as social groups. Stamps characterized the groups as "snobbish and intellectual." He nevertheless strongly desired to join one, and felt great pride in being selected to join the Dunbar Club, headed by Dawson. He had a special affection for Dunbar's more melancholy poems, and Stamps recollected that he "could quote Dunbar by the volume."[62]

Like DuBois, Dawson was nominated by the faculty to serve as editor of the *Fisk Herald,* where he expressed views that reflected faculty opinion as well as moved toward his own personal philosophy.[63] In an April 1908 editorial, for example, Dawson wrote that the faculty and administration of Fisk generally had the interests of the students at heart. Therefore, when students received new guidelines designed to improve behavior, rather than question the faculty, they should examine their own behavior for the source of the new rules.[64] In a more personal piece, Dawson waxed rhapsodic on the virtues of utter commitment to an ideal, revealing an ambitious young man who thought hard about how to make a contribution to the world even if doing so took great self-sacrifice.[65]

Differing from DuBois who called athletics a "distraction," Dawson's athletic prowess brought him just as much attention as his facility with the written word.[66] Stamps remembered Dawson's time as captain of the school's intramural basketball squad, and recalled that Dawson's team generally won. Stamps recollected, "He seemed to have that kind of leadership ability that made you want to be on his team, so *you* could be a winner."[67] At 5 feet, 8 inches tall and 140 pounds Dawson also played quarterback and halfback on the football team. In 1906 he led the team as quarterback in the annual contest between Fisk and Lincoln University. By 1908 he had moved to halfback, and the *Fisk Herald* reporter wrote, "His long consistent gains were remarkable. His tackling and breaking up plays were his specialty."[68] Every year the game between Fisk and Meharry Medical College generated the most excitement, said Stamps. As medical school students, the members of Meharry's team tended to be larger than those from Fisk, and they "played rough," but Dawson—with his smaller stature—"showed that football was a thinking man's game . . . [since] we outplayed them during William's time."[69]

Dawson 's prioritization of athletics appeared not only in his activities but also in his *Fisk Herald* columns. He began a March 1908 essay by discussing the intense work needed to master a Fisk education.[70] Although he called these efforts profoundly valuable, he cautioned students to take advantage of the opportunities they had at Fisk for physical development. A strong mind, he wrote, "can never give the best results when placed in a body weak and infirm." Moreover, modern America demanded such qualities from them, "for where the world once expected to find in the college graduate a person with an abnormal intellect and weak small body, it now expects to find the perfect mental and physical man."[71]

With all of these activities it would seem that Dawson hardly had time for a social life, and to a certain extent the faculty wanted socializing to be the least of their students' concerns. Like their colleagues at other black universities, Fisk students took part in a tough daily schedule designed to impart a strong work ethic, Christian morality, and middle-class social graces. The day's first study period went from 5:30 to 7:00 a.m. Mandatory morning church services came next, and the school held an extra afternoon service on Wednesdays. Following church, students went to their second study period from 8:30 to 12:00 p.m. The third and fourth study periods ran from 1 to 4:00 p.m. and 6:30 to 9 p.m. The school prohibited visiting between students during study periods and forbade visits between men and women at any time. All coed situations had to occur in public places in the presence of a faculty member. No Fisk student could drink alcohol, gamble, or smoke tobacco, on or off campus. Violations of any of these rules generally led to expulsions, but on some occasions faculty members meted out other chastisements, including corporal punishment. Students did not appear to resent these rules, even though the average student at this time was twenty-six years old, for the opportunity to attend Fisk provided reward enough.[72]

In addition to its rigid rules, the university designed a system of room and board specifically to impart morals and manners to the students. Fisk built boarding homes (i.e., dormitories) in which students lived with faculty. The university held each student responsible for his or her own set of required daily chores, arguing that these habits developed the students'—particularly the female students'—understanding of household economy. The chores also helped the poorer students pay their tuition. The faculty also used a common dining hall, which allowed the students to develop the manners and habits of their Northern white instructors.[73]

Dawson's favorite teacher, Professor Dora Scribner (master of arts) hosted his table. Scribner appointed Dawson the student host during his senior year, which meant that he had to guide conversation among the dozen or so diners into respectable yet interesting topics.[74]

All of these structured activities, though, should not imply that Dawson did not partake of the whimsies of young adulthood. He was, after all, the same young man who pretended to catch the spirit so that he could go play ball with his friends. Stamps remembered Dawson as a sharp dresser who took particular pride in his appearance. Most African American men today know of or have used a wave-cap (a stocking cap designed to keep freshly styled hair in place), but Dawson was first person that Stamps had ever seen using one. Dawson also led a fashionable clique of young men who wore particular striped slacks and cutaway coats to church and other social activities. This sense of style suited Julia Mae Williams, a young lady from South Carolina whom Dawson courted, perhaps under the watchful eye of Professor Scribner.[75]

Despite his frenetic social and academic life, Dawson remained during his years at Fisk essentially a loner. In this way he again differed from DuBois, who formed many close relationships during his college years.[76] In each of Dawson's activities, from editing the *Fisk Herald* to serving as student body president in 1909, he held leadership positions in which he interacted with his peers but remained justly slightly apart and above them. Stamps called Dawson a "very single minded person." He also remembered Dawson as "quite independent, and not very sociable." This characteristic extended to family as well. Julian soon followed his brother to Fisk, where he excelled academically and played even more sports than his brother, including baseball, football, and gymnastics. Although he and William acknowledged each other, they did not room together and rarely socialized with one another.[77]

As Dawson's years at Fisk passed he had to consider his future. Several examples of African American life must have been apparent to him. There was, of course, his father, a successful barber in Albany. He could also probably envision life as an educator. Fisk's normal (education) curriculum played a major role in the college's academic life, and Fisk turned out considerable numbers of teachers.[78] Perhaps he considered examples from Fisk's faculty, which in 1909 included two black professors, D.A. Williston and T.W. Talley. He also could have looked toward Booker T. Washington, who visited Fisk in 1908, and W.E.B. DuBois, who also came in 1908 and gave a militant speech to a group of Fisk alumni. Then there were the Chicago families like the Griffens, the working-class family with whom he stayed over the summers as he worked as a waiter in Chicago, or the Careys, a middle-class family he had befriended in Chicago and prominent leaders in Republican politics.[79]

Daniel Hale Williams, one of the nation's leading heart surgeons, most likely sparked the greatest interest in Dawson's mind. Williams, a graduate of what is now known as Northwestern University Medical School and founder of Chicago's Provident Hospital, visited Nashville every year between 1899 and 1912. During each of those visits, Williams spent time at Meharry Medical College, where he conducted a model heart surgery for the faculty and students.[80] In light of the small world of Nashville's middle class, Dawson must have known of this annual event.

Thus, after graduating from Fisk in 1909 with a bachelor of arts degree summa cum laude, Dawson tried to go into medicine. Despite having a classical education Dawson applied to Harvard and prepared to take the medical school examination by memorizing an anatomy textbook. The plan worked and Harvard accepted Dawson's application. But while in Cambridge, Dawson witnessed a woman and child on the verge of being struck by an oncoming car. The former football star rushed to save them but shattered his hand in the process, rendering him unable to train in surgery.[81]

So Dawson moved back to Albany and resumed working part time as a porter and occasional hotel worker in Chicago to pay for his siblings' educations, including Julian, who soon matriculated at Northwestern Medical School.[82] Nevertheless this unsatisfying situation coupled with the Jim Crow's ruinous effects on black families finally led Dawson away from the South for good. While Dawson worked a stint at the Chicago Beach Hotel, a white man in Albany raped his sister Janie. Dawson knew that he could not return to Albany without seeking revenge for the assault. Moreover, another white man sexually assaulted his aunt, and Levi Dawson apparently avenged her, but this move forced the family to leave Albany.[83] These incidents, on top of a lifetime's worth of griev-ances, convinced Dawson to leave Dougherty County and the Black Belt. Everything in his life, from his parents' emphasis on education and indi-vidual efficacy to his successful tenure at Fisk University, made Dawson unsuited to the South's racial hierarchy. The South afforded few oppor-tunities to educated and ambitious black men, much less for those who could not hold their tongues in the face of racism. Thus, Dawson headed to Chicago for good in 1912.[84]

Although moving to Chicago reshaped his life, Dawson would soon participate in one of the most important historical epochs of the African

American experience: World War I. The war shook Dawson's soul and revealed his life's purpose. Attuned to the hypocrisies inherent in U.S. race relations from his time in Albany and at Fisk, Dawson nonetheless volunteered in the American Expeditionary Force, believing that he should help defend the country from external threats despite its institutionalized racial inequality.[85] Unfortunately, his time in the military only brought more disappointments as the army remained fundamentally racist and thoroughly degraded its black soldiers.[86] Years after the war Dawson claimed that this treatment proved more devastating to his soul than the injuries he received to his body and that he was particularly dismayed that he and his comrades had no black elected official to whom they could turn for support. Conversely, he indicated that black soldiers' willingness to face down death when under the guidance of fair leadership, black or white, gave him hope that the Constitution still provided a framework which could bring about "a full and free citizenship" for all Americans. After this experience, he returned to Chicago dedicated to using politics to remedy the inequalities experienced by black soldiers in the war.[87]

When he moved to Chicago in 1912, Dawson joined the trickle of migrants that had been moving north since the 1890s: the so-called Migration of the Talented Tenth. Although the majority of the migrants in this period came from farm and labor stock, it also contained an educated contingent of African Americans who found life within the South's racial hierarchy untenable.[88]

The Migration of the Talented Tenth significantly expanded Chicago's black population and, in doing so, exacerbated the city's latent racism and catalyzed the development of a large segregated black community. In 1893, 16,000 blacks lived in Chicago, but by 1910 the black population had grown to 44,103, making blacks 2 percent of the city's total population.[89] Residing in small block-sized enclaves across the city, many blacks in early twentieth-century Chicago claimed that little friction existed over issues of race and housing. Nevertheless, these so-called Old Settlers commonly noted that race relations remained harmonious as long as few blacks lived in any given white neighborhood.[90] As the migration continued, white Chicagoans pressed blacks into densely populated and physically decaying neighborhoods running south from 21st Street to 39th Street—the Black Belt.[91] Middle- and upper-class blacks attempted to avoid this area by heading to the southern fringe of the black enclave, but distraught whites reacted to them with mobs and legal bullying through residential housing associations.[92] In the mid-1920s white

Chicagoans discovered another legal obstacle in restrictive covenants, real estate contracts that prohibited the sale of property "to any member of a race not Caucasian," and by 1930 restrictive covenants covered 75 percent of the city's homes.[93]

Despite these obstacles, the Old Settlers created a number of strong community institutions and established multiple centers of black leadership that subscribed to a mix of Washingtonian internal community development and DuBoisian external racial advocacy.[94] Representing the most refined strata of Chicago's black leadership, Dr. Daniel Hale Williams worked with Booker T. Washington to create the National Medical Association for black doctors in 1904.[95] On the DuBoisian end of the spectrum, Ida B. Wells led protests against lynching in southern Illinois in 1909, advocated for the establishment of a Chicago branch of the NAACP, and participated in women's suffrage and settlement work.[96]

The topmost level of black religious leadership in Chicago included eloquent college-educated theologians who attended to the social needs and political concerns of their increasingly southern congregations in varied ways.[97] Wallace Best notes, for example, that the Reverend Archibald J. Carey's Institutional AME Church and Social Settlement backed his spiritual goals for the migrants with "a concern for more material aims such as black civil rights, equality in housing, employment, and general social betterment." After coming to AME in 1909, he brought in a staff trained in social work to assist the migrants' acclimation to city life. He also built a preschool and kindergarten and set up an employment agency that placed job seekers in the Chicago public schools, the Pullman Company, and the stockyards. In contrast, J. B. Massiah, rector of St. Thomas Episcopal Church, typically avoided participation in racial and political matters. Nevertheless, he vigorously admonished the National Negro Business League for its accommodationist stance when it met in Chicago in 1912.[98]

These leaders coexisted with another group of notables who, for various reasons, did not fit the refined Afro-Saxon model like the individuals discussed above.[99] Most black Chicagoans, for instance, would have identified Jesse Binga as their most prominent entrepreneur. Despite having little formal education, Binga became a successful real estate broker and established the Binga Bank in 1908. In 1912 Binga married Eudora Johnson, sister of John "Mushmouth" Johnson—one of the city's gambling kingpins. Their marriage pointed to the extent to which "respectables" such as Binga shared the upper class with even wealthier "shadies" such as Johnson. The picture becomes even more complicated when one realizes that Chicago's black gambling kingpins invested heavily in their own communities, gave financial and personnel support to black politicians, and provided venture capital to the financially underserved African American community.[100]

Chicago's leading black newspaper, the *Chicago Defender,* closely followed the exploits of the city's policy kings. Its editor and founder, Robert S. Abbot, espoused a mix of both the DuBoisian and Washingtonian philosophical camps. Expressing a strong belief in the ability of the common black person to succeed if given a chance, a strenuous objection to DuBois's "talented tenth," and a caustic dismissiveness of all aspects of southern segregation, Abbot staked out a complex position that articulated the hopes and frustrations of middle- and working-class blacks.[101]

Evidencing Abbot's contentions regarding black ambitions, Chicago's black political leadership would soon begin their struggle to create an independent political domain on Chicago's South Side. At the time, Chicago politics operated as a complex web of factional, patron-client relationships that divided roughly along ethnic and racial lines.[102] Since the Civil War, blacks had maintained an uneasy alliance with the Republican Party. They quietly moved up its ranks, while white Chicagoans battled over which type of progressive reform would guide local government. Catholic and Jewish working-class immigrants generally aligned themselves with the Democratic Party and social reform that emphasized political power for the lower classes, accepted European cultural diversity, backed organized labor, and supported increased city services. These newcomers battled against more established middle- and upper-class Chicagoans of northern European stock, who, by and large, sided with Republican business reform programs that promoted commercial interests as central to governance and decried working-class political participation in what they derisively called the "machine." Although blacks, like their fellow migrants from southern and eastern Europe, saw business reform as little more than a veiled attack on working-class life, they generally sided with the GOP because of its abolitionist heritage.[103]

In the nineteenth century, black Chicagoans' small voter base gave them little power to strive for political independence, but in the 1910s a group of young black Republicans realized that the migration provided sufficient numbers of black voters to play a critical role in citywide elections. At the turn of the century, black Chicagoans received a token number of political offices. They had held seats in the Illinois state legislature since 1882, garnered the appointment of a prominent black lawyer as assistant state's attorney, and secured spots on the county commission in 1894 and 1896.[104] But the individuals who held these positions generally did so as a sideline to their careers as lawyers and businessmen rather than as professional politicians.[105] This state of affairs neared its end as a quartet of black Republicans—Ed Wright, Oscar DePriest, Robert R. Jackson, and Louis Anderson—began to organize the black population as a viable political force. By the mid-1910s they would establish the predominantly black Second and Third wards on the city's South Side as strongholds of black political leadership.[106]

Despite its cadre of educated black professionals, the majority of black Chicagoans toiled on the economic fringes. In 1893 black Chicago's working population numbered approximately 10,000 and labored overwhelmingly in the nonindustrial service sector. A small segment of this population held skilled jobs as musicians, carpenters, and plasters, whereas virtually no blacks could find clerical employment outside of the Black Belt. Except for foundry workers, the city's powerful trade unions prohibited black participation. Black women faced even more limited opportunities, with 75 percent involved in domestic services. In 1910 this economic picture remained virtually unchanged, with more than 51 percent of black males working in personal services. Meanwhile domestic service remained the dominant occupation for black women, and, to the extent that they worked in manufacturing, it was out of their homes as dressmakers and seamstresses.[107]

For all of its complexity, black Chicago probably did not catch Dawson unawares. Although he lacked direction, his early years in Chicago essentially continued patterns begun during his summers there as a college student. He moved back with the Griffins, secured a job as Pullman porter on the Santa Fe run, and resumed sending money to his family to help his remaining siblings attend school and to pay for his sister Janie's medical care. Meanwhile the Dawson boys seemed to continue the intellectual contests from their childhood, with Julian attending Northwestern Medical School in downtown Chicago and Dawson taking night classes at Chicago Kent College of law.[108] Dawson frequently socialized with the prominent Carey family, who also came from Georgia. Although Carey ministered at Institutional Church, Dawson went to singles activities at Grace Church and Olivet Baptist Church, where the Griffins worshipped. He also often played poker, where he enjoyed listening to the older men's bull sessions.[109] Dawson's ambitions remained somewhat unfocused, however, and he opened a tailor shop on Wabash Avenue. Perhaps the shop took too much of his time, for he discontinued his legal studies after only three semesters.[110] This period would not last, and William and Julian would soon throw themselves into the Great War.

As it became clear that the United States would support Great Britain and France in the war against Germany, black leaders debated whether they should participate in a war to secure democracy for Europeans when equality did not exist for blacks in the United States.[111] Even so, the community generally supported the war effort. Civil rights leaders and black journalists did not question participation as much as whether blacks should leverage their involvement to agitate for civil rights during or after the conflict, a discussion highlighted by the controversy surrounding W.E.B DuBois's surprise endorsement of black participation in the war effort.[112]

Black leaders had ample reason to engage in such debates, for throughout preparations for the war, white Americans' racial psychoses resulted in hypocritical pronouncements and incoherent policies by government and military leaders regarding black military participation. On the eve of U.S. entry into the war more than 10,000 blacks on active duty participated in four Jim Crow units and another 10,000 blacks, including Julian Dawson, held positions in various segregated National Guard units. Meanwhile, no blacks could obtain admission into the Army Corp of Engineers, Army Field Artillery, Marine Corps, or the Army Air Corps.[113] When the United States considered the possibility of participating in the war, it mandated that the regular Army bring itself to full strength through the National Defense Act of 1916. The four black units filled up with 4,000 volunteers within a week, and, unable to conceive of blacks in integrated units, the army stopped the enlistment of black soldiers. Meanwhile, it allowed whites to continue their enlistments, with 650,000 white recruits joining.[114]

Despite their certitude regarding white superiority, the U.S military nevertheless enlisted a higher proportion of blacks than at any time in the past. After Congress declared war on Germany in April 1917, it became clear that the number of volunteers obtained would not suffice to wage hostilities overseas. As a result, Congress instituted a draft in May 1917 with the Selective Service Act.[115] Despite persistent white-held myths of African Americans as physically inferior, mentally deficient, and disease prone, the U.S. military enrolled blacks at a significantly greater rate than whites, with an acceptance rate of 34.1 percent for blacks compared to 24.04 percent for whites. The army also gave more deferments to whites, except in the South, where local planters feared that they could not survive without their black tenants.[116]

Their lopsided registration processes notwithstanding, military leaders still refused to accept blacks as combat troops, and civil rights leaders had to press the government to allow blacks to fight. Mississippi Senator James K. Vardaman, for instance, complained that "several million" armed blacks would undoubtedly "menace" the South.[117] While Wilson administration and military officials fallaciously asserted that it had been "customary" for blacks to operate solely in service capacities and declared it impracticable to use existing black regiments, such as 8th Illinois Infantry and the Ohio 9th Infantry.[118] Black civil rights leaders nevertheless organized a nationwide movement—which included the NAACP, black college administrators and professors, the black press, and the Central Committee of Negro College Men (CCNCM)—to secure a place for blacks as officers in the army.[119] Their efforts won the day, and on May 17 Secretary of War Newton Baker approved plans for a black officers training camp at Fort Des Moines, Iowa.[120]

William, Julian, and several future Chicago politicos numbered among the 1,250 men who gained acceptance to the pioneering Jim Crow officers training camp. Just over 400 of the men came from civilian life, whereas the remainder had been noncommissioned officers in the four existing black units. A civilian, Dawson knew of the racism surrounding the army's grudging acceptance of black soldiers, but he felt that the potential threat to the United States outweighed racial concerns.[121] Already a member of the U.S. Army Medical Reserve, Julian became one of the first black recruits the army selected for the medical indoctrination course. Like his brother, Julian had more than enough preparation to succeed in the military, and, unlike his brother, he had always wanted the opportunity to do so. Several Chicagoans joined Julian and William including Earl Dickerson and Christopher Wimbish.[122] Regardless of their backgrounds all of the men knew that they played a critical role in an important racial experiment; as their commanding officer Major General Charles C. Ballou indicated, "Your race will be on trial with you as its representatives during the existence of this training camp."[123]

The training that William and Julian received matched that of white officers, and, ironically, possessed a daily rigor similar to that of life at Fisk. Monday through Saturday, the candidates awoke to reveille at 5:45 a.m. Breakfast commenced precisely at 6:00 a.m., and training lasted from 7 a.m. to 12 p.m. The men ate lunch at 12:15 p.m. and took further instruction from 1:30 to 4:30 p.m. Dinner came at 6:00 p.m., and then the candidates went to a study period from 7:00 to 9:30 p.m., with taps at 9:45. Their training included bayonet, saber, infantry and physical drills, equipment maintenance, signaling, musketry, and trench warfare. If any of the men failed to live up to required standards of behavior they received a black mark, and three marks meant expulsion from the program. For their efforts, the army paid $100 per month in gold coin.[124]

Although black observers such as Robert Russa Moton, president of the Tuskegee Institute, reported that the camps operated under good conditions, prejudice followed the men to Fort Des Moines. General Ballou, for instance, responded to instances of discrimination by asking the men to refrain from engaging in any actions that pushed the race issue.[125] At the end of their training the candidates received a surprise announcement stipulating that they would not receive their commissions. Several reasons accounted for this policy shift, but, essentially, the army, facing resistance from white commanders and complaints from southern legislators, did not know what to do with the black officers.[126]

This ridiculous state of affairs resolved itself when manpower needs pressed the men into service, and the army finally commissioned them on October 17, 1917.[127] A total of 629 men graduated from this first class. Abiding by an arbitrary ceiling placed on black officers, the army commissioned 106 captains, 329 first lieutenants, and 204 second lieutenants. Captain Julian Dawson and First Lieutenant William Dawson sent graduation photos to their parents.[128] Then they, along with First Lieutenant Christopher Wimbish and Second Lieutenant Earl Dickerson, awaited their first assignments.

While the Dawson boys, Dickerson, and Wimbish waited for sensible leadership, the Department of War and top military leaders fumbled for a policy regarding the placement of black soldiers. Assuming that black combat troops could fight only under white leadership and fearing the reoccurrence of racial hostilities such as those that occurred with black soldiers in the 24th Infantry Battalion in Houston, a committee of generals proposed that the department immediately suspend the black draft and disperse the men into the Quartermaster Corps.[129] The committee favored this plan because it allowed for little training under arms and would prevent any trouble stemming from racial conflicts. A month later, Major General Tasker Bliss added that the military should perhaps create a token combat division for black troops. This move, Bliss argued, would distract from the military's intent to use blacks in primarily non-combat operations.[130]

Bliss's suggestion led to the creation of the segregated 92nd and the 93rd divisions.[131] Black combat troops would fill the ranks, graduates from Fort Des Moines would serve as junior officers, and whites would make up the divisions' senior command.[132] The army assigned William, Julian, Earl Dickerson, and Christopher Wimbish to the 92nd. William went to a company in the 365th Regiment. Julian became the regimental surgeon for the 365th, where, as the only black doctor in the 92nd Division, he led an entire regiment. The military noted Dickerson's fluency in French and made him an advanced billeting officer, sending him to France a month before the rest of the 92nd to prepare for their arrival.[133]

In the interval between its creation and its deployment to France, the 92nd was plagued by racism. For unexplained reasons, military command dispersed the division for training throughout the United States; each locale employed its own set of unique racial insults. Lieutenant Charles Houston, for example, reported that the army forced black soldiers stationed in Fort Meade to reside with conscientious objectors in decrepit quarters under armed guard, and Houston, a lawyer, was almost lynched when he tried to dismiss charges against black soldiers involved in an altercation with a group of whites.[134] Elsewhere, Fort Des Moines graduates dealt with white officers who plotted to undermine their authority in the so-called Camp Meade conspiracy, and black officers in Camp Funston in Fort Riley, Kansas, received reprimands from their commanding officer when they encountered racism in the small local town of Junction City. In Camp Alexander, Virginia, black troops received old Civil War uniforms but no overcoats, antique or otherwise, and several died of hypothermia in the exceptionally harsh winter of 1917–18.[135]

Contemporary observers, such as W. E. B. DuBois, learned of the treatment received by the prospective black combat soldiers and wondered whether the military actually wanted the 92nd to fail. DuBois and others' doubts must have been exacerbated by the fact that the army did not bring the 92nd to full strength until six days before its departure. Its individual units had been trained in an incomplete and inconsistent fashion in various camps across the United States. The army, for example, had only recently organized the 92nd's 317th Trench Mortar Battery on May 20. No other division in the army had been dealt with in such a careless fashion.[136]

As elements of the 92nd departed for France on June 7, discrimination went with them. En route white officers reserved the ship's first-class accommodations for themselves and ordered black officers to mess and second-class cabins. Earl Dickerson remembered that a "terrible rainy day" greeted Dawson 's group as it landed in Brest and white senior officers ordered their black colleagues to a set of Napoleon-era barracks, while they stayed in local hotels.[137]

Respite from their senior officers came from French locals, who welcomed the black troops. The 92nd soon left Brest for Saint-Nazaire, where they could stay in better hotels, patronize local restaurants, and enjoy a lively social life with the local ladies. The men continued this pattern when they moved to the Lorraine region.[138] As Earl Dickerson noted: "When we took leave we would go to St. Die, a city at the foot of the mountains where were stationed. Since I knew French, I could help make dates for the fellows with the girls. . . . [But] Dawson didn't need an interpreter. He had good use of the language, so that he was very popular. He was so well groomed and vigorous."[139]

Unable to convince the French of black troops' alleged inhumanity, U.S. Army officials attempted to enforce segregation on their own.[140] Army liaisons pressed French hotel and restaurant owners to prohibit black patronage of their facilities, and military police officers arrested blacks attending French functions even if they had been invited.[141] Then, in a bizarre move that smacked of Reconstruction era black codes, the commander of the 92nd ordered an hourly check on the whereabouts of all black soldiers between daybreak and 11 p.m. and a prohibition on travel away from base without a pass. These draconian and racist mandates were in large part motivated by white officers' fixation on black male sexuality. This fear was unfounded, for the army convicted only one soldier out of 25,000 of rape during the 92nd's six-month tenure in France.[142]

Suspicious of the white leadership at their backs, the men of the 92nd nevertheless had to prepare to face the German enemy at their front.[143] In the first week of July the army assigned the 92nd to work under the French 87th Division of the 38th Corp near Bourbonne-les-Bains, a spa town that sits on the southeastern border between the Champagne-Ardenne and Lorraine regions near Belgium and Luxembourg. The division expected to finish a three-stage training program, but, like most U.S. divisions, they received only partial instruction in phases one and two: allied offensive and defensive techniques. As the men approached critical training in divisional maneuvers, they received orders to head toward the front lines in Lorraine.[144]

On August 12, the 92nd headed east to Bruyères and Saint-Dié-des-Vosges for combat operations. When the 92nd arrived in Lorraine, the region possessed a reputation as a quiet sector along a battle line stretching from the North Sea to Switzerland. Alsace lay to the east, and beyond forests covered a mountain range that made military maneuvers nearly impossible. The inability to move made the sector a relatively quiet staging ground for inexperienced divisions. French troops stared down German guns in Saales, just east in northern Alsace, but the action rarely escalated beyond light shelling.[145]

The arrival of the 92nd shifted this delicate balance and led to Dawson's first combat experiences. On August 30 the army ordered the division to relieve the French 87th of an area approximately twenty-five kilometers wide just north of Saint-Dié. Companies from the 365th, 366th, 367th, and 368th consequently took over the frontline trenches and carried out a series of nighttime raids against the Germans. As a junior officer in the 365th Dawson led his squad in combat operations that included offensive raids, patrols, and repelling German attacks.[146]

The type of frontline warfare faced by Dawson and his fellow infantrymen can only be described as hellish. The soldiers lived in muddy, verminous, corpse-filled trenches. They remained wary and alert for days on end as their bodies suffered through trench foot, a disease that could eventually cause the feet to become numb and gangrenous, and trench fever, a disease spread by lice that caused headaches, leg pain, painful rashes, and inflamed eyes. The soldiers faced terrifying new weapons including flame throwers, machine guns, 150-mm shells, and *Minnenwerfers* (mortars filled with scrap metal). All of this occurred in a barren landscape of poisonous gas, barbed wire, and mangled bodies.[147]

In spite of their senior leadership, the 365th succeeded in its first missions. On August 31, the 365th fought off a German attempt to capture Frapelle, just east of Saint-Dié. The attack began with a bombardment of more than 12,000 shells between 12:30 and 3:00 p.m., followed by a German charge with flame throwers and mustard gas. Although the attack killed four and wounded thirty-four Americans, the 365th held their line and later received a commendation for their efforts. When the 92nd left on September 19 they had fought off eleven raids and carried out approximately thirteen patrols per day.[148]

This first battle tested the bond between Julian and William. As chief medical officer, Julian served in the rear. Yet, at some point during the fighting in and around Saint-Dié, a call came out for medical volunteers, and Julian, worried about his brother, left the combat hospital for the front lines of the Saint-Dié sector without notifying his commanding officer. Julian could not find William, but he remained at the frontline station for three weeks before being recalled.[149] His concern made sense, for black soldiers did not receive the same medical treatment as whites. During battle a piece of shrapnel lodged itself in Dawson 's shoulder. He retreated to the frontline hospital to receive care, but the white medical officers told him to report to the medical section for blacks further to the rear. He never made it to the hospital and carried that shrapnel for the rest of his life.[150]

After their successful defense of Saint-Dié, the men of the 92nd prepared to join the ill-fated Meuse-Argonne offensive. General John J. Pershing hoped to take the Argonne forest. Unfortunately, it became clear that as the French and American armies advanced through the forest they also veered away from each other, creating a gap in the front line. Pershing indicated that a unit from each army would have to fill the breach and he selected the 368th for the U.S. unit. Although assigned to the 365th, Dawson somehow received orders to go with the 368th in what would become one of the army's most shameful misuses of black troops.[151]

Because of poor planning and inadequate leadership by white officers the 368th failed in its mission. First, the 368th, which had been used solely in a patrol capacity, did not have the experience necessary for forest combat, and upon arrival, its units received between a few hours and two days to prepare. As if the mission of connecting two advancing armies that spoke different languages in wooded, rainy, muddy, combat terrain was not difficult enough, German divisions outnumbered the French and U.S. forces almost two to one. Moreover, the army did not provide the 368th maps or the wire cutters necessary to make their way through miles of barbed wire. Both armies neglected to give the black troops sufficient artillery support, and even if firing batteries had responded it would have been difficult for them to provide proper cover since the 368th had no maps with which they could deduce their coordinates. Adding insult to injury, the white commander of the 2nd Battalion, Major Max Elser of the 92nd Division, suffered a nervous breakdown during the battle and the commander of the 3rd Battalion of the 92nd, Major B. F. Norris, confessed to "hiding in a ditch during the attack." Under these circumstances, it is not surprising the 368th failed, with 58 killed and 200 wounded.[152]

Despite white officers' outrageous performance, the army blamed the alleged racial qualities of its black soldiers. Critics such as General Robert Bullard, head of the U.S. 2nd Army, called the division a failure and accused the men of sneaking to the rear to wait for a retreat. Bullard's critique differed greatly than those made of the white 35th Division, which also broke during the battle. In their case, though, military evaluators pointed to logistical problems, an inefficient leadership organization, and poor morale as the cause of the division's retreat.[153] One can only imagine

Dawson and the other black soldiers' shock at hearing the military leadership engage in such scurrilous attacks against their fallen comrades, assign all the blame for 368th's failure on black officers, and cite the Meuse-Argonne offensive as a rationale against black combat troops.[154]

In the wake of this disaster, Dawson had little time to reflect, for he received orders to what would be one of the last battles of the war: the Marbache offensive.[155] After the Meuse-Argonne fiasco, the army ordered the 92nd Division, now a part of the 2nd Army, to defend the frontline trenches near Dieulouard and to prepare for a final attack. The Marbache offensive produced some of the highest casualties of the war, and, as had been the case throughout black soldiers' participation in the conflict, the military's senior staff gave little concern to their well-being.[156] For their part in the offensive, the 92nd received orders to push east through the heavily defended Bois Fréhaut (Fréhaut Woods) to retake the town of Metz, which Emmett J. Scott, special adjutant to the Secretary of War, described as "a network of barbed-wire entanglements, and the big guns in Metz had to do nothing but sweep the woods with a murderous fire . . . it was worse than hell . . . it had become a sepulcher of hundreds."[157]

The final battle began in earnest for the men of the 365th on November 5. By November 10, they had driven east to the edge of the Bois Fréhaut as part of a full-scale offensive by the entire allied force in France to push the Germans back.[158] Dawson and his men fought nearly to the last minute of the last day of the last battle of the Great War.[159] On November 11, at 5 a.m., the 1st and 2nd Battalions of the 365th resumed their attack under heavy artillery fire and Dawson's platoon remained in the full pitch of battle until the reports of the Armistice came at 10:45 a.m.[160]

As Dawson drew his men together, death surrounded them. At that moment the senselessness of war coupled with the inexcusable racism of his white superiors steeled the young lieutenant's resolve to make a difference when he returned home. Doris Saunders reported that as Dawson gazed upon the destruction, his emotions welled up and he exclaimed, "O father God, if you will just take me back home, I will give my life to teach my fellow man to use the ballot so that these kinds of things, these atrocities will not happen again. If you will, I promise you, God, I'll die teaching them how to use the ballot."[161] Regardless of whether he uttered these specific words, they capture the transformation that the Great War wrought in the young man from Albany. His mission had been revealed: He would dedicate himself to teaching blacks how to use the ballot.[162]

(left) Chicago's most popular black Republican of the early twentieth century and Dawson's second mentor, Oscar DePriest. Doris Evans Saunders Papers, folder 256

(below) Louis Anderson, a founder of black politics in Chicago and the link between black Republicans and the emergent Democratic organization of the 1930s. Doris Evans Saunders Papers, folder 255

The creators of the party-building philosophy, William Dawson, Christopher Wimbish, Corneal Davis, and an unidentified gentleman. Doris Evans Saunders Papers, folder 189

The backbone of the early Dawson organization of the 1940s. From left to right: Fred Smith, William Harvey, Fred Wall, Christopher Wimbish, Corneal Davis, and William Dawson. Doris Evans Saunders Papers, folder 110, George H. Myles Photography

(above) An example of the Dawson organization's effort to integrate Democratic politics into the social fabric of the black South Side. Dawson crowning the winner of the Second Ward Popularity Contest, Edna Latson. Doris Evans Saunders Papers, folder 175

(left) Truman Gibson, Jr., a critical ally in Dawson's push for black equality in the military during World War II. Doris Evans Saunders Papers, folder 111

Dawson shaking hands with former federal judge William Hastie, who proved a critical Truman supporter in the 1948 campaign. Doris Evans Saunders Papers, folder 102

Dawson and President Harry Truman apparently enjoying a punch line. The two maintained a particularly cordial relationship after the 1948 presidential campaign. Doris Evans
Saunders Papers, folder 101

Dawson conferring with Martin Luther King at an unidentified venue. King's youthful appearance next to Dawson highlights the generational differences between the two.

Doris Evans Saunders Papers, folder 203

Dawson on the stump during a reelection campaign. Doris Evans Saunders Papers, folder 104

Dawson chatting with House Speaker Sam Rayburn at a testimonial dinner for the Texas representative circa 1955. A part of the network of committee chairmen and the House leadership, Dawson sat at the head table. Doris Evans Saunders Papers, folder 207. Photographer: Gaffney Photographers, 1811 Benning Rd. N.E. Washington 2 D.C. Taken by Theodore M. Gaffney.

Wire spectacles in his right hand and his characteristic cigar in the left, Dawson's portrait communicates an impassive authority. Doris Evans Saunders Papers, folder 208. Photographer: Harris & Ewing.

Dawson, Mary Bethune, Helen Gahagan Douglas, and an unidentified man at a rally for Douglas's failed 1950 senatorial campaign in California.

One of Dawson's key allies in the late 1940s and 1950s, *Chicago Defender* editor, John Sengstacke.

One of Chicago's earliest female judges, one of the first African American delegates to the United Nations, and a Dawson protegé, Edith Sampson. Doris Evans Saunders Papers, folder 261

Dawson throwing out the first pitch of a negro baseball league game.

Dawson and his daughter
Barbara Dawson Morgan at a
formal engagement. Doris Evans

Saunders Papers, folder 285

Dawson with Mayor Richard J.
Daley to his left and the members of the Illinois delegation
to the House delegation circa
1960. Given Daley's relatively
recent undermining of the
congressman's local influence,
one is left to wonder at Dawson's distinctly reserved body
language relative to that of his
colleagues. Daniel Rostenkowski Papers,

Loyola University, Chicago

Dawson and members from the Illinois delegation from Cook County in March 1960.

Chapter Two

BIG BILL, THE IRONMASTER, AND THE OLD ROMAN

I want you to think about taking your money and using it to save your property. . . . You had better know that "Mr. Charlie" wants your property. It's good land and he thinks it's too good for you. If you mess up, he will get it back.[1]—*William L. Dawson*

By birth, training, and experience I am better fitted to represent the district in Washington than any of the candidates in the field. Mr. Madden, the present Congressman, doesn't even live in the district. He is a white man. Therefore, for those two reasons, if no others, he can hardly voice the hopes, ideals and sentiment of the majority of the district.[2]—*William L. Dawson*

When William Dawson decided to change African Americans' fortunes through politics he reflected a militancy that had captured the imagination of black Americans in the late 1910s.[3] For better or worse, in Chicago this sentiment found particularly strong expression through electoral politics.[4] Starting in 1917, a generation of Chicago's black political leaders, particularly Dawson's mentors Ed Wright and Oscar DePriest, a Chicago alderman and member of Congress, attempted various moderately successful strategies to leverage the South Side's growing black vote and exploit the city's decentralized, factional party politics to bring black Chicagoans the benefits of participating in local politics.[5] Although Dawson worked closely with Wright and DePriest in the 1920s, he remained a mere foot soldier in their political battles. Regardless of his low rank, he could not fail to notice that neither methodical organizing nor racial militancy provided a foundation sufficient to promote African American interests consistently in light of the unstable nature of the local Republican Party's factional politics. Indeed, Dawson's observations of his mentors' failures fueled his desire to create an independent black organization that could demand greater respect from the white political leadership.

Before the start of the Great Migration in 1917, black Chicago had few voters and little clout in local politics. Their alliance with the Republican Party had yielded blacks a few token appointments. In 1898, for example, the Democratic mayor, Carter Harrison II, nominated a black lawyer, S.A.T. Watkins, to be an assistant prosecuting attorney. Also, Chicago sent a string of black Republicans to the state legislature between 1894 and 1900.[6] Still, the black men who held elective and appointive office in the late nineteenth and early twentieth centuries engaged in politics as a sideline to their legal and business careers. Their political activities represented their responsibilities as community leaders more than systematic endeavors to lobby for their communities through the ballot.[7]

This situation proved inadequate for achieving any semblance of political autonomy. As long as the black vote remained small and reliable, white Republicans saw no need to grant any significant political power to black leadership. White disregard became apparent in 1906, when prominent black Republican Ferdinand Barnett ran for a seat on the municipal court. Barnett had won the Republican nomination based on his history of Republican activism, but his campaign aroused intense resistance from Chicago whites. Although Barnett won the initial count by 500 votes, Democratic officials alleged fraud and demanded a recount. Demonstrating black Republicans' expendability, the new tally deemed Barnett the loser by 304 votes, making him the only local Republican nominee defeated in that election cycle.[8] The Barnett case shocked black Chicago, and they realized that no black candidate could win citywide elective office.[9]

White voter resistance seemed insurmountable until the first Great Migration began drastically changing the city's demographic landscape. Drawn to Chicago by wartime production needs and the *Chicago Defender's* "Great Northern Drive," approximately 50,000 southern blacks migrated to Chicago between 1917 and 1918. The new arrivals raised the city's black population to 110,000.[10] As indicated previously, as early as 1910 blacks could find housing only in relatively segregated, often rundown, areas. The Great Migration rapidly accelerated this pattern, transforming the nascent South Side slum into a densely populated and increasingly large black ghetto. In 1910, practically no black Chicagoans lived in areas with a population of more than 75 percent black, but by 1920 more than 45 percent of black Chicagoans lived in such areas.[11] These segregated housing patterns concentrated the new arrivals into the South Side's 2nd and 3rd Wards and presented black political leaders with the potential to mobilize black voters into a unified voting block.[12]

The growing flood of black migrants came as a godsend to Ed Wright, who had been seeking a means to boost the power of the black vote for over a decade.[13] Dubbed "The Ironmaster" by political observers for his rigorous political organization, Wright first realized the power of a unified black voting bloc in 1894. That year Wright urged blacks in the 1st Ward to vote for a straight Republican ticket. They responded and helped elect the Republican mayoral candidate, George B. Swift. Swift acknowledged Wright's role in garnering this support by recognizing him as an important political player on the South Side. Wright used Swift's backing to nominate several blacks to important posts, including Theodore W. Jones as county commissioner in 1894 and Ferdinand Barnett as assistant state's attorney in 1896. Wright expanded his political power in 1896 by engineering his own election to the county commission. Later, he manipulated his fellow board members into electing him president of the county board.[14]

A string of Democratic administrations (1899–1905, 1911–1915) slowed Wright's drive, but he remained in the spotlight as a promoter of black political power when he ran a series of racially militant campaigns for alderman of the 3rd Ward in the 1910s. When Wright ran for the seat in 1910, blacks constituted 25 percent of the ward. Wright hoped to unify them and draw in a few whites for an upset victory. Although the regular Republican leadership gave him no support, Wright won 18 percent of the vote to finish in third place. He ran again in 1912, but the South Side's second most prominent black politician and Wright's primary rival, Oscar "The Old Roman" DePriest, opposed him. Without DePriest's support, Wright could not win.[15] Wright's break finally came in 1914, when he supported another black candidate, William B. Cowan, for the alderman's seat. Like past black candidates, Cowan did not receive the endorsement of white Republicans, but this time Wright exploited white Republicans' lack of enthusiasm as a battle cry for black control of the Republican Party in the 3rd Ward. Although Cowan lost the election, he pulled in 45 percent of the vote.[16]

Cowan's significant percentage indicated that the Republican leadership could no longer ignore black voters. As local Republicans began to charm black voters more vigorously, Wright asserted himself and built a substantial black Republican faction in the South Side's 2nd and 3rd Wards.[17] After being appointed assistant corporate counsel in 1915, Wright earned immense gratitude from white party leaders by successfully defending several prominent Republicans against charges of voting irregularities. In 1917, Wright took the presidency of the 2nd Ward regular organization, and in 1918 he managed William "Big Bill" Thompson's short-lived senatorial campaign in the black wards. Mayor Thompson, who was immensely popular among Chicago blacks for his vocal opposition to Jim Crow and copious dispensation of patronage, acknowledged Wright as the dominant leader of the 2nd Ward by backing his successful bid for 2nd Ward committeeman in 1919.[18]

Just as Wright began his tenure as the leading power in black politics, Chicago, like the rest of the nation, convulsed from ethnic and racial tensions.[19] In 1918–1919, newly arrived European immigrants played out conflicts reflecting those manifested during the postwar negotiations in Versailles. In the spring of 1918 Lithuanian nationalists clashed with Lithuanian Bolsheviks over the future of their mother country. Later that summer, more than 200,000 people greeted Czechoslovakian nationalist Thomas Masaryk when he visited Chicago to rally support for an independent Czechoslovakia. In June and July of 1919, antagonisms escalated between the city's Jewish and Polish populations over dominance of neighborhoods on the West and Southeast Sides, generating mob conflicts numbering up to 5,000. Meanwhile, Irish nationalism rose to a fever pitch when Irish independence leader Eamon De Valera visited Chicago in early July.[20] European immigrants to Chicago shared their nationalist fever with African Americans who joined Marcus Garvey's Universal Negro Improvement Association. With his message of liberation and pride for all people of African descent, Garvey found several thousand black Chicagoans eager to hear his ideas.[21] Job competition, an economic recession, and increasing violence at the boundaries of black Chicago brought this volatile mixture to a boiling point in the Chicago race riot in July 1919, which left thirty-eight dead and several hundred wounded—blacks and whites.[22]

In an act of great bravery DePriest personally executed the rescue of several blacks trapped by white mobs. DePriest's actions during the riot, perhaps reminiscent of the valor of black soldiers in the war, inspired Dawson and led to his movement into the South Side's black Republican organization:

I remember seeing him put on a policeman's uniform and drive a patrol wagon into the stockyards and bring out the Negroes who were trapped inside during the riot of 1919. He was respected as a former alderman, and he did what not a single policeman had the courage to do. . . . I sat down and wrote Oscar a letter. I told him I thought he had performed a great deed and I personally wanted to congratulate him. I also told him that he could always depend on me for support in anything he would undertake in the future and that I was ready to stand behind him.[23]

DePriest took Dawson seriously and found a place for him in the Wright organization. While the author could find little information regarding Dawson's earliest political jobs, it does appear that Dawson began under the tutelage of the renowned blind precinct captain "Crip" Woods.[24]

As a would-be Republican leader, Dawson immediately saw the value of a law degree and quickly resumed his legal studies as a second-year student at Northwestern University. His war injuries rendered him eligible for educational benefits through the Federal Vocation and Training Board, which paid for his tuition and supplies. Midway through his third year, though, Dawson apparently wanted to move on to his legal practice, so he requested permission from the faculty to take the bar exam in January 1920. They denied his petition, but Dawson applied again and successfully passed the bar in November.[25]

Without finishing his degree—a common practice in the period— Dawson joined four promising lawyers in their Loop offices at 184 West Washington. Dawson's partners, William H. Haynes, Herman E. Moore, Irvin C. Mollinson, and J. Ernest Wilkins, had also migrated from the South and their firm's reputation for aggressive legal advocacy grew quickly. Then one day Moore went downstairs to get some lunch and the restaurant refused him service. Moore sued the establishment, with his partners acting as his legal counsel. The building management retaliated by serving them with an eviction notice, but the attorneys laughed it off and signed a lease with a building next door. In the future all of the men, with the exception of Hayes, who died before the others, would go on to exceptional careers: one as a congressman, two as federal judges, and one as a subcabinet appointee.[26]

Dawson had more concerns than just his career at the time though, namely, his future wife, Miss Nellie Brown of Washington, D.C. In the summer of 1921, Nellie came to Chicago to visit a family friend, Dr. Mary Waring. Another lawyer from Detroit, Percy Piper, introduced Brown to Dawson, who she said "was all gentility and Southern grace and manners." The pack headed over to the Sten Inn for dinner and then another party. Dawson could not go because of a prior engagement, but he would not let Nellie get too far out of his sight. He asked Nellie of her plans for the rest of her time in Chicago, and she replied that she did not have anything definite. While their friends looked on and teased that Dawson would try to take up all of her time, he replied that she should let him know everything she wanted to do and "then consider that it would be done."[27] Before she left to Indianapolis to continue her vacation, Dawson caught up with Nellie and begged her to come back to Chicago before she went back to Washington. She agreed, and that September Dawson asked her to marry him. Brown said, "I knew I would, but I knew that I would have to work on Papa. Bill was brownskin, and my father, like so many of that day, didn't want any black grandchildren."[28]

Brown possessed a more urbane upbringing than her fiancé. The Browns originated from Louisville, Kentucky, where Nellie's father, the Reverend Thomas Jacob Brown, had married Nellie's mother, Sallie. Mrs. Brown passed away during Nellie's childhood, and her father accepted an appointment to St. Luke's Protestant Episcopal Church in Washington. Home to the influential intellectual Alexander Crumell in the nineteenth century, St. Luke's boasted a refined and intellectual congregation. Reverend Brown then married Lucretia Minor, daughter of Howard University professor John L. Minor. Unlike Dawson, Nellie's childhood did not include chores and economic struggles; in her home the "help" did the laundry. Nellie regularly interacted with the District's black elites, including Carter G. Woodson, who apparently favored her in his classes. Her social life as a teenager involved concerts, vacations, and trips to the seashore. After sending her to Minor Teachers College for her bachelor's degree, Nellie's parents expected her to look for a husband among the upper class of Washington, D.C., or the East Coast.[29]

In May 1922, Dawson went to Washington to meet the Browns and ask for their daughter's hand in marriage. Surprisingly, his color posed no problem for Reverend Brown, for the two men hit it off immediately. Nellie remembered, "Papa said he was a wonderful man," and her "stepbrother adored him." Later during the trip the newly engaged couple went to visit a family friend in Maryland, and as they ran to catch the streetcar home the excitement of it all overwhelmed Dawson who yelled, "Miss Nell Brown of Washington town, I'm going to bring you back here as the wife of the first Negro Congressman from the 1st Congressional District of Illinois." This odd exclamation prompted her to think, "Oh, my God! Am I marrying a nut?"[30] Dawson returned to Washington in

December 1922 for the wedding. As she walked down the aisle to meet her groom, who, at thirty-six, was nine years her elder, Nellie wore a white satin dress with a garland of orange flowers atop her wavy, brown hair. The Reverend Brown performed the ceremony in St. Luke's. The Browns held a reception for the newlyweds, who left on a midnight train to Chicago that evening.[31]

Nellie described the early years of their marriage as "wonderful in a way," but her husband's political ambitions and Nellie's distaste for Chicago impinged upon their relationship from the start. Chicago's black elite immediately welcomed the Dawsons, with the Barnetts holding a reception in their honor. Yet the evening did not suit Nellie. Ida Wells-Barnett's preoccupation with social causes made the evening weightier than Nellie expected. As a member of the exclusive 40 Club and a founding member of Chicago's graduate chapter of Alpha Phi Alpha fraternity, Dawson's connections kept their social calendar full, but the South Side did not possess the gentility of Washington's more established black community. Nellie said, "There was always so much dirt and so much ignorance and I was unaccustomed to it, but Bill loved people, all kinds and in the beginning I went with him. . . . I was with him the night he made his first speech at a school on 41st Street." Not yet a politician, but clearly political, Dawson, who specialized in real estate, went to a political rally with Oscar DePriest, where he addressed the crowd. Foreshadowing a militancy and pragmatism that would reveal itself more fully in a few years, Nellie remembered her husband saying, "I want you to think about taking your money and using it to save your property. . . . You had better know that 'Mr. Charlie' wants your property. It's good land and he thinks it's too good for you. If you mess up, he will get it back."[32]

Though the exact date is unclear, it seems that this event occurred relatively soon after Ed Wright had brought Dawson into the main organization as his protégé in 1922. Nellie said that Wright became a singularly important influence on her husband, "Mr. Wright gave Bill things . . . he would never have known in the political world. Things he could apply. Ed Wright spared him nothing."[33] Wright's mentoring, coupled with Dawson's ability to work well with others, enabled him to move quickly through the Republican organization's ranks. He served first as a precinct captain, where he ascertained the needs of community members, connected them to city services, and drummed up their votes on Election Day.[34] Dawson's ability to connect with constituents and to bring in the vote eventually led to his appointment as supervisor of several precincts. Throughout this time Dawson kept friendly ties with all of the Republican factions. Although he prioritized his relationship with Wright, for example, Dawson remained cordial to DePriest.[35] One contemporary mused, Dawson "wasn't too sociable. He was friendly, but there's a difference between friendly and sociable." Ferdinand Barnett noted, "Dawson knew how to treat people. How to talk to them, how to ask them for things."[36] Indeed, Dawson's ability to connect with people while conducting shrewd politics distinguished him from his mentor. Aaron Payne, who later opposed Dawson in a city council race in 1933, said that Wright "lacked heart" and was "cold and austere." Dawson, by contrast, possessed a certain kind of warmth.[37]

As a lieutenant for the Iron Master, Dawson operated more as an observer than a leader in the politics of the 1920s, and he learned that Chicago's white Republican leadership would only support expanded black political representation under pressure that threatened their hold on power. At first, Wright seemed poised to move beyond racial limitations. With his newfound influence and support from two powerful white Republicans, Wright quickly pushed for more black employment and appointments in local government.[38] Although DePriest left the city council in 1917 amid allegations of conspiracy, Wright remained aware of his activities. Wright then secured his flank by supporting his friend and political ally, Louis Anderson, for DePriest's old seat. With one man already in the city council, Wright sent two other allies, Charles A. Griffen and William E. King, to the state legislature in 1924. Wright then pushed for black appointments in the sanitation districts controlled by Mayor Thompson, in the sheriff's department, county coroner's office, and state's attorney's office. Finally, Wright became the first black member of the Illinois Commerce Commission with Governor Len Small's backing, but this move put Wright in an awkward position. He now had obligations to two powerful white Republicans: Mayor Thompson and Governor Small.[39]

Unfortunately Wright's belligerent advocacy for expanded black participation in government rendered him vulnerable to his political enemies. In 1923, for instance, he obtained the Republican nomination for judge of the superior court for corporate and civil rights lawyer Edward H. Morris by threatening to withdraw his support for the congressional campaign of Martin B. Madden, whose 1st Congressional District contained the increasingly black 2nd and 3d wards. Morris lost the election, but Wright had made his point.[40] One year later, Wright pushed for another African American judge, successfully backing Albert B. George to a coveted spot on the municipal court. Yet, he again relied on bullying and humiliation to counter the party's unwillingness to nominate a black candidate. During a meeting of the Cook County Republican Committee, Wright insisted that the committee put up a black nominee for the municipal court. The state's attorney, Robert Crowe, faced reelection that year, and he expressed his white colleagues' fears when he said that putting up a black attorney would hurt the ticket. Wright responded to Crowe:

> Look, Bob you can't carry your own precinct. . . . Let me tell you, you can't carry your own precinct. I'm the committeeman of the 2nd Ward, and the 3d Ward is all Republican and black. . . I want you to know that these two wards will give the Republican Party a 50,000 majority. . . . You can't tell me about who's going to hurt the ticket. It will be Albert B. George. . . . Albert B. George will be the candidate for judge. And I'm going to go a little further than that. I'm going to watch the returns from every ward in the city of Chicago. And any ward that doesn't give Albert George an equal vote to the white candidates, I don't want anybody from that ward ever to ask the support of black people. I'll see that they don't get it.[41]

The committee nominated and supported George, making him the first black judge in the municipal court, but the episode did not endear Wright to his white colleagues.[42] Also in 1924, Wright suggested that corporation counsel Sam A. Ettleson retire from his seat in the state senate to make room for Aldebert H. Roberts, one of Wright's allies. Ettelson complied, and Roberts served in the senate for the next ten years.[43]

Wright exhibited the same aggression toward white politicians of national stature as he had with local leaders. In 1920 black postal employees created the Phalanx Club and the National Alliance of Postal Workers to lobby for equal opportunities within the U.S. Postal Service. Blacks in Chicago had held positions in the post office since the 1880s, but management rarely promoted them to managerial positions. The alliance had petitioned Congressman Madden to use his influence as chairman of the House Appropriations Committee—charged with dispersing funds throughout the federal government—to secure one black managerial position in the post office. Madden responded positively but never followed through. As a result, a delegation including Corneal Davis visited Ed Wright in his City Hall office. They discussed their negotiations with Madden and presented Wright with a list of all the recent vacancies that had occurred in the Chicago post office. Davis recollected that Wright responded with his characteristic "bug eyes" popping out in indignation, "You mean to tell me that these vacancies have occurred and no Negro has been appointed supervisor yet?" Wright then told his secretary to call Madden, leaving Davis and the others to hear Wright's end of the conversation:

> Hello, Congressman Madden, this is Ed Wright of Chicago. You promised me that when a vacancy occurred in the Chicago Post Office, you would see that a black man was appointed supervisor. Congressman Madden, I have before me conclusive evidence that several vacancies have occurred and no black man has been named supervisor in the Chicago Post Office. . . . Congressman Madden, it is now 11:00 a.m. in the morning. I want you to appoint one Dave Hawley to the Chicago Post Office before the sun goes down. Good-bye, Congressman Madden.[44]

By 5 p.m. Dave Hawley received an appointment as the first black supervisor in a Chicago Post Office.[45]

In 1926, however, Wright's fortunes declined when he picked the wrong side in a factional squabble between his two patrons and the states' leading white Republicans, Thompson and Small. The problem originated three years earlier when DePriest challenged Wright's control over black politics. That year both men's white sponsor, Mayor Thompson, did not seek reelection, and the two black leaders supported rival candidates for the mayor's office. Neither man's candidate won, but the difference revealed DePriest's resistance to Wright's control. When Thompson lost office, he also relinquished his control of government patronage. Without access to municipal jobs, Wright could neither solidify his followers' support nor execute a program to install more blacks in government. He consequently shifted his allegiance to incumbent governor Len Small—a dangerous move, because Small and Thompson despised each other. Then, in 1926, Wright opposed Thompson's ally for 1st Ward committeeman, Daniel A. Serritella, and Thompson accused Wright of attempting to establish a South Side dictatorship. When Thompson ran for mayor again in 1927, Wright backed Small's associate, John Dill Robertson. DePriest, however, saw a Thompson victory as an opportunity to return to electoral politics and backed the former mayor.[46]

As fate would have it, Thompson won the election and cut down Wright—an episode that devastated Dawson and showed him black politicians' vulnerability when involved in the factional struggles of their more powerful white patrons. Immediately after the election Thompson ordered Wright to send his patronage workers to Dan Jackson, the man whom Thompson designated to take Wright's place in the next election for 2nd Ward committeeman. Addressing his precinct captains at the 8th Regiment Armory, Wright said, "I have chosen my own course. I am not asking any of you to quit your jobs. I am able to take care of myself. You go over to Dan Jackson. . . . He is your new leader." State Senator Roberts left first. Soon after, all of the men filed out, even his friend Alderman Louis Anderson, leaving behind Davis and Dawson. Seeing Wright's career destroyed broke their hearts. Davis said, "That was one of the most moving things I have ever seen in my whole life. Wright knew that he was sealing his political doom. When a man comes big enough to do a thing like that [sic] they don't come any bigger." It was a lesson, said Davis, that he and Dawson would never forget.[47]

Later that year, Wright mounted an independent campaign against Congressman Madden with assistance from Dawson, Earl Dickerson, and several other young black lawyers, but, without a white sponsor, Wright had no chance, and he never again played a role in Chicago politics. White politicos would not readmit Wright to the fold, for he used the burgeoning black vote in a way that too strongly threatened their political dominance. By 1927, Wright had already moved beyond the leadership of a minor Republican faction. He had gained statewide recognition and attempted to influence appointments at the federal level. He secured government jobs for blacks who did not work in local politics and strong armed the appointments of several others. Calculating and fearless, Wright threatened to "cut" white Republican candidates if the party did not support the black candidates he suggested for various offices, and he did not hesitate to shout down colleagues who disagreed with his claims to patronage positions. Most dangerous of all, though, claimed Davis, was that Wright was a "big, bad man pushing Thompson," whose popularity among black voters outshone even Wright's.[48]

In sum, although Ed Wright attempted to make blacks a legitimate force within the state and local party, two factors prevented him from becoming the city's first party builder. First, Wright did not temper his ambition with recognition of the importance of building stable relationships within his party. He made numerous enemies, including the powerful and charismatic William Thompson, as well as dozens of others whom he intimidated in the course of his career. Thus, many of Illinois's top GOP leaders considered him a risk. Second, in the 1920s, the growth of a single black power base on the South Side benefited white leaders of neither party. The Republican Party possessed a long and unchallenged history of black activism and electoral support. Without the need to hold or recruit black voters, the GOP leadership saw Wright as expendable. Moreover, a host of ambitious young black Republicans vied for his power. Within the context of the intense factionalism that characterized Chicago Republicanism, this cohort of black politicians had numerous opportunities to attach themselves to competing white sponsors and potentially "cut" each other, as DePriest cut Wright in 1927.

Contrasting with Wright's aggressive wielding of the black vote, DePriest used racially militant rhetoric to cultivate an independent power base and more subtly exploited divisions among white political factions to bring himself back into the political limelight. Although DePriest left office under the shadow of corruption charges in 1917, he bided his time by forming the People's Movement, an independent race-based political organization. The People's Movement won appreciation from insurgent white Republican factions when it opposed aldermen sponsored by the Wright and Madden blocs in 1918 and 1919. Conversely, it honed the usage of racially militant critiques against the dominant white organization to draw admiration from black voters. Indeed, DePriest's rhetoric of racial solidarity against black leaders allegedly handpicked by whites brought him a significant number of votes in both elections.[49] These attacks, however, did not return DePriest to office. As a result, DePriest gambled the People's Movement and all of his remaining political capital on Thompson's 1927 mayoral campaign. Thompson won and rewarded DePriest by making him committeeman of the 3d Ward, the dominant leader of black Republican politics, and Dawson's new boss.[50]

Despite DePriest and Thompson's popularity, black Chicagoans in the 1st Congressional District, which included the overwhelmingly black 2nd and 3rd Wards, chafed under the leadership of their aging white Republican congressman, Martin Madden. Madden had secured an appointment for Dave Hawley as a supervisor at the Armour Avenue Post Office, but this move did not quell discontent over the persistent dearth of black appointments to administrative level positions in the postal service. As chairman of the Committee on Appropriations Madden ran perhaps the most powerful committee in the House, yet he refused to push for blacks to receive managerial positions. This incongruity begged the question of why blacks in the 2nd and 3rd wards tolerated his representation in the first place.[51]

Indeed, Madden's unacceptability to black voters factored into several years of frustration with local politics as white voters moved toward allegedly cleaner politics that ignored black interests. In 1923 the leaders of the three most prominent Democratic factions, Roger Sullivan,

Carter Harrison II, and Edward Dunne momentarily united to support Judge William E. Dever for mayor. Dever's acceptance stemmed less from his political acumen than from his spotless reputation among watchdog groups such as the Municipal Voters League. The Republicans nominated Arthur C. Leuder, a similarly clean candidate whose record as a business- man and postmaster generated none of the enthusiasm that blacks had felt for Thompson.[52]

The stunningly bland candidates, who led no political organizations of their own, left the city's black political operatives to make allegiances of convenience. In a move that demonstrated his willingness to cross political lines to maintain black electoral strength, Republican Alderman Louis Anderson agreed to generate black votes for Dever, if he and other black leaders could keep their patronage positions in a Democratic ad- ministration. Dever agreed and subsequently won the election with a considerable percentage of black votes, which established Anderson as a conduit between the South Side's black Republicans and the leadership of the Democratic Party.[53]

In Dever's four years as mayor, Anderson and later DePriest retained some influence over city hiring, but black voters had little else to cele- brate. Dever initiated a series of raids focusing on South Side that lead to the arrests of 1,000 blacks, although illegal gambling existed throughout the city. In 1927 Dever angered many black Chicagoans when he visited Biloxi, Mississippi, and praised the notoriously segregated state for educat- ing black children to have such good manners. In the election that year his campaign hired calliopes to play "Bye-Bye Blackbird" in downtown Chicago to rekindle fears that a Thompson victory meant black control.[54]

Dever's disregard for black voters made up one strand in a tightening noose of racism and segregation that characterized the late 1920s. By the end of the decade the black population had risen to 233,903 from 109,594 in 1920, and African Americans made up 7 percent of the city's total popu- lation. Simultaneously, segregation worsened, with 66 percent of all black Chicagoans residing in areas with concentrations of blacks in excess of 90 percent. This state of affairs encouraged neglect by slumlords and fostered significant deterioration of housing across the Black Belt.[55] As a result, although blacks increased their presence throughout the industrial labor force, they could not live near their jobs in the same manner as their Eu- ropean counterparts.[56] Furthermore European workers' embrace of Ameri- can-style racism precluded their acceptance of blacks in the emergent labor movement and rendered black workers particularly vulnerable to unsafe working conditions as well as the vagaries of the economic cycle.[57]

Well aware of black Chicagoans' frustration, Dawson used combative rhetoric and grassroots organizing to mount an independent campaign against Congressman Madden in 1928. In so doing, he joined a number of black leaders who challenged the city's white political leadership along racial lines and attempted to consolidate black Chicago's voting power. With the memories of the Great War still vibrant, Dawson and Corneal Davis donned their World War I uniforms to become the "Army Buddies." The two men trooped across the 1st Congressional District, from its pool halls to precinct meetings, trying to convince the voters that they needed a black congressman:

> By birth, training, and experience I am better fitted to represent the district in Washington than any of the candidates in the field. Mr. Madden, the present Congressman, doesn't even live in the district. He is a white man. Therefore, for those two reasons, if no others, he can hardly voice the hopes, ideals and sentiment of the majority of the district.[58]

A Mississippi native, Davis spoke directly to black Southerners' desires to realize their goals in coming north: "This is the only district north of the Mason Dixon Line where a black man can be elected to Congress and you ought to elect him."[59] Ida B. Wells gave her approval by sharing the stage with Dawson early in the primary season as she ran her own independent campaign for delegate to the Republican National Convention (RNC). And another World War I veteran, C. C. Wimbish, ran against the regular ticket for a position as alternate delegate to the RNC. Meanwhile, Ed Wright gave as much assistance as he could, and as the primaries drew near Dawson's crowds grew.[60]

Despite his message, heavy canvassing, and growing popularity, Dawson's campaign could not defeat the array of regular Republican forces deployed against him. He received, for instance, almost no coverage in the *Chicago Defender*. Voters who wanted to know anything about Dawson's campaign had to rely on the much smaller *Chicago Whip* or handbills.[61] The *Defender* did report on the speeches and activities of Thompson's America First coalition, which included almost all of the city's prominent black politicians: 2nd Ward Committeeman Dan Jackson, Alderman Louis Anderson, Alderman William E. King, Civil Service Commissioner Bishop Archibald Carey, State Senator Aldebert H. Roberts, 3d District Representative George T. Kersey, State Representative George W. Blackwell, and State Representative Harris B. Gaines. These men signed a pamphlet entitled "An Appeal to Reason," which praised Madden for his efforts to protect his new black constituents. The *Defender* also ran a dramatic article on Madden's sickbed defense of Howard University's appropriation against southern legislative attacks.[62]

Despite conjecture by contemporary scholars that Dawson coordinated his attack on Madden with Oscar DePriest, no definitive evidence exists to point to such collusion.[63] To the contrary, the Thompson-DePriest faction came down hard on Dawson—rhetorically and physically. DePriest frequently commended Madden as a bulwark against southern bigots. He recounted Madden's rebuffing of southern representatives' attempts to cut the number of blacks in the postal service and argued that the South would rejoice at Madden's defeat.[64] Thompson joined DePriest's attack by coming to the South Side to rally votes for Madden. "A Negro might go to Congress and after serving there for twenty years *might* become chairman of the powerful finance committee," Thompson proclaimed with incredulity, "perhaps he might—*perhaps.*" Much to his surprise, the crowds reacted with a chorus of boos and hissing.[65] Finally, the regular organization escalated their offensive to physical attacks on Dawson and Davis. First, Republican regulars routinely destroyed their campaign materials. Then police harassment came into play. The Army Buddies particularly feared two black policemen, Big Six and Starks, who gave them a few harsh thrashings as they campaigned against Madden.[66]

Unsurprisingly, Dawson lost to Madden in the March 14 primary, but he sent a strong message to the white political establishment. Despite a nonexistent budget, no regular support, and reports of voter fraud, Dawson won a third of the vote—7,910 to Madden's 19,615.[67] True to his parents' warning to keep his mouth shut, Dawson did not protest: "Well, I didn't get mad. I learned a lesson. You not only have to get the votes into the box, you have to protect the box too."[68] Besides, Dawson had, to a certain extent, accomplished his goal. His campaign pointed to a clear and growing determination on the part of blacks in the 1st Congressional District to elect a black congressman, and it had the secondary effect of establishing Dawson as a rising star in local politics.[69]

A month later Madden died unexpectedly and DePriest seized the opportunity to set himself up to become the first black congressman since Reconstruction. At the time, DePriest, Anderson, and other black politicians vacationed at a resort in West Baden, Indiana. While Anderson and the rest of the crew played cards, DePriest looked on and then left the room to answer the phone. As it turned out, the caller wanted to notify the men of Madden's death. When DePriest did not return, his associates assumed he had gone to bed. Little did they know that he had rushed to the local telegraph office and contacted the men on the committee charged with replacing Madden, which included 1st Ward Committee-man Dan Seritella and 2nd Ward Committeeman Dan Jackson—both of whom played a role in Wright's downfall.[70] DePriest quickly drafted support from the mayor and the city's leading Republicans to receive the nomination to replace Madden. He would go on to win the election in the fall with 4,000 more votes than his closest rival.[71]

Attempting to shore up black Republicanism against Democratic surges in the 1st Congressional District, DePriest reconciled with Dawson and sponsored him for a spot on the Republican State committee in 1929.[72] Dawson soon became one of DePriest's primary representatives, and politics consumed his life. In 1931, as Dawson hurried through the train station at 63rd Street and Stony Island his shoulder caught a platform turnstile, causing him to trip and fall onto the tracks below. As he tried to get up an oncoming train severed his foot. Later that day when Aaron Payne visited him in the hospital, Dawson responded glibly, "What's a leg?"[73] Nellie visited him throughout his six-week hospital stay, and she thought the injury might cause Dawson to give greater consideration to his family, whom he rarely saw. Nellie reflected that in the early years of their marriage she would say, "Husband, can't we go out together just you and me, to a show, or to dinner?" Dawson, however, always had a commitment to this or that organization. He no longer had a social life, having long since dropped his activities in social clubs and fraternities, and the amputation did not slow him down. Instead, he grew increas-ingly irritable, and got himself back in the game as soon as possible.[74]

His work paid off in 1933, when Anderson announced his retirement as 2nd Ward alderman, and rumors circulated that DePriest would nominate Dawson for the seat. Citing Dawson's work as an attorney and praising his war record, DePriest formally endorsed Dawson's campaign. He argued that Dawson came from a younger generation of black leaders, including 2nd Ward Committeeman William E. King and 3d Ward Alderman Robert Jack-son, who possessed a burning desire to lead blacks into the future. Unlike the 1928 campaign, Dawson now had the backing of all of the black regular Republicans and he beat his opponent, Edgar G. Brown, 14,032 to 2,002.[75]

Thus, in 1933, twenty years after leaving the South, Dawson won a spot on the city council as alderman of the city's 2nd Ward. Yet a dis-cordant tone marred his celebrations. Shortly after the election, *Chicago Defender* writer A. N. Fields advised his readers that they should not expect miracles from the new alderman or his colleague Robert Jackson, because they had no access to patronage.[76] For while Chicago's black Republicans had been fighting each other on the South Side, Chicago's Democratic Party had taken control of the city, the state, and the nation's politics.

Chapter Three
"SECOND WARD FOR THE SECOND WARDERS"

Dawson built his following among us by the most vigorous anti-white speeches you have ever heard. His theme was, "No black man who had to lick from a trough fed by white hands can be effective." That is why he felt it was so crucial for a political organization to be able to run under its own steam and not have to ask for money from downtown to keep your organization together.[1]—*Fred Wall*

Halt the Rent Hog, Fight the Real Estate Gouger, Protect Your Home and Family. Don't Pay High Rent for Run-Down Property. Join the Consolidated Tenants Association.[2]
—*Tenants' War Cry*

There can be no question that the aims, interests and aspirations of all Negro citizens in America are identical with those of the 275,000 on Chicago's South Side. All must stand together united as one in striving to attain full integration into American life.[3]
—*William L. Dawson*

Although Ed Wright failed to consolidate an African American political base in the Republican Party, the 1930s provided a decidedly different political landscape. The ravages of the Depression brought Democratic victories in Washington, D.C., and Illinois. President Roosevelt began the New Deal, and the local Democratic Party apparently provided the best access to its benefits.[4] These circumstances fostered the continued evolution of black Chicagoans' perception of themselves as political actors by unleashing an unprecedented wave of black protest as well as loosening the Republican Party's grip on African American voters.[5] Many young, black would-be politicians began to consider the Democratic Party a more appropriate arena for their personal ambitions. For two such men, Christopher Wimbish and Corneal Davis, the Democratic Party became more than just an organization that could further their careers. It increasingly became *the* party through which they could carry out their vision, crafted with William Dawson during World War I, of an autonomous black political base. Although Dawson's party loyalty led him to struggle for political survival in the waning local GOP, Wimbish and Davis fought for a place with the ascendant Democrats and repeatedly asked Dawson to go in with them. Dawson finally joined them in 1939, and the three veterans took advantage of competition between white Democratic factions to lay the foundation for one of the nation's strongest black political organizations.

Dawson's election to the City Council in 1933 came at a time of transformation within Chicago politics. Throughout the 1920s, Catholic and Jewish migrants had taken over most of the wards within the city, while Protestants moved to the city's periphery. Although most of the new immigrants distrusted the Republicans' business or moralistic progressivism, the Democrats failed to reconcile tensions between the city's European ethnic groups to their advantage. Nevertheless by the late 1920s, the city's foreign born made up two-thirds of the city's population, presenting an opportune moment for Chicago's new migrants to assert control over the city's politics.[6]

After taking the top position of the Cook County Democratic Party in 1928, Anton Cermak shifted the party's orientation. Prioritizing multiethnicity, Cermak reduced interethnic political tensions and emphasized the benefits to be gained through electoral cooperation. Cermak promised that Democrats would provide representation and patronage jobs to individual ethnic groups in exchange for their votes. His organization permitted individual ambition as long as contenders mediated their aspirations through the local Democratic Party.[7] Although this arrangement indicated a new level of acceptance of recent immigrants in local politics, it did so by siphoning their most radical political energies. Thus, Cermak's Democratic organization remained an essentially conservative force designed to stabilize rather than alter the city's systems of power, including race relations.

Cermak's successful challenge of Mayor Thompson in 1931 established a Democratic ascendancy in Chicago politics. In the election, Cermak invoked reform themes, such as government efficiency, but by disavowing temperance he retained white ethnic support. This tactic allowed him to soundly defeat Thompson, whose only backing came from the staunchly Republican black wards. As mayor, Cermak continued to emphasize administrative reform. Meanwhile as head of the local party, Cermak along with Cook County Central Committee chairman Pat Nash established the business-like manner that characterized Chicago politics for the next forty years and made the Democratic Party the main vehicle for political change for all of the city's ethnic groups. Party leaders charged their subordinates with delivering votes, and, without exception, failure to do so meant dismissal from the organization.[8]

Because black voters posed an obvious threat to Cermak's fledgling coalition, he attempted to destabilize black Republicanism on the South Side. Cermak fired 2,500 civil service employees, targeting black patronage recipients in particular. He launched a crackdown on criminal activity, which, in typical Chicago fashion, focused inordinate attention on the black community. Cermak then attempted to make inroads into the South Side's politics. Although he failed to convince Dawson to shift his political allegiance, he successfully installed a newcomer, Mike Sneed, as the first black Democratic committeeman of the 3d Ward and ordered Committeeman Joe Tittinger to organize black Democrats in the 2nd Ward.[9]

Cermak executed his strategy during the early years of the Depression, which had hit black Chicagoans especially hard. In October 1932, 750,000 workers in Chicago remained unemployed, whereas the majority of the 800,000 with jobs worked only part time.[10] In light of the instability of black economic fortunes in the 1920s, the Depression represented an extension of negative economic trends more than a radical departure. Nevertheless, it took a tremendous toll. With a 45 percent unemployment rate—compared to 40 percent for white Chicagoans—blacks accounted for nearly a quarter of the city's relief cases. Unemployment left blacks even more vulnerable to disproportionately high rents, and evictions on the South Side skyrocketed.[11]

With no relief coming from the Cermak administration and no viable response from its established leadership, black Chicago produced a new, more aggressive cohort to fight against the Depression. Although these new leaders situated their campaigns within the struggle for civil rights, they did not develop a broad analysis that connected systemic inequality in the urban North to segregation in the South and white supremacy within an international context as would be the case in New York's civil rights campaigns of the 1940s or the Chicago Freedom Movement in the

1960s.[12] Rather, the new leadership, in which Dawson played an important role, focused primarily on more immediate, short-term goals such as economic relief, access to public housing, and expanded employment opportunities within specific industries.

The transition to the new leadership and more confrontational style began in the early 1930s. In 1930, *Chicago Whip* editors Joseph Bibb and A.C. MacNeal ushered in the new phase with a boycott against Woolworth stores—dubbed the "Don't Spend Your Money Where You Can't Work" campaign.[13] Also in 1930 the Chicago branches of the NAACP, the Urban League, and the Brotherhood of Sleeping Car Porters, as well as Congressman DePriest, coordinated their efforts to block the Supreme Court nomination of North Carolinian William Parker.[14] In 1931, though, more confrontational protests erupted during the "Streetcar Riots," when loosely organized groups of black workers protested their exclusion from employment in the construction of new streetcar lines. Demonstrations such as these made it clear to the local branch of the Communist Party that Chicago's economic collapse offered an opportunity to connect to the black community if they could create agendas that addressed blacks' economic situation. As a result, communist organizations staged several major protests in the early 1930s. In March 1931, for example, they presented a petition to the mayor's office, allegedly signed by 500,000 workers who demanded $75 million dollars for unemployment relief, an end to evictions, and free gas, electricity, and food for the unemployed. Although the communist surge diminished when the state government approved increased funding for relief in 1932, their activities pushed black activists to new heights.[15]

As black Chicagoans found new ways to express their social discontent, black Republicans faced rapidly diminishing returns in what had become a nearly completely Democratic city. The black Republican cohort consequently descended into a chaotic period characterized by intense destructive competition and near total disregard for party allegiances. In characteristic fashion, Alderman Louis Anderson quickly recognized growing Democratic power, and he, along with several of Thompson's other floor leaders, endorsed Cermak.[16] More than any of the black Thompson-DePriest Republicans, Anderson possessed significant intraparty experience as Thompson's floor leader and the head of the powerful finance committee. This history, however, meant little after the 1931 mayoral election, when Cermak replaced Anderson with Alderman John Clark as finance committee chair.[17] Two years later Cermak died in an assassination attempt on President Roosevelt, and Anderson backed Nash's play to install sanitation chief Ed Kelly as his replacement. This move created an important link to the incoming mayoral administration.[18] After the election, Nash handed Anderson a blank check and told him to write in the amount. Tearing up the check, Anderson replied, "Mr. Nash you ain't going to get off this easy. . . . We got the mayor. We'll both use him."[19]

The debt that Kelly owed to black Republicans marked a major difference between his and Cermak's administration. Where Cermak's efforts to woo blacks were conflicted, Kelly made a determined attempt to draw black support. He repudiated Cermak's harsh policing of the South Side, gave positions of honor to notable South Siders, such as boxing champion Joe Louis, and criticized the racist imagery in the still-popular film *Birth of a Nation*. More important, Kelly opposed segregation, particularly in education, and provided blacks with even more patronage than Thompson.[20]

Although these efforts considerably improved relations between blacks and the Democratic Party, Kelly and Nash remained far from solidifying any sort of black Democratic organization. Sneed began a credible black Democratic cohort, but from the start community leaders criticized him for obtaining insufficient patronage positions, having too many mob ties, and being Kelly's puppet. Committeeman Tittinger faced similar charges, as well as a constant push for black representation. Sounding much like Dawson in 1928, Christopher Wimbish wrote, in a pamphlet entitled "The Truth," "Many of you left the South because you desired to exercise the right of suffrage. . . . The fact that you reside in the 2nd Ward and that your political opportunities and privileges are controlled by one not of your group should be proof positive to you that you are still being denied the proper rights of suffrage."[21] Further confusing matters, Republican Aldermen Dawson and Jackson became two of Kelly's strongest supporters on the city council, where they backed Kelly's implementation of New Deal programs and pushed for patronage positions for blacks in their wards.[22] As helpful as their support may have been to the mayor, Jackson and Dawson's political affiliation nevertheless limited their involvement with the Kelly-Nash organization.

Though unwieldy, the networks between the Kelly-Nash administration and the South Side's black Republican leadership were not unprecedented. The successful efforts of a newcomer, Arthur Mitchell, to become part of the Kelly-Nash faction, however, proved far more unusual. Indeed, given the insular nature of Chicago politics, Mitchell's move into the regular organization revealed the extent to which the city's white Democratic leadership desperately sought to connect to the city's black population—

a desperation that Wimbish, Davis, and Dawson would eventually exploit to establish their own black Democratic faction.

Mitchell, who came from Roanoke, Alabama, possessed great intelligence, ruthless ambition, and a considerable ego. He began his education at Tuskegee Institute, where he worked as Booker T. Washington's assistant. After earning his teaching degree, he founded Alabama Normal and Industrial Institute. In 1908 he received a donation of eighty acres of land from a local white planter and built much of the school through his own effort.[23] The institution, however, got off to a rocky financial start, and Mitchell constantly bickered with the local black population, which accused him of using donations for his personal benefit. He left Alabama Normal under a cloud of corruption to head Armstrong Agricultural Institute. There, Mitchell's haughty and condescending behavior thoroughly alienated blacks and whites and he compounded a bad situation by absconding to Washington, D.C., with $10,000 of the school's money and the deeds to several hundred acres of land that the local populace thought he had purchased under the school's name.[24]

Although Mitchell pursued a lucrative real estate career in Washington, he closely monitored national politics. After making a small fortune by blockbusting white neighborhoods, Mitchell sought political opportunities, first in the GOP and then the Democratic Party. His initial break came when he went on a speaking tour for Herbert Hoover in 1928. During the tour, Mitchell learned of Chicago's black Republicans and their apparent access to patronage, which proved to be more than he could resist. The GOP, however, possessed too many established black politicians for Mitchell to advance as quickly as he desired, and he soon offered his services to Democratic Party leaders. This tactic landed him another speaking tour in 1932. This time Democratic Party Chairman James Farley hired Mitchell to attack DePriest, who toured the nation trying to rally blacks for President Hoover. A polished orator, Mitchell unnerved the Old Roman and secured himself an introduction to Chicago's Democrats.[25]

Mitchell then executed an intense personal lobbying strategy among Democratic leaders in Chicago and Washington, which eventually brought him a seat in Congress. Through a persistent letter-writing campaign to national and local Democratic leaders, Mitchell came into contact with 2nd Ward Committeeman Tittinger.[26] With steady attacks against his leadership, the beleaguered committeeman needed to enhance his organization's relationship with local blacks, but he refused to run a black candidate. In response, Mitchell ran an independent campaign against Tittinger's pick, Harry Baker, who had already lost to

DePriest in the previous three elections. Mitchell lost to Baker in the primary 6,182 to 7,236, but Baker unexpectedly passed away and Tittinger, given the clamor for black representation, had little choice but to go with Mitchell.[27] Thus, with almost no background in politics and even less experience in Chicago, Arthur Mitchell became Chicago's first black Democratic nominee for Congress.

Mitchell's candidacy came during a crippling rivalry between DePriest's lieutenants, 2nd Ward Alderman Dawson and Illinois Senator and 2nd Ward Committeeman William King. With DePriest's backing, Dawson ran for 2nd Ward committeeman against King, who received support from Louis Anderson. Dawson also attacked King's senate seat through his proxy Bryant Hammond. Finally, Dawson took over the management of DePriest's campaign. Although Dawson secured DePriest's primary fight, he lost to King in the committee race, and his candidate lost to King for Illinois State Senate. Four months later, King still felt the sting, calling Dawson "overambitious."[28] Thus, going into the general election DePriest's organization remained too divided to give him adequate support.

With support from the regular Democratic organization and Louis Anderson's guidance, Mitchell beat DePriest in the general election.[29] In a 1933 letter to the dean of Howard University, Kelly Miller, Mitchell articulated the issues he would stand for as a candidate for elective office: (1) programs to create work; (2) the elimination of racial discrimination; (3) a national program to promote higher standards of living for black Americans; (4) the elimination of discrimination in government departments; (5) equal hiring in New Deal programs; (6) the reenfranchisement of southern blacks; and (7) preference for American citizens in employment.[30] Mitchell's campaign cohered with this statement. He also condemned DePriest for his alleged corruption, unpolished political style, and unwillingness to engage in political debate.[31] DePriest's campaign, which consisted of attacking Mitchell's southern connections and criticizing the New Deal, proved inadequate. Despite DePriest's retention of the black vote, Mitchell won over whites and a smattering of blacks, allowing him to take the district with 27,963 votes to DePriest's 24,829.[32]

As the nation's first black Democratic representative and Dawson's immediate predecessor, Arthur Mitchell's time in office deserves our attention for it reveals the Democratic Party and black America's expectations of black congressional leadership. In and out of Chicago, African Americans wanted Mitchell to represent all of the nation's blacks, advocate for civil rights, coordinate with the black press and civil rights leadership, and support President Roosevelt's New Deal. Black Chicagoans in particular demanded that Mitchell use his influence to obtain patronage positions for black applicants. Meanwhile the local Democratic Party hoped that Mitchell could quell the anti-Tittinger uprising, and the national party expected Mitchell to lead the effort to draw in black voters during presidential elections.

Unfortunately, with the exception of supporting the New Deal, Mitchell's ego and conservative political tendencies made him inadequate to nearly all of these tasks. His inflated sense of importance rendered him unable to negotiate when he saw himself as the victim of offensive behavior, whether that behavior came from the black press, black civil rights leaders, or racist white politicians. Two weeks into his first term, Mitchell declared that he would not "tolerate any foolishness from the press and would not use the press for his political campaigns." He eventually decided to refrain from sending out press releases altogether except to select publications.[33] His relations with various black organizations fared even worse. In January 1935 Mitchell met with a local black social group, the Musolis Club, and at some point they indicated that they saw Mitchell as a representative of all blacks. Completely misunderstanding black Americans' desire for some sort of federal representation, Mitchell countered that he served only Chicago's downtown Loop. An argument followed in which the Musolis Club members began to refer to him as "Arthur," and Mitchell responded, "My name is Mr. Mitchell to you. . . . You don't know me well enough to call me 'Arthur.'" At which point, the *Defender* reported, Mitchell "left in a huff."[34] These sorts of episodes led a writer in the *Crisis* to chastise Mitchell on his "silly" fights with the press and his unwillingness to address black issues outside of his district.[35]

The new congressman's self-centeredness also trumped obvious intraparty civil rights issues. Georgia Governor Gene Talmadge refused to attend the Democrats' annual Jackson Day Dinner because of Mitchell's race, and planners attempted to dissuade Mitchell from going. Rather than recognize the episode as a civil rights matter, Mitchell took it as a personal affront:

> Your request has greatly embarrassed ME. You can chose to return my check if you choose. Certainly I will not request its return. And if the check IS returned, I will see to it that every Negro in the United States knows about it. It will have a most "embarrassing" effect at the next election.[36]

In the end Mitchell attended; Talmadge did not. And nothing else came of the matter.[37]

Although most African Americans, particularly those in Chicago, assumed that the congressman would use his influence to obtain patronage positions for blacks, Mitchell refused do so. Moreover, he does not appear to have attempted to gain the ability to control any patronage positions. This was a stunning position, because in the early twentieth century patronage tied the lowest-ranking precinct worker to his or her party's highest officials. Many reform-oriented observers saw patronage as little more than another form of graft, but their critiques presupposed that the United States ensured access to government resources on the basis of merit.[38] To the contrary, by allowing regional racial biases to skew its hiring processes, the U.S. government actually maintained and spread discrimination.[39] As a result, patronage greatly facilitated African Americans' movement into mainstream politics, as it had for generations of ethnic Europeans before them.

Indeed, many blacks viewed patronage appointments as civil rights gains and saw Mitchell's unwillingness to obtain patronage positions as a major shortfall. Mitchell not only denied that he possessed the ability to facilitate such matters; he also contended that it was absurd for anyone to think he had the power to do so. He consistently—sometimes mockingly—told supplicants that he would not look into matters outside of his congressional district, and upon receiving entreaties from within his district he typically told the writer to see their ward committeeman.[40] Mitchell apparently did not understand that, in Chicago, political leaders routinely assisted job seekers. Although it was true that congressional representatives generally did not have the power to appoint individuals to positions, Mitchell's deficient attempts to work the party apparatus toward that end could only be seen by his constituents as a severe failing.

In addition, Mitchell's conservative political bent led him to make statements and submit legislation that many blacks viewed as questionable. The press condemned Mitchell early in his tenure, when he stated that the "Southern white man is the Negro's best friend." Mitchell's fortunes with the press dropped even further when he sponsored a bill to create the Negro Industrial Relations Commission.[41] At first the bill sparked little controversy and several black leaders endorsed it.[42] The NAACP and many in the press, however, balked at concentrating all black labor issues in a five-person commission. Associated Negro Press reporter William Pickens typified their responses when he wrote that the committee would ghettoize black labor issues, and that Mitchell's bill was "the dumbest thing ever offered as a threat to the Negro Race."[43]

In 1936, the Democratic leadership tried to use Mitchell as a leader to organize African American support for Roosevelt, but his management produced strife and division. Democratic leaders apparently considered Mitchell an important symbolic figure for rallying black voters, as indicated by several requests for him to speak around the country.[44] The Democratic National Committee (DNC) appointed Mitchell to head its Western Division, which included all of the states between Ohio and California. Mitchell coordinated and distributed funds for speakers to work throughout these states, but as late as September he criticized the DNC for providing insufficient monies to cover the area.[45] In October, black Democrats in Colorado and Missouri complained that they had not received any campaign literature or money, and Mitchell informed them that they needed to send their concerns to the chairman of the DNC, James Farley.[46] In Ohio and Kansas, black Democrats criticized Mitchell for creating dissension, while doing nothing to move the campaign. Mitchell called these critics opportunistic and "silly."[47] Finally, Mitchell feuded with Julian Rainey, head of the eastern division of the Democratic campaign.[48] Although the DNC dragged its feet in getting Mitchell the proper funds—on some occasions Mitchell paid for speakers out of his own pocket—Mitchell clearly did not have the skills to handle the demands of a national campaign.[49]

Whereas Mitchell failed at becoming the congressional representative that blacks and the Democratic Party wanted, Dawson and other black Republican leaders in Chicago became more actively involved in Democratic factionalism. Mayor Kelly initiated much of the interparty flirtation by opposing educational segregation and asking Louis Anderson if he would again rally blacks to the Democratic cause during the 1935 primaries. Anderson complied, praising the incumbent mayor in speeches across the South Side as "another Bill Thompson."[50] Kelly also supported Robert Jackson and William Dawson in their reelection bids and ordered Tittinger to refrain from running Earl Dickerson, now an assistant attorney general for northern Illinois, as a Democratic candidate for 2nd Ward alderman. Jackson and Dawson reciprocated by publicly endorsing Kelly's mayoral campaign.[51]

By the 1936 election, the relationship between Chicago's black Republicans and the local Democratic Party was blurred, and bickering between the state's leading white Democrats only created more political uncertainty. Among Democrats, Kelly's victory did not mean domination over the party statewide, and a feud soon erupted between the mayor and Democratic governor Henry Horner. Tensions between the two men rose over the so-called bookie bill, which would have allowed Chicago to license and tax handbooks. Horner vetoed the bill, and Kelly pushed the regular organization to nominate Chicago's health commissioner, Herman Bundesen, for governor instead of Horner. Horner consequently ran an independent campaign, which he framed as a fight against "Boss Kelly."[52]

The Democratic schism gave Corneal Davis and Christopher Wimbish an entry into Democratic politics and a chance to fill the void left by Mitchell's incompetent leadership. Davis had already considered switching parties as early as 1928 when the Thompson-DePriest Republicans opposed Dawson's congressional campaign. Davis also appreciated the Democrats' work to elect Henry Horner, a South Side German Jew, in the 1932 gubernatorial race. Reflecting upon the powerlessness of local Republicans and the growing relationship between Kelly and the two black Republican aldermen, Davis and Wimbish often urged Dawson to switch parties, but he refused. Although Davis and Wimbish had not yet announced their change in party allegiance, they worked for Horner and began planning an independent organization to beat the Tittinger-Mitchell faction out of the 2nd Ward.[53]

For his part, Dawson had little time to think about his friends' Democratic crusade, because he and King soon recommenced open warfare. Characteristic of the bitter, chaotic infighting between black Republicans at the time, the two men sponsored opposing slates for several offices in the April primaries. Dawson's organization endorsed Louis Anderson for Congress and Dawson for 2nd Ward committeeman, while King slated himself for 2nd Ward committeeman and DePriest for Congress. King also backed DePriest's attempt to take Jackson's place as 3rd Ward Republican committeeman. King's slate beat all of Dawson picks, as well as Dawson's ally Robert Jackson. King and DePriest, in particular, trounced Dawson and Anderson by more than 5,000 votes each, leading the *Chicago Defender* to call King the "Undisputed Republican Leader on the South Side."[54]

In the general election, King's management of DePriest's primary campaign made little difference, for Mitchell beat DePriest handily in a nationwide Democratic landslide.[55] Mitchell's campaign, with assistance from Louis Anderson and Corneal Davis, emphasized his ability to work with his congressional colleagues, a racial discrimination suit Mitchell had filed against the railroads, and Mitchell's connection to the New Deal.[56] DePriest emphasized his long political career, his unequivocal opposition to segregation, and Mitchell's suspicious friendships with southern politicians. After making a call for unity, most of the city's prominent black Republicans expressed support for DePriest on paper, but these public statements meant nothing when even DePriest publicly acknowledged the dissension between his top lieutenants.[57] Mitchell called the DePriest campaign backwards and believed that he would beat DePriest two to one.[58] Although Mitchell did not beat DePriest by that margin, he did win decisively: 35,330 to 21,182.[59]

Now on his own, with neither a political mentor nor a supportive political party, Dawson focused his energies on black struggles for housing and employment. By the 1930s, black housing opportunities in Chicago had diminished because of overcrowding and neglect of existing stocks. There were 287,000 units constructed in the 1920s, but in the 1930s only 15,500 new residential units were built. Starting in 1934, the city demolished over 18,000 dilapidated residences, but new construction brought back fewer than 8,000 units. More than 6,500 of the demolitions by the city occurred in the Black Belt. Meanwhile, restrictive covenants forced the ever-increasing stream of southern migrants to live in that very area, permitting landlords to abandon maintenance of the remaining homes. Despite the deplorable condition of their housing, blacks paid, on average, twice the rent paid by whites, and poor housing led to disproportionately high rates of tuberculosis, insanity, and infant mortality in the black community.[60]

Attempting to address these circumstances, Dawson began to emphasize community development during his second aldermanic campaign in 1935, when he employed the slogan "Second Ward for the Second Warders." The motto ostensibly referred to a program to revitalize the 2nd Ward through self-help, community organization, and housing improvement. At the same time, it sent a warning to carpetbagger Democratic leaders such as Tittinger and Mitchell, who did not have a community base within the ward.[61]

As an alderman Dawson's most aggressive work in housing started through some of his organizations' youngest political organizers and speakers. Dawson's relationship with Kelly afforded him some influence in the dispensation of jobs in the Works Progress Administration (WPA), and he secured work for some of his men, including Joseph Jefferson, at the Wabash Avenue YMCA. One day in 1937 Jefferson complained about a rent increase to his colleagues, and all agreed that Jefferson should not pay the raise. This conversation led the young men to organize the Consolidated Tenants Association (CTA), with Dawson as its president and Jefferson its secretary. They met with Dawson nearly every morning for a free breakfast and a strategy session. With Dawson's know-how, the young men organized rent strikes in apartment complexes where landlords increased rents. If landlords retaliated with legal proceedings,

Dawson gave the CTA free counsel. He also took on pro bono work for tenants evicted through dubious leases.[62] In April 1938, Dawson captured the attention of the local media when he became the first black alderman to push the council to consider black housing issues by packing a city council meeting with black CTA members. Mayor Kelly responded creating a commission to investigate and make recommendations on the crisis.[63]

Encouraged by their successes in housing, Jefferson and his colleagues began to consider employment discrimination after one of their charges at the YMCA complained that he could deliver newspapers but could never grow up to be a carrier manager. They discussed this situation with Dawson and decided to fight for equal employment opportunities in a new group, which Dawson named the Negro Labor Relations League (NLRL). With Jefferson as its president and Dawson as legal counsel, the NLRL organized several buying power campaigns, including a boycott of the Chicago *Daily Herald* (to force the *Daily Herald* to employ black carrier managers), another boycott against the local milk companies (to force them to hire blacks as delivery truck drivers), and demonstrations against Illinois Bell (to force the telephone company to place blacks as switchboard operators). Dawson also walked the picket lines with the NLRL in their successful protest against South Side movie theaters that refused to train blacks as projectionists.[64]

Though characterized by protest and racial militancy, Dawson's experiences with the NLRL actually heightened his belief that the most effective change would only come through electoral politics. Fred Wall, co-chairman of the NLRL and Dawson's future executive secretary, recollected that even as Dawson's reputation for activism grew, his ultimate goal remained building an independent black political organization:

> Dawson built his following among us by the most vigorous anti-white speeches you have ever heard. His theme was, "No black man who had to lick from a trough fed by white hands can be effective." That is why he felt it was so crucial for a political organization to be able to run under its own steam and not have to ask for money from down-town to keep your organization together.[65]

Throughout the various protest campaigns Dawson argued that militancy could not be an end unto itself. Although he supported the "Don't Spend Your Money Where You Can't Work" campaign, joined the pickets to obtain black projectionists in the theaters, and laid down in front of city trains during the streetcar riots, he always pushed his young colleagues to think about what they would do once they got inside. Corneal Davis recalled that Dawson would often say, "When you get inside you change. That's what you're fighting for . . . to get inside."[66]

Personal needs probably also played a role in his unwillingness to commit to protest. M. Earl Sarden remembered that during one of the daily breakfast meetings with the NLRL, Dawson expressed frustration at the personal instability incumbent with protest leadership. He noted that despite years of street protests they had little to show for all of their work and that he would have to take better care of himself and his family. This announcement did not mean he would abandon the group, but he intended to pull away from the front lines of protest.[67]

Indeed, as the 1938 election approached, Chicago politics provided more than enough stimulation to require Dawson's attention. Hastening the disintegration of black Republicanism, Dawson and King continued their civil war. Four major black Republican leaders sought Mitchell's seat, including Dawson, Anderson (backed by King), DePriest, and Roscoe Conkling Simmons. Mitchell won the Democratic primary with 16,682 votes, while Dawson won the Republican primary with 4,295 out of 12,000-plus votes cast. In addition to Dawson's primary victory, Dawson's man, S. Timothy Washington, won his race for state central committeeman; however, two King-sponsored candidates A. Andrew Torrence and attorney Richard Harewood, beat two Dawson-sponsored men for seats in the State Senate and House.[68]

Meanwhile, among the Democrats, C. C. Wimbish laid plans for an uprising against white control of the 2nd Ward. Although Governor Horner and Mayor Kelly had reconciled, State's Attorney Thomas J. Courtney and County Judge Edmund Jarecki remained intransigent in their opposition to the Kelly-Nash faction. Now a fully committed Democrat, Wimbish aligned himself with the Courtney-Jarecki bloc. He then exploited the factional split and established an independent 2nd Ward Democratic organization to challenge Tittinger and Mitchell's leadership.[69]

Between the primary and general election, Dawson turned his attention back to the housing struggle, and played a leading role in securing the much-needed Southside Gardens housing project. The 1933 National Recovery Act stipulated that the federal government construct four projects in Chicago, one of which would be built in a black South Side community, but the plan faced major obstacles. First, white Chicagoans from Kenwood, Oakland, Woodlawn, and Hyde Park, with support from the Chicago Real Estate Board, formed the Allied Civic Clubs to oppose the project. Second, downstate legislators had to be convinced to give the project the tax-exempt status necessary to meet federal requirements.[70]

The effort to obtain tax-exempt status for the Southside Gardens project represented a high point in coordination in Chicago's black politicians, activists, journalists, and business leaders' fight against the effects of the Depression within civil rights framework. The *Chicago Defender,* the Consolidated Tenants Association, the Cook County Physicians' Association, the Council of Negro Organizations, and the Social Service Roundtable all lobbied legislators in Springfield for passage of the legislation. Dawson and Chicago Urban League representative Frayser T. Lane addressed the first committee meeting discussing the legislation in the Senate, while the Senators William King and T.V. Smith, a white legislator from Hyde Park, lobbied behind the scenes. When their efforts failed, the *Defender* circulated 50,000 fliers urging people to wire Mayor Kelly and Governor Horner in support of the bill, which finally passed in July.[71]

This victory, however, brought no respite on other civil rights fronts. Indeed, the NLRL's fight against the theaters had only intensified. By August 1938, only one theater had hired a black projectionist. Jefferson informed the theaters that the NLRL planned demonstrations to get at least sixteen more blacks hired. The Motion Picture Operators Union asked Dawson to stop the demonstrations, but Dawson replied that it would be impossible to do so without compliance to League demands.[72] In late September bystanders attacked one picketer and police arrested two others at the Metropolitan Theater on South Parkway and 47th Street, where Dawson also walked the line. He secured their release and defended them in court the next day. Tensions rose as the protests continued into October, and the theaters banned picture-taking by journalists. Finally, in November the NLRL and the Motion Pictures Operators Union negotiated a plan to hire four blacks immediately and ten more as positions became available.[73] Meanwhile, Dawson pushed the city council to grant tax-exempt status to the Southside Gardens housing project. Their vote guaranteed the construction of 1,700 South Side homes.[74]

As valuable as the protest efforts may have been, they simply did not compare to the immediate benefits of the New Deal and Democratic patronage nor could they draw black Chicagoans away from their interest in politics as a tool for racial advancement.[75] Consequently, Dawson's activism could do nothing to stem the Democratic tide in the general election. By November Wimbish and Mitchell had reconciled. With help from Wimbish, Mayor Kelly, Tittinger, Louis Anderson, and Corneal Davis, Mitchell's campaign focused on the value of the New Deal and beat Dawson 30,207 votes to 26,396.[76] Continuing the Democratic sweep, a

Tittinger Democrat, William Wallace, defeated Dawson's nemesis William King and 3rd Ward Committeeman Ed Sneed became the first black Democrat elected to the county commission.[77]

These Democratic victories confirmed Wimbish and Davis's belief that the Democratic Party offered the best opportunity to establish an independent black faction. The two men thus labored to sway South Side blacks from their loyalty to the GOP. The task proved difficult, but they dogged Republican speakers across the 2nd and 3rd Wards, arguing that voting Republican meant attacking the party that had made black survival possible through the New Deal. When black Republicans brought up loyalty to President Lincoln, recollected Davis, comical debates often ensued:

> Roscoe [Conkling] Simmons used to go around and tell them that he went down to Springfield, knocked on Mr. Lincoln's tomb. Mr. Lincoln told him go back, don't desert the party, vote the Republican ticket. And I'd go back and I'd say, "I was down in Springfield and there's 90 tons of concrete on Lincoln, Lincoln didn't say a word to me. . . . I tried to get him to talk to me and he's never said nothing." That's the kind of debates we had. It was funny.[78]

Mocking blacks' allegiance to the GOP was one prong of Wimbish and Davis's plan to bring Dawson to the Democrats and to end carpetbagger leadership of the 2nd Ward. While undermining 2nd Ward blacks' commitment to the GOP, Wimbish, in particular, consistently undercut the authority of the Tittinger-Mitchell faction. Although Dawson agreed with their goals, he would not join Wimbish and Mitchell, for he felt that he could not be an effective Democratic leader with so many blacks in the Republican Party. So Wimbish and Davis worked hard to demonstrate to their "friend" and "buddy" Dawson that he could not win with the GOP, or, as Davis put it, "We want Dawson to come into the Democrat party. And we're going to whip him into the party. He—we're going to run this thing."[79] Mitchell's successful campaign against Dawson, despite Dawson's extensive community connections, made this final point abundantly clear.

Mitchell's victory, nevertheless, did not point to his growing popularity. Indeed, Mitchell's political choices in Washington, D.C., remained controversial. To his credit, Mitchell attacked the notorious Dies Committee, also known as the House Investigative Committee on Un-American Activities. Created in 1938 to investigate communist and fascist activities in the U.S., the Dies Committee became infamous for Red-baiting pacifist, civil rights, and other liberal organizations.[80] He also received press attention for consistently supporting New Deal measures, and he joined a chorus of criticism against the Daughters of the American Revolution (DAR) who denied contralto Marian Anderson the opportunity to sing in Washington's Constitution Hall because of her race.[81] Nevertheless, Mitchell's relationships with civil rights groups remained testy. The same month Mitchell criticized DAR, for example, he received a telegram from the NAACP's Walter White urging him to sign a discharge petition to push a controversial antilynching bill to the floor for a vote. Mitchell replied that White should have known that he had already signed the petition and irritably asked, "Are you stone crazy?" Mitchell also submitted a bill to resettle northern blacks in the American South. The bill possessed sound ideas—for example, not all blacks had succeeded to their expectations in the North and land ownership for agricultural purposes could provide stability for many blacks—but its tone totally overlooked the emotional content of the Great Migration.[82] Mitchell's insensitivity and seeming inability to even communicate with civil rights leaders such as Walter White did not play well at home, but the Democrats had yet to offer a viable alternative.

Although it was unclear at the time, a new alignment that would eventually supplant the Tittinger-Mitchell faction began to coalesce when the 1939 aldermanic race brought together multiple trends that led Dawson to finally join Wimbish and Davis's Democratic crusade. That year Wimbish and Davis escalated their assault on the regular organization by running Davis as the Courtney faction candidate for 2nd Ward alderman against the Tittinger-Mitchell pick: attorney and civil rights crusader Earl Dickerson. Mayor Kelly, however, did not think Dickerson could function well within the organization and refused to support him. Instead, Kelly gave Dawson "silent support" as he had in the last three election cycles. Tittinger nevertheless moved the 2nd Ward Democratic Organization behind Dickerson, who would have already drawn considerable support for his civil rights credentials.[83] On the Republican side, Dawson once again faced his perennial nemesis William King. This time, however, the committeeman and ex-senator ran himself for alderman, and he marshaled the black GOP's remaining forces behind his campaign. Neither Davis nor Dawson could overcome the power of the local, regular organizations, and they had to watch as King and Dickerson fought it out in the general election.[84]

It appears, however, that either in concert or as individuals Dawson, Wimbish, and Davis may have engineered Dawson's loss to facilitate his entrance into the Democratic Party. Davis, for example, indicated that, although Dawson's defeat disappointed Mayor Kelly, he and Wimbish told the mayor that they could not "build a Democratic Party by electing Republicans" and that they planned to bring Dawson into the party as their leader.[85] Davis and Wimbish were two of several prominent black leaders urging Kelly to accept Dawson.[86] Their years of agitation against Tittinger as members of an insurgent Democratic faction and their abilities as political organizers must have given their opinion significant weight. Moreover, Davis's assertion that he and Wimbish expected Dawson to be their "leader" and "master" dovetails with later assertions by Dawson and his lieutenant, William Barnett, that Dawson never intended to win the race. Instead, both claimed that Dawson intentionally lost the primary to allow him to cut ties to the Republicans while out of office.[87]

In any case, Dawson began to execute his strategy to join the Democrats the morning after the primary. He paid a visit to Dickerson and indicated he would only support his campaign if Dickerson backed Dawson for Democratic 2nd Ward Committeeman.[88] Although it is impossible to ascertain what exactly Dawson planned or what Dickerson thought of this invitation, interviews of both men and analysis of the political calculus involved is revealing. Because Dickerson hoped to use political office as a platform to mobilize black citizens for civil rights change, he had only participated in politics to the extent it allowed him to pursue a civil rights agenda.[89] In the primary Dickerson (9,236 votes), King (9,219 votes), and Dawson (8,575 votes) ran a close race, with the majority of the votes going to the two GOP candidates. Thus, without Dawson's voters, Dickerson had no chance of beating the much more experienced King and no chance of bringing his civil rights program to city hall.[90] Furthermore, in later interviews Dickerson indicated that he had no desire to be ward committeeman. This conforms to Dickerson's history, because the committee seat, although an extraordinarily powerful position, could only be linked to civil rights work indirectly. Finally, Dickerson claimed that Dawson promised to use his influence as Ward committeeman to support Dickerson for Congress in 1940 where he would have greater opportunities for civil rights leadership.[91]

In offering to nominate Dickerson for Congress, Dawson illustrated his ability to exploit the weaknesses of his political opponents. One of their contemporaries, Truman Gibson Jr., indicated that Dickerson "was the supreme egoist" with a "high opinion of himself."[92] In a none-too-humble fashion, Dawson once said, "God gave me the key to understand men and to know them. If you learn to handle men, the right ones—all men for that matter—you can get what you want." Dawson's offer apparently clouded Dickerson's ability to see that as 2nd Ward committeeman Dawson could control his fate.[93] After this first meeting, said Dawson, Dickerson visited him often to make sure that Dawson would go through with the deal: "One day Dickerson came to me again. I told him that I was going to be the new committeeman in the Ward, and I asked him if he was with me. He said he was. I leaned over and said, 'Shake hands, Mr. Alderman. You're elected.'"[94]

After dealing with Dickerson, Dawson went to Wimbish and Davis to forge a pact that would bring all of them to political power. He told his old friends that he wanted to join them in the Democratic Party and become committeeman of the 2nd Ward, but he left out any indication that he agreed to put Dickerson in Congress.[95] At that moment, said Davis, the three men decided that they would build their own faction in the ward:

> Wimbish and I had helped to build the Democratic Party. [laughs] Dawson had no alternative, it was our party. He came in the Democratic Party after we did. He was still a Republican alderman, and he came to us. Well, we had a place for him of course, but he came to us. And we knew that he wanted to go to Congress because he had already run for Congress on the Republican ticket and we said, "Come on, were going to make you the congressman, but you've got to declare a Democrat." See he had been elected alderman as a Republican and he was afraid because blacks hadn't fully adopted the Democratic Party. . . . But when he came into the party, he just marched in, [sic] all he had to do was come on in. His friends had the organization—we had the organization of independent Democrats and Dawson brought his Republican organization and we became powerful.[96]

Another deal had been set, but this one did not include Dickerson.

In a move that should have aroused suspicion, Wimbish and Davis quickly lent their support to Dickerson. With neither the stature of Republican affiliation nor the patronage of the regular Democratic organization, Davis's earlier campaign for alderman clearly had no chance of victory and only could have been designed to undermine Dickerson. Moreover, when Wimbish opposed the Tittinger-Mitchell organization in 1938, it took six months, a reconciliation dinner, and significant negotiations to get Wimbish to support Mitchell's candidacy.[97] This time, however, no conciliatory measures occurred. Dawson, Wimbish, and Davis's support gave Dickerson, a relative newcomer to electoral politics, the 2,000 extra votes he needed to beat the much more experienced King.[98]

After Dickerson's victory Dawson approached Kelly about becoming the 2nd Ward committeeman. Dawson already had the inside track for the post because of his prior work with Kelly on the city council. Visits by Wimbish, Davis, and other black leaders urging Kelly to sponsor Dawson as the next ward committeeman would have only reinforced this predisposition.[99] Thus, it does not take great sagacity to see the wisdom of supporting Dawson. Although Dawson would likely arouse opposition from the ranks of many black 2nd Ward Democrats, those same Democrats already loathed Tittinger. Dawson's votes could not be ignored, either; with no patronage inducements his totals nearly equaled Dickerson's, who could boast civil rights credentials, an association with the New Deal and the dominant local Democratic faction. Dawson also would be able to bring Wimbish and Davis into the regular organization. When considered from this perspective Kelly's support for Dawson came almost as a foregone conclusion.

Ironically, the only major black politician who harbored any misgivings about Dawson's entry to Democratic politics was Arthur Mitchell. Although Mitchell possessed ample reasons to distrust Dawson, whom he considered "treacherous," perhaps he should have turned his attention toward Dickerson. Dickerson's campaign retained the services of Edgar Brown, who, Mitchell complained, spent too much time criticizing him. Moreover, although Dickerson thanked Mitchell for his help in securing him the nomination, he did not indicate that he would quiet Brown and he made no mention of his recent deal with Dawson to run for Congress.[100]

From Mitchell's perspective, the transition in 2nd Ward appeared chaotic. Since January, black precinct captains continually challenged Tittinger's leadership, and in May Tittinger pleaded to Nash that he needed more jobs to swing the upcoming judicial elections. Nash, though, would hear nothing of it, replying: "I don't give a —— what you do in the judicial election, but if you don't deliver, you had better resign." When Mitchell learned of this state of affairs he agreed that Tittinger needed to look after his men. Nevertheless, even as Tittinger's fortunes sank, Mitchell sent out letters of support for his sponsor and held a tribute banquet with the 2nd Ward's precinct captains.[101] Tittinger could not be redeemed, though, and Kelly officially made Dawson head of the 2nd Ward in November 1939.[102]

While Dawson brought order to the raucous ward, Dickerson continued some of the initiatives begun by his predecessors. Like Dawson, Dickerson's dedication to improving the lot of black Americans stemmed in large part from his experiences of Jim Crow violence as a child in

Redemption-era Mississippi and with segregation in the U.S. armed forces in World War I.[103] It came as little surprise then when he picked up where Dawson and Robert Jackson had left off in the housing struggle. A leading fighter against restrictive covenants, Dickerson initiated investigations on the housing situation, lobbied for increased public housing, and asked the council to propose remedies for deteriorating educational facilities in the Black Belt.[104]

Unlike Dawson, Dickerson used his city council seat to articulate a wide-ranging liberal/civil rights ideology that went beyond meeting Depression-era economic and welfare needs. Prefiguring the model that would later emerge in Harlem's Adam Clayton Powell Jr., whose philosophical origins connected more directly to 1930s Communist Party agitation and a postwar critique of American racism,[105] Dickerson privileged demands for immediate black equality over short-term alliances and used his office as a base for mobilizing citizen support for his reform initiatives. When the American Federation of Labor (AFL) protested a 17 percent cut from the WPA's budget, for example, Dickerson recognized that the reduction would have particularly deleterious effects on black workers and urged the city council to send a petition to Congress in support of the AFL. He opposed, however, many white rank-and-file union members when he pushed the city council to include an antidiscrimination clause in the creation of the new Chicago Transit Authority. Finally, he created a 2nd Ward Advisory Council to help him execute a civic responsibility program to get African American representation on every city board and to arouse mass action on civil rights issues.[106]

Again foreshadowing Powell's testy relationship with his Democratic colleagues, Dickerson did not place great emphasis on forming productive political relationships. He urged the 2nd Ward Advisory Council, for example, to organize a mass mailing of civil rights grievances to city hall. After winning the battle to include an equal hiring clause in the transit bill, Dickerson later threatened to derail the legislation if the council did not create a grievance policy to enforce it and he brought 200 supporters to a closed city council meeting to back him up.[107] In keeping with his principled stance on civil rights, the fight for an antidiscrimination clause sought to allow black workers in general to apply for low-level employment in the renovation of public transportation lines. Yet Dickerson does not appear to have ever requested traditional patronage appointments in municipal government for his supporters and 2nd Ward constituents, which could have cemented the allegiance of ambitious, younger politicians, and broadened his popular base. Finally, he alienated his former ally Mitchell by calling him Kelly's puppet—a truthful, albeit impolitic, statement.[108]

Taking a route different from Dickerson's and diverging from his work as an alderman, Dawson focused almost entirely on his political organization. Kelly's support apparently did not translate into any kind of funding, for Dawson started by mortgaging his home to gain the funds needed to put things in order.[109] Then, he appointed Wimbish president of the 2nd Ward Organization—a move that guaranteed Wimbish a position of leadership worthy of his struggle against Tittinger. He offered an olive branch to the ward's white residents by slating Tittinger for the state legislature. He promised black Democrats who initially refused to accept his leadership that they would not lose their jobs. Because they had virtually no patronage positions under Tittinger anyway, they had nothing to lose in that regard.[110] Meanwhile, Dawson simply waited out an apprehensive Mitchell, who watched from Washington and tried his best to skirt Dawson's authority.[111]

Next Dawson made the Democratic Party part of the social fabric of the 2nd Ward. Within his first month in office, Dawson established an ex-servicemen's league and a woman's auxiliary to the regular organization, the Eleanor Roosevelt Club. He installed his supporters in precinct offices. He promoted a female basketball team called the "Dawson Coeds" and a male team called the "Dawson Boosters."[112] He kept his headquarters open at all times, and during the day he could always be found in its offices. Staff members served on call to advise on any types of problems his constituents had, ranging from legal assistance to advising on New Deal programs.[113]

Finally, by initiating a strict training program for all the precinct captains, Dawson, Davis, and Wimbish brought discipline to the ward's politics. The organization sponsored classes in which ward leaders reviewed all aspects of running a campaign. Davis indicated that they stressed that the precinct captains should not get mad at people who rejected the Democrats. Instead the captains should try to find out if voters needed help with anything, and even talk to their friends to determine whether they could use assistance. They prepared the captains for election day, as well, by discussing election laws, noting the differences between good and bad ballots, and informing the election judges of their responsibilities and limits.[114]

These efforts won over even Mitchell, who finally acknowledged Dawson as leader of the ward early in 1940. Unlikely as they may have been, rumors that the Kelly-Nash faction planned to run Dickerson for Congress might have accounted for Mitchell's change of attitude. Having taken the presumptive step of writing a ten-point platform for all African Americans in the upcoming 1940 election, Dickerson did nothing to quell the buzz.[115] Fearing that Dawson would back Dickerson, Mitchell held a party in Dawson's honor, and two days later the two men held a conference in which Dawson easily persuaded Mitchell to run for a third term. Dawson led Mitchell's campaign, handily beating off a primary challenge from union leader Willard Townsend and easily dismissing William King in the general election.[116] Elated with Dawson's handling of his campaign and his organization of the ward, Mitchell became one of Dawson's biggest supporters.[117] Mitchell also shifted from his previous position of support for Dickerson to a critique of him as "the most conceited man in the United States."[118]

Although Dawson brought restraint to black Democratic politics in Chicago, Mitchell remained unable to bring any stability to black Democrats at the national level. As the presidential election approached several black operatives, including Mitchell, Dickerson, William J. Thompkins, Bishop R.R. Wright, and Julian Rainey, vied for dominance—a rather remarkable throng considering that black voting nationally still trended Republican.[119] Polls disagreed over black voters' allegiance, and the Republican candidate, Wendell Wilkie, made strong anti-segregation statements.[120] With black Democratic leaders unable to agree on one or even two national leaders, the DNC appointed Bishop R. R. Wright to head the western division and Julian Rainey to run the eastern division.[121] But these moves caused more discord as members of the National Colored Democrats Association vigorously opposed Rainey's appointment and other members broke off to form the National Council of Negro Democrats.[122] Thus to the extent that the Democratic Party won the black vote in 1940, it could not be credited to effective leadership on the part of white or black politicians.

By 1942, both Dawson and Dickerson felt equipped to replace Mitchell and provide a new model of black Democratic leadership at the national level. Neither an effective civil rights advocate nor a potent political organizer, Mitchell had fallen short of all expectations. Dawson, however, had a history of community activism as a Republican and had demonstrated strong organizational skills since his Democratic conversion. Dickerson for his part possessed a national reputation as a staunch defender of civil rights. Nevertheless, it would be their history as local politicians that determined which man could move to the national stage.

Dickerson may have hurt his chances by giving mixed signals regarding the Congressional nomination. In 1938 and 1940 Dickerson indicated that he wanted the job. Yet, in February 1942, Dickerson told the Draft Dickerson for Congress committee that he would not seek congressional office. By March he shifted again when he approached Dawson about sponsoring him for the nomination, but Dawson asked Dickerson to wait until he had cleared up some other party issues.[123] In actuality, Dawson had no intention of running Dickerson. Instead, he slated himself for congressman of the 1st Congressional District, Davis for 1st District assemblyman, and Wimbish for the Illinois State Senate.[124] Dickerson protested and urged the Ward's precinct captains to support his run for Congress, but the move backfired. Instead of rallying to support Dickerson, organization members attacked him. They criticized him for not supporting Kelly in the city council, for not working with the rest of the organization, and for being an arrogant "silk stocking."[125]

This move so angered Dickerson that he used his own money to launch an independent campaign.[126] His platform supported equal opportunity, the extension of the New Deal, additional low-cost housing projects, support for labor, the establishment of a permanent fair employment practices committee, enforcement of existing civil rights laws, and abolition of the poll tax.[127] Dickerson also questioned Dawson's integrity and masculinity.[128] In the *People's Voice,* a publication Dickerson created, Dickerson called Dawson "Wee Willie," accused him of skimping on the number of charity baskets given to each precinct during Thanksgiving, and questioned Dawson's handling of money made from boxing tournaments in the 2nd Ward.[129]

Dawson ran an equally negative campaign. The *Voice,* the regular organization's paper, routinely called Dickerson "Early B" and "Little Dick."[130] Although these representations may have been spiteful, the campaign's strongest barb questioned Dickerson's legitimacy as a representative for South Side blacks. Calling the alderman "Hi-Hat Dickerson" and "Silk Stockings" the *Voice* accused Dickerson of initiating numerous programs but not following through on them so that he could reap the praise of being known as a race man. *Voice* writers also insisted that Dickerson boasted of his service on racially mixed civic boards, which were mixed only by his presence.[131] Years later Dickerson admitted the charge that he worked for the people but was not of the people proved particularly harmful, because it was more or less correct. Despite humble origins, Dickerson never really became comfortable with the common African Americans whom he claimed to represent.[132]

Dickerson's go-it-alone attitude damaged him as much as his inability to relate to working-class African Americans. Corneal Davis blamed

Dickerson for putting himself in a position that allowed Dawson to turn on him. Had Dickerson included Wimbish and Davis in his negotiations with Dawson, they would have opposed Dawson when he reneged on the deal. "But," continued Davis, "Dickerson went without us. He forgot who put him there. So when the committeeman decided to go to Congress, we didn't back Dickerson."[133]

In addition to attacking Dickerson's personality, Dawson combined considerable party backing with his reputation as a community activist. Dawson received endorsements from the Cook County Democratic Central Committee, the 1st, 2nd, 4th, and 11th ward regular organizations, Arthur Mitchell, and the former Republican 1st District representative, William Gaines. A group of 2nd Ward mothers touted Dawson's campaign for community development initiatives, such as the creation of a child welfare program, slum clearing efforts, and establishment of the ward's first juvenile program. Dawson also drew in organized labor when he received an endorsement from Willard Townsend, the only black American on the Congress of Industrial Organization's executive board. Townsend's move nullified the importance of Dickerson's approval from the Council at large and gave some substance to Dawson's contention that Dickerson was a "race man" in the eyes of liberal whites but not the black masses.[134] With all of these guns pointed at Dickerson, his loss in the primary surprised no one. Dawson beat Dickerson in the primary 13,789 votes to 4,187. In the general election he beat his old rival William King 26,593 votes to 23,628.[135] Moreover, Dawson's entire slate, including Wimbish and Davis, won.[136] The new faction made good.

The 1942 elections marked a culmination of efforts begun by Ed Wright back in the early twentieth century and the realization of a vision crafted by Dawson, Wimbish, and Davis on the battlefields of southeastern France. During the preceding years, several leaders offered competing though ultimately unsuccessful models of black electoral leadership. Remaining doggedly loyal to the party of Lincoln, William King stayed closest to Wright's style. Despite his remarkable staying power, no black Republican with electoral aspirations could have withstood the Chicago Democrats' overwhelming political power. An outsider to Chicago, Mitchell attached himself to the relevant centers of white Democratic power, but he relied upon them entirely to consolidate his base. African Americans in the 1st Congressional District immediately chafed at this imposition (not to mention Mitchell's eccentric behaviors), and it was only a matter of time before they would remove Mitchell in a quest for more authentic representation. As a Chicago civil rights crusader, Dickerson, by contrast, could have provided that leadership. Although his civil rights endeavors made him popular with liberal elites and the black press, he did not take the appropriate steps to establish a political organization. He could have chosen, like DePriest did with the People's Movement, to cultivate a base that could circumvent his party's established apparatuses, but he never deepened his connection the South Side's grass roots.

Dawson, Wimbish, and Davis eventually chose a strategy that was simultaneously pragmatic and idealistic: to harness the voting power of South Side blacks for the creation of a powerful black political organization that they believed could provide the same benefits to its constituents as politics had provided for ethnic white Chicagoans. From Dawson's run for Congress in 1928 to Wimbish and Davis's steady attacks on Tittinger, they framed their vision in civil rights terms as they infiltrated the Democratic Party through cracks in its white leadership. In 1942 they consolidated their first major victory. Only time would tell if the delicate balance between electoral politics and civil rights could be sustained.

Chapter Four

A NEW ERA IN THE POLITICAL LIFE OF THE NATION

Black America and the
National Democratic Coalition, 1944–1952

The Negro vote in the North is already of some importance. It could become of much greater importance were it more wisely used. As the educational level of the Negro people is being raised and as the northward migration is continuing it might become the instrument by which the Negroes can increasingly use the machinery of federal legislation and administration to tear down the walls of discrimination.[1]—*Gunnar Myrdal*

Although scholars have argued that the New Deal forged a strong relationship between blacks and the Democratic Party, Dawson's role within the party reveals that a black/Democratic alliance remained questionable throughout the 1940s.[2] Rather than moving easily into the Democratic fold, blacks had a tenuous relationship with the party, torn as it was between its segregationist and moderate leadership. The postwar era battle between the party's liberal and conservative blocs has received ample historical attention, likewise the efforts of civil rights groups to influence both parties. Scholars, however, have ignored the role of black electoral officials in transforming the party.[3] Nevertheless, black Democrats met the party's powerful southern contingent head on in the fight for full integration into party politics. No politician figured more prominently in this group during the 1940s than William Dawson. Dawson pushed blacks to use the Democratic Party as their primary vehicle for civil rights and reminded the party of its debt to black voters—demonstrating that black Democratic leadership should be recognized, alongside the efforts of liberal insiders and outside civil rights groups, for moving the party toward a more racially inclusive agenda.

Dawson's crusade produced mixed results within the local, congressional, and national contexts. Although he often played a role in blocking overtly racist congressional legislation, Dawson consistently found himself unable to push forward any civil rights bills in the House (see the appendix). In Chicago Dawson could do nothing to ward off Mayor Martin Kennelly's racially insensitive policing and housing policies, but he significantly influenced the local party's decision to remove its support for the mayor. Dawson's greatest successes came within the party's national leadership, where he pushed the Democrats toward a more racially inclusive national agenda in the 1944 and 1948 election cycles. These victories encouraged him to reach out to black voters in a series of voter registration drives and to aid fledgling black Democratic organizations throughout the country. Consequently, Dawson supported the increased politicization that characterized southern and northern urban black communities in the late 1940s and early 1950s.

After winning the 1942 election, Dawson quickly secured his political position at home by replacing Dickerson with former social worker and fireman William Harvey for 2nd Ward alderman and sponsoring Christopher Wimbish for 3rd Ward committeeman.[4] Feeling safer at home, Dawson could turn his attention to his decidedly precarious situation in Washington, D.C.: serving as the nation's only black representative in a House greatly influenced by a network of southern committee chairs.[5] Unlike his predecessor, Dawson remained generally wary and distant from his white colleagues, particularly during his early years in the House. Congress did not present a black legislator with many potential allies, much less friends, but Dawson established a rapport with John W. McCormack, a congressman from Massachusetts who had also supported Arthur Mitchell.[6] Despite their collegiality, Dawson said of white representatives, "I won't break bread with them. They invite me to big dinners and the like. I won't go. Why should I? I know what they want from me. I don't need a meal from them, and I am not flattered by their company."[7] Of southern legislators he said, "Sometimes if I am offered a cigarette—particularly from a white southerner—I'll take it. Then I'll stand there and make him light it."[8]

This attitude came as no surprise considering that Dawson pursued race issues (in line with the liberal wing of the Democratic Party), only to have those efforts blocked by a coalition of northern conservatives and southern segregationists. Over the course of the 1940s, the *Congressional Record* indicates that Dawson submitted numerous civil rights bills, including several bills for equal employment opportunities, two anti-lynching bills, two bills to desegregate public accommodations in Washington, D.C., and a bill to prevent statements inciting racial hatred, none of which made it out of its initial committee assignment. Dawson also consistently coordinated with the House's liberal cadre, Vito Marcantonio and Arthur G. Klein (New York), Louis Ludlow (Indiana), and Mary T. Norton (New Jersey), on civil rights legislation. Yet their joint efforts proved no more successful in obtaining anti-lynching, equal employment, or other civil rights legislation.[9]

Although the liberal allies could not pass civil rights bills, Dawson held and even advanced the line in several race skirmishes in the House. For instance, in his first speech in Congress, Dawson blocked a drive by the Dies Committee to dismiss William Pickens, a black employee in the Treasury Department, for his association with radical organizations.[10] Also in March 1944, Dawson introduced legislation that served as a precedent for using congressional powers to investigate blacks' treatment in the military and the future desegregation of the Army, both of which will be discussed shortly.[11]

Even if he wanted to, Dawson could not focus solely on the House. The presidential election overshadowed all political activity in 1944, and as the nation's only black congressman as well as the apparent head of black politics in Chicago, Dawson became a crucial point man in the Democrats' push for African American votes.[12] Sensitive to black voter demands, the Democratic leadership increasingly sought Dawson's opinion on strategic matters. During the 1944 election cycle, for instance, Roosevelt consulted the freshman congressman on how to attract the black vote and asked him to approve James F. Byrnes's vice-presidential campaign.[13] Dawson's subsequent rejection of Byrnes and his later efforts in support of the liberal incumbent, Vice President Henry Wallace, represented two of Dawson's earliest attempts to push the national Democratic Party toward an acceptance of civil rights.

Although most Democrats welcomed Roosevelt's decision to run for a fourth term, the selection of a vice presidential candidate generated far more controversy.[14] Extremely liberal and outspoken, Henry Wallace divided the party faithful. He had important allies, including blacks, labor, and liberal Democrats, yet he aroused animosity from southern Democrats and frustration among party strategists.[15] Thus, by 1944, a powerful group of Democratic politicians, including White House Press Secretary Stephen Early, Democratic National Committee Chairman Robert Hannegan, and Chicago Mayor Edward Kelly, tried to dump Wallace.[16] Unwilling to reveal any disapproval of Wallace, Roosevelt approved his run for the nomination with an ambiguously worded letter of support, leading Wallace to believe that he could win the nomination.[17]

In addition to backroom plotting against his candidacy, the vice president faced competition from James F. Byrnes, a former senator from South Carolina whom black and liberal Democrats despised. Head of the powerful Office of War Mobilization (OWM), Byrnes sought the nomination for himself and he had received a vague nod of support from the president, who saw Byrnes as key leader in the war effort.[18] Black voters remembered, however, that Byrnes neglected the controversial Fair Employment Practices Committee (FEPC), the precedent-setting government agency charged with investigating reports of discrimination in wartime industries. Moreover, many black pundits noted that Byrnes ignored requests from civil rights groups to issue a statement supporting equal employment opportunities.[19]

The Democrats could not overlook Byrnes's unpopularity among blacks. Because rural whites in the West and Midwest had begun to move toward the GOP, the Democratic leadership needed urban black votes for a presidential victory.[20] Despite Roosevelt's increasing popularity among blacks, he still could not claim their full allegiance. After all, it was only in recent elections that blacks had seriously considered voting Democratic rather than Republican. Born out of frustrations with President Hoover's neglect of black voters, some black political pundits began to push for blacks to use their votes in a strategic fashion to make both parties consider race issues as early as the 1932 general election. Leaders such as *Pittsburgh Courier* editor Robert L. Vann, Bishop Reverdy Ransom of the African Methodist Episcopal Church, popular newspaper columnist Lester Walton, and prominent black historian Carter G. Woodson contended that vote splitting indicated political maturity and that blacks needed to free themselves from the GOP. By the 1936 general election, writers in the black and the white press speculated that blacks held the balance of power in several states, a situation that drew unprecedented attention to black issues by both parties.[21]

Doubts regarding which party would receive the black vote remained in 1944, and Dawson attempted to take advantage of them by pushing a civil rights agenda on the Democrats in exchange for black support. To this end, Dawson convened a meeting of black political leaders from around the country to draft a list of black political concerns. The meeting's participants, including Dawson, Herbert Bruce (New York), Emmett S. Cunningham (Michigan), and Joseph F. Albright (Minnesota), sent a list of demands to the Democratic National Committee: passage of an anti–poll tax law; passage of the Green-Lucas soldier voting bill; passage of the Dawson-Scanlon bill for a permanent FEPC; the passage of a financial package to prevent inflation; and "passage of the Wagner-Murray-Dingel bill intended to broaden the benefits of Social Security."[22] A *Chicago Defender* reported that Dawson closed the conference with a "fire eating" speech urging the Democrats to rid the party of southern segregationists:

> [The] only obstacle to forward progress to social and economic legislation has come from collusion between the southern bloc and reactionary Republicans. . . . If the South doesn't want Negroes in the Democratic Party, let them get out for we are here to stay—If the Republicans want them, they can take them. For every vote we lose, the Northern Democratic Party will get them back two-fold.[23]

Sentiments such as those expressed by Dawson and other black leaders confirmed a potential for black nonalignment that worried white Democratic strategists. Their apprehension was justified, considering the Republicans' strong appeals to black voters. The Republican nominee, Governor Thomas Dewey of New York, possessed a relatively solid civil rights record and the Republican platform pledged anti-lynching legislation, repeal of the poll tax, and a permanent FEPC.[24] With these concerns in mind, Roosevelt met with several Democratic heavyweights, including party chairman Robert Hannegan, party secretary George Allen, and Edward Kelly on July 11 to discuss the choice of a vice presidential nominee. Kelly argued strongly against Byrnes, claiming he would cost too many black votes. Worried and undecided, the group even tried to call Dawson to ask his opinion on the matter.[25]

In acknowledgment of the increasing importance of the black vote to the Democrats' national strategy Roosevelt met with Dawson and another black Democrat, Crystal Byrd Faucett, to formulate a response to the Republicans' civil rights pledges and to discuss the vice-presidential nomination on July 12th. Dawson assured the president that he would most likely receive black support because of the popularity of the New Deal, but he emphasized that the Democrats needed to write a strong civil rights plank. Roosevelt replied that he did not want the party platform to articulate specific civil rights pledges. Instead, he would campaign on his record to prevent any further alienation of the South while allowing him to make a strong bid for black votes. Roosevelt hoped that Dawson would explain this strategy to a meeting of leading black Democratic delegates during a meeting in his 2nd Ward headquarters before the convention. Roosevelt then asked Dawson's opinion of former Senator Byrnes. Dawson said he would back whomever the Illinois delegation chose, but he preferred Wallace whom he called "a great liberal, who has continued to grow in stature, bringing honor and strength to our country."[26]

At the start of the convention one week later, disagreements regarding the vice-presidential nomination and civil rights plank generated differences of opinion that threatened to polarize convention delegates, and Dawson played a role in Roosevelt's plans to keep the party together. In so doing, Dawson attempted to reconcile political and civil rights concerns. On the one hand, Dawson supported a somewhat moderate civil rights platform to mollify southern Democrats. On the other hand, he blocked Byrnes's vice-presidential aspirations and rallied black Democrats in support of Wallace.

After giving an address to the convention that emphasized the contributions of all races to the U.S. war effort, Dawson tried to mediate between the party's warring factions.[27] Southern delegates argued that the platform should not make any mention of civil rights, much less contain an entire plank on the subject.[28] Opposing the southern contingent, black and white liberal delegates demanded a plank stronger than the 1940 version with specific civil rights pledges.[29] Dawson, Kelly, and other party strategists tried to intercede between the two groups. Kelly and Dawson contended that Roosevelt had been a president for all Americans and his "record for Negroes ought to be a guarantee of his stand on matters affecting them in the future."[30] The *Chicago Defender* reported that these conflicting positions led the Committee on Platform and Resolutions into an "all-night deadlock," but the moderates prevailed in retaining a rather cautious civil rights plank: "We believe that racial and religious minorities have the right to live, develop and vote equally with all citizens and share the rights that are guaranteed by our Constitution. Congress should exert its full constitutional powers to protect those rights."[31] For the black delegation that appeared before the civil rights committee, the plank did not come near the specificity needed.[32] Nevertheless, the plank represented a disturbing defeat to southern delegates, who wanted to remove civil rights entirely.[33]

Although Dawson worked with the moderates in calming the fight over the civil rights plank, he gave vigorous support to the vice-presidential campaign of Henry Wallace, whose liberal stances on civil rights and the New Deal drew Dawson's unqualified admiration. Over the course of the convention, Wallace realized that a group of party leaders conspired against him by lobbying for the nomination of Missouri Senator Harry S. Truman. Wallace countered by giving a fiery speech seconding the president's nomination and aligning Roosevelt with racial and economic liberalism.[34] In one of the most passionate points of his oration, during which massive applause drowned out the boos of disgruntled conservatives, Wallace acclaimed liberalism, demanded an end to the poll tax, and called for equal educational opportunities.[35] Wallace's speech threw the convention into an uproar. No one had ever come out so strongly for equal rights at a party convention. Indeed, with his job in jeopardy, political observers expected Wallace to console the South by offering a timid position on civil rights.[36] Instead, the speech ignited a boisterous liberal rally in which Dawson led the black delegates to swing the vote for Wallace.[37] The pro-Wallace surge so alarmed the party leadership that Chairman Hannegan convinced Kelly to invoke city fire regulations, shutting down the convention before a vote could occur.[38]

The powerful anti-Wallace faction seemed to improve Byrnes's chances, but his position on civil rights made him an untenable candidate. Just prior to the convention, Byrnes's prospects looked good. Truman, who did not know that he was being considered for the nomination, had pledged his support, and Byrnes believed that this endorsement would keep Truman out of the running. Byrnes also knew that a survey in Illinois indicated that blacks would vote for Roosevelt even with Byrnes as the vice-presidential nominee, yet Byrnes's plans fell apart when he arrived at the convention. A group called the Progressive Democrats picketed the South Carolina delegation, the one most likely to nominate Byrnes, for its support of segregation. Then, in a jab at Byrnes, Walter White of the NAACP, Reverend Maynard Jackson of Dallas, and Edgar G. Brown of the National Negro Campaign warned the Democratic leadership that any candidate with a poor civil rights record would face intense black opposition.[39]

These protests caused Roosevelt alarm, for he needed black votes to offset his declining popularity with rural midwestern whites. Because most political leaders believed that Dawson controlled not only the votes of black Chicago, but also black votes in downstate Illinois, the party leadership needed to know how Dawson would react to a Byrnes nomination.[40] Dawson had after all assisted the party moderates in finding a compromise on the civil rights plank. Would he also support Byrnes, allowing the party leadership to use Dawson to force Byrnes on the black Democrats? Or would he oppose Byrnes, thus aligning himself with the black civil rights leadership against the resultant Roosevelt-Byrnes ticket.

Despite his willingness to cooperate on the civil rights plank, Dawson could not support Byrnes's candidacy, and he virtually sank the former senator's vice-presidential candidacy. Roosevelt asked Kelly whether he could deliver Illinois with Byrnes on the ticket, and Kelly responded that he needed assurances from Dawson that he would support Byrnes.[41] The crucial moment came when Kelly arranged for the two men to meet at the Blackstone Hotel in Chicago. Dawson and Byrnes talked in private for three hours, after which Dawson slowly and deliberately walked out to an anxious Ed Kelly. Dawson turned to look directly at Byrnes and said, "Mr. Justice, you cannot be my candidate." He then turned back to Mayor Kelly and said, "He cannot be my candidate." Without saying another word Dawson walked out.[42]

Byrnes dismissed Dawson's disapproval, but it nonetheless spelled the end of his drive for the vice presidency. More important, this episode marked the first instance of an African American leader having direct influence on the selection of a major party's presidential ticket and highlighted the growing power of black voters within the Democratic coalition. A Byrnes biographer notes that the meeting between Dawson and the former senator did not happen by chance. Rather, Roosevelt intended from the start to sacrifice Byrnes's vice-presidential aspirations to a coalition of blacks, labor, and northern urban voters.[43] Because Byrnes possessed considerable support from several party leaders and presumably from southern voters, however, Roosevelt could not dismiss him out of hand. Dawson's negative appraisal thus gave the president another strong reason to put Byrnes's candidacy aside.

After the meeting Dawson went back to the convention to push for Wallace, but the vice president had little chance of victory.[44] Just as Roosevelt engineered Byrnes's defeat, he also had conspired against Wallace, whose intense commitment to liberalism posed an equally significant threat to party unity.[45] Like Byrnes, Wallace gradually learned of the Truman insurgency. On the third day of the convention Truman obtained the nomination after three rounds of balloting, sealing Roosevelt's plan of a compromise plank and a moderate ticket.[46]

Dawson's role in this stratagem revealed the Democrats' recognition of blacks as a critical part of their coalition and marked the beginning of Dawson's ascent to national campaign leadership. Shortly into the national campaign, Democratic National Committee Chairman Robert Hannegan appointed Dawson assistant chairman of the DNC, at that time the highest party position obtained by a black Democrat. The *Defender* argued that Dawson's appointment made him the number one "man in the Democratic publicity drive to retain the Negro vote for the New Deal." Dawson headed up the drive in the eight large urban areas in particular where either party could have won the black vote: Baltimore, Chicago, Cleveland, Louisville, Detroit, Los Angeles, New York, and St. Louis.[47] The Democrats needed Dawson in these cities to counter the GOP's strong appeals to black voters. In New York, for example, Dewey's reputation as a civil rights–friendly governor rivaled Roosevelt's popularity.[48]

In his new leadership role, Dawson attacked the GOP nominee's stance on military desegregation—a particularly sensitive topic, given black Americans' desire for full and equal participation in the war effort. Unsatisfied with his past achievements as governor of New York, black journalists asked Dewey to take a stand on segregation in the military.[49] He refused to do so, stating that he did not have the expertise to judge the military's racial policy. To which Dawson replied,

> It does not take a "military expert" to know that segregation in the armed forces is against the full rights of Negro Americans and is not in accord with the freedom granted in the Constitution. . . . Every answer Governor Dewey has made on the race issue has either been evasive or showed a complete lack of knowledge or sympathy with the aspirations of the Negro people.[50]

Dawson's criticism drew upon the deep anger that black Americans felt toward discrimination in the U.S. armed forces, as well as their high expectations for an end to segregation upon the war's conclusion.[51] Despite government propaganda, blacks remained segregated in every aspect of the war effort, from the battlefield to the war industries.[52] This state of affairs led to constant criticism from black leaders, an organized protest at the 1940 Democratic convention, and the *Pittsburgh Courier's* immensely popular "Double-V" campaign for victory over "fascism abroad and racism at home." Meanwhile the national headquarters of the NAACP directed its local branches to target protests against segregated defense industries.[53]

Several Chicago black politicians and civil rights groups had joined the fight against segregation in the defense industries. The Chicago branch of the NAACP picketed the Bauer and Black plant, and later assisted A. Philip Randolph in organizing the March on Washington Movement

(MOWM) to pressure the Roosevelt administration to end discrimination in the nation's defense industries.[54] On June 25, 1941, Roosevelt capitulated and issued Executive Order 8802, which directed government agencies to administer defense programs on an equal basis and created the Fair Employment Practices Committee (FEPC) to investigate and recommend solutions to instances of discrimination in wartime industries. Earl Dickerson was one of two blacks on the five-member committee, and he pushed the commission to hold public hearings in several major cities, including Chicago in January 1942.[55] Dawson's Second Ward Organization also joined in. Citing 8802 Davis, Wimbish, and Harvey pushed the People's Gas and Light Company to hire more blacks. Later Davis, Wimbish, and Illinois State Representative Charles Jenkins led the fight for a state FEPC in Illinois.[56]

In keeping with the mainstream civil rights leadership of the era, Dawson actively used the war as a wedge to break down America's defense of black inequality. Although he coordinated with the NAACP by sponsoring a bill for fair employment practices in January 1944, he focused most of his efforts on securing equal rights in the military.[57] Repeating the inanity that gripped them during World War I, segregationists insisted on limiting black enlistment through a quota system. After obtaining the quota system, southerners then feared that young, single black males would prey on southern white women while southern white males participated in the war effort. As a result, southern politicians began to demand that blacks be drafted into the military. Once blacks enlisted, though, those same southerners insisted that blacks be kept out of combat situations. Trapped in convoluted southern racial paradigms, the army tried to calm Dixie's fears by putting southern white officers in charge of black troops and placing most black training facilities in the Deep South. These efforts to keep black soldiers "in their place" angered black civil rights leaders, who remained adamant that blacks participate in combat situations just like white soldiers.[58]

Starting in 1943, Dawson worked closely with Truman Gibson Jr., a fellow Chicagoan and the civilian aide to the secretary of war, to fight the army's segregationist policies. Gibson believed that, as a veteran of World War I, Dawson possessed a fervent interest in blacks' military affairs, which fueled his drive for military integration:

> We whipsawed the Army. Bill was a veteran of World War I and had been an officer from the old Jim Crow officer's course in Des Moines, Iowa. . . . He was extremely helpful in putting pressure on the War Department, because then we started the whole battle for inclusion, ostensibly led by

the *Pittsburgh Courier* with the "Double V Campaign": victory at home and victory abroad. And with the inclusion came problems, because the Army was resistant to the use of blacks in any combat roles. . . . Dawson was a part of this whole pressure movement long before Randolph.[59]

During his time at the war department, Gibson wrote several reports condemning racism in the military. Indeed, when Gibson won the Medal of Merit Award, the nation's highest award for civilians, a *Defender* reporter wrote that Secretary of War Henry Stimson had been most impressed "by the number of statements critical of Army policy and procedure which Gibson had submitted to him, adding, perhaps it would have been easier for all concerned had the pleasant things been emphasized" instead.[60] Gibson's recollection that Dawson's efforts preceded Randolph's MOWM is most likely incorrect, since Randolph's planning preceded Gibson's arrival in Washington, D.C., by two years.[61] Nevertheless, the fact that a leader as cogent and well informed as Gibson remembered it as such points to the intensity of Dawson's effort.

Indeed, Dawson criticized the military even more harshly than Gibson. In 1944 Stimson justified the usage of black troops in primarily support capacities by citing their lower educational qualifications. An infuriated Dawson joined the Chicago Citizens Committee of 1,000 and the National Negro Council in calling for Stimson's resignation:

> Either willfully or ignorantly, Secretary Stimson is playing hand-in-glove with that element in the Army, which has done everything through the years to handicap, or discredit Negro troops. Mr. Stimson's statement could not be based on facts. Every valid record shows the valor and fighting courage of our boys.[62]

Twelve days later, Dawson introduced House Resolution 472 to convene a special committee to study and make recommendations to Congress regarding race relations and the country's war effort.[63] A March 1944 article in the *Chicago Defender*, "Cong. Dawson's Bill Seeks Causes of Racial Tensions," spelled out the proposal: to establish a Congressional investigating committee to investigate the extent to which the military used blacks in the war effort, the types of services they performed, the extent to which they were being rejected from the services because of illiteracy, the effect of lowered black enlistments on manpower, the degree to which black skills were being used in essential wartime industries, and the causes of recent race riots.[64]

Although the House Rules Committee did not let the measure go to the floor, in time the resolution would be seen as setting the precedent for the establishment of the President's Committee on Civil Rights in 1946. In 1958 Dawson received a nomination for an Americanism award from the American Veterans Committee (AVC), whose membership included Ralph Bunche, Eleanor Roosevelt, and Harry Truman. In a letter supporting Dawson's nomination the AVC's national counsel, Phineas Indritz, wrote,

> Congressman Dawson has been particularly active . . . to correct injustices and discrimination against Negro servicemen, and . . . [i]t should be added that his bill in 1944 to have a special committee established to investigate the utilization of colored Americans in the military service and in defense industries laid the foundation for the President's Committee on Civil Rights.[65]

After the campaign, Dawson did not let go of the issue. The following year he proposed House Resolution 48, also intended to "create a special committee to make a full and complete study of race relations in the United States."[66]

In 1944, though, Dawson tied his crusade for military desegregation to the national campaign. Dawson noted, for instance, that the administration had supported a bill Dawson introduced to investigate the effects of discrimination in the military, and argued that electing more liberal congressmen would lead to an end to the poll tax and improvements for blacks in the defense industries.[67] As head of the DNC's drive to target black votes in major urban areas, Dawson likely organized the party's effort to spread this campaign material to the black press. Advertisements in papers such as the *Chicago Defender,* the *St. Louis Argus,* the *Philadelphia Afro-American,* the *Washington Afro-American,* the *New York Age,* the *Cleveland Gazette,* the *Michigan Chronicle,* and the *Chicago Bee* described Roosevelt's support of integration during the Philadelphia Rapid Transit system strike and noted several black accomplishments during FDR's administrations. The strategy succeeded, and, wrote St. Clair Drake and Horace Cayton, blacks began to feel that "Dr. Win the War would write an effective prescription for his Negro patients."[68]

If blacks needed more proof of Roosevelt's commitment to civil rights issues, they got it when Roosevelt and Wallace, who campaigned for the party despite his removal from the ticket, made several civil rights pledges during campaign stops in Chicago and on the South Side. Blacks listened attentively to Roosevelt's position on civil rights, and he did not let them down. He called for a permanent FEPC, supported equal employment opportunities, and condemned the poll tax.[69] To reinforce the president's visit, Wallace came to Chicago's Bronzeville the following day, making him the highest party official to visit a major black community. With Dawson, New York congressional candidate Adam Clayton Powell Jr., and Mary McCleod Bethune joining him onstage, Wallace pointed to FDR's establishment of the FEPC and his leadership in the Depression while criticizing Dewey for allegedly promising southerners that he would "soft-pedal" civil rights in exchange for their support. Dawson heavily criticized the contemporary Republican leadership. Echoing his local partners, Wimbish and Davis, Dawson told the audience of 5,000 that they owed no allegiance to Lincoln: "If they can bring Lincoln back, I'll vote for him. That failing I'm for FDR."[70]

On election day, Roosevelt received remarkable support from black voters, earning them a more prominent place in the Democratic coalition. In Chicago, Roosevelt's share of the black vote increased from 52 to 65 percent. Scholars have argued that the civil rights pledges blacks received in the 1944 elections from both parties resulted from their intense competition for the black vote.[71] Dawson's experience in the 1944 election adds another dynamic. Democratic Party leaders not only attempted to bring in black voters by making civil rights pledges but also saw the need to involve an African American in decision making. The leadership saw Dawson as the logical choice for this role. Although Roosevelt surely used Dawson in his own machinations, Dawson's inclusion indicated blacks' growing power in the national Democratic coalition.

Yet playing an important role in national politics did not translate to more influence over white Chicago politicians whose constituents demanded that they maintain white supremacy, and no political issue in Chicago made Dawson's lack of power more apparent than his inability to check the array of whites in Chicago and Illinois who demanded segregated public housing. Throughout the 1940s adequate housing, in terms of quality and quantity, remained out of reach for most black Chicagoans. Hemmed in by white phobias, antipathy, and violence, approximately 375,000 blacks lived in a South Side area with housing stock capable of accommodating only 100,000. As Black Belt landlords took advantage of desperate home seekers by charging exorbitant rents for shabbily constructed "kitchenette" apartments, health and safety standards all but disappeared. Rat attacks on South Side children resulting in injuries and death became common, and fires killed more than 180 blacks between 1947 and 1953.[72]

Despite Mayor Kelly's support, Chicago Housing Authority (CHA) director Elizabeth Wood's efforts to gradually and modestly integrate public housing in the late 1940s touched off massive aggressive white resistance.[73] For example, in 1946, when the CHA attempted to move an African American veteran and his family into the Airport Homes housing project, white mobs numbering between 1,500 and 3,000 fought police in protest. Kelly nevertheless gave Wood's attempts at gradual integration his steadfast support.[74] If Kelly could not stem white resistance, it should come as no surprise that Dawson's organization could do no better. Still, it appears that black Chicagoans did not expect it to. The press gave no attention to the black political corps during this fiasco, focusing instead upon supporting Elizabeth Wood and Mayor Kelly.

Black Chicagoans, nevertheless, could do little but watch as indignant white voters, civic leaders, and local Democrats deposed Mayor Kelly and steamrolled the proponents of integrated, scattered-site housing. These forces not only drastically exceeded the powers available to Dawson's organization but also made short work of the mayor. In the 1947, when polling made it abundantly clear that white Chicagoans would not re-elect Kelly because of his modest support of integration, the Democratic organization dropped Kelly for Martin Kennelly, a prominent businessman and alleged reformer.[75]

Most black Chicagoans saw Kennelly's reformist programs as thinly veiled harassment of the black community. The new mayor's anticrime efforts generated headlines, but his strategies did not relieve community problems on the South Side, and his attack on the so-called jitney cabs undermined an important element of black Chicago's underground economy.[76] Black businessmen in Chicago created the jitney cab system because whites provided black neighborhoods inadequate transportation services and because white-owned cab companies would not hire black drivers. Since white banks refused to loan black businessmen the startup capital necessary to start a profitable cab company, blacks created their own system in which individuals bought a small number of cab licenses and then leased the cars for a twelve-hour period. Complaints against the unregulated system drew the attention of the Internal Revenue Service in 1943, and Dawson led a legal defense of several jitney operators against IRS attempts to shut them down.[77] Although materials in Dawson's files do not indicate who won the case, it is most likely that the defense succeeded, because jitney cabs remained pervasive on the South Side well past 1943.

Starting in early 1947 Kennelly, reform-minded South Side whites, and upper-class blacks aligned themselves against the million-dollar industry, which now employed between 200 and 500 South Side blacks. In 1948 a local improvement association and the Illinois Commerce Commission filed suit to close several jitneys, and Kennelly supported their efforts. Many black observers saw the attack as an attempt by the city to put the jitneys out of business and as a distraction from such serious ghetto problems as inadequate political representation and health care. Others argued that Chicagoans' use of the cabs demonstrated the service's value. Finally, a class element appeared when working-class blacks suggested that black doctors and lawyers should be satisfied driving their expensive new cars without limiting transportation for their poorer counterparts.[78] Dawson understood the value of the jitneys for his constituents and lodged angry protests with the mayor against his attempts to undermine the cabs' operation, but Kennelly ignored him.[79]

Kennelly's disregard for Dawson had even greater ramifications in the area of public housing. Dawson's work for the Southside Gardens Project in the late 1930s pointed to his interest in obtaining more public housing for his desperate constituents. Yet, because Kennelly's mandate repudiated the previous administration's relationship with the African American community, the mayor could easily squeeze out Dawson, as well as any other black leader, from participating in housing negotiations. Only two months into Kennelly's term, the Metropolitan Housing Committee, composed of representatives of powerful downtown interests, secured Kennelly's support in passing the Blighted Areas Redevelopment and Relocation Act of 1947. The act allowed the CHA to acquire blighted land with the city council's approval through eminent domain and sell the property to private developers for new homes. But only 15 percent of that land could be used for low-income public housing.[80] In view of the city council's unwillingness to approve sites that disturbed the racial status quo and a mere 15 percent allocation for low-income homes, critics saw that the new law would improve housing stocks only through massive displacement of black Chicagoans.[81] This prediction came true with the first redevelopment effort, the New York Life Insurance Company's Lake Meadows project. Marshall Field's, the Chicago Title and Trust Company, Michael Reese Hospital, and the Illinois Institute of Technology designed the project to head off the growing black slum on the near South Side. Plans estimated that the project would displace 29,500 families, but only 6,530 would have access to public housing. The remainder of the largely impoverished population had to fend for themselves. Although the planners did not explicitly exclude blacks, pricing made it clear that they intended the new properties for middle-class ownership.[82]

Blacks could not mount a serious challenge to the forces supporting the project. The city council brushed aside a bill by the 3rd Ward's
independent black Republican alderman, Archibald Carey, Jr., to require
all new housing constructed with public funds to be open to all applicants regardless of race.[83] Dawson vocally opposed Lake Meadows, but
Kennelly's "progressive" inclinations rendered him unsympathetic to an
organization-man like Dawson. Recently historians have cited Dawson's
unwillingness to lead a "racial confrontation" against Lake Meadows and
subsequent housing projects as evidence that the projects served Dawson's interests by retaining racial boundaries.[84] Although such a state of
affairs did not hinder Dawson and his cohorts' ability to retain office,
there is no evidence that their political territory faced any real threats
at the time. Moreover, no proof exists that his organization would have
found this situation morally desirable. To the contrary, even as all of this
occurred, Dawson fought discrimination within his party's caucuses and
in various legislative actions, including support for a permanent FEPC,
desegregation of the armed forces, anti–poll tax legislation, and open
housing for black veterans.[85] Meanwhile, Wimbish and Davis pursued
state FEPC legislation and faced off lynch mobs in an attempt to get equal
pay for black teachers in downstate Illinois.[86] It is difficult to imagine that
the men who engaged in these actions would happily embrace their exclusion from housing policy formation because of political expediency.

With practically no voice in the development of slum renewal, Dawson's organization could only attempt to mitigate the project's negative
effects. Alderman Harvey, a former social worker, became a frequent and
vocal critic of slum renewal programs' inadequate apportionment of
replacement housing. He executed stalling tactics in the city council to
slow down the projects while assisting displaced black families in finding
a place to live. The organization also pushed for displaced homeowners
to receive the best prices possible for their condemned properties.[87]

In light of Chicago Democrats' callous disregard for blacks and continued southern intransigence, it should have come as little surprise that
the argument for political nonalignment to defeat segregationists continued to resonate among black political leaders.[88] As early as the 1946
congressional elections, John Sengstacke, the publisher of the Chicago
Defender, pushed the "*Defender* Vote Crusade," a slogan that urged blacks
to protect their interests through the ballot.[89] In 1947 Sengstacke wrote an
editorial encouraging Republicans to heed black concerns in 1948: "The
Republican Party will need our vote, but it will have to earn it, not by
words of the mouth and empty promises, but by actual accomplishments

and deeds."[90] Finally, in 1948 NAACP publicist Henry Lee Moon raised a stir among black intellectuals and politicians with his book *Balance of Power*, which claimed that blacks held the swing vote in seventy-five northern congressional districts.[91]

Black voters' continued emphasis on political nonalignment as well as as southern whites' increasing discontent with the party's racially liberal elements caused trepidation among the party leadership and gave Dawson an opening to leverage black votes for increased Democratic attention to race issues. In 1948 the Democrats faced not only Thomas Dewey but also a challenge from Henry Wallace, now a member of the Progressive Party.[92] Wallace's campaign, with his strong appeal to blacks, heightened the competition between the two major parties for black support.[93] Because of these dynamics, Dawson implemented a two-front strategy: first, he urged blacks to resist the temptations of Wallace's third-party campaign; second, he demonstrated to the white Democratic leadership that blacks could provide the votes needed to replace southern whites' support. His work in this area proved critical to Truman's success and helped legitimize civil rights as a national political issue. As the election approached, this scenario seemed unlikely, because many pundits had already dismissed Truman, who faced difficulties in his foreign policy and in domestic civil rights. His Russian policy had faltered, and fellow Democrats had attempted to recruit Eisenhower for the ticket.[94] Meanwhile, race issues presented Truman with a particularly vexing problem. Increasingly alarmed about racial injustice, Truman established the President's Committee on Civil Rights in December and the committee's 1947 report, *To Secure These Rights*, called for sweeping changes to the nation's race policies.[95] Predictably, northern and southern white Democrats divided over the report. Black leaders, though, praised Truman's courage in presenting the issues.[96]

Truman's turn toward civil rights came amid a campaign by civil rights leaders to push segregation into the international spotlight. The NAACP had recently filed a petition with the United Nations entitled "An Appeal to the World: A Statement on the Denial of Human Rights to Minorities in the Case of Citizens of Negro Descent in the United States of America and an Appeal to the United Nations for Redress," which embarrassed the United States in its capacity as "the leader of the *free* world."[97] Truman also faced criticism from Henry Wallace, whose willingness to attack segregation generated intense black support.[98]

On February 2, 1948, Truman presented a bold civil rights agenda to Congress.[99] In his address, Truman called attention to the hypocrisy of claiming to support equality while maintaining segregation. Truman challenged Congress to remove the poll tax, establish a permanent FEPC and Commission on Civil Rights, pass federal protection against lynching, and grant home rule to the District of Columbia. He also promised to sign an executive order banning discrimination in employment and asked the defense secretary to hasten military desegregation.[100]

Although several northern and black newspapers praised Truman's position on civil rights, many Americans opposed it. A Gallup poll showed that only 6 percent of Americans supported Truman's agenda. Broken down between North and South, the numbers still looked bad. Only 21 percent of nonsouthern whites approved the program, whereas 15 percent opposed it, and the remaining 64 percent had not even heard of it. Fifty-one percent of southern whites argued that Truman unfairly condemned the South, and the Southern Governors Conference declared its intention to oppose Truman, or any other pro–civil rights candidate, in the upcoming election. Even though the South did not unite in its opposition to Truman, the governors' announcement caused alarm among Democrats.[101]

Once again disagreement over civil rights threatened to divide the party along its northern and southern seam. Although the Republican nominees, Thomas Dewey and Earl Warren of California, received guarded praise from black intellectuals and journalists, their civil rights positions did not cause the coming Democratic crisis.[102] Unlike the 1944 election, most of the pressure came from within the party. A pall hung over the July convention as Truman faced the daunting task of placating disgruntled southern Democrats without losing northern liberal support, labor, or black voters.[103]

Things quickly fell apart as the Democrats' pro– and anti–civil rights factions lined-up against one another. An acrimonious debate ensued during the Platform Committee's sessions as southern forces defeated liberals' efforts to draft a civil rights plank with the same specificity as Truman's civil rights message to Congress. Knowing that Truman wanted a strong civil rights plank, Andrew Biemiller, head of the Americans for Democratic Action (ADA), Hubert Humphrey, and Esther Murray (the only black woman on the civil rights subcommittee) vowed to continue the fight to the floor, where they proposed an amendment for a strong civil rights plank.[104] Despite blocking the liberal wave, several southern delegations also rejected the majority report. The Mississippi, Texas, Tennessee, and Alabama delegations submitted their own amendment to the platform to include a statement upholding the principle of states' rights.[105]

In the end, the convention adopted the more liberal plank, leading southern delegates to abandon the proceedings.[106] The delegates first went through a roll call vote and then several voice votes on the states' rights plank, all of which failed. Then the chairman of the California delegation requested a roll call vote on the Humphrey-Biemiller-Murray plank. One by one, the chairman asked each delegation for its position and a scramble followed to round up enough support for the civil rights amendment.[107] Americans for Democratic Action chairman Leon Anderson quickly polled each delegation for its intended vote. When he asked Jake Arvey, the party leader in Cook County, for Illinois's position, Arvey replied that he could make no comment until he met with Dawson, who, the *Defender* reported, did much of the "groundwork for adoption of the minority report." When Illinois's turn arrived, it cast all sixty of its votes for the amendment, which won by only sixty-nine votes.[108] Immediately after the reading of the platform half of the Alabama delegation and the entire Mississippi delegation stalked out of the convention.[109]

Although the southern walkout seriously threatened Truman's election chances, black Democrats and civil rights leaders reacted to their defection and the civil rights plank with elation. NAACP Executive Secretary Walter White, for instance, praised the earnestness with which the Democrats addressed civil rights and claimed that the platform "marked the greatest turning point for the South and America since the Civil War." When asked his feelings on the platform, a jubilant Dawson said, "[It] is the most heartening experience I've ever had since I've been in politics. It marks a new era in the political life of the nation."[110] Dawson correctly pointed out the importance of the civil rights plank, but the plank alone would not lead to this "new era." Rather, in 1948, black Democrats, led by Dawson, proved that they could be a critical swing vote in presidential elections.

As the general election got underway, the Truman campaign realized that it had no chance for success without the black vote, for it faced attacks from the Right and the Left. With their prosegregation positions, the States' Rights Party or Dixiecrats ran a backward-looking campaign.[111] Although the Dixiecrats did not have complete southern support, they threatened to cut into Truman's vote totals and push the election to the House of Representatives, where southern strength could force concessions from whomever the eventual President would be. On the other end of the Democratic spectrum, Truman faced Wallace's Progressive Party campaign, which strongly advocated black civil rights.[112]

These threats to the Democratic base made black support critical and forced the party to grant more attention to black concerns. Like Roosevelt did in 1944, Democratic leaders again came to Dawson. In 1948, however, the need for black votes surpassed that of the past election, and Dawson took the opportunity to push the party's racial stance further toward civil rights. Indeed, the 1948 campaign marked a highpoint in the Democrats' attempt to secure black votes. The party officially disbanded its Negro Division and spread black workers throughout its apparatus, arguing that segregation would not be tolerated within the party structure. John P. Davis, assistant director of publicity, created a newspaper entitled the *Truman Record*, which contained articles by Dawson and other leaders who connected Truman and the Democratic Party to civil rights.[113] Finally, DNC chairman and Rhode Island Senator Howard McGrath promoted Dawson to vice chairman of the party, the highest Democratic position yet achieved by a black American.[114]

In one of the most critical moves of the 1948 campaign, Dawson arranged a speaking tour on behalf of the Democratic Party for William Hastie, a Harvard law school graduate, the first black circuit court judge, former dean of the Howard University Law School, and an uncompromising civil rights advocate. Hastie approached party officials about helping the campaign. None of them, however, including McGrath, recognized that Hastie's prominence could assist Truman's quest for black support. To the contrary, Hastie said that white party officials acted disheartened and apathetic. So Hastie went to Dawson, who arranged for Hastie to go on a mid-Atlantic speaking tour, which continued right up to the day before the election and climaxed with a rally in Madison Square Garden. Thus, Dawson arranged what White House aide Stephen Springarn called the Democratic Party's most important move to attract black voters in the 1948 campaign.[115]

Dawson's most lasting contribution, though, was his formation of the National Citizens Committee for the Reelection of President Truman (NCCRPT), which marked the first time that blacks organized to help finance a campaign for a major political party and demonstrated the plausibility of African Americans replacing the southern segregationist contingent of the Democratic Party. When the Dixiecrats withdrew their support, Truman faced a significant drop in funding. *Defender* editor John Sengstacke responded to their defection in an editorial telling that blacks voters to "put up or shut up" and start a nationwide fundraising campaign for Truman. A few weeks later, Dawson and Sengstacke announced the formation of the NCCRPT with its goal to raise a million dollars for Truman.

Dawson presided over the group and Ann Hedgeman, an executive with the Young Women's Christian Association, the former executive director of the National Council for a Permanent FEPC, and a leader in the March on Washington Movement, served as its director. The committee sought vice chairmen from black population centers across the country, and the list of respondents read like a who's who of black America, including leaders from New York, Florida, Mississippi, Kentucky, Alabama, Pennsylvania, Washington, D.C., and Louisiana.[116]

The NCCRPT gave black leaders and Democratic activists a conspicuous opportunity to flex their political muscle. More than eighty black leaders of local and national prominence from New York to Mississippi responded enthusiastically to Dawson and Sengstacke's call. Mary McCleod Bethune, founder of Bethune-Cookman College and former Black Cabinet member, wrote, "You do not need to ask me. I am standing in the front ranks with Truman." Other contributors included J. Raymond Jones, a Harlem political leader; C.A. Scott, an Atlanta publisher; Percy Greene, editor of the *Jackson Advocate;* Venice T. Spraggs, a political correspondent with the *Chicago Defender;* R. O'Hara Lanier, president of Texas State University for Negroes (currently Texas Southern University); and William Houston, a prominent Washington, D.C., attorney.[117] Although it had widespread support, the NCCRPT does not appear to have coordinated specifically with civil rights or black religious organizations. Rather, the group named a series of vice chairmen who supervised the work of local fundraising activities. This plan succeeded, and, by the end of the election, the *Defender* put Dawson on its 1948 honor roll "for raising more funds for the President's campaign than any other single individual."[118]

In November, after intense campaigning, the black vote helped Truman win the election in what some consider the greatest political upset in U.S. history.[119] Labor and small-town America claimed to be the swing vote, but blacks had as much of a stake as either of these groups.[120] Truman beat Dewey by a significant margin in the Electoral College (303 to 189), but the election hinged upon Illinois and Ohio, which held a total of 53 electoral votes. Had Dewey won these states, the Electoral College returns would have been 250 to 242, meaning that neither candidate would have possessed the absolute majority of 270 electoral college votes needed to secure the presidency, and the House of Representatives would have decided the election. Had this been the case, the body's array of dominant southern chairpersons would have certainly demanded a conservative stance on black rights from either candidate. The black vote, however, carried Truman in both of these states. Dawson, in particular, deserved the credit for delivering Truman an overwhelming 128,541 votes in Illinois, where Truman won by only 33,612 votes overall.[121] As one black journalist put it, "The Negro vote holding the balance of power has returned President Harry S. Truman to the White House. Ignored by all of the nation-wide polls as an 'insignificant minority' whose opinion needed no consideration this minority has again demonstrated that 15 million Negroes can swing any national ticket."[122]

Truman acknowledged Dawson's assistance, and the two remained allies through the duration of Truman's time in office. Discussing their travels around the country to raise money for the president, Corneal Davis said that "Truman thought a lot of William L. Dawson." Days after the election Truman thanked him for his "work in the national ticket" and his faith in Truman's ability to win.[123] This letter marked the beginning of a cordial political relationship. In 1950, in response to a letter from Davis, who was organizing a "National Dawson Day," President Truman wrote, "[Those] who have worked with him know that he is always ready to throw his strength on the side of justice and fair play. I have called on him often and he has never failed me. He is a great public servant and I am pleased to be counted among those celebrating National Dawson Day."[124] Two years later, Truman thanked Dawson again for his help in the 1952 Democratic convention,[125] and in September 1952 he wrote to praise a moving speech against the segregation of veterans hospitals Dawson gave in Congress—a speech that Truman hailed as "one of the great documents of the age."[126] Finally, when he left office in 1953, Truman thanked Dawson for his support during his terms in office.[127]

During the heady aftermath of Truman's victory, African Americans perceived the Democrats' recognition of Dawson as an important national figure as an advance for the nation's blacks. Black journalists, for instance, celebrated the fact that one of their own was the object of a gala tribute dinner chaired by Senator Howard McGrath and Senator Scott Lucas of Illinois. The tribute, organized by Representative Helen Gahagan of California, celebrated Dawson's contributions to the Democratic ticket.[128]

Dawson brought African Americans an even greater symbolic victory though, when he used his influence to push for the desegregation of the president's inaugural ball.[129] A second home to many southern legislators, Washington, D.C., of the 1940s adhered to segregation as rigorously as any city in Dixie.[130] Dawson attacked this tradition, however, when he used his newfound political clout to end the whites-only inaugural ball.[131] John Sengstacke saw the 1948 ball as a sign of hope and coming equality, when he wrote, "[For] the first time in history Negro citizens were fully integrated in the inaugural celebration and it was obvious to everyone that the lily white era of Washington's social life had come to an abrupt end."[132] Although the desegregation of Washington would be a long and difficult process—and one that many would say remains incomplete—the integration of the inaugural ball was an unprecedented first step.

Despite these successes, Dawson remained focused on the tangible goals of the party-building agenda: increased black electoral participation through the Democratic Party and greater access to government employment for black workers. Truman's promotion of civil rights as a national issue had no significant effect on hiring in government agencies. Racist hiring practices continued, primarily because of southern Democratic committee chairs' tendency to attack federal agencies that even considered integrationist agendas.[133] Moreover, systemic racism corrupted any stated goals of meritocratic hiring, whereas the few blacks that did make it through civil service hoops could generally count on being restricted to the most menial positions.[134]

DNC correspondence and articles in the black press indicate that by 1948 Dawson possessed great influence over the appointment of blacks in government.[135] In light of the apparent inequity in government hiring, it should come as no surprise that Dawson saw the acquisition of patronage jobs for black Americans as one of the most important civil rights tools available to him as an elected official: "I have tried to fight for civil rights where it is most effective, within the caucuses of my own party. I have helped to get good jobs for qualified colored people and many of the big posts we hold in government today were obtained through this technique."[136]

Contemporary reform-oriented elites and modern critics have routinely disparaged patronage for its connection to political corruption, but their appraisals overlooked its central role in providing black Americans' access to government employment. Defined as "the allocation of the discretionary favors of government in exchange for political support," patronage pervaded the American political process at mid-century. Politicians of Bill Dawson's era used patronage as a multipurpose glue to attach the lowest ranking precinct worker to his or her party's highest-ranking officials and to facilitate outside interest groups' movement into mainstream politics. Most political reformers, pundits, and intellectuals, though, saw patronage as little more than another form of graft that granted "favors on the basis of favoritism not merit."[137] These critiques assumed, however, that American democracy created systems ensuring access to government resources based on merit.[138] Yet this situation simply did not exist for the majority of blacks' history in America and certainly not in the postwar era, when the U.S. government did more to sustain racial inequality than to fight against discrimination.[139]

While scholars have pointed out that Dawson, like his contemporaries of both races and parties, used patronage to secure his political position, they have ignored how Dawson's patronage efforts responded directly to appeals grounded in civil rights arguments by everyday blacks. Many of the petitions Dawson received, for instance, reflected a sense of patronage as a civil rights tool, particularly in cases where blacks sought promotions in government agencies. Percy P. Creuzot of New Orleans, for example, wrote Dawson on behalf of his associate, George E. Mohns, who had been a customs inspector for twenty-two years while less-qualified white colleagues routinely received promotions.[140] A letter from Victor R. Daly provided another example. Daly wanted assistance in getting an upgrade to GS 12 in the Personnel and Fiscal Division in the U.S. Employment Service. With this promotion, Daly wrote, he could ensure fair treatment for other blacks in the civil service.[141]

Prominent black leaders also combined racial and political appeals regarding patronage positions. In 1950, for instance, NAACP chairman Walter White asked that Dawson ensure that a black businessman be chosen as the new president of the Virgin Islands Corporation, arguing that putting a black businessman in this position would inspire blacks generally, boost Democratic votes, and protect the black Haitian population from predatory white businessmen.[142] Likewise, Cleveland councilwoman Jean Murrel Capers wrote Dawson in 1952 to help get black attorney Paul D. White into the district attorney's office. Capers asked Dawson to point out the importance of the black vote to Cleveland congressman Robert Crosser and how the appointment of a black American to a high government post would stimulate votes in his favor.[143]

After receiving a request for a patronage position, Dawson used several criteria to evaluate a candidate. Merit, Dawson indicated, ranked high among them.[144] Dawson, however, held party loyalty and political competency of equal importance. This emphasis stemmed from Dawson's experience in Chicago, where he learned that racial crusading alone did not guarantee political results.[145] Indeed, by the time Dawson had won his own congressional seat, he had an explicit bias against involving nonelected civil rights leaders in the patronage process. Instead, Dawson generally selected blacks who "had come up the hard way through party ranks," and who, in times of conflict between race and party goals, followed the party.[146]

Dawson's emphasis on merit and political loyalty in evaluating patronage candidates represented an important step in the evolution of black politics on the national level. It indicated a shift from the selection of isolated black notables to symbolic positions, such as those in Roosevelt's so-called Black Cabinet, to an expectation that a black applicant not only possessed the expertise to perform the task at hand, but that the applicant would also be able to serve the needs of the party in power.[147]

Using these criteria Dawson helped an innumerable number of blacks obtain lower level civil service positions while supporting dozen's into higher ranking appointments.[148] The black press kept a close eye on the more prominent positions Dawson obtained. They included Municipal Court Judge Fred "Duke" Slater; consultant to the U.S. Employment Service Thomasina J. Norford; Social Security Administrator Ann Arnold Hedgeman; Recorder of Deeds Dr. Marshall L. Shepard; Federal Housing Agency Officer Frank S. Horne; First Deputy Recorder Oliver Thornton; Selective Service Director Colonel Campbell C. Johnson; New York District Federal Customs Court Judge Irvin C. Mollinson (Mollinson was the first black American to sit as a federal judge in the continental United States); Pennsylvania District Judge William Hastie; Virgin Islands District Federal Judge Herman E. Moore; and alternate delegate to the United Nations Edith Sampson.[149]

While Dawson expended political capital for these patronage positions, he spent his own money to preach the gospel of political participation to blacks in the South and urban North.[150] In doing so, Dawson encouraged the wave of southern black voter registration that began in the 1930s with the Supreme Court's prohibition of the white primary in *Smith v. Allwright* (1944).[151] Aware that many blacks felt that whites impeded their ability to make a change, Dawson strongly urged blacks to avoid apathy and to stop seeking white political approval. Instead, if blacks used their votes to influence politicians, white or black, whites' personal opinions on black political aspirations would not matter. "Obligate them," he told the Virginia Civil Rights Organization in 1949. "That's one of the rules of politics. Obligate 'em before the election and they'll owe you something after the election." In the end, Dawson claimed, only votes mattered to politicians.[152]

Dawson's forceful attitude to the ballot did not mean that he saw blacks and whites as political enemies. Instead, he argued that animosity hurt both races. Hatred lowered blacks morally and lessened their chances for achieving civil rights.[153] At the same time, he urged whites to drop the bitterness engendered by the Civil War and recognize that they shared the South with blacks.[154] Oppressing blacks, Dawson asserted at a rally in Virginia, only damaged southern whites: "Negroes have been held down here in the South, and today the South is the most backward part of the country—all because its brains, its leadership have been busy keeping us down—and staying down here with us."[155] But, he told a Cleveland audience, times were changing and blacks were on the march.[156]

Dawson knew, though, that aggressive rhetoric would not reach all of his listeners, for, after years of disfranchisement, many blacks felt great cynicism toward politics. He frequently argued, therefore, that blacks needed to stop treating politics as if it was inherently corrupt. In May 1951, for instance, Dawson spoke at an engagement sponsored by the Dallas Council of Negro Women. After being met by a motorcade that included representatives of the Dallas Negro Chamber of Commerce, the YMCA, and the YWCA and other black civic leaders, Dawson spoke before a crowd of 800 packed in the Good Street Baptist Church:

> Next to religion itself, there is no better device through which we can make progress than through politics. It is the root of all civic benefits, better jobs, and better living. . . . We can have no political emancipation until we quit taking money out of politics and we put some into it.[157]

The applause after this line forced Dawson to stop speaking. When he resumed, he pushed the audience to think of themselves as voters, not as complainers. "It's time," he told the audience, "to stop getting mad and start getting smart."[158]

Dawson's unswerving belief in the Constitution and politics provided the foundation for these appeals.[159] The Constitution gave U.S. citizens the ballot to cause change, and, Dawson argued, only the ballot could move whites to share power. As long as southern white politicians answered only to whites, blacks would continue to see their civil rights goals denied.[160]

Although there is no way to quantify Dawson's impact on his target audiences, Dawson's trips in the late 1940s should be considered among the factors that primed many southern black communities for the arrival of the young activists in the late 1950s and early 1960s who did the dangerous work of registering black voters. In *Local People,* John Dittmer argues that there was a "flurry of activity" for voting rights in Mississippi, which received "no support from traditional civil rights allies such as the federal government and labor." Dittmer places particular emphasis on the formation of the Regional Council of Negro Leadership

(RCNL) in 1951 as a benchmark of Mississippi blacks' increased political awareness.[161] Yet he fails to mention that the participants proclaimed the meeting "Dawson Day" and that Dawson's speech on increased black participation at all levels of government had received "round after round of applause."[162] Therein lay an important story. Although the U.S. government gave little support to southern black political efforts, Dawson, as a representative of the Democratic Party, the Congress, and the U.S. government, served during the critical years between World War II and the civil rights movement as an inspiration to blacks determined to retake their place in U.S. politics.[163]

Dawson's outreach in the early 1950s efforts capped just over six years of work to shift the Democratic Party's stance on race. This process generated minimal progress at the local level but gradually saw results in the national party and reached its zenith in 1948, when Dawson organized black leaders across the nation to support Truman. Following these victories, Dawson turned his efforts toward bringing more blacks into the party as both voters and leaders. Thus, it is clear from Dawson's experiences in these years that the changes in the Democratic Party did not result simply from struggles between northern white liberals, southern conservatives, and civil rights groups. Effective black electoral leadership pushed the party to change as well. Still, little had changed in Chicago and the southern contingent had not yet surrendered and the question remained: would this trend last?

Chapter Five
A DREAM DEFERRED
*Party-building from the Late
1940s through the 1950s*

The whole Southern wing of the party is a definite handicap to us locally and we would rather see a clean split between the two—else we're damned.[1]—*John F. Kennedy*

4th Ward Alderman Holman—a fighter . . . his plight is unique. . . . The man on the 5th floor (Mayor DALEY) is his albatross . . . and you know that alliance was responsible for the old man (Cong. WILLIAM DAWSON) not chopping his head.[2]—*Mattie Colon Smith*

Although some progress had been made in the 1940s, events in Chicago, on Capitol Hill, and within national Democratic politics in the 1950s revealed severe limitations in the party-building strategy. In 1955 Dawson had some success in influencing the removal of Mayor Martin Kennelly, whose politics angered black Chicagoans. Nevertheless, Kennelly's dismissal drew criticism from many reform-oriented whites who had supported the incumbent mayor. Moreover, in removing Mayor Kennelly, Dawson helped elect Richard J. Daley, who decisively isolated Dawson by making the city's black politicians responsible directly to City Hall rather than the 2nd Ward.

The inadequacies of Dawson's electoral strategy became increasingly apparent at the national level too. At first Dawson's emphasis on increasing blacks' electoral strength yielded several tangible results: Dawson's appointments as vice chairman of the Democratic National Committee and chair of the Committee on Government Operations in 1948 and a marked increase in southern black voters in 1952. Yet both of these appointments generated extraordinary scrutiny and notable resistance from white colleagues. Meanwhile, southern Democrats shifted to more extreme segregationism, and Adlai Stevenson, the Democratic presidential nominee in 1952 and 1956, only expressed a moderate commitment to civil rights. Despite these steps backwards, Dawson remained committed to his party. Many black voters, however, did not, and they punished the Democrats by voting Republican in the 1956 election.

In the wake of Truman's 1948 victory, party building at the national level still appeared promising and black journalists wrote with confidence regarding their community's value to the Democrats. This sentiment came to the fore particularly during the racially motivated debacles that ensued over Dawson's assumption of two unprecedented leadership positions: chairman of the Congressional Government Operations Committee (CGO) and vice chairman of the Democratic National Committee.

After the 1948 elections southern Democrats still controlled a significant number of committee chairmanships in the House and continued to ally themselves with GOP conservatives to ensure that the government upheld segregation.[3] The CGO, though not an exclusive committee, had been a part of southern representatives' arsenal of tools in this effort.[4]

Thus, when Dawson became chairman of the CGO in 1948, it caused an uproar that led some white representatives to challenge the House seniority system. When the Democrats won control of the House in 1948, Dawson ranked third on the CGO, behind Republican Clare Hoffman and Democrat John McCormack. McCormack, however, had been elected House majority leader. Because custom required that the majority leader refuse committee assignments, Dawson stood next in line to assume the chairmanship. Assumption of the chair made Dawson the first black American to lead a standing committee in the House, and, although reveling in the racial significance of Dawson's promotion, black journalists indicated that party leaders saw the move as experimental. Some white legislators, however, wanted no part of the trial. A Texas member resigned, and a non-southern member tried to incite Southerners on the committee to bypass Dawson. Speaker of the House Sam Rayburn, also a Southerner, rebuffed the malcontents, arguing that Dawson possessed the most qualifications and the necessary seniority. McCormack added to Dawson's legitimacy by announcing that he would remain on the CGO "to show what a great pleasure it is for me to serve under him as chairman."[5]

Obtaining the committee chair did little to forward a racial agenda, however, because Dawson rarely used it to investigate civil rights issues. Rather, the CGO under Dawson saved the government billions of dollars through legislation promoting increased government efficiency.[6] For the most part, the committee's mandate had little direct influence over civil rights issues in government.[7] True, in 1938 a white CGO chairman used his influence to reinforce discriminatory hiring by the U.S. Employment Service, but he did so with the blessing of his prejudiced colleagues (a majority of the House to be sure). Congressman Dan Rostenkowski remembered that Dawson, however, operated within a "sea of sharks" who constantly hoped that he would make a misstep as committee chair.[8] I have found no evidence for why Dawson so infrequently used his committee chairmanship to lobby for civil rights, but one can safely speculate that doing so would have entailed considerable more jeopardy for Dawson than that encountered by predecessors who used the committee to enforce inequality and that Dawson's caution regarding maintaining his own power precluded this kind of risk taking.[9]

If Dawson needed another reminder of his tenuous position as a leader of black *and* white Democrats he received it in 1950 when a scandal emerged regarding the Democratic leadership's attempt to conceal his status as vice chairman of the party. During the 1948 general elections, DNC chairman Howard McGrath acknowledged black voters' importance to the Democratic coalition by appointing Dawson vice chairman.[10] Yet, rather than publicizing Dawson's promotion, DNC publicity director Jack Redding decided to quietly test the reactions of prominent white Democrats.[11] As the news of the appointment spread, southern Democrats complained vigorously to the new DNC chairman Robert Boyle and threatened to leave the party. Thus, DNC officials referred to Dawson as Boyle's "special assistant" instead of vice chairman.[12]

Dawson's status remained in limbo until February 1950, when the black press exposed the affair in a list of several Democratic bungles.[13] The *Defender* disparaged local Democrats for assuming that they owned the black vote while slating candidates in black districts who did not meet with the community's approval. The paper also accused the Truman administration of making a lackadaisical effort to get Congress to strengthen the Fair Employment Practices Committee and ignoring qualified black candidates for governor of the Virgin Islands.[14] In a letter sent to black newspapers across the nation, Boyle quickly apologized and publicly acknowledged Dawson's appointment. Nevertheless, the *Defender* warned that the South did not only mean white voters, but also 10 million black voters "who swear by Dawson's leadership."[15]

The apparent instability of Dawson's authority in both the House and the party did not lend themselves to proactive civil rights efforts—at least not to someone of Dawson's increasingly risk-averse temperament. If Dawson did have some power to alter the course of civil rights in Congress it was based on his ability to help block passage of explicitly racist legislation, such as the 1951 Winstead amendment. Two months after the Air Force completed its integration program in February 1951, Congressman William Winstead of Mississippi submitted an amendment to the Universal Military Training and Service Act that would have allowed inductees to request assignment to racially segregated units.[16] The amendment received strong support from southern Democrats and conservative Republicans. The NAACP sent forty-four representatives from eleven "key states" to urge their congressmen to oppose Winstead's legislation and to vote instead for an amendment by California representative Franck Havenner that would have made assaulting or murdering a member of the armed forces a federal offense. Havenner's amendment did more than challenge white violence against black soldiers; it attempted to push civil rights gains from the military into the civilian sector, for the amendment targeted the white civilian population, not white military officers. Things looked grim when southern Democrats and conservative Republicans defeated the Havenner amendment. Yet, just as quickly, the Congress's liberal contingent beat back a southern push for an array of segregationist amendments.

Who then would win the final battle over the Winstead amendment? At this moment Dawson took the floor. Citing his experience in the First World War, Dawson asked his colleagues, "How long, how long, my conferees and gentlemen from the South, will you divide us Americans on account of color? Why will this body go on record to brand this section of citizens as second class?" After admonishing his colleagues with the assertion that God did not curse him by making him black, a *New York Times* reporter wrote that Dawson told a hushed House, "Give to me the test that would apply to make anyone a full-fledged American, and by the living God, if it means death itself, I will pay it—but give it to me."[17] As conservative and liberal representatives rose to their feet, a tremendous wave of applause broke out from every corner of the House and swept away the segregationist measure. Reflecting on Dawson's career years later, James Free wrote in the *Champaign-Urbana Courier* that Dawson's speech rebuffed the Winstead amendment, "More than any one man, he was responsible for the defeat in 1951 of a draft law provision that would have allowed inductees to choose whether they would serve in segregated units."[18]

Later that year, Dawson and New York's black Congressman Adam Clayton Powell Jr. helped to defeat a bill to construct a segregated hospital for black veterans. The bill in question was H.R. 314, introduced by another Mississippi segregationist, John E. Rankin, who received support from an odd coalition: segregationists as well as liberals who genuinely believed that the hospital could provide professional opportunities for black medical professionals. An even larger group of legislators opposed Rankin, arguing that the bill blatantly enforced racial prejudice. The bill's supporters had claimed that it would fill a need for the Veterans' Administration (VA); the VA, however, responded that it already faced a deficit of medical staff to oversee the administration's existing patient capacity. Moreover, argued Kenneth Keating (D-NY), eight VA hospitals within a 200-mile radius of the proposed Georgia site already existed and no black veterans complained about using these facilities.[19]

Keating's argument pointed to the bill's racist orientation. Dawson and others supported this argument by noting that the new hospital could not help black medical school students because its proposed location was nowhere near the nation's two black medical schools Meharry and Howard.[20] Furthermore, Dawson argued, Booker T. Washington did not need further honors; he had already received countless accolades throughout the South. Moreover, the government did not need to build a hospital for blacks because all doctors "learned anatomy, not black anatomy."[21] Powell followed Dawson and threatened that he would propose an amendment to strike the bill's enacting clause unless the House removed the word "Negro" from the bill.[22]

Congressmen Jacob Javits and Emmanuel Celler, both from New York, echoed Dawson's arguments. Javits argued that the bill turned "the clock back toward segregation instead of directly away from it, the direction it must go if we wish to have freedom."[23] Celler added that Rankin's tendency to use the word "nigger" cast the bill's validity in doubt: "His calling it a 'nigger' hospital is sufficient to encourage a vote against the bill."[24]

Celler's remarks scratched the thin veneer covering race dynamics in the House as the discussion rapidly descended into near absurdity. At one point, two representatives engaged in a heated debate over each other's attitude toward the word "Negro." A comical moment occurred when Representative Abraham Multer of New York sarcastically asked Rankin whether black doctors practiced special surgical techniques on black veterans as compared the practices of white doctors on white veterans. Rankin didn't get the joke and retorted that Multer should read the works of Dr. George Washington Carver, who had "brought information that Negroes had gathered in Africa for a thousand years. The gentleman himself would probably be amazed if he would get that book and read it." The image of an arch-segregationist and race baiter like John Rankin spending his evenings curled up by the fire reading books on ancient African science stretches credulity. Back in character, Rankin argued in his closing remarks that the communists in the NAACP incited opposition to his bill. George Washington Carver, communist conspiracies, and ancient African science aside, the bill's racism proved too much to swallow, and Congress voted down the enacting clause 233 to 117.[25]

Although Congressional politics generated mixed results, Dawson remained committed to reshaping the Democratic Party into a suitable vessel for the aspirations of black Americans.[26] As the 1952 national elections approached, Dawson advocated the removal of southern segregationists from the party. "We plan to rid the Democratic Party of Dixiecrats because they are of no assistance to us in Congress," he told the *Washington Afro-American*. The *Afro-American* noted Dawson's statement because it echoed similar statements by President Truman and because Dawson was an acknowledged Democratic strategist. If the Democrats stopped appeasing segregationists, the reporter observed, they could craft a strong civil rights platform that would retain black northern votes and generate enough black votes in the South to make up for segregationist defections.[27]

Unfortunately for those proponents of black political strength, the presidential field in 1952 differed significantly from that of 1948. The Democrats had no clear nominee, and the frontrunner, Adlai Stevenson of Illinois, evinced little desire to run. With pressure from the Democratic leadership and a small group of supporters who operated without his approval, Stevenson eventually won the nomination. He selected John Sparkman, a moderate senator from Alabama, as his running mate, hoping that Sparkman could satisfy southern conservatives and northern liberals.[28]

Nominating a reluctant candidate may have been problematic, but the 1952 convention produced the strongest civil rights plank to date. Dawson urged the assemblage to continue Truman's civil rights legacy and, with John McCormack, John Sparkman, and Brooks Hayes, pushed the southern delegates on the platform committee to compromise.[29] The new plank placed a higher priority on creating equal employment opportunities, complemented the Justice Department's efforts to attack "illegal discrimination," and included previously ignored minority groups.[30] Walter White hailed it as a "signal victory for the forces of liberalism," and Truman thanked Dawson for helping to secure a strong civil rights plank without splitting the party.[31]

The candidates' weak civil rights positions, however, concerned civil rights advocates more than the plank. On the state level, Stevenson favored strong executive and legislative actions to address civil rights issues. He had, for example, utilized the National Guard to quell race rioting in Cicero, Illinois, and he tried hard to pass fair employment practices legislation. Stevenson hesitated, though, to endorse the use of federal mechanisms to address what he perceived as a personal, individual issue. This reticence damaged his prospects with both liberal whites and black civil rights leaders.[32] Moreover, Stevenson excluded Dawson from his campaign.[33] One can only speculate that Dawson's close ties to Truman, his position in the DNC, and his prominence in the Chicago organization gave Stevenson pause, because the nominee wanted to appear independent of the Democratic leadership.[34]

Sparkman's southern background presented serious concerns for black voters and pundits, who feared a revival of Dixiecratic power and took any indication of alliances with the South very seriously. The *New Jersey Times Herald*, for instance, ran a story in which it pointed out that Sparkman had twenty-three opportunities to vote against discriminatory bills but did not.[35] Thomas Dewey, for his part, attacked Sparkman for being a segregationist and a "Jim Crow Agent."[36] Stoking these fears, the Republicans ran ads implying that Sparkman would be in charge of the government's civil rights programs.[37]

Thus, the new Democratic ticket aroused great suspicion among blacks. No one highlighted this anxiety more than Powell, who condemned the Democratic ticket, its plank, and Dawson's role in backing both.[38] Powell, who had pushed for an even stronger plank, called Dawson an "Uncle Tom." The plank, Powell claimed, did not give the FEPC enough support and Sparkman lacked commitment to civil rights. Although Powell's anger originated in part from being overshadowed by Dawson at the convention, he did represent more militant black Americans who wanted the Democrats to produce a no-compromise ticket and platform. Yet the 1952 platform, if not the ticket, represented a definite gain. Black leaders such as A. Philip Randolph, Walter White, Joseph Pickney, and Herbert Bruce all criticized Powell's threats, and Powell eventually supported the ticket.[39]

Nevertheless, black Democratic leaders knew that black voters had not fully accepted the ticket. To assuage their fears, the black press contrasted Stevenson and the Republican nominee, General Dwight Eisenhower. The *Black Dispatch* and the *Defender,* for example, wrote that Stevenson's speeches to integrated audiences in the South bridged the gap between the races, whereas the Associated Negro Press (ANP) circulated stories that several former Dixiecrats had aligned themselves with the GOP candidate.[40] Finally, Dawson brought together 150 key black political leaders from 26 states for a workshop on increasing Democratic vote totals. He told the group that the election represented a battle in which blacks had to demonstrate their political might and argued the "Negro is a mature citizen who can no longer be bullied or bamboozled."[41]

When all was said and done, white Americans liked Ike, but black voters overwhelmingly backed Stevenson.[42] Indeed, blacks voted at record rates that year. With 81 percent of the black vote, Stevenson benefited most from these gains.[43] These results seem odd given blacks' lukewarm reaction to the Stevenson campaign. One of Dawson's precinct captains, for instance, remembered that it was difficult to stir up excitement for the candidate who many black Chicagoans called a "sourpuss." Not to mention Powell's early critiques.[44]

Three other factors most likely accounted for black support for Stevenson. First, many blacks remained committed to Roosevelt and Truman. Second, after giving key support to Truman in 1948, black voters remained excited regarding their effectiveness as members of the Democratic coalition. Finally, the late 1940s and early 1950s witnessed an increase in black politicization facilitated by local black leaders, the black press and Dawson. So, even as the GOP took both the House and the Senate, Dawson argued "national black support for the Democratic ticket demonstrated that blacks were grateful for 20 years of Democratic progress."[45] At the time Dawson was correct. Blacks did appreciate the Democratic Party, not Stevenson's party, but the party of the 1940s: of Wallace, Truman, Franklin and Eleanor Roosevelt, and the New Deal.

Although a victory of sorts for black voters, the election of 1952 illustrated one of the limits of black electoral participation: even high black voter turnout could not put a less than popular candidate in the White House. Black voters, the black press, and civil rights leaders by themselves simply could not set the tone of national debates.

Meanwhile, more limitations on black electoral power arose back in Chicago during Martin Kennelly's administrations.[46] Kennelly did not care at all to negotiate with Dawson regarding the fate of blacks displaced by the Lake Meadows Project, and he backed an attack on the South Side's jitney cab system. Yet Kennelly continued to foist his reform efforts on black Chicago when he attacked the "policy": a large-scale illegal lottery that contributed significantly to the South Side's underground economy. Players bet on various numbers, and three times a day wheel operators drew the winning numbers at approximately 500 different policy stations across the South Side. The policy employed more than 5,000 people and in 1938 had "an annual gross turnover of at least eighteen million dollars." During the Depression, when blacks made up 40 percent of Chicago's welfare rolls, policy wheel operators provided blacks with steady employment.[47] Moreover, the policy assisted the black community at large. In addition to supplying jobs for individual blacks and enriching the lives of a few select wheel operators, policy money granted critical venture capital to black entrepreneurs who could not have obtained support from mainstream institutions like white-owned banks, whose discretionary (that is, prejudicial) lending practices generally excluded black Americans.[48] Nearly all policy owners reinvested their profits in local black enterprises, and in the 1930s, policy money backed approximately 20 percent of the city's largest black businesses.[49]

The policy needed protection, though, from the police and the mafia, which Dawson attempted to provide. In 1931 policy operators formed "the syndicate" to organize the city's random assortment of policy wheels and protect themselves from exploitative politicians. To this end, the syndicate paid out a complex set of bribes to the police, neighborhood politicians, and court officials. In 1938, at least $7,500 dollars per week went to "downtown" politicians to prevent police crackdowns.[50] As chief of the city's black wards, Dawson became the policy's principal protector—a fact he freely admitted.[51] In exchange, wheel operators gave Dawson's organization political contributions (independent of the white-dominated Chicago machine), patronage jobs that Dawson could dole out to his supporters, and workers to use for canvassing at election time.[52]

When Ed Kelly still held the mayor's office, Dawson furnished policy operators significant political protection. In 1946, for example, Dawson used his influence over policing in the South Side to rebuff a takeover attempt by the syndicate.[53] Dawson and Kennelly, however, consistently clashed over South Side gambling. Black Chicagoans knew that whites-only gambling resorts and illegal gambling dens flourished throughout the city.[54] Blacks also understood that attacking the policy brought Kennelly acclaim in the mainstream press while allowing him to ignore organized crime among whites. Dawson argued that Kennelly's crime strategy was hypocritical because he did nothing to curb gambling rings operated by the white mafia. In a twist on Washingtonian economic nationalism Dawson contended, "If anybody is to profit out of gambling in the Negro community it should be the Negro. It is purely an economic question. I want the money my people earn to stay in the community." Without political backing, the policy would be vulnerable to the Italian mafia, and then, Dawson predicted, it would receive police protection.[55]

Dawson understood and tried to protect the delicate relationship between the illegal, underground economy sustained by the policy, the legitimate ends to which policy bosses employed their profits and the security afforded to the policy through political patronage. Although Dawson realized the corruption and illegality of that relationship, he made what his contemporaries would call the "race choice"—as well the political choice—to support the institution. Dawson's decision made little difference, though, without mayoral support. During the Kennelly administrations, constant police harassment weakened "the syndicate" sufficiently and allowed the Italian mafia to wrest control from black operators. This, in turn, mortally wounded the project to create an autonomous black political organization, because it ended whatever economic independence Dawson's submachine had previously enjoyed from the white-dominated regular Democratic organization.[56]

Further aggravating matters, Kennelly focused so intently on Bronzeville that he virtually ignored the white rioters who attacked blacks over housing in the late 1940s and early 1950s. In August 1947, for example, between 1,500 and 5,000 whites fought police officers in their protests against the placement of black veterans in the Fernwood Park Homes, and an even larger mob of 10,000 went on a destructive rampage after hearing a rumor that another black family intended to move to the area.[57] In 1953 whites panicked and mobbed again when Donald and Betty Howard moved in the Trumbull Park public housing project. On August 5, six days after moving in, locals heaved a brick through the Howard's living room window. Neighborhood hooligans followed with several more bricks and sulphur bombs. So many firecrackers went off near their barricaded residence that the *Defender* said it looked like "Soldier Field on the Fourth of July" and groups of wannabe white hoodlums attacked individual blacks passing by. Rank and file police only stopped the harassment if a senior officer arrived on the scene, and it eventually took 750 officers working triple shifts to stop the violence.[58]

Kennelly's attacks against the South Side's underground economies, his slow action against racial violence, and his unwillingness to address rising police brutality against black Chicagoans led blacks to call for his resignation and pushed Dawson to withdraw the support of his Democratic faction.[59] Thus, Dawson joined a group of powerful committeemen dedicated to removing Mayor Kennelly in the 1955 election. During the meeting of the Cook County Regular Democratic Organization to decide on the 1955 mayoral candidate, committee member Joe Gill asked whether Dawson would support Kennelly. Dawson replied, "Mr. Gill, I can't support him. . . . I can't support Mayor Kennelly. He made it plain he'd rather not have me in his office. He didn't want anything to do with patronage and that's—that's how we live out there. I just can't support him." Dawson then walked out and brought the voting to a standstill.[60]

At the next meeting, Dawson and most of the powerful committee-men thought they had found a replacement in Clarence Wagner, but Wagner's untimely death would allow Richard J. Daley a chance at the nomination. Daley, with the support of the smaller West Side Irish block, competed with Wagner for the organization's support, but all accounts predicted an easy victory for Wagner. In a twist of fate, Wagner died in an auto accident before the committee vote, leaving Daley to win the nomination and the election. Dawson saw no reason to oppose Daley, especially since Wimbish and Davis both told him that Daley had been a good colleague in the Illinois House. Daley, of course, had observed Dawson and the committeemen engineer Kennelly's removal from pow-er and had no intention of allowing a set of "powerful dukes" become a threat to his mayoralty. In particular, argued former alderman and fair-housing activist Leon Despres, Daley had deep mistrust of Dawson—a mistrust that hinged less on race than on Dawson's reputed control over black votes across the city.[61] For now, though, Daley had to bide his time as all the Democrats prepared for the 1956 presidential elections.

As the primaries approached, only Stevenson prepared to take on Eisenhower, but his moderation angered much of the Democratic co-alition, including blacks, white liberals, and segregationist Democrats. Because of his refusal to make a strong stance on black and Jewish con-cerns, for instance, both groups gave his candidacy what one Steven-son biographer characterized as "lukewarm support."[62] Blacks concerned themselves most with Stevenson's position on the *Brown* decision, which, with its unequivocal denunciation of segregation, removed the legal basis for "separate but equal."[63] Indeed, both black and southern white voters wanted to know political candidates' intentions for its implemen-tation. Hoping to maintain a coalition of blacks and southern whites, Stevenson favored *Brown,* but not the use of federal power to enforce it. Stevenson also angered blacks when he refused to condemn the lynch-ing of Emmett Till, a fourteen-year-old Chicago boy who was murdered by a white mob in tiny Money, Mississippi.[64]

As early as November 1955 Dawson pointed out the black hostility toward another Stevenson run. *Defender* reporter Louis Martin indicated that Stevenson had failed to convince Dawson that he would work for civil rights. Dawson argued that Stevenson spent too much time telling voters "what he was going to do to them instead of telling them what he was going to do for them" and that he should not have allowed amateurs to run his 1952 campaign.[65]

America's most junior African American representative, Charles Diggs of Detroit, warned the Democrats that black support for the Democratic Party stood at its lowest since 1932. Elected in 1954 from a mixed black and white, working-class district, Diggs pursued a coherent, broad liberal agenda that gave particular attention to civil rights.[66] Eisenhower, Diggs contended, had "established a pretty good record among blacks," whereas Stevenson's moderation alienated them.[67] Finally, a *Chicago Defender* editorial asserted that blacks would probably vote Republican, because of segregationist Democrats.[68]

Why this shift in party loyalties by 1956? Despite Diggs's comments, Eisenhower articulated a more moderate position on civil rights than Stevenson. Except for desegregating the military, where his administration made slight progress, Eisenhower demonstrated a reluctance to push for racial equality in American life, particularly in housing or in the enforcement of *Brown*.[69] Still, the administration drew less attention than white Southerners' resistance to integration in the mid-1950s.

After *Brown* southern segregationists intensified their opposition to civil rights. In March 1956, eighty-four southern congressmen issued the "Southern Manifesto," which called the *Brown* decision a blatant abuse of power by the Supreme Court, asserted the primacy of states rights, and warned against intrusions by "outside instigators" pushing racial equality. State governments rapidly brought injunctions against the NAACP. Meanwhile, groups such as the Ku Klux Klan and the White Citizens Councils rose in defense of the color line. Composed of the South's middle and upper class, the White Citizens Councils began a legal assault on integration and black politicization that caused a tremendous drop in black voter registration throughout the rural "Black Belt." Although the Citizens Councils refrained from using violence, the Klan did not. The Klan brought a terrorist temperament to the resistance and was linked, for instance, to the bombing of a home in North Carolina in 1959, the shooting of three civil rights workers in 1964, and the killing of a white civil rights worker during the 1965 march from Selma to Montgomery, Alabama.[70]

Black political and civil rights leaders reacted to this situation by pressuring the Democrats to rebuke their southern wing. On July 21, fifty-five black Democrats met in Chicago to construct a list of "no compromise musts" for the civil rights plank committee, on which sat Dawson and Diggs.[71] In August, Roy Wilkins, chairman of the Leadership Conference on Civil Rights, sent a civil rights plan to both parties. The plan urged an end to state-sanctioned segregation, a strengthening of civil rights laws, protection for black voters in elections, the passage of a fair employment practices law, revision of the Senate's cloture rule to end filibusters, and the selection of congressional committee chairmen by merit rather than seniority. Furthermore, Wilkins argued, both parties needed to endorse *Brown.*[72] The Americans for Democratic Action (ADA) joined the NAACP and advised the Democrats to "stand firm" for civil rights in 1956.[73]

Black America's intense desire to take a firm stance regarding *Brown* led to the first major split in the black congressional delegation; Dawson and Powell disagreed on Powell's amendment to the 1956 Federal Aid to Education Bill—a $1.5 billion package that would have refurbished and built new schools across the United States. Citing southern resistance to *Brown,* Powell tacked on an amendment that would have cut federal funds to any school that did not fulfill *Brown's* mandate.[74] The amendment's emotional subtext led civil rights proponents to some extreme characterizations of the players involved. The NAACP, for example, supported Powell's amendment and declared that any congressman who voted against it supported segregation. The *Defender* characterized the debate as an epic battle between southern reactionaries and liberal crusaders, and as a struggle for power between the nation's two most important black elected officials: Dawson and Powell.[75]

Although the two congressmen never worked closely and the press characterized them as "friendly enemies," it was something of a leap to contend that a rivalry would lead these two men, both of whom possessed deep civil rights convictions, to gamble on a bill as important as the Aid to Education Bill.[76] Rivalry or no, Dawson and Powell had no prior reservations in coordinating against segregationist legislation. Moreover, only two weeks after their alleged struggle for supremacy in the fight over the Powell amendment, Dawson defended Powell's integrity against other representatives who resented Powell's tactics.[77] It was more likely that the high stakes involved in 1956 stimulated the strong feelings surrounding the Powell amendment. The amendment forced Congress to decide if it would actively enforce the Court's mandate in *Brown.* It posed the same challenge to President Eisenhower, who could have attempted to use his influence to sway Republicans to vote for the bill.[78] The NAACP's willingness to risk the entire construction bill highlighted its desire to see *Brown* implemented immediately.

The Powell amendment, well intentioned as it may have been, ripped apart liberals within the Democratic Party.[79] Dawson and others agonized over the possibility of losing the new schools. President Truman, for example, wrote that although he believed both in civil rights and the school aid bill, he knew that conservative Republicans intended to use the amendment to sink the whole bill. West Virginia Congressman Cleve Bailey, also a liberal, agonized over the Powell amendment and eventually chose schools for all students over a bill destined for defeat.[80]

Even Powell himself had backed off his amendment in past instances when it appeared to jeopardize education funding for black students. In 1949 Powell attached his amendment to the National School Lunch Act but accepted a modification by Representative John H. Folger that effectively neutralized the amendment's power to withhold federal school lunch funds from schools that practiced segregation. The new amendment, with Powell's backing, assured instead that black schools would receive an unstipulated "fair share of the school lunch program fund." This early version of the Powell amendment angered the NAACP because it implicitly accepted separate schools. After *Brown,* Powell strengthened the amendment to remove this loophole; nevertheless the amendment's evolution indicates that the New York representative recognized the perils involved with risking education funding in the fight for civil rights.[81]

Thus, the Powell amendment apparently never had the unalloyed support of the nation's liberal politicians or Powell. For Dawson, the possibility of killing the education-funding bill posed too great a loss. Remembering his childhood, Dawson described how his mother and grandmother "worked their fingers to the bone cooking and washing clothes in order to give" him and his siblings their educations. His willingness to pay for his siblings and his niece's tuition evidenced deep commitment to education, and this commitment must have made consideration of the Powell amendment intensely problematic.[82]

Truman's prognosis regarding the amendment proved correct. When the Powell amendment came up for a vote, the House accepted it 225 to 192, with Dawson voting against and Powell and Detroit Congressman Diggs voting for it. Once Dawson saw that the amendment was going to stay on the bill, he gave it his support, but it made no difference. On the final vote a combination of conservative Republicans and southern Democrats, many of whom supported the Powell amendment simply for an excuse to vote against the school bill, easily voted the legislation down. A statement for desegregation had been made, but at a tremendous cost.[83]

Similar attempts to utilize the amendment in future congresses continued to split the black delegation. By 1960, in fact, the NAACP opposed its use.[84] Despite being well within the range of congressional liberal and civil rights thought on the Powell amendment, Dawson's opposition to Powell became a point of tension between himself and incipient civil rights activists in Chicago.

The fight over the amendment highlighted fault lines between Democrats that would split their 1956 convention into moderate, liberal, and conservative factions. Adlai Stevenson, Eleanor Roosevelt, labor leader Walter Reuther, and southern delegations believed that a pro–civil rights platform would alienate the South and cause southern defections. They wanted a platform that ignored *Brown* and a candidate who would not push for civil rights. Harry Truman, Congressman Diggs, Roy Wilkins, civil rights groups, and other labor leaders, wanted a "no compromise" civil rights plank that explicitly upheld the *Brown* decision, and Averell Harriman emerged as a viable candidate for this group.[85] Between these powerful forces stood Dawson and a group of congressmen—including John McCormack, Paul Dever, Joseph O'Mahoney, Emanuel Celler, and John Moss—who hoped to keep the party from tearing itself apart.[86]

These pressures stretched the party-building strategy to its limits, catching Dawson between the determination of African Americans for a strong civil rights plank and the expectations of the Democratic Party that he would try to prevent a breakdown reminiscent of 1948.[87] This time, however, two viable presidential contenders representing opposing Democratic points of view struggled for the nomination, and a satisfactory compromise proved impossible.[88] Representing the Harriman forces, Congressman Diggs threatened to lead a challenge against the platform if it did not contain a plan to implement *Brown,* whereas Virginia Governor John H. Battle promised to take his delegates out of the convention if it did.[89] This situation clearly distressed Dawson, who, rumor had it, received intense pressure from Lyndon Johnson, Stevenson, and other Democratic leaders. When questioned about the civil rights committee meeting, which finally ended at 1 a.m., Dawson uncharacteristically snapped, "I am fighting for all I can get without jeopardizing the unity of the party."[90]

As it became clear that Stevenson had the most support, the moderates eventually won, but not without a fight on the convention floor. On August 15, the majority reported a civil rights plank similar to the 1952 version, but with a vague reference to *Brown,* which stipulated the decisions of the Supreme Court as the "law of the land." A minority report on the plank stating that the party should work to carry out the Court's recent decisions on public schools received both boos and applause.

Delegates argued for and against the two reports, but after some adroit gavel work by Convention Chairman Sam Rayburn—which led several delegates to sarcastically question Rayburn's ability to count—the Democrats accepted the moderate plank.[91] Dawson went along with those hoping to make a platform tepid enough to be supported by both wings of the party, but, like Stevenson's moderation, the civil rights plank pleased hardly any one.

Immediately after the proceedings, Dawson and the DNC faced severe condemnation. A *Defender* article accused Dawson and other party leaders of contriving the entire convention. It claimed that Truman supported Harriman only to push Stevenson toward a position more acceptable to blacks and labor. Regardless of whether he expressed stronger civil rights credentials, claimed the article, Stevenson's nomination had already been decided by party insiders.[92] The Chicago NAACP rejected the Democrats' civil rights plank and reserved particularly strong criticism for Dawson. Willoughby Abner, president of the Chicago branch, sent Dawson an open letter questioning his dedication to civil rights. Abner wrote that the NAACP first became concerned over Dawson's silence regarding the shooting deaths of Emmett Till and others. Dawson then opposed the Powell amendment and did not voice support for the program of the Leadership Conference on Civil Rights. After his recent allegiance with party moderates, the NAACP could no longer accept Dawson's leadership. A few days later *Defender* reporter Lee Blackwell argued that what blacks needed was a spokesman who put "loyalty to the race a little above loyalty to the party."[93]

Further exacerbating the Democrats' relationship to black voters, Powell defected to Eisenhower. On October 13, Powell announced that he would form an organization to work for the incumbent president. The reasons for his switch were unclear. Contrary to the GOP platform, Powell announced that Eisenhower had expressed interest in pushing for another Powell amendment, an assertion that the administration later forced Powell to retract. Rumors also circulated that the White House had pressured Powell to support Eisenhower in exchange for ignoring a kickback scandal involving Powell's former secretary, Hattie Freeman Dodson. (The White House emphatically denied any relation between the case and Powell's endorsement.)[94]

The black press and leadership community divided over Powell's switch, whereas black politicians, including Diggs and Dawson, raised serious questions about Powell's credibility. In an interview with the *Chicago Defender*, Dawson asserted that Powell's shift would not cost the Democrats any votes, because he had been threatening to support Eisenhower for years and because Powell's move stemmed from his being left out of the party's decision-making processes. Furthermore, Dawson continued, Powell now supported a candidate that he had recently charged with "trying to segregate the United States Armed Forces in Germany."[95]

In any case, Powell's move underscored both Eisenhower's extreme popularity and Stevenson's inability to connect with blacks. Stevenson's advertisements targeted to the black community discussed his civil rights initiatives as governor of Illinois, including his efforts to integrate school's in downstate Illinois, his proposals for state FEPC legislation, his support of Truman's 1948 civil rights package, and his order to desegregate the Illinois National Guard.[96] Yet Stevenson still did not include any blacks in the top circle of his campaign team, and he never made a clear statement on *Brown*. Dawson even had to write Stevenson an open letter questioning the candidate on "school desegregation and other civil rights matters." Stevenson replied that although he did not favor "restrictive provisions on legislative measures for federal aid to education," he "would take the position that any school district which defied a federal court desegregation order would become ineligible for government funds."[97]

With hemming and hawing like this, the campaign failed to excite the black community in Chicago or the South. Attendees at a meeting of the Baptist Ministers Conference of Chicago and Vicinity booed Dawson during a speech for Stevenson, and Dawson could not easily brush aside Republican attacks. In fact, reporters speculated that a significant number of South Siders would vote for Eisenhower to punish Dawson's opposition to the Powell amendment and his support for a moderate civil rights plank. With such turbulence in Chicago, where the local Democratic organization exercised extraordinary power, it was little wonder that the campaign did not pull in blacks in other parts of the country.[98]

Black disaffection predicted Stevenson's impending defeat. The Democratic nominee received only 73 Electoral College votes to Eisenhower's 457. In the popular vote, Eisenhower beat Stevenson 35,590,472 to 26,029,752. Except the seven states he carried, Stevenson lost by a greater margin than in 1952. Even Illinois backed Eisenhower. Stevenson blamed the press and a lack of funds for his loss, while pundits pointed to confusion among Stevenson's campaign team and disturbances in foreign affairs that stimulated a rally behind the president.[99]

Blacks' abandonment of Stevenson pointed to serious Democratic failures. Blacks came out in record numbers in 1956. In Shelby County,

Tennessee, a startling 73 percent of the county's 53,000 black voters turned out, yet Eisenhower received 9,000 more votes in Tennessee that year than he won 1952, with Tennessee's Republican chairman, Guy Smith, claiming that the black vote accounted for "a good segment of the victory." Poll watchers reported ballot splitting in Baltimore, where blacks voted for Eisenhower at a five-to-four margin, but supported their white Democratic congressmen. In 1952, these same districts went for Stevenson three to two. Likewise, Richmond, Virginia, and the all-black community of Mound Bayou, Mississippi, went Republican.[100]

These results indicated that the Democrats' moderate strategy repulsed the party faithful. White Southerners used the election as an opportunity to protest the party's liberal tendencies, whereas blacks used the election as an opportunity to reject the party's indulgence of its segregationist malcontents. Indeed, after the election results came in, Democratic Senator John F. Kennedy predicted an outright split between the party's northern and southern branches, arguing that the "whole Southern wing of the party is a definite handicap to us locally and we would rather see a clean split between the two—else we're damned."[101]

Mayor Richard J. Daley's strong support for a civil rights plank during the convention indicated that he would have agreed with Kennedy regarding national politics. The mayor's position regarding the plank, ironically, bore practically no relation to his agenda in Chicago, where he used his unprecedented power as the local party chairman and mayor to centralize all of the city's patronage in City Hall and undercut the ward committeemen's influence. By 1958 he stood ready to take on Dawson, who had previously influenced patronage in all of the city's black wards.[102]

Former independent Alderman Leon Despres argued that Daley used the fair housing issue to topple Dawson. Throughout the 1950s, Despres had pushed hard for a fair-housing ordinance to allow the unmolested movement of black Chicagoans out of the city's South and West sides. Such a change, however, would have destabilized the Democratic organization, for it conflicted with the interests of second and third generation white ethnics who made up the majority of the local coalition and who had already shown a willingness to use violence in racial issues.[103] Thus, Daley had no intention of violating "neighborhood integrity."[104] Daley claimed instead that blacks could channel their growing demands through the gradualist mechanisms of the local Democratic Party, as had been the case for white ethnics.[105] The migration, however, outpaced the regular organization's ability—not to mention desire—to channel blacks' needs through politics, and blacks began to assail the city council in protest. Daley responded by prohibiting any discussion of fair housing, and Dawson told his subordinates that none of them were to support or draft an open-housing bill.[106]

In response, Despres drafted his own ordinance in 1958, and in a curious move a so-called Dawson alderman, Claude Holman of the 4th Ward, joined him.[107] Holman and Despres agreed not to introduce the ordinance immediately, for they knew it would fail. They conducted a publicity drive first, which entailed speaking to various civil rights and real estate groups. Throughout their labors Despres wanted to defer to Holman, but Holman rarely spoke. Then, much to Despres's surprise, Holman unilaterally submitted their bill in March 1958.[108]

The only way to make sense of this move, Despres reasoned, was to assume that Daley and Holman had made a deal to cut Dawson and contain open housing. Holman's work with Despres defied a direct order from Dawson. This move put Dawson in a vulnerable position, for his subordinate had violated an imperative from the top. Dawson quickly demanded that the central committee punish Holman, but Daley rebuked Dawson instead and stripped him of any patronage outside of the 2nd Ward. This move, combined with the loss of policy money during the Kennelly administrations, removed all of Dawson's independent power in local politics. Daley never punished Holman though, and in 1960 Holman introduced a resolution to investigate open occupancy. The 1960 resolution possessed none of the enforcement mechanisms contained in the original Despres-Holman ordinance, but all of the black aldermen, now firmly aligned with Daley, hurriedly signed the Holman resolution, and Holman, with his newfound power to control the patronage in his ward, just as quickly lost any interest in a strong fair-housing law.[109]

Ironically, although Daley used the ambitions of younger black aldermen to cut Dawson, Dawson's political opponents began to argue that the congressman caused the majority of black Chicago's negative circumstances. In the 1958 congressional election Dawson faced Dr. T. R. M. Howard, one of Mississippi's earliest civil rights leaders and founder of Regional Council of Negro Leadership (RCNL). Through the RCNL, Howard took on the extremely risky task of raising Mississippi blacks' political awareness, making him a natural ally with Dawson, whom he invited to speak at the organization's first annual meeting in 1952.[110] Despite their cooperation, southern whites' massive resistance to *Brown* and the burgeoning civil rights movement wrought differences between the two men. Unlike Dawson, Howard reacted strongly and publicly to

Emmett Till's murder in 1955 and had been forced to flee Mississippi after his family received numerous death threats.[111]

Dawson, however, did not discuss the Till case in public. Instead, he became the "secret benefactor" of Mamie Bradley (Till's mother). Dawson provided Ms. Bradley with money and moral support. Then he drew on political connections to prevent Till's hasty burial in Mississippi and arranged for Mississippi authorities to release the body for public viewing in Chicago.[112] When asked why he did not publicize his efforts, Dawson indicated that he did not seek to make "political capital" out assisting others during unfortunate times.[113]

Although Dawson's actions cohered with his political history, he underestimated the cultural impact of the Till murder, which figured most prominent in a larger pattern of increased southern violence that had dashed blacks' hopes for a swift end to discrimination. Called a "moment of simultaneity" by Adam Green, the public mourning of Till in Chicago drew American blacks together in an unprecedented, singular expression of pain and outrage that became the touchstone of a generation of artists, intellectuals, and activists dedicated to the eradication of racial oppression. Under these circumstances, black Americans needed to hear their leaders issue strong condemnations of Till's murderers and the southern legal system that freed them. Although Dawson's secretiveness certainly allowed for the public viewing of Till's body, the strong sentiments provoked by this episode rendered Dawson's silence unacceptable.[114]

After Till's murder, Howard went on a national speaking tour criticizing segregation and eventually fled Mississippi because of death threats to his family. Upon coming to Chicago in 1956 he continued his activism in local politics. Two years later, Howard won the Republican nomination for the 1st District congressional seat and based his campaign rhetoric in large part upon the argument that Dawson bore responsibility for segregation in Chicago. As a candidate, he criticized housing discrimination and unequal education. He argued that civil rights was the "bread and butter" issue for all blacks and called for a national conference on jobs and civil rights. Howard placed most of his emphasis, however, on attacking Dawson. *Defender* columnist Louis Martin wrote that Howard's campaign responded to a charge by members of Dawson's camp that Howard exaggerated the threats on his life in Mississippi by arguing that Dawson "helped to make Chicago the most segregated city in the nation. They also dump all of the ills of the Negro community on the Congressman's doorstep."[115] Although Howard's candidacy did not succeed (Dawson defeated Howard nearly three to one), his run was

Dawson's first notable challenge and it would set the tone for a string of political opponents through the 1960s.

Despite his loss, Howard pointed to the growing obsolescence of Dawson's party-building strategy. Although it had not failed in every instance in the 1950s, Dawson's defeats outweighed successes at both the local and the national levels. *Brown* changed everything by eradicating many black Americans' willingness to accept any type of gradualist rights strategies and convincing segregationists that slow mechanisms of electoral politics could not protect white supremacy. Thus, Dawson's efforts to push the Democratic Party or congressional wing toward civil rights could not overcome the opposition of segregationist Democrats, whereas Chicago civil rights leaders increasingly viewed Dawson's method of working within party circles as another obstacle to social change. Howard's campaign strengthened this sensibility at a time when Mayor Daley, who had already countermanded Dawson's authority, increasingly alienated the black community. As the 1960s approached, there was no sign that these trends would slow and whether Dawson's strategy would remain at all relevant to black liberation in the new decade remained to be seen.

Chapter Six
"WHERE IS THE INVISIBLE MAN?"

How is it that after fighting all of my life for the rights of my people I suddenly awaken in the September of my life to find myself being vilified and abused, and those who know me well and what I have stood for are accusing me of being against civil rights.[1]
—*William L. Dawson*

As a younger generation of black civil rights and political leaders experimented with direct-action techniques and pushed race to the front of America's consciousness in the 1960s, Dawson remained committed to the now decades-old party-building strategy—an approach that alienated him from the increasingly militant sentiment of civil rights leaders in Chicago while yielding only mixed results with the national party. In the presidential election of 1960, for instance, Dawson attempted to retake the offensive by pushing for a candidate more amenable to a civil rights agenda and playing a role in crafting the strongest civil rights plank in the nation's history. Ironically, John Kennedy's presidency instigated Dawson's decline as a party-based broker for civil rights while advancing only a small portion of the civil rights agenda.

Mirroring the disappointing developments at the national level, the Democratic Party in Chicago likewise failed to meet the civil rights needs of its black constituents. The local party's unwillingness to grant blacks equality in housing and education invigorated a portion of black Chicago and led to the Chicago Freedom Movement in which Dawson could not or would not play a part. Instead, Dawson's organization eschewed the protest style and continued the type of government-based support that characterized the civil rights agenda of a bygone era. Although

these efforts espoused mild and isolated forms of community empowerment through government programs, they did not address Chicago's
systemic racial inequalities or black Chicagoans' increasing desire for
control over their own community's institutions, in particular schools.[2]
Thus, by the end of the decade, Dawson found himself marginalized in
Chicago and Washington by the very forces he helped bring about.

As the 1960 presidential elections approached various black political and civil rights leaders wondered whether John F. Kennedy, then an
aspiring senator from Massachusetts, could usher in a new relationship
between Washington and the civil rights community. Nevertheless, although Dawson and various civil rights groups had praised Kennedy's
civil rights stance as early as 1946, their attention did not mean that
Kennedy could count on black votes in 1960.[3] Black pundits and leaders
frequently criticized Kennedy for being long on talk but short on action, and one acerbic *Defender* editorial accused Kennedy of compromis-
ing civil rights goals for political expediency.[4] Moreover, many blacks,
the majority of whom were Protestant, did not believe that a Catholic president would support their issues. Martin Luther King Sr. typified
black clergymen when he opposed Kennedy because of his religion and
backed Senator Hubert Humphrey, an established liberal and civil rights
proponent.[5] Kennedy's religion mattered little to Dawson, but he did
question the young senator's experience and promised his support to
Lyndon Johnson instead. Johnson's efforts to make Dawson the DNC
vice chairman convinced him of the Texas senator's racial goodwill, and
he doubted that Kennedy had the acumen to beat him.[6]

Dawson could not have been too committed to Johnson, however,
because he allowed Corneal Davis, who had been approached by Kennedy supporters in Chicago, to campaign for the Massachusetts senator in
the Wisconsin primary. Kennedy had difficulty arranging meetings with
black Democrats there and Sargent Shriver, head of the Chicago school
board and a Kennedy backer, thought that Davis's Masonic and religious
connections could overcome black resistance. After receiving Dawson's
approval, Davis organized several rallies for Kennedy in Wisconsin, helping him to win the black vote. He then did the same in West Virginia.
Davis believed that a Kennedy victory would strike a blow against religious—and implicitly, racial—prejudice, and he used this argument successfully in both states to convince reluctant black Protestants to support
Kennedy.[7] Kennedy's victories here convinced Humphrey to withdraw

from the race; his success with black voters in Wisconsin and West Virginia demonstrated to party leaders that he could be a viable candidate for black and liberal Democrats.[8]

Kennedy's image needed this boost, for he did not have a strong grasp of race issues and significant black notables still preferred Humphrey.[9] Moreover, although the candidates for both parties' nominations tried to get in front of the civil rights issue (instead of dodging it like the candidates did in 1956), the Democrats faced pressure to draft a civil rights program acceptable to their southern wing. A week before the convention, a group of black spokespersons went before the Democratic Platform Committee to demand that the committee add strong civil rights guarantees into its 1960 planks. The petitioners submitted a ten-point civil rights plan, signed by black leaders including Martin Luther King Jr. and A. Philip Randolph. Liberal members of the committee responded by announcing that they intended to push for a civil rights plank that supported the sit-ins and called for greater federal action on civil rights.[10]

Once the convention got underway, Kennedy used Johnson's southern origins to sway to black delegates. Adam Powell and several southern delegations had already pledged their first ballot votes to Johnson, who did not run in the primaries. Most black leaders, however, questioned Powell's decision and viewed Johnson's close ties to conservative Georgia Senator Richard Russell with trepidation. In contrast, Kennedy painted himself as the Democrats' best liberal alternative. An endorsement from a group of Stevenson supporters, a Kennedy pledge to win the nomination without a single southern vote, and a promise to a black newspaper that he would not abandon a strong civil rights position eventually clinched support from blacks, liberals, and labor.[11]

Nevertheless, Kennedy did not alienate southern whites. He assuaged segregationists' delicate sensibilities at the start of the convention with the carefully worded pledge to support sit-ins as long as they remained "peaceful and legal." Reading between the lines, several southern delegations promised Kennedy their vote in a second or third balloting. As it turned out, he did not need their support, for the coalition of blacks, liberals, and labor secured Kennedy the nomination on the first vote. Kennedy then chose Johnson as his running mate. Although this selection shored up southern support, it also alienated the black delegates who had supported Kennedy against Johnson in the first place.[12]

Dawson attempted to put a positive spin on Johnson's southern origins and his history as a moderating influence on civil rights bills when he nominated Johnson for the vice presidency.[13] First, he tried to give some unity to the fractious delegates by urging them to "lay aside all local, sectional, religious and racial differences in one common force." Then Dawson attempted to shift attention from Johnson's public record as a moderating influence on civil rights bills to his personal views on civil rights and his interactions with blacks:

> I have been in the Congress of the United States for some eighteen years. As a newcomer, I came to know Lyndon B. Johnson. My delegation from Illinois named me as their representative to the Democratic National Committee. The name of Lyndon B. Johnson, then a young man in the Congress, was presented to the Committee. Lyndon B. Johnson, in his speech declining the nomination, seconded the nomination of Dawson, a fellow member, and I hold that office today. He wasn't thinking of the Vice Presidency then. He wasn't thinking of anything that could come to him then. But what he did was an indication of the character of the man. The question of race, loyalty, or religion, did not enter his mind then, and it will not enter his mind with the many vexing problems that our beloved country must face now.[14]

With this speech, Dawson joined Adam Clayton Powell Jr. in vouching for Johnson's civil rights credentials.[15]

If the Democratic ticket provoked anxiety among civil rights activists, the strong civil rights plank calmed their fears. In May, Congressman Chester Bowles, who chaired the platform committee, Kennedy aide Harris Wofford, Martin Luther King Jr., and Bayard Rustin met secretly to draft an ideal civil rights plank for the Democratic platform. Although Bowles expected delegates to water down the plank in the negotiations process, King and Rustin intended to push for its full acceptance. To that end King, Rustin, and Randolph organized a rally of approximately 5,000 people, as well as a round-the-clock picket line, urging the ratification of the Bowles plank.[16]

The plank's eventual passage resulted from a miscalculation by Robert Kennedy, for the statement, with its pledges to end segregation and to ensure equal employment opportunities, promised far more than John Kennedy wanted. In the confusion of the convention, Robert Kennedy did not see the Bowles plank. Unaware of Bowles's expectation that convention would curtail the plank's promises, Robert Kennedy commanded his brother's delegates to push for the plank without any alterations. A group of southern delegates submitted a weaker minority plank, but they could not defeat the coalition of blacks, labor, and liberals behind the Bowles measure. When Wofford reached Robert Kennedy to explain what happened, it was too late. The Democrats had already accepted the "strongest civil rights plank in party history."[17]

The Democratic plank generated strong feelings in both factions of the party. The *Chicago Defender* wrote that the Democrats' civil rights pledges excited civil rights leaders around the country, Chicago mayor Richard Daley called the plank "the greatest document ever presented to any convention," and Congressman Diggs called the plank the "most tremendously far-reaching and far-sighted document ever adopted in the history of the party." As for segregationists' attitudes, a southern delegate questioned about the platform simply replied, "Go to Hell."[18]

Dawson, who sat on the platform committee, apparently played an important role in the plank's acceptance, and he reveled in its passage. One *Defender* article noted that Dawson "consolidated his position as one of the great Negro leaders of our times during the 1960 party convention here, emerging as a central figure in the shaping of a civil rights plank that is easily the strongest worded declaration of principles in that field since the Magna Carta and the Declaration of Independence."[19] Likewise, Chester Bowles thanked Dawson for his "help and cooperation" and for working "closely" with him to obtain the new plank.[20] When asked about the plank, Dawson told a reporter, "I'm happy. This demonstrates once again that the Democrats believe in action—not promises."[21]

Dawson had long awaited this moment: a promising Democratic candidate who prioritized civil rights and a close election that made black votes crucial. Indeed, the circumstances of this election appeared to provide the perfect opportunity for Dawson to bring black electoral leadership into the conference rooms of the White House. Because the Republican nominee Richard Nixon was popular among blacks and could stand upon a strong civil rights plank, Kennedy realized that he had to make a serious effort on civil rights.[22] To that end, he put together a team of specialists that included Dawson; Frank Reeves, a lawyer from Washington, D.C., and a black member of the Democratic National Committee; Wofford, a white lawyer with ties to Martin Luther King Jr.; R. Sargent Shriver, Kennedy's brother-in-law, who had worked on race relations in Chicago; and Louis Martin, a black journalist. Finally, at the behest of Richard J. Daley, the Kennedy campaign asked Dawson to head its civil rights efforts. Comprising a stronger cast than its predecessors in previous elections, this group also had greater access to the candidate.[23]

The Kennedy campaign, however, ridiculed Dawson and used him only as a figurehead. Kennedy aides Wofford and Shriver believed that

Dawson practiced an old-fashioned political style unbefitting the young liberals in the Kennedy campaign. In particular, they thought that Dawson was too conservative on race issues, because he worried that Kennedy needed southern white voters to beat Nixon. When Dawson indicated that he did not feel comfortable working in the large open-air room that housed the civil rights section, campaign staffers closeted Dawson in a private office, which they derisively dubbed "Uncle Tom's Cabin." They also limited Dawson's participation to ceremonial events.[24] Thus, although Dawson had finally achieved what he thought would be an ideal political situation at the national level, the victory proved pyrrhic. Considered too old-fashioned by Kennedy's race strategists, Dawson, the twenty-year champion of black electoral power, had only an honorary title and the jibes of the young, liberal, whites in Kennedy's campaign to mark his triumph.

As a result, Dawson did not play the same active role in the presidential campaign of 1960 as he had for Roosevelt and Truman. Outside of Chicago, he did little campaigning, although it would have been difficult for the seventy-four-year-old, handicapped congressman to hit the trail as he had in years past. As during the primaries, Dawson sent agents to work against black voters' anti-Catholic prejudice. He also recruited Chicago clergymen to work in this effort. Reverend Paul E. Turner of Gregg Memorial Church in Chicago, for instance, briefed Dawson on a meeting he attended at the Ohio Conference of Ministers, where he encountered great difficulty diverting the ministers' attention from Kennedy's religion and Johnson's Texas background.[25]

The Dawson organization nevertheless made strong efforts for Kennedy at home. They blanketed the South Side with campaign material and Dawson organized a massive rally of 10,000 supporters in Lake Meadows.[26] In a display of the same pragmatism that had enabled him to bring political organization to the 2nd Ward in the early 1940s, Dawson and his assistant Lawrence Woods created a campaign to use black beauticians' social network. Woods explained that they targeted beauticians because of their centrality to the black community. Black women, Woods argued, spent considerable time in the beauty parlor and heeded the advice of their beauticians, who had standing in the community as independent women of means. Dawson's organization contacted approximately 50,000 black beauticians around the country and held each responsible for getting four people to vote for Kennedy, for a total of 200,000 votes.[27] Considering that Kennedy won by just over 100,000 votes, this campaign certainly must be listed as one factor in his slim victory.

Dawson's efforts to popularize Kennedy in the black community fit the general objective of the Civil Rights Section (CRS) to increase Kennedy's exposure among blacks. Early in the campaign Louis Martin, a former *Defender* editor, believed that the single most important step in getting the black vote was to hit the black newspapers, and the CRS saturated the black press with Kennedy advertisements.[28] The ads often compared Kennedy with Roosevelt, whose New Deal attracted many blacks to the Democratic Party in the first place.[29] The CRS also tried to show Kennedy's relationships with major black leaders and entertainers, including Dawson, Nat King Cole, Pittsburgh *Courier* editor P. L. Prattis, Mahalia Jackson, Billy Eckstine, Harry Belafonte, Lena Horne, T. D. McNeal, Gene "Big Daddy" Lipscomb, Jersey Joe Walcott, and Ralph Metcalfe.[30] Finally, the CRS emphasized the strong Democratic civil rights plank and the ticket's commitment to black rights, with even Texas's Lyndon Johnson pledging, "You will, before the end of the next Democratic Administration, see that we will make more progress in the field of civil rights than we have made in the last century."[31] The volume of these advertisements dwarfed any previous Democratic public relations campaigns in the black press. They also far exceeded efforts in the Republican camp, where the GOP spent little to no money on advertising directed toward blacks and where Nixon concentrated more on garnering southern white support.[32]

These overtures, nevertheless, had not won over black voters, and it was the CRS's publicizing of an empathetic gesture by Kennedy to Coretta Scott King that pulled blacks into Democratic camp. In October, Dr. King received a sentence of four months hard labor on trumped-up trespassing charges. Fearing that her husband would not survive, a distressed Coretta King called her friend Harris Wofford. Wofford suggested to Kennedy that he call Mrs. King to offer his sympathy, which he did. Although the call received little coverage in the white press, it became a significant event in the black community. The CRS quickly put together a pamphlet detailing the episode and distributed it through black churches around the country. Kennedy's call not only belied blacks' fears of Kennedy's Catholic background but also characterized the type of attention blacks hoped they would receive from a new president after eight years of relative indifference from Eisenhower.[33]

In the final analysis, the black vote played an important role in Kennedy's slim victory over Richard Nixon.[34] Of the 69 million votes cast, Kennedy received 34,221,463 to Nixon's 34,108,582. Although European ethnic voters—such as Italian, Irish, and Polish Americans—as well as American Catholics and Jews could lay claim to giving Kennedy his margin of 0.2 percent, the black vote proved equally crucial.[35] For example, in the key cities of Chicago, Cleveland, and New York, blacks gave Kennedy 82, 75, and 66 percent of their votes, respectively.[36] These high percentages gave Kennedy a 40 percent margin among blacks. Even the Republican National Committee Chairman Thruston B. Morton later admitted that the Republicans "had taken the Negro vote too much for granted."[37]

That Kennedy owed some debt to blacks generally, and to Dawson in particular, became evident when Kennedy nominated Dawson to his cabinet as postmaster general.[38] Dawson's nomination, which came at the behest of Lyndon Johnson, marked the first time a U.S. president invited a black American to join the highest reaches of an administration.[39] Yet debate arose immediately after the nomination: many pundits argued that Kennedy made the nomination for purely political reasons. Chalmers Roberts of the *Washington Post,* for example, wrote that Kennedy nominated Dawson to pay off blacks for their support. A septuagenarian, Dawson did not fit the profile of the other cabinet members, whose average age was fifty. Moreover, Roberts claimed, Dawson possessed no training for the job. An article in the *Chicago Daily News* went further, alleging that Dawson's nomination stemmed from some alleged "wrong doing" in obtaining black votes for Kennedy.[40]

If the accusations in this debate did not raise eyebrows, Dawson's decision to decline the nomination captured attention nationwide. President-elect Kennedy told a group of reporters that, after "some reflection," Dawson decided to remain in the House of Representatives, where he believed he could do more for blacks as head of the Committee on Government Operations.[41] Kennedy's statement did not ring true, however, in light of the inability of black legislators to make much difference in the creation or passage of civil rights legislation. Rather, Dawson apparently saw the cabinet position as a symbolic office, and he had no interest in symbolism. Dawson privately called the position a "political graveyard" that would keep him from his primary interests: politics and people.[42] Dozens of letters in Dawson's files indicate blacks reacted strongly both for and against his decision. Many criticized Dawson for refusing Kennedy's powerful symbolic offer, whereas an equally large group believed that Dawson did the right thing by remaining in Congress, where true power lay. Moreover, argued the latter group, blacks had surpassed the need to accept every honorary position offered to them.[43]

Although Dawson declined the postmaster general position to retain the power and prestige he believed he had as a congressman, Kennedy's election transformed the Democrats in ways that reduced Dawson's party influence. From this point forward, the national leadership of the party clearly identified itself with the principle, if not the methods, of civil rights. Conservative white Southerners began their migration to the Republican Party, and, although civil rights issues remained contentious, storms over the civil rights plank would not ravage future Democratic conventions as they had in the 1940s and 1950s. Furthermore, Kennedy's establishment of the Equal Employment Opportunities Commission (EEOC) in 1964 and the election of six more blacks to Congress over the following eight years darkened the complexion of Washington, D.C., such that the Democratic leadership could no longer treat Dawson as the sole leader of black Democrats.[44]

Although Dawson adjusted to the new realities of the Kennedy administration, his organization in Chicago had to accommodate its exclusion from the construction of high-rise public housing complexes, which led some poor blacks to determine that Dawson colluded with Mayor Daley against their interests and thus further alienated black Chicagoans from their political leadership. As a result of near unanimous white resistance to integrated public housing in the 1940s and 1950s, the Chicago Housing Authority (CHA) built racially segregated public housing almost entirely in the city's black ghettos.[45] In 1949 the CHA, under city council guidance, selected a tract of land, two blocks wide and two miles long that cut due south through the Black Belt ghetto along State Street. The CHA originally proposed a scattered set of eight- and two-story units with a series of playgrounds and parks dispersed throughout the selected area. The Federal Housing Authority rejected the plan, however, because of its cost, and the CHA submitted a backup plan for twenty-eight sixteen-story high-rises.[46]

Although it represented a significant improvement over the slum it replaced, the project—the Robert Taylor Homes—received considerable criticism from the outset. Detractors decried the builders' use of mediocre construction materials. They also pointed to the tremendous amount of so-called dead space—the massive vacant tracts remaining because the buildings only used seven of ninety-six available acres. Moreover, community and structural problems arose very early in the nation's largest public housing project, including the presence of youth gangs, inadequate playground equipment, and rickety elevators.[47]

Nevertheless, when the Robert Taylor Homes opened in 1962, black Chicagoans saw it as a much-needed rest stop for working-class blacks on the road to home ownership. The CHA maintained a rigorous screening process for entrance into the project and residents exhibited a strong sense of community pride. Moreover, a network, primarily of women, emerged in groups such as Mothers on the Move against Slums, building councils, and resident councils to create social programs for the youth, communicate residents' needs to the city government, and fight for more effective building management.[48]

Indeed, the project from suffered increasingly slipshod oversight, immersed as it was in Chicago politics, patronage, and nepotism, and some project residents blamed Dawson. Project lore held that the eventual deterioration of the Robert Taylor Homes stemmed from Dawson's desire to further consolidate his political base, as these remarks by two former residents indicate:

> I think that political machinations affected the decisions for public housing, causing deteriorated, segregated public housing. I believe that there was an agreement with Dawson and Mayor Daley. While on one hand I laud Daley for pushing for more public housing in the city of Chicago, I also decry him for the collusion, which forced so many underprivileged poor people into what I call "concentrated ghettos."[49]

> Dawson went to Daley, and they came up with this plan. Each of those buildings is a precinct. It was for political expediency. The problem is that it is a rotten situation to the core, because it makes the project building a site of political favors.[50]

Apparently the façade of leadership that Mayor Daley allowed Dawson combined with the very real presence of Dawson's political workers gave project residents, and black Chicagoans generally, a false sense of Dawson's power on local politics. Yet a Dawson-Daley organization never existed, and Dawson had no real political power to affect the design of the new housing project.

On the contrary, Dawson's organization accommodated a situation over which it had virtually no control and most likely saw the establishment of each building as an individual precinct as its only recourse to provide support for its residents. Chuck Bowen, the top precinct captain in Dawson's organization between 1955 and 1966, proudly recounted some of the activities his organization carried out in his project precinct. His men regularly provided food baskets to needy families on Christmas and Thanksgiving. Because few project families could afford a luxury such as candy, Bowen's organization threw Halloween parties for the kids. Bowen could not recall how many children had been born in his car on the way to the hospital, a consequence of the slow ambulance service in the black ghetto. Project families who faced eviction because of roach or mouse infestations often called Bowen's office. He would send a team to clean and fumigate the apartment. An inspector would soon follow, whose approval allowed the family to keep their home. Although he could not say that every precinct captain provided such services, he remembered that organization leaders emphasized giving help of this caliber.[51]

These small things were not only of crucial importance to many poor black South Siders, but also to most working-class Chicagoans. Twenty-fifth Ward committeeman Vito Marzullo, for example, offered similar services to his constituents, ranging from free legal advice to helping people find jobs to giving money to the needy.[52] This exchange was simply how local politicians used their offices in most of Chicago. The system certainly wasted resources and allowed individual politicians to amass small fortunes in graft. Although no evidence exists supporting the contention that any Chicago voters explicitly supported corruption, "clean" politics did not appear to be the top agenda of Chicago's working class of European ethnic or African American derivation.[53]

In spite of a willingness to overlook corrupt politics, black voters did expect the political system to provide them the same social and economic advancement that it had allowed for European immigrants whose children and grandchildren eventually left inner-city slums for better neighborhoods. Black Chicagoans, by contrast, found few opportunities to move to areas unlike the declining communities they sought to leave behind. Thus, even successful middle-class black families stayed only a few steps ahead of ghetto-related problems.[54] With the construction of the high-rise projects in the heart of the black ghetto in the early 1960s, the city government openly allied itself to the project of black residential segregation. When continued segregation resulted in a visible detriment to their children's education, however, black Chicagoans began an unprecedented wave of protests against the political system.[55]

Starting in the 1961 and lasting through 1964, black Chicagoans targeted school segregation through a series of large-scale protests in which Dawson and the city's black aldermen played no substantive part. As blacks continued to migrate to Chicago, the number of children enrolled in the city's schools grew from 375,000 to 520,000. Although white schools in neighborhoods surrounding the Black Belt often functioned below capacity, school superintendant Benjamin Willis refused to violate "neighborhood integrity" if it meant school integration. Instead, Willis instituted a double-shift program and installed mobile classrooms, dubbed "Willis Wagons," near overcrowded black schools to alleviate overcrowding.[56]

In response to these moves, black Chicagoans attempted to remove Superintendent Willis. In 1961 black parents from Chatham, a middle-class neighborhood, filed a class-action suit against the school board for blocking parents' efforts to transfer their children to lesser-populated schools in nearby white neighborhoods. The next year a group of parents from Vernon Park staged a sit-in to protest school overcrowding.[57]

When the Citizens School Committee (CSC) nominated six whites to fill vacancies on the city's already all-white school board in April 1962, Dawson joined local activists' protests for black membership. The CSC's move set off a wave of black condemnation because blacks made up 43 percent of elementary school and 35 percent of high school enrollments. Moreover, black critics argued that the school board rubber-stamped Willis's racially insensitive policies. Dawson criticized the CSC for its secret deliberations and supported the black aldermen in their criticism of Superintendent Willis. Dawson had a private meeting with Mayor Daley, after which the mayor met with a black delegation that included Carl Fuqua and Charles Davis of the NAACP, Edwin Berry of the Urban League, Richard Cooper of the Chatham-Avalon Council, Mark Jones of the Coordinating Committee of Community Organizations (CCCO), and Aldermen William Harvey and Ralph Metcalfe. After the meeting, Daley announced that he would urge the CSC to consider adding at least two black members.[58]

This minor skirmish in the Chicago freedom struggle was Dawson's last stand in the local civil rights fight, after which he would no longer play a role in leading the city's cohort of black politicians, whose alliance to the mayor pulled them further away from the increasingly radical sentiments of local civil rights leaders.[59] Although Dawson referred to the black city councilmen as "my aldermen," he had not controlled or led all of the black aldermen since 1956.[60] This language alluded to the façade of control that Daley allowed the elderly congressman. In a more telling, yet still guarded statement, Dawson, a politician whose local reputation rested on his open-door policy, uncharacteristically admitted that he was out of touch with the situation because of his work in Washington. He added, "This is a local problem and I must concern myself with the problems of my constituents at the national level." *Defender* reporter Kenneth C. Field challenged Dawson directly on this point, arguing that Dawson's position as 2nd Ward committeeman made him directly responsible to local concerns.[61] It is unlikely that Dawson was unaware of the reaction the comment would provoke. Instead, Dawson's comments were the closest he could go toward a public capitulation to Mayor Daley's control of black politics in the city without directly condemning the mayor.

Daley's subjugation of Dawson was great indeed, since Dawson showed as much interest as ever in civil rights in Washington—so much so that he even censured the Kennedy administration's slow movement on black equality. As Chicago's various civil rights protests escalated, a broad band of civil rights, community, and religious groups formed the CCCO. By 1965 CCCO allied with Martin Luther King and the Southern Christian Leadership Conference to execute the Chicago Freedom Movement, a series of protests centered around open housing.[62] Dawson said nothing. This silence in Chicago pointed to Dawson's unwillingness—or inability—mount a challenge to Mayor Daley. In Washington, however, Dawson strongly criticized Kennedy for refusing to submit strong civil rights legislation to Congress out of fear of reprisals by the strong southern congressional bloc.[63] In October 1963 Dawson took the unusual step of calling a press conference and presenting thousands of petitions in support of his recent civil rights bill, H.R. 7453. At the conference the aging congressman sounded like the young veteran who made a name for himself with street corner speeches across Chicago's South Side, "We have borne these cruel and unjust burdens for 100 years since the Emancipation Proclamation. Time has run out! These burdens can no longer be borne. Our patience is gone!" Yet southern influence over the House kept Dawson's bill from ever making it to the floor.[64]

Dawson's press conference and submission of H.R. 7453 contrasted sharply with his accommodationist stance at home. In January 1964 the city's black ward committeemen formed the Assembly to End Prejudice, Injustice, and Poverty (ATEPIP). Bertel W. Diagre represented Dawson, who, although listed as the group's vice president, took no active role in any of the group's activities. Most local political pundits and civil rights advocates chuckled at the organization's plans to create programs for improving education, housing, and employment. Ironically, despite Dawson's absence, and the apparent leadership efforts of aldermen Kenneth Campbell (president) and Claude Holman, observers argued that the new group represented an attempt by the "Dawson-Daley machine" to co-opt the new movement.[65]

Despite its questionable origins, ATEPIP reflected the ambivalence felt by more established black leaders in Chicago toward the methods of the Chicago Freedom Movement. When Chicago activists joined forces with Martin Luther King Jr. and the Southern Christian Leadership Conference, for example, Alderman Ralph Metcalfe led the city's black politicians and other Daley-allied civic leaders to form another opposition civil rights group: the Chicago Conference to Fulfill These Rights (CCFTR). Observers expressed the same skepticism toward this group as they had toward ATEPIP and recognized that it too served as a proxy for Mayor Daley.[66] Nevertheless, ATEPIP and the CCFTR represented a large portion of Chicago's black leadership, including clergymen, politicians, and various other civic leaders who had eked out a modicum of political power and opposed the new movement's direct attack on Daley and his allies.[67] Indeed, the inability of protest organizers to connect with these established black civic leaders factored in the Chicago Freedom Movement's failure to realize its goals, and after working out a fairly weak open-housing agreement with Mayor Daley, King retreated from Chicago.[68]

Dawson gave virtually no support to the rapidly evolving direct action campaigns of the mid- and late 1960s. Instead Dawson remained committed to his New Deal–era conception of improving the community through government and party apparatuses, which contrasted greatly to the recent shift left by Chicago's civil rights leadership toward a vision of investing power in indigenous community leaders.[69] There is no way to tell whether Dawson would have joined the younger generation of protesters if he were not so tightly circumscribed by Mayor Daley's power, which had isolated Dawson by forming bilateral allegiances with the city's younger black elected officials rather than dealing with the black politicos as a single entity. Nevertheless, it is clear that his decision to stay within established political frameworks fit within Mayor Daley's demand that control of Great Society community programs remain in the hands of Democratic regulars.[70] As one might expect, these efforts did not reflect the temper of the era and received little attention in the black press.

One such program was the Dawson Plan for Education. The Dawson Plan called for providing three- and four-year-old children in poverty-stricken areas of Chicago with "educational and cultural experiences designed to prepare them for successful transition into regular educational programs and to increase their likelihood of continued success throughout their school careers." The program would also provide medical and dental care, as well as good nutrition, rest, and play. The program would strongly encourage parents of children involved in the program to learn more to aid their children's educational development outside of school. Apparently the plan had the support of the Chicago Teachers College (CTC) and the U.S. Department of Education. The education department provided the Chicago Teachers College a grant to study the program's feasibility, and if the CTC deemed the plan economical, the Department of Education would provide another grant to implement the Dawson Plan.[71] No evidence exists, however, that the plans ever came to fruition.

Dawson also played an important role in the establishment of the OUTREACH employment program. OUTREACH, in conjunction with Illinois State Employment Services and the U.S. Department of Labor's Chicago Plan (CHIP), sought to turn the unemployable into the employed by going to pool halls, street corners, and other areas to reach out to disadvantaged groups. The OUTREACH program gave advice on grooming, conducting an interview, and completing job applications. It also paid transportation costs for going to interviews. A *Chicago Tribune* article indicated that Dawson developed the program and convinced "the Business and Professional Men's club of his district into supplying rent-free facilities and to use its funds to advertise the office." Dawson provided an office for OUTREACH out of his Chicago headquarters at 3435 South Indiana Avenue, as did Chicago settlement houses, labor organizations, and churches for a total of twenty-three offices in underprivileged communities throughout Chicago. As of January 1967, CHIP and OUTREACH had found gainful employment for 1,500 "hard core unemployables" and had 500 more in training.[72]

Finally, in addition to the OUTREACH job placement center, Dawson requested that the Small Business Administration (SBA) establish a unit in his South Side headquarters. In connection with the SBA office, Dawson then operated the so-called Dawson School of Business Management, in which SBA officers and members of the 1st Congressional District Business and Professional Men's Club taught workshops on business administration. Instructors designed these courses to help underclass entrepreneurs learn how to take advantage of the benefits of the Economic Opportunity Act.[73] Still, as well intentioned as these programs may have been, they in no way challenged the Democratic organization's racial prerogatives.

Dawson's unwillingness to confront the Daley organization provoked anger among civil rights leaders and young activists who had moved away from integrationist sentiments toward a demand for greater community control, and their expressions of frustration led many would-be challengers to the mistaken conclusion that all of black Chicago's voters wanted Dawson out of office.[74] The 1964 congressional elections, for example, appeared to put Dawson's seat in serious jeopardy, but the protest model followed by Dawson's opponent proved inadequate to the task of creating an organized political unit. Two years had passed since Dawson involved himself in the effort to put more blacks on the school board, and some black Chicagoans resented Dawson's silence on the continuing standoff regarding education.[75] Dawson's primary opponents zeroed in on Superintendent Willis as the pivotal issue of the campaign. A. A. Sammy Rayner and Brenetta M. Howell announced their respective candidacies—against Dawson and 6th Congressional district representative Thomas J. O'Brien—as an attack on "Willisism." Specifically, they opposed gerrymandered school districts, construction of new schools in ghetto areas, use of mobile schools, and the establishment of so-called upper-grade schools to prevent the overflow of black students into white schools.[76]

Of the two candidates, Rayner most ardently adhered to the protest model and was dubbed by the press as Dawson's greatest challenge since T.R.M. Howard. Like Howard, Rayner came to the campaign with business experience as a partner in the undertaking firm of A.A. Rayner and Sons and with a civil rights background as the treasurer of Protest at the Polls, a group the *Defender* called the political arm of the Chicago Freedom Movement.[77] The Independent Voters of Illinois endorsed Rayner for his liberal agenda, particularly his plans for desegregating the Chicago public schools and a massive public works program he would submit to boost black employment. James Meredith, who spearheaded the integration of the University of Mississippi, also announced his support for Rayner, arguing that he did not appreciate Dawson's association with ATEPIP. Rayner's other supporters included Lawrence Landry of the Chicago Friends of the Student Non-Violent Coordinating Committee, Albert Raby of the CCCO, Timmuel Black of the Negro American Labor Council, and activist/comedian Dick Gregory.[78]

Boisterous, youthful opposition to Dawson led protest organizers to believe that he would lose the election. Awash in the early stirrings of militancy that would grow into a wave of Black Power sentiment in Chicago within a couple of years,[79] a mixed-race group of fifty unaffiliated high school students picketed against Dawson on April 1, calling him an "old guard, Uncle Tom, handkerchief-head politician." The students ridiculed Dawson and yelled, "Ain't Gonna Let No Uncle Tom Turn Me Round!" Commenting on Dawson's silence one of protesters mocked Dawson as "clinically senile."[80] Later that month, the Chicago Area Friends of the Student Nonviolent Coordinating Committee held a protest against the "Daley-Dawson machine" at another Dawson campaign rally, where they chanted, "22 Years of Uncle Tomism Is Too Long! Dawson Must Go! Where Is the Invisible Man?"[81] During the protest a fight broke out between some of Dawson's supporters and the protesters, while leaders Dick Gregory and Lawrence Landry looked on.[82] Youthful enthusiasm for Rayner, attention from the press, and the anti-Dawson protests convinced Landry that Rayner would win by more than 10,000 votes. Furthermore, former State Representative Charles M. Skyles claimed that Dawson's unwillingness or inability to keep up with civil rights demands would cost him the election.[83]

Dawson, however, still had supporters. As usual, all of the city's incumbent Democrats backed Dawson, with Daley disingenuously claiming that he owed much of his political success to Dawson's counsel and guidance.[84] Basing his campaign on the Great Society and the need to broaden community services, Dawson had the support of an interdenominational group of religious leaders who backed Dawson for his "long record of outstanding service and his message of love and togetherness." The group, which included Bishop Louis Henry Ford, a prominent civic leader and activist who gave the sermon at Emmett Till's funeral, and the Reverend Louis Bodie, a well-known antipoverty activist, particularly appreciated Dawson's unwillingness to snipe at his critics. As Bishop Ford indicated, "We are proud of the manner in which this great statesman has carried himself in the face of the attacks upon him by forces who are attempting to malign him."[85] Meanwhile, the Reverend Bodie remembered Dawson's walking the picket line with him against sweatshops and argued that the South Side owed a debt for Dawson's work to pass the recently passed Food Stamps Act.[86]

As Election Day approached, Rayner's backers overestimated their support and presumed that Dawson's organization could only win by resorting to election fraud. Rayner requested that Attorney General Robert Kennedy send official monitors. Yet foul play did not seem to be necessary, for Dawson easily beat Rayner, 45,737 to 20,577. Observers later complained that Rayner pursued a good cause but marred it by enlisting the support of young people who did not know how to comport themselves. *Defender* columnist Chuck Stone, for example, noted that the Rayner campaign illustrated that enthusiasm could not substitute for organization.[87] He then offered a disturbing contention that scorned the poor for their voting choices:

> Negroes in the comparatively lower income areas and in low-income project housing are blindly loyal to the Democrat machine. Their bellies are still telling them what to do and Negro decency, self-respect, freedom and achievement don't mean a thing compared to a basket of food and a dollar.[88]

In the general election, newspaper headlines proclaimed that Dawson's Republican opponent, the Reverend Wilbur Daniel, did not fear going into the "Lions Den" to fight the congressman. Echoing the young protesters who supported Rayner, Daniel attacked Dawson's mental acuity and challenged him to a debate, but he lost by an even wider margin than Rayner, 40,000 to 8,000.[89]

With no serious challengers, Dawson's congressional seat remained safe, but he and the other black representatives still did not play an important role in the passage and formulation of civil rights legislation. By the mid-1960s the number of black Congressional representatives had grown to six. Yet, when the Johnson administration passed the strongest civil rights legislation of the twentieth century, with the Civil Rights Act of 1964 and the Voting Rights Act of 1965, there is no indication that any of them played an important part.[90] Indeed, a bipartisan coalition in the House easily fended off "over one hundred crippling amendments" to pass the bill 290 to 130.[91] The real battle for these bills came in the Senate, where Johnson had to maneuver to prevent southern filibusters of his legislation.[92] Thus, although the administration may have welcomed black support, it appears to have been unnecessary.

The congressional calendars of the late-1960s did not possess the same number of intense civil rights battles that marked the 1940s and 1950s, for neither Dawson nor the rest of the black delegation. Although the delegation continued to submit voting rights legislation, bills to end employment discrimination, anti-lynching bills, and proposals to outlaw the use of cattle prods as a method of crowd control, the number of strictly civil rights–oriented bills submitted by the black representatives declined after 1965.

This decline, however, should not be interpreted as belief by the black representatives that the role of Congress in securing civil rights was finished. On the contrary, Dawson and the black delegation opposed the party leadership by supporting the Mississippi Freedom Democratic Party's (MFDP) controversial challenge to the seating of the all-white Mississippi congressional delegation in 1965.[93] Then, in 1966 and 1968, Dawson and the black delegation backed the major omnibus civil rights packages the Johnson administration submitted in those years. In discussion of these bills Dawson gave particular attention to the issue of open housing as means to cure violent unrest in black ghettos in the short term, and a way to ensure the long term stabilization of a black middle-class by allowing blacks to "inherit, purchase, sell, hold and convey personal property" in the same manner as whites.[94] He also supported various bills to allow Washington, D.C., home rule and, in coordination with the Johnson administration, he used one of his subcommittees to obtain limited home rule for Washington in 1967.[95]

Although support for the 1968 and 1969 civil rights bills, as well as efforts to pass legislation for political autonomy in the District of Columbia, sought civil rights goals, the diffusion of energy that afflicted contemporary civil rights leadership also affected the black congressional delegation. The handful of blacks in Congress appeared to cooperate somewhat prior to 1965. Their bills shared common themes, such as protecting voting rights; instituting desegregation in public facilities, the workplace, and in the military; and exacting more stringent punishment for violent mob actions against black soldiers and civilians. After 1965, however, the black congressional delegation pursued a broader liberal agenda emphasizing antipoverty programs.[96] Dawson, for example, frequently spoke in support of the Great Society. Still, he argued that elements of it needed adjustment, particularly the tendency of Aid to Families with Dependent Children and then Social Security Act of 1967 to reduce support for families in which the father worked.[97]

The congressman's tenure would end before he could act on these concerns, but there is little reason to believe that any legislation he would have submitted to adjust Great Society programs would have passed, for Dawson never possessed much power in Congress—considerably less than he ever wielded in the party, where his vote-getting power proved critical in several presidential elections. Thus, in the House Dawson could only use his influence as a representative of black interests to weaken bills that would put the party in a bad light and thus undermined its presidential chances. When it came to proactive civil rights action, though, Dawson faced not only the limitations that any pro–civil rights legislator would face but also a far lower ability to engage in the coalition building needed to get a bill through the House. These constraints led him to rely on congressional norms such as seniority and cordiality. Although these traditional paths to leadership brought him to chair the House Committee on Government Operations, the "experimental" nature of Dawson's chairmanship hardly indicated a mandate to use the committee as a civil rights platform. Moreover, Dawson's status as a committee chairman did nothing to gain a hearing for any of the civil rights bills he submitted.

In the House, Dawson's party-building strategy proved mostly ineffective for passing civil rights laws, and other black representatives in the 1960s had an equally discouraging record. Recognizing the limitations of working as individuals, black legislators began to caucus as the Black Eight in the late 1960s. Dawson did not participate, though, arguing that he just did not see himself as part of the new "black movement." Thus, Dawson stood alone in June 1969 when he publicly challenged President Nixon's poor enforcement of civil rights laws. Five months later the Black Eight followed with a similar declaration of grievances, yet neither complaint had any effect.[98] Although thirty years of working within the Democratic Party let Dawson to push for civil rights advances during critical elections and through party mechanisms, blacks' civil rights aspirations in Chicago remained frustrated and black power in the Congress had yet to live up to its promise. These were indeed the ties that bind.

Conclusion
"TIMES ARE DIFFERENT NOW"

Woods was Dawson's administrative assistant. . . . Dawson had to know what kind of man he was if the other people in the ward knew, and they did, that's why he wasn't liked and why the precinct captains of the ward "revolted" and lost him the election intentionally.[1]—*Charles Chew*

His quick intelligence gave him an extraordinary grasp of the many problems we face. He was a man of political sophistication who appreciated what his government could do and what it could not do in relation to our needs and desires. . . . He opened doors that had never been opened before, and widened others not by shouting and bragging.[2]—*Olive M. Diggs*

For nearly thirty years William J. Dawson had fought single-mindedly to implement his vision of black advancement through party politics. The party-building strategy found ready acceptance and yielded victories in the 1930s and 1940s. Yet its inadequacy as an overall strategy became apparent in the decades that followed, as black Chicagoans watched their hopes for advancement shatter against white Chicagoans' defense of systemic inequalities and as civil rights activists across the nation witnessed segregationists' refusal to yield to anything short of mass protest. Nevertheless, Dawson remained committed to his program, even after Mayor Daley severely undercut his power in Chicago, Kennedy's campaign staff relegated him to "Uncle Tom's Cabin," and a series of political opponents heaped scorn upon his political legacy. Through it all, the organization established by Dawson, Christopher Wimbish, and Corneal Davis in 1938 continued to satisfy the majority of voters in the 1st Congressional District, as indicated by Dawson's easy victories throughout the 1960s.[3]

Still, the organization required firm leadership, and as 1970 approached the aging congressman simply did not possess enough strength to carry on the fight.

Dawson appears to have been a man of good health for most of his adult life, but starting in 1957 his vigor began to decline.[4] Perhaps it was Dawson's weakened condition that allowed an opportunistic newcomer to slip into his organization: Lawrence Woods of Hot Springs, Arkansas. Woods came to Dawson as a refugee of the Arkansas Democratic Party, which, because of a paroxysm of racist sentiment surrounding the integration of the public schools, proved an inhospitable base for black Democrats. Woods's specific connection to the Arkansas Democratic Party is unclear, but he had an arrest record that pointed to his reputation as a hustler and he did not reveal any of this information to Dawson.[5]

In any case, shortly after his arrival Woods became a top precinct captain and Dawson's executive assistant in Chicago, but his presence proved cancerous to the organization.[6] By 1959 Woods had obtained a position in the county assessor's office, but soon lost his job from charges of extorting bribes from local businesses.[7] Within the organization, Woods alienated the other precinct captains by focusing on building a faction around himself rather than attending to the needs of constituents. One *Commonweal* reporter indicated that Woods, known as Dawson's hatchet man, relished power and "made a lot of enemies."[8]

As Dawson's health worsened, Woods's desire for influence became apparent. In 1969 Woods ran in a special election for alderman of the 2nd Ward, which had been held by Alderman Harvey who moved on to the county board.[9] Woods announced his campaign early and claimed several high-profile supporters, including Dawson, Daley, John Sengstacke, John Johnson, Dr. T.K. Lawless, Jesse Jackson, and Truman Gibson Sr.[10]

The contest between Woods and his opponent, Fred Hubbard, focused on Dawson's care of the ward and revelations of Wood's tainted history. Hubbard, a Korean War veteran and director of the Clarence Darrow Center, ran as an independent candidate. He had already unsuccessfully challenged the Dawson organization on two occasions, and he quickly turned the 1969 race into a referendum on Dawson.[11] Hubbard argued that Dawson spent too little time with the people of the ward. He also received endorsements from the city council's small independent block, which included Leon Despres (5th Ward), A.A. "Sammy" Rayner (6th Ward), and William Cousins Jr. (8th Ward).[12] Woods, who ran on his history of work in the community as Dawson's representative, received backing from two progressive black organizations: the Black Independent Voters of Illinois and the New Breed. In a surprising twist, both groups argued that Hubbard's candidacy received too much white support and praised Woods's involvement in various community-based endeavors, such as the Dawson School of Business and Operation Breadbasket's Black Christmas project.[13] Finally, near the end of the campaign, *Chicago Daily News* reporter Mike Royko exposed Woods's unsavory past and found that Woods had fabricated many of his endorsements, including those attributed to John Johnson and Truman Gibson Sr.[14]

On election day, Hubbard beat Woods 6,924 to 4,600. Independents and reporters saw Hubbard's victory, in Dawson's home district, as a massive blow to the regular Democratic organization.[15] Yet, as much as Hubbard's win highlighted Dawson's inability to run his organization, it also marked contempt for Woods. Indeed, many of Dawson's precinct captains defected to Hubbard just to beat Woods. As one precinct captain put it, "Dawson is still our leader. . . . I've been a precinct captain for Dawson for 16 years, but I can't stand Woods. . . . Woods didn't serve the constituency. He built a new organization around him . . . [that's why] so many of us went for Hubbard. . . . Dawson is still our leader."[16]

In spite of this support, Dawson was vulnerable and several black elected officials declared their intentions for his seat, including 3rd Ward Alderman Ralph Metcalfe, 20th Ward Alderman Kenneth Campbell, and the independent 6th Ward Alderman Sammy A. A. Rayner Jr.[17] As the young lions circled and as Daley looked on impassively, Dawson realized that his time to bow out had arrived:

> Now I feel the time has come to pass on the responsibilities of the high office you have given me to another whom you may deem worthy to represent you. Upon the completion of my term in Congress, I shall not seek reelection. The memories of my long tenure in office, of the friendships, of the challenges, of the defeats and victories which all of us have shared will sustain me all of the rest of my life.[18]

But he never made it to retirement. After spending most of the next year in the hospital with a respiratory infection stemming from pneumonia, Dawson died on November 9, 1970. At eighty-four, he was the oldest member of Congress.[19] Noting that flags flew at half mast over all of the federal buildings in Washington, D.C., and at Chicago's city hall, a *Chicago Defender* reporter wrote that it was "the first time in the history of this country that so much acknowledgement has been given to a black man."[20] An array of dignitaries spoke at the funeral, including Mayor Daley, California Representative Chet Hollifield, Circuit Court Judge Archibald Carey,

Representative Charles Diggs Jr., gospel singer Mahalia Jackson, and State Representative Corneal Davis. Meanwhile, Dawson's old friends Presidents Lyndon Johnson and Harry Truman served as honorary pallbearers.[21]

Dawson's death generated an outpouring of praise, criticism, and analysis that capped a series of discussions regarding the congressman begun by intellectuals, pundits, activists, and ordinary citizens in the mid-1960s. One of the most subtle evaluations came from activist and *Chicago Defender* reporter Warner Saunders. Saunders praised Dawson's activist roots and acknowledged the wisdom of Dawson's vision regarding rigorous political organization, yet he maintained that Dawson's commitment to the Democratic Party and electoral politics amounted to a Faustian bargain that stifled new black leadership and ultimately kept black Chicagoans in an oppressed condition.[22]

Saunders accurately criticized Dawson's career in Chicago after 1956, but the roots of Dawson's party-building strategy went back much further. They began in his southern upbringing, where his parents, Rebecca and Levi, themselves witnesses to the removal of the ballot by white supremacists, inculcated a strong sense of self-worth in their children and emphasized the value of a rigorous education and economic self-sufficiency. Moreover, Rebecca and Levi taught their children to actively support African Americans in need. If William felt any uncertainty on this point, Levi Dawson provided his son an example when he, William, and Julian spent the night protecting a neighbor from a potential lynch mob. As a young adult, William's time in Fisk University only strengthened his sense of duty to the race and provided a first-class education toward that end.

After a freak accident prevented him from attending Harvard Medical School, Dawson drifted for a few years until the Great War pointed him to his life's work. Like several hundred thousand African American volunteers, Dawson looked at participation in the war as a way to demonstrate black loyalty and ability. The U.S. government, however, treated its black soldiers with inexcusable and despicable contempt, as it relegated the majority of them to menial jobs and issued detestable warnings of black male sexuality to its European allies. Moreover, as a combat officer, Dawson also saw the army routinely humiliate black combat soldiers, providing them with inadequate training, shoddy materials, and inadequate support during critical missions. As the humiliations piled on, Dawson, his fellow officer Christopher Wimbish, and Cornel Davis, a younger enlisted man, debated the future of black Americans and asked what could be done to make sure that the degradations they experienced as soldiers would not happen again. The three of them decided on politics and vowed to make a change when they returned.

Dawson joined the political game almost immediately upon his return in 1919 and learned that neither black Republicans' highly factionalized politics nor black radicals' protest campaigns could exert much influence against the local political leadership. During the decade that followed, the pioneers of black politics in Chicago, Ed Wright, Oscar DePriest, and Louis Anderson, deemed political participation the ultimate expression of civil rights and aggressively leveraged a growing black voter base to exploit factionalism between white political leaders in the execution of their agenda.[23] Then, in the 1930s, Dawson witnessed a flurry of protest activities in Chicago and tested the viability of direct action protest for himself, but the protests of those years yielded underwhelming results when compared to the powers of a Wright, who could force the hiring of more blacks at multiple levels in government, or a DePriest, who could take civil rights issues to Congress. Nevertheless, the vulnerabilities faced by Dawson's mentors, Wright in particular, supported Dawson, Davis, and Wimbish's vision of creating a powerful black political faction that could demand concessions from white political leaders.

Dawson's program to improve the situation of African Americans solely through Democratic Party politics essentially represented an extension of the tactics created by Wright, DePriest, and Anderson.[24] Dawson achieved greater success than his mentors because he formed his organization within the Democratic Party—which had recently consolidated its control of local politics, established a strong connection to the New Deal programs, and wanted to include black voters within its ethnic coalition. Dawson's career makes it clear that black voters in Chicago did not join the Democratic Party solely for New Deal benefits nor did white politicians draw former black Republicans by doling out patronage.[25] Rather, Davis and Wimbish actively undermined the unstable coalition of white Democratic leaders and their black clients in the predominantly black 2nd Ward for their own ends. When Dawson left the Republican Party and joined Davis and Wimbish, the triumvirate worked to shift black Chicagoans away from the GOP to their new Democratic organization the old-fashioned way—person to person, house to house, block by block, and precinct by precinct.

With the establishment of a refurbished black Democratic political network, Dawson's organization eventually achieved its goals, which included extension of social welfare benefits, increased black patronage, and increased black political representation. Through Davis, the organization taught its precinct captains to commit themselves to the needs of their constituents and gained a reputation for providing a range of support to its constituents, from free in-house legal services to expert advice on New Deal social programs to rides to the emergency room for expectant mothers.[26] The triumvirate eventually established black political representation in all of the South Side's predominantly black wards and obtained patronage appointments in city government nearly in proportion to black Chicago's percentage of the population. Moreover, Dawson sought not only low-level service positions but also upper-level offices that both he and the local press noted as important civil rights gains for the race.[27]

Dawson's strategy, however, with its emphasis on using blacks' votes as tools for social change within an intensely competitive political environment, did not anticipate the ways in which white racism in Chicago would, or could thwart even minor attempts to address structural inequality. The obstinacy of Chicago's white ethnic population to black advancement and the volatility their racial neuroses posed for elected white officials became apparent with the removal of Mayor Kelly in 1947. Thus, by the late 1940s, the new rules became clear: the regular Democratic organization would support blacks holding political office and the extension of individual benefits such as patronage, but it would not permit any attacks on structural inequality that could disturb white voters' fragile sense of superiority.[28] This conservative position, coupled with shifting factional leadership, restricted the Dawson organization, committed as it was to party politics, to an ineffective defensive posture within Chicago. Dawson and his organization fought, for example, Mayor Kennelly's anticrime initiatives, which did more to hurt the Black Belt's underground economy than to reduce crime, and Kennelly's slum clearance programs, which did more to buffer downtown from the ghetto than improve black housing stocks. Yet, by the time Dawson and the members of the Cook County Central committee removed Kennelly, his initiatives had already established the precedent of excluding African American leadership from local housing policy discussions and had facilitated seizure of the policy by the (white) mafia—a move that made the Dawson organization utterly dependent on white Democrats for financial support.

Just as important as Dawson's underestimation of white resistance to removing systemic inequality, his organization also did not predict Mayor Richard J. Daley's consolidation of political and governmental power in the mid-1950s. Daley effectively eliminated factionalism between white Democratic leaders while instigating struggles for power among

Dawson's lieutenants—a stratagem that removed any space in which the Dawson organization could jockey for position and undermined its ability to function as a unit. Daley's unprecedented tenure as the mayor and head of the local party centralized governmental and political power to himself.[29] Under these circumstances, the Dawson organization could no longer function as a strong player among competing white factions; rather, they stood as black Chicagoans' sole representative against the city's combined white interests under Daley organization. Daley then began eroding the Dawson organization in 1958, when he used Alderman Claude Holman's ambition and the open-housing issue to cut Dawson's influence outside of the 2nd Ward and shift all black political loyalties directly to city hall. Thereafter, neither Dawson nor his organization engaged in any noteworthy civil rights efforts in Chicago.

This state of affairs differed somewhat from Dawson's continued, albeit less than successful, engagement with civil rights on Capitol Hill. In Congress, Dawson played roles in blocking the passage of unabashedly racist legislation, such as the Winstead Amendment and the bill for a Booker T. Washington veterans' hospital. Nevertheless, the difficulties of passing legislation rendered a single black representative almost powerless to initiate, promote, and pass a civil rights bill. During his time in Congress, Dawson submitted forty-three civil rights bills, none of which made it out of their initial committee assignments.[30]

The contradiction between Dawson's ability to block racist bills and his failure to pass civil rights legislation stemmed from the difference between party building and House coalition building. From the 1940s through the early 1960s, the Democratic Party increasingly needed blacks' votes to win presidential elections. Blacks held the keys to elections in urban centers such as Chicago, New York, Detroit, and Philadelphia, and the Democrats needed these cities to win the electoral votes of Illinois, New York, Michigan, and Pennsylvania. Thus, the party could not afford to pass legislation that explicitly violated the sensibilities of its newest coalition members, black urban voters. In Congress, Dawson, Powell, and later Charles Diggs represented this segment of the coalition, and thus they possessed considerable influence in stopping racist bills. Passing legislation, however, differed significantly and required the agreement of several hundred representatives with different, locally based interests.[31] It took the moral urgency stemming from President Kennedy's assassination and President Johnson's political will to push through the civil rights legislation of the 1960s. Yet, because the bills passed the House with overwhelming support, the black representatives had little substantive effect.[32]

If Dawson's party-building strategy eventually failed in Chicago and yielded mixed results in Congress, it proved more successful in pushing the national party leadership toward accommodating black voters. Dawson essentially took the model crafted by Wright, DePriest, and Anderson to the national Democratic leadership at a time when African Americans' political affiliation teetered between the two parties. Although Dawson's effort was one among a number of forces molding the party, it nonetheless influenced several key moments in the era, including the blocking of James Byrnes's vice-presidential aspirations and the rally of black Democrats in support of Henry Wallace's vice-presidential bid in 1944; the demonstration of black voters' ability to replace segregationist southern whites; the appointment of Dawson as the first black vice chairman of the Democratic Party; the desegregation of the presidential inaugural ball in 1948; a series of speeches supporting and the active efforts to organize black Democrats across the South between 1948 and 1952, which provided the only federal validation of southern blacks' increasing politicization; the strong Democratic civil rights plank and record-breaking black voter turnout in 1952; the efforts to undermine black religious prejudice against Kennedy during the primaries and writing of the Democrat's near categorical statement in support of civil rights in 1960; and finally, Kennedy's nomination of Dawson for postmaster general, the first such nomination for an African American.

Dawson's experiences in these years indicate that changes in the Democratic Party did not result simply from struggles between northern white liberals and southern conservatives. Nor did blacks influence the party only from the outside through civil rights protest. Rather, effective black electoral leaders partnered with white liberals during the party conventions, leveraged the uncertainty surrounding the black vote for a more accommodative stance by the Democratic Party, and played an important role in the increased politicization of black Americans that characterized the late 1940s and early 1950s.

Finally, Dawson's career legitimized black political leadership and influenced the professionalization of black politicians. After becoming both 2nd Ward Democratic committeeman and representative from the 1st Congressional District, Dawson moved into uncharted political territory. Because no black American had reached the levels of power Dawson achieved, he had no examples for guidance, and most of his white contemporaries doubted his abilities. This underestimation of Dawson as a (black) politician evidenced itself at several critical moments, particularly when the Democratic Party nominated him as an experimental vice chairman and when his white congressional colleagues viewed his chairmanship of standing committee in Congress as a trial.[33] Under the intense scrutiny of whites and blacks, Dawson charted a path that eventually brought praise from his white colleagues and mixed assessments from black Americans.

In his decades-long effort to promote African Americans' rights within electoral politics, Dawson left a legacy of political organization, professionalism, and power for generations of black politicians. It was not coincidental that Charles Chew, the first independent alderman to fight and beat the Daley organization, received a great deal of advice from Dawson in the early stages of his career.[34] It was not an accident that a young Ralph Metcalfe admired Dawson's fights for increased black representation on the Cook County Democratic Committee and that Congressman Ralph Metcalfe would later engage in a bitter feud with Mayor Daley over police brutality.[35] It was not chance that frequently brought William Dawson to the childhood home of future independent mayor Harold Washington, that Washington learned the basics of political organization at his father's side in the 3rd Ward, or that Washington's classes on politics within the 3rd Ward resembled classes designed by Corneal Davis nearly thirty years earlier.[36] And destiny did not determine that two of the three African Americans elected to the U.S. Senate since Reconstruction and that the only successful presidential bid by an African American candidate originated from the South Side of Chicago.

In an interview discussing the array of black politicians and government officials connected to him in the 1940s and 1950s, Dawson laughingly replied, "I'm the granddaddy of them all."[37] Like real children, Dawson's political offspring faced unforeseen circumstances and made different choices than their forbearers. Yet, like their predecessor, who stood on the shoulders of Ed Wright, Oscar DePriest, and Louis Anderson, the black politicians who followed Dawson grappled with the same tensions between executing an agenda that addresses African Americans' historical oppression while conforming to the rules of white-dominated, American electoral politics. As *Chicago Defender* reporter Ethel L. Payne wrote,

> There is a new breed of black politicians mostly young, voice furious, and up front in the limelight. Like it or not, they got where they are now because there was a Bill Dawson 30 years ago who helped pave the way for their coming. . . . Who knows but that thirty years from now some young and eager blacks entering the political lists will say of the present group, "Well they were all right for their day, but times are different now."[38]

APPENDIX

Civil Rights, Resolutions, Remarks and
Legislation & Committee Legislation
and Remarks, 1941–1950

1943

H. Res 724: to create a commission to study race relations; detained in the Rules Committee

Defense of William Pickens, a member of the NAACP and government employee, facing investigation by the Dies Committee

Gave remarks critiquing assertions that blacks had engaged in rioting in Washington, D.C.

1944

H.R. 4004: to provide for equal employment opportunities detained in the Education and Labor Committee

Gave remarks supporting the FEPC

H. Res. 472: to create a commission to study race relations; detained in the Rules Committee

1945

H. Res. 48: to create a commission to study race relations; detained in the Rules Committee

Made remarks supporting anti–poll tax legislation

Made remarks opposing legislation designed to liquidate the FEPC

H.R. 700: for equal employment opportunities, detained in the Education and Labor Committee

1947

H.R. 228: antilynching legislation; detained in the Judiciary Committee

H.R. 229: for equal employment opportunities, detained in the Education and Labor Committee

H.R. 230: anti–poll tax legislation; detained in the Administration Committee

H.R. 231: desegregation of public accommodations in Washington, D.C.; detained in the D.C. Committee

H.R. 2902: for equal employment opportunities, detained in the Education and Labor Committee.

1949

H. Res 213: to authorize U.S. participation in the celebration of Haitian independence; detained in Foreign Affairs Committee

H.R. 382: desegregation of public accommodations in Washington, D.C.; detained in the D.C. Committee

H.R. 383: anti–poll tax legislation; detained in the Administration Committee

H.R. 384: for equal employment opportunities, detained in the Education and Labor Committee

H.R. 385: antilynching legislation; detained in the Judiciary Committee

H.R. 2217: to prohibit the transportation or importation of false statements designed to arouse intergroup conflict; detained in the Judiciary Committee

A dozen remarks and thirteen bills on government efficiency, four of which passed, including the Reorganization Act

1950

Gave remarks supporting a permanent FEPC

Nine bills on government efficiency, two of which passed

1951

H.R. 3687: to provide for a competitive civil service hiring procedure based on open competition and merit

Sixteen government efficiency bills, none of which passed

Gave remarks opposing the Winstead amendment to create segregated veterans hospitals in the famous speech "If it Means Death Itself, I Will Pay It."

NOTES

Introduction—"Don't Get Mad! Get Smart. Vote!"

1. Doris E. Saunders, "Black Politics and Chicago: The Bill Dawson Story," TS, DSP-CGWL, n.p.

2. "Mississippi Regional Council of Negro Leadership Reveals New Approach to Problems of Negro Life in the State. Cong. Dawson Cites Value of Voting and Political Participation at the State and Local Levels," *Jackson Advocate*, May 10, 1952, 1, WLDP-FUL.

3. John Dittmer, *Local People: The Struggle for Civil Rights in Mississippi* (Urbana: University of Illinois Press, 1994), 32–33; Charles M. Payne, *I've Got the Light of Freedom: The Organizing Tradition and the Mississippi Freedom Struggle* (University of California Press, 1995), 7–15; James C. Cobb, *The Most Southern Place on Earth: The Mississippi Delta and the Roots of Regional Identity* (Oxford: Oxford University Press, 1992), 208–29; Neil McMillen, *Dark Journey: Black Mississippians in the Age of Jim Crow* (Urbana: University of Illinois Press, 1990), 28–32.

4. Robert Weisbrot, *Freedom Bound: A History of America's Civil Rights Movement* (New York: Penguin, 1991), 92–97; Steven F. Lawson, *In Pursuit of Power: Southern Blacks and Electoral Politics, 1965–1982* (New York: Columbia University Press, 1985), 16, 20, 31, 40; Payne, 290–301.

5. Dittmer, 33.

6. "Mississippi Regional Council of Negro Leadership Reveals New Approach to Problems of Negro Life in the State. Cong. Dawson Cites Value of Voting and Political Participation at the State and Local Levels," *Jackson Advocate*, May 10, 1952, 1, WLDP-FUL.

7. Ibid., 1.

8. Biographical Sketch, Archives, Fisk University Library, Fisk University, Nashville, Tennessee; Charles Branham, "The Transformation of Black Political Leadership in Chicago, 1864–1942," Ph.D. diss., University of Chicago, 1981, 378; Louis Lautier, "Rep. Dawson-From Georgia Bootblack to Congressman," *Journal and Guide* October 7, 5, 10, 1950, WLDP-FUL; Adam Cohen and Elizabeth Taylor, *American Pharaoh. Mayor Richard J. Daley: His Battle for Chicago and the Nation* (Boston: Little, Brown, 2000), 58, 96; "Mississippi Regional Council of Negro Leadership Reveals New Approach to Problems of Negro Life in the State. Cong. Dawson Cites Value of Voting and Political Participation at the State and Local Levels," *Jackson Advocate*, May 10, 1952, 1, WLDP-FUL.

9. Corneal Davis, interview by Horace Waggoner, IGAOHP-BL; Bill Booker, Chicago, to John H. Hamilton, Washington, D.C., May 12, 1938, CBP-CHS; *Tenants' War Cry*, April 17, 1937, CBP-CHS; "Dawson Opens Campaign for Re-Election," *Chicago Defender*, January 28, 1939, 7; Branham, 384; Doris E. Saunders, "Black Politics and Chicago: The Bill Dawson Story," TS, DSP-CGWL, n.p.; Reed, "Study of Black Politics and Protest," 324–27; M. Earl Sarden, interview by Christopher Manning, tape recording, July 30, 2002, recording in possession of the interviewer, Chicago; "Theatre Hires Race Operator After Sunday Demonstration," *Chicago Defender*, September 24, 1938, 7; Bill Booker, Chicago, to John H. Hamilton, Washington, D.C., May 12, 1938, CBP-CHS.

10. Corneal Davis, interview by Horace Waggoner, IGAOHP-BL; Roger Biles, *Big City Boss in Depression and War: Mayor Edward J. Kelly of Chicago* (DeKalb: Northern Illi-

nois University Press, 1984), 98, 180; Branham, 393, Christopher Robert Reed, "A Study of Black Politics and Protest in Depression-Decade Chicago: 1930–1939," Ph.D. diss., Kent State University,, 251; Joseph Tittinger, Chicago, to Arthur Mitchell, Washington, D.C., March 10, 1938, AWMP-CHS; Robert J. Blakely, with Marcus Shepard, *Earl B. Dickerson: A Voice for Freedom and Equality* (Evanston, Ill.: Northwestern University Press, 2006), 68; Saunders, n.p.; Truman K. Gibson Jr., with Steve Huntley, *Knocking Down Barriers: My Fight for Black America* (Evanston, Ill.: Northwestern University Press, 2005), 48.

11. "Virginia Negroes Are Urged to Concentrate on Politics By Dawson Speech Here," *Richmond Times Dispatch*, March 21, 1949, 2, WLDP-FUL; *Richmond Afro-American*, December 18, 1948, n.p., WLDP-FUL; "Dawson Thrills 800 Dallasites," *Texas Edition of the Call*, May 4, 1951, 1, WLDP-FUL; "Dawson Thrills 800 Dallasites," *Dallas Express*, May 5, 1951, 1, WLDP-FUL.; Speech given by William L. Dawson before the North Carolina Regional Council of Negro Leadership, North Carolina, May 2, 1953, WLDP-CHS; Louis Martin, "Dawson Opened the Door for Black Politicians," n.t., November 14, 1970, 3, WLDP-FUL; "Independent Voters Back Dawson's Fine Record," *Chicago Defender*, October 26, 1946, 1, 9; Political advertisement, *Chicago Defender*, October 26, 1946, 16; Political advertisement, *Chicago Defender*, November 2, 1946, 3.

12. John Dittmer, for example, notes the significance of the RCNL meeting as a critical moment in Mississippi's nascent civil rights movement. Yet despite the RCNL designating their first convention "Dawson Day," Dittmer makes no mention of the Illinois congressman and writes that the growth of voting rights activities in Mississippi's black community in the 1950s had "no support from the traditional civil rights allies such as the federal government and labor." Dittmer, 31–34.

Several scholars have pointed to Dawson as more or less derivative product of Chicago politics with little interest in black rights. For examples see Arnold R. Hirsch, "The Cook County Democratic Organization and the Dilemma of Race, 1931–1987," in his *Snowbelt Cities: Metropolitan Politics in the Northwest and Midwest Since World War II* (Bloomington: University of Indiana Press, 1990), 64–69; William J. Grimshaw, *Bitter Fruit: Black Politics and the Chicago Political Machine, 1931–1991* (Chicago: University of Chicago Press, 1992), 82–86; Roger Biles, "Edward J. Kelly: New Deal Machine Builder," in *The Mayors: The Chicago Political Tradition* eds. Paul M. Green and Melvin G. Holli (Carbondale, Illinois: Southern University Press, 1995), 116; Charles V. Hamilton, *Adam Clayton Powell, Jr.: The Political Biography of an American Dilemma* (New York: Antheum Books, 1991), 481; and William Haygood, *King of the Cats: The Life and Times of Adam Clayton Powell, Jr.* (New York: Houghton-Mifflin, 1993), 111.

13. For more nuanced, yet still Chicago-focused, analyses see, Dianne M. Pinderhughes, *Race and Ethnicity in Chicago Politics: A Reexamination of Pluralist Theory* (Urbana: University of Illinois Press, 1987), 63–65; Reed, 194, 198, 209, 241–53, 261–65, 314; Charles Branham, "The Transformation of Black Political Leadership in Chicago, 1864–1942," Ph.D. diss., University of Chicago, 1981, 133, 286–90, 374–80, 383–409, 433–34, 442–47; Nicholas Lemann, *The Promised Land: The Great Black Migration and How it Changed America* (New York: Vintage Books, 1991), 75; Adam Cohen and Elizabeth Taylor, *American Pharaoh: Mayor Richard J. Daley: His Battle for Chicago and the Nation* (Boston: Little, Brown, 2000), 93–97.

Only Donald R. McCoy and Richard T. Reuten have taken extensive note of Dawson's activities as black intercessor for civil rights in the national Democratic Party. See their *Quest and Response: Minority Rights and the Truman Administration* (Lawrence: University Press of Kansas, 1973), 34, 107, 139–40, 209, 237, 323–25.

14. Pete Hamill, "Man of the People," *New York Post*, August 26, 1966, 5, 45, DSP-CGWL.

15. See also Stokely Carmichael and Charles V. Hamilton, *Black Power: The Politics of Liberation in America* (New York: Vintage Books, 1967), 10–11; Chuck Stone, *Black Political Power in America* (New York: Dell Publishing, 1968), 176, 177, 178, 179–83.

16. Roy Wilkins, to Nellie Dawson, Chicago, November 1, 1979, WLDP-FUL.

17. Richard Slusser, November 11, 1970, WLDP-FUL; Toni Anthony, "Dawson Is Laid to Eternal Rest," *Chicago Daily Defender,* November 14, 1970, 2.

18. Richard Slusser, November 11, 1970, WLDP-FUL; Anthony, "Dawson Is Laid to Eternal Rest," 2; Michael Killian, "2,000 Led By Mayor Daley Attend Rep. Dawson's Funeral," *Chicago Tribune,* November 13, 1970; Edward T. Clayton, *The Negro Politician* (Chicago: Johnson Publishing, 1964), 71.

19. Louis Martin, "Dawson Opened Door for Black Politicians," *Chicago Daily Defender,* November 14, 1970, 3.

20. James Q. Wilson, *Negro Politics: The Search for Leadership* (New York: The Free Press, 1960), 50–56; Alden Whitman, "Rep. William l. Dawson Dies; Served Chicago since '42,'" n.t, November 10, 1970, 46 DSP-CGWL; Chuck Stone, *Black Political Power in America* (New York: Dell Publishing, 1968), 183; Warner Saunders, "William Dawson: A Really Great Man in His Time," *Chicago Defender,* December 8, 1970, 8; Simeon Booker, "Nation Mourns Dawson's Death as Capitol Flag Flies Half Mast," *Jet,* November 26, 1979, 20–27, WLDP-FUL.

21. On the transcript, Saunders noted that the white committeeman in question was John D. Arco of the First Ward. Ralph Metcalfe, interview by Doris Saunders, transcript, February 25, 1970, DSP-CGWL.

22. Simeon Booker, "Nation Mourns Dawson's Death as Capitol Flag Flies Half Mast," *Jet,* November 26, 1979, 20–27, WLDP-FUL.

23. Black businessmen in Chicago created the so-called jitney cab system because black neighborhoods received inadequate transportation services and white-owned cab companies would not hire black drivers. Because white banks would not loan black businessmen the startup capital for a profitable cab company, blacks created their own system in which individuals bought a small number of cab licenses and then leased the cars for twelve-hour periods. See "The Struggle for Existence," *Chicago Defender,* April 26, 1941, 14; "Cab Driver Loses $2,000 Damage Suit," *Chicago Defender,* November 25, 1939, 12.

24. Stone, 177–78.

25. Whitman, "Rep. William L. Dawson Dies; Served Chicago since '42,'" n.t, November 10, 1970, 46 DSP-CGWL; Eleanor L. Payne, "Dawson: Master Quiet Politician," n.t., November 14, 1970, WLDP-FUL; Simeon Booker, "Nation Mourns Dawson's Death as Capitol Flag Flies Half Mast," *Jet,* November 26, 1979, 25–27, WLDP-FUL.

26. Whitman; Eleanor L. Payne, "Dawson: Master Quiet Politician," n.t., November 14, 1970, WLDP-FUL; Simeon Booker, "Nation Mourns Dawson's Death as Capitol Flag Flies Half Mast," *Jet,* November 26, 1979, 25–27, WLDP-FUL.

27. Whitman; Warner Saunders, "William Dawson: A Really Great Man in His Time," *Chicago Defender,* December 8, 1970, 8; Booker; Ellen Hoffman, n.t, November 10, 1970, n.p., WLDP-FUL; Edward T. Clayton, *The Negro Politician* (Chicago: Johnson Publishing, 1964), 39–57.

28. Dawson's experiences with the party during these years contradict historians who have indicated that the New Deal's social welfare programs and Eleanor Roosevelt's dedication to civil rights inextricably linked black voters to the Democratic Party in the 1930s. See Nancy Weiss, *Farewell to the Party of Lincoln: Black Politics in the Age of FDR* (Princeton, N.J.: Princeton University Press, 1983), 120–36; Harvard Sitkoff, *A New Deal for Blacks: The Emergence of Civil Rights as a National Issue.* Vol. 1: *The Depression Decade* (New York: Oxford University Press, 1978), 139–69, 331–33.

29. In 1949 Dawson told an audience of Virginia blacks, "Negroes must pick their candidates with care, but then support your candidate—put your money behind him and put your vote behind him. Do that whether the candidate is black or white. Obligate them—that's one of the rules of politics. Obligate them before the election and they'll owe you something after the election." This statement is clearly indicative of

a believe in the power of the vote to shape the political will of elected officials and not a simple endorsement of the Democratic Party. "Virginia Negroes Are Urged to Concentrate on Politics By Dawson Speech Here," *Richmond Times Dispatch,* March 21, 1949, 2, WLDP-FUL.

30. William L. Dawson, Washington, D.C., to Richard M. Nixon, Washington, D.C., June 30, 1969, WLDP-FUL; Ethel L. Payne, "Dawson Tells Why He Nixed Black Paper," n.t., September 29, 1969, 2, DSP-CGWL; Larry Bryant, "'Black Eight' Rap Nixon's Domestic Policy," n.t., November 11, 1969, n.p., WLDP-FUL; N.A., "Cong. Dawson Hits HEW in Letter to President," n.t., June 10, 1969, n.p., DSP-CGWL.

31. Jervis Anderson, *A. Philip Randolph: A Biographical Portrait* (Berkeley: University of California Press, 1972), x.

1—"A Greater Understanding of Humanity"

1. Doris E. Saunders, "Black Politics and Chicago: The Bill William Story," TS, 110, DSP-CGWL.

2. Biographical Sketch, WLDP-FUL; Branham, 378; Louis Lautier, "Rep. Dawson—From Georgia Bootblack to Congressman," *Journal & Guide* October 7, 1950, 5, 10, WLDP-FUL.

3. Nunan V. Bartley, *The Creation of Modern Georgia,* 2nd ed. (Athens: University of Georgia Press, 1990), 139, 143, 147–48; Eric Foner, *Reconstruction: America's Unfinished Revolution, 1863–1877* (New York: Harper & Row, 1988), 424; Steven Hahn, *The Roots of Southern Populism: Yeomen Farmers and the Transformation of the Georgia Upcountry, 1850–1890* (New York: Oxford University Press, 1983), 194; William Warren Rogers, "A Reconstruction Referendum in Southwest Georgia: Richard Whiteley Versus Gideon Wright in 1872," *Journal of Southwest Georgia History,* 15 (2000): 3; Deton J. Brooks Jr., "Fame Brings Dawson Chance to Help," *Chicago Defender,* April 3, 1943, 13.

4. I will use the definition of southwest Georgia given by Lee W. Formwalt in "Planter Persistence in Southwestern Georgia, 1850–1870," which included Dougherty (the county in which Albany is located), Miller, Calhoun, and Mitchell Counties. See Lee W. Formwalt, "Planter Persistence in Southwestern Georgia, 1850–1870," *Journal of Southwest Georgia History,* 2 (1984): 42.

5. Saunders, 13–14.

6. Blanche Dawson Roney, to William Levi Dawson, Chicago, November 11, 1943, WLDP-FUL.

7. Indeed a history of Albany written in the 1920s lists a Judge W. W. Kendrick as one of the first justices of the Inferior Court when the Georgia state legislature formed Dougherty County in December of 1853, and this Kendrick was most likely the Judge Kendrick in question. In *History and Reminiscences of Dougherty County, Georgia* an A. S. Kendrick is listed as one of Albany's original settlers in the mid-1830s. See Daughters of the American Revolution Georgia State Society Thronateeska Chapter, *History and Reminiscences of Dougherty County, Georgia* (Albany: Daughters of the American Revolution Georgia State Society, 1924), 7, 22; Saunders, 7.

8. Blanche Dawson Roney, to William Levi Dawson, Chicago, November 11, 1943, WLDP-FUL; 1900 and 1910 Census Soundex, CS-DCPL; Leonard Farkas, to William L. Dawson, March 3, 1944, WLDP-FUL.

9. Saunders, 14. The town census listed the entire Dawson family in 1900 and 1910 as mulattoes. See 1900 and 1910 Census Soundex, CS-DCPL; Branham, 377.

10. Free blacks were a rarity in Dougherty County. In 1850 the census listed only seventeen free black males and seven free black females. Daughters of the American Revolution Georgia State Society Thronateeska Chapter, Albany, *History and Reminis-*

cences of Dougherty County, Georgia (Albany: Daughters of the American Revolution Georgia State Society, 1924), xv–xviii, 4.

11. Perhaps the power of naming worked, since the Dawson boys would go on to successes in music, medicine, and politics. See William Levi Dawson, interview by Nathaniel C. Standifer, transcript, n.d., available at www.umich.edu/~afroammu/standifer/dawson.html, Nathaniel C. Standifer Video Archive of Oral History: Black American Musicians, African American Music Collection, University of Michigan, Ann Harbor, Mich., retrieved October 6, 2006; Saunders, 6.

12. John D. Fair, "Nelson Tift: A Connecticut Yankee in King Cotton's Court," *Georgia Historical Quarterly*, 88, no. 3 (fall 2004): 338–74; Daughters of the American Revolution, Albany, 5; John D. Fair, n.a.; Daughters of the American Revolution, Albany, 72, 77; DuBois, 92; Ramsey B. Carlyle, "History of Albany State College," Ph.D. diss., Florida State University, 1973, 5; County Government of Dougherty County, Georgia, *Albany and Dougherty County Georgia: A Descriptive and Illustrated Pamphlet Issued under the Auspices of the City and Council Authorities* (Albany, Ga.: H. T. McIntosh & J. A. Davis Jr. Publishers, 1904), 7, 54.

13. Formwalt, "Planter Persistence," 48, 41; Woolfolk, 26.

14. Lee W. Formwalt, "Petitioning for Protection: A Black View of Reconstruction at the Local Level," *Georgia Historical Quarterly* 73 (1989): 309; Foner, *Reconstruction,* 70–71, 104, 163, 183–84; Paul A. Cimbala, *Under the Guardianship of the Nation: The Freedmen's Bureau and the Reconstruction of Georgia, 1865–1879* (Athens: University of Georgia Press, 1997), 2–9, 29–34, 77–79; Paul A. Cimbala, "Reconstruction's Allies: The Relationship of the Freedmen's Bureau and Georgia Freedmen," in *The Freedmen's Bureau and Reconstruction,* ed. Paul A. Cimbala and Randall M. Miller (New York: Fordham University Press, 1999), 319; Hahn, *Southern Populism,* 208; Formwalt, "Origins," 212, 214–19.

15. Formwalt, "Petitioning," 311–13; Foner, *Reconstruction,* 276, 331; Cimballa, "A Black Colony," 86; Formwalt, "Origins," 218–19; Lewis Nicholas Wynne and Milly St. Julien Vappie, "The Camilla Race Riot and the Failure of Reconstruction in Georgia," *Journal of South Georgia History* 16 (2004): 40, 42–43; Edmund L. Drago, *Black Politicians and Reconstruction in Georgia* (Baton Rouge: Louisiana State University Press, 1982), 23, 34–51; "Georgia Constitution of 1868," available at www.cviog.uga.edu/Projects/gainfo/con1868.htm, GI-CVIG, retrieved October 6, 2006; George Gordon Meade, Atlanta, Ga., to Rufus Bullock, Atlanta, Ga., October 2, 1868, available at dlg.galileo.usg.edu/camilla/cam045.php, CUCG-DLG, retrieved October 6, 2006; George Gordon Meade, Atlanta, Ga., to Ulysses S. Grant, Washington, D.C., October 3, 1868, available at dlg.galileo.usg.edu/camilla/cam044.php, CUCG-DLG, retrieved October 6, 2006; Hahn, 212–13; Hahn, *Southern Populism,* 204, 211–13; Bartley, 35, 65, 73; Charles L. Flynn Jr., *White Land, Black Labor: Caste and Class in Late Nineteenth Century Georgia* (Baton Rouge: Louisiana State University Press, 1983), 43, 53; W. Fitzhugh Brundage, *Lynching in the New South: Georgia and Virginia, 1880–1930* (Urbana: University of Illinois Press, 1993), 6.

16. Fair, n.a.; *History and Reminiscences of Dougherty County Georgia,* 62; Caleb Chase Sibley, Atlanta, Ga., to Major General Oliver Otis Howard, Washington, D.C., October 12, 1868, available at dlg.galileo.usg.edu/camilla/cam020.php, CUCG-DLG, retrieved October 6, 2006; 2005 Republican Freedom Calendar, available at policy.house.gov/2005_calendar/sep.cfm, retrieved October 6, 2006; Formwalt, "Petitioning," 306, 312; O. H. Howard, Albany, Ga., to Colonel John Randolph Lewis, Atlanta, Ga., September 20, 1868, available at dlg.galileo.usg.edu/camilla/cam016.php, CUCG-DLG, retrieved October 6, 2006; Captain William Mills, Albany, Ga., to Brigadier General R. C. Drum, Atlanta, Ga., September 29, 1868, available at dlg.galileo.usg.edu/camilla/cam021.php, CUCG-DLG, retrieved October 6, 2006; Christian Raushenberg, Albany, Ga., to Major O. H. Howard, Atlanta, Ga., September 28, 1868 available at dlg.galileo.

usg.edu/camilla/cam006.php, CUCG-DLG, retrieved October 6, 2006; "Riot at Camilla, Mitchell County," *Albany Semi-Weekly News,* available at dlg.galileo.usg.edu/camilla/cam005.php, CUCG-DLG, retrieved October 6, 2006; Flynn, 38–39; Drago, 51–56; Mary Ellen Bacon, *Albany on the Flint: Indians to Industry, 1836–1936* (Albany: Albany Town Committee of the Colonial Dames of America in the State of Georgia, 1970), 63; Foner, 343; George Gordon Meade, Atlanta, Ga., to Rufus B. Bullock, Atlanta, Ga., October 2, 1868, available at dlg.galileo.usg.edu/camilla/cam045.php, CUCG-DLG, retrieved October 6, 2006; Formwalt, "The Camilla Massacre," 402, 417–22, 425; Drago, 148–54; Hahn, *Southern Populism,* 194.

17. Drago, 161–62; Bacon, 67; Bartley, 80; Foner, 423–27, 508; Rogers, 3, 11; Johnetta Cross Brazzell, "Brick without Straw: Missionary-Sponsored Higher Education in the Post-Emancipation Era," *Journal of Higher Education* 63 (1) (1992): 29; Cimbala, *Guardianship,* 226.

18. Hahn, *Southern Populism,* 2–11, 40–49; Drago, 93–95; Flynn, 150–66; Charles Crowe, "Tom Watson, Populists, and Blacks Reconsidered," *Journal of Negro History* 55 (2) (1970): 106; Frances M. Wilhoit, "A Interpretation of Populism's Impact on the Georgia Negro," *Journal of Negro History* 52 (2) (1967): 116, 118; John Hope Franklin and Alfred A. Moss, *From Slavery to Freedom: A History of African Americans* (New York: McGraw-Hill, 1994), 257–58, 314; Sarah A. Soule, "Populism and Black Lynching in Georgia, 1890–1900," *Social Forces* 71 (2) (1992): 434; Bartley, 148–49; Bacon, 91–92.

19. W.E.B. DuBois, *Souls of Black Folk* (New York: First Vintage Books/Library of America Edition, 1990), 102; County Government of Dougherty County, Ga., 35; DAR, 320; *History and Reminiscences of Dougherty County, Georgia,* 320.

20. W.E.B. DuBois, *The Souls of Black Folk: With an Introduction by Randall Kenan* (New York: Signet Classic, 1995), 145–47.

21. Lee W. Formwalt, "Planter Persistence," 43, 46, 57.

22. Saunders, 7; *History and Reminiscences of Dougherty County, Georgia,* 65–67, 200–203, 206, 208, 210.

23. County Government of Dougherty County, Ga., 7, 17–18.

24. *History and Reminiscences of Dougherty County, Georgia,* 26, 59, 62, 141. Despite the fact that blacks outnumbered whites in Albany and the surrounding areas by over four to one. The local chapter of DAR saw fit to limit the section of the text discussing the area's black population to just under five pages—the last pages of the book. See *History and Reminiscences of Dougherty County, Georgia,* 408–11.

25. Ibid., 62. Another telling anecdote comes from a work published nearly fifty years after *History and Reminiscences.* In *Albany on the Flint,* published by the Albany Town Committee of the Colonial Dames of America, Mary Ellen Bacon wrote that no lynching had ever occurred in Albany. She pointed to the hanging of Gus Courts, an African American carpenter sentenced for murder and the first person to be hanged in Dougherty County. She noted that because the hanging had not been properly announced, the local paper lamented that only a thousand people showed up for the affair. See Bacon, 68.

26. The National Association for the Advancement of Colored People, *Thirty Years of Lynching in the United States, 1889–1918* (New York: Negro Universities Press, 1969), 10; Ida B. Wells, *Selected Works of Ida B. Wells,* comp. Trudier Harris (New York: Oxford University Press, 1991), 14, 19, 20–28; Walter White, *Rope and Faggot: A Biography of Judge Lynch* (Notre Dame, Ind.: University of Notre Dame Press, 2001), 54–81; Leon F. Litwack, "Hellhounds," introduction to *Without Sanctuary: Lynching Photography in America,* comp. James Allen (Santa Fe, N.M.: Twin Palms Press, 2000).

27. Bacon, 91–92; DuBois, 87–97.

28. Carlyle B. Ramsey, "History of Albany State College, 1903–1965," Ph.D. diss., University of Michigan, 1973, 7–8.

29. DuBois, 103–5.

30. 1900 Census Soundex, CS-DCPL; Saunders, 6.

31. The Dawson's children were as follows: Dee Potter, born February 1881; Wallace, born May 1883; Willie (William), born March 1886; Julian born March 1888; Janie May, born May 1890; Blanche, born February 1891; and Lillian born March 1894. See 1900 Census Soundex, CS-DCPL.

32. Saunders, 12–13.

33. Ibid., 13.

34. Crowe, 106.

35. Saunders, 12–13; Charles Branham, "The Transformation of Black Political Leadership in Chicago, 1864–1942," Ph.D. diss., University of Chicago, 1981, 378.

36. 1900 and 1910 Census Soundex, CS-DCPL.

37. Saunders, 15.

38. Ramsey, 9; Saunders, 20–21; James D. Anderson, *The Education of Blacks in the South, 1860–1935* (Chapel Hill: University of North Carolina Press, 1988), 240–41; Johnetta Cross Brazzell, "Brick Without Straw: Missionary-Sponsored Higher Education in the Post-Emancipation Era," *Journal of Higher Education* 63 (1) (1992): 31–32.

39. Congress, *Congressional Record: Proceedings and Debates of the 78th Congress First Session,* vol. 89, part 4, *May 14, 1943 to June 14, 1943* (Washington, D.C.: Government Printing Office, 1943), 4853; Speech given by William L. Dawson before the House of Representatives, Washington, D.C., July 3, 1956, WLDP-FUL.

40. Saunders, 22.

41. Ibid., 14–15; Standifer.

42. Edward T. Clayton, *The Negro Politician* (Chicago: Johnson Publishing, 1964), 84–85; Saunders, 17–18.

43. Joseph Winthrop Holley, *You Can't Build a Chimney from the Top: The South Through the Life of a Negro Educator* (New York: William Frederick Press, 1949), 24–25, 32–39, 42, 48, 50; Daughters of the American Revolution, 411.

44. In a Congressional speech, Dawson specifically indicated that his mother and grandmother took in laundry and cooked for whites to pay for his schooling, although the 1900 Census Soundex listed Patsy Gill as a nurse. Apparently, both Patsy Gill and Rebecca Dawson passed away by the enumeration of the 1910 census, for neither is listed. And a speech by Dawson in 1956 indicates that his mother had died in the 1900s, either just before or after he began secondary school. See Congress, *Congressional Record: Proceedings and Debates of the 78th Congress First Session,* vol. 89, part 4, *May 14, 1943 to June 14, 1943* (Washington, D.C.: Government Printing Office, 1943), 4853; Speech given by William L. Dawson before the House of Representatives, Washington, D.C., July 3, 1956, WLDP-FUL; 1900 and 1910 Census Soundex, CS-DCPL, Albany, Ga.; Speech given by William L. Dawson before the House of Representatives, Washington, D.C., July 3, 1956, WLDP-FUL; Blanche Roney, Boston, to William L. Dawson, Chicago, January 11, 1945, WLDP-FUL; Blanche Roney, Boston, to William L. Dawson, Chicago, November 1, 1945, WLDP-FUL.

45. Saunders, 15; 1910 Census Soundex, CS-DCPL.

46. Saunders, 23; Holley, 24; Deton J. Brooks Jr., "Fame Brings Dawson Chance to Help," *Chicago Defender,* April 3, 1943, 13.

47. Franklin and Moss, 312.

48. Brundage, 107–9.

49. Branham, 378.

50. Charles M. Payne, *I've Got the Light of Freedom: The Organizing Tradition and the Mississippi Freedom Struggle* (Berkeley: University of California Press, 1995), 235.

51. Biographical Sketch, WLDP-FUL; Branham, 378; Louis Lautier, "Rep. Daw-

son-From Georgia Bootblack to Congressman," *Journal & Guide* October 7, 1950, 5, 10, WLDP-FUL.

52. Darnell Hunt, "A Different World," available at www.museum.tv/archives/etv/D/htmlD/differentwor/differentwor.htm, retrieved October 10, 2006, from.

53. Charles Webster Smith, "Statistics of the College Class of '09," *Fisk Herald*, June 1909, FUL.

54. Ronald E. Butchart, "'Outthinking and Outflanking the Owners of the World': A Historiography of the African American Struggle for Education," *History of Education Quaterly*, 28 (1998): 334.

55. Joe M. Richardson, *Christian Reconstruction: The American Missionary Association and Southern Blacks, 1861–1890* (Athens: University of Georgia Press, 1986), ix, 130–35; Henry Allen Bullock, *A History of Negro Education in the South: From 1619 to the Present* (Cambridge, Mass.: Harvard University Press, 1967), 31, 76. For a similar argument regarding Baptist missionaries see Johnetta Cross Brazzell, "Bricks Without Straw: Missionary-Sponsored Higher Education in the Post-Emancipation Era," *Journal of Higher Education*, 63 (1992), 26–49; Ronald E. Butchart, "Mission Matters: Mount Holyoke, Oberlin, and the Schooling of Southern Blacks," *History of Education Quarterly* 42 (2002), 14–16; Ronald E. Butchart, "Remapping Racial Boundaries: Teachers as Border Police and Boundary Transgressors in Post-Emancipation Black Education, USA, 1861–1971," *Pedagogica Historica* 43 (2007), 76–77.

56. Joe M. Richardson, *A History of Fisk University, 1865–1946* (Tuscaloosa: University of Alabama Press, 1980), 135; Bullock, 31; Richardson, *Christian Reconstruction*, 9.

57. *Catalogue of the Officers, Students, and Alumni of Fisk University Nashville, Tennessee, 1908–1909* (Nashville: Press of Marshall & Bruce, 1909), 31–33, FUL. See also James D. Anderson, *The Education of Blacks in the South, 1860–1935* (Chapel Hill: University of North Carolina Press, 1988), 240–41; Doris E. Saunders, "Black Politics and Chicago: The Bill William Story," TS, DSP-CGWL.

58. Anderson, 240–43, 264–66.

59. "1500 Salute Veteran Solon," *The Voice*, August 9, 1964, WLDP-FUL; "William Dawson Decides He Won't Run for Re-Election," *Washington Afro-American*, November 25, 1969, WLDP-FUL.

60. Doris E. Saunders, "Black Politics and Chicago: The Bill Dawson Story," TS, DSP-CGWL, 28.

61. Charles Webster Smith, "Statistics of the College Class of '09," *Fisk Herald*, June 1909, FUL.

62. *Fisk Herald*, May 1908, 10, FUL; Saunders, 28; "Chicago Fisk Club Greets Dr. T.E. Jones," *Chicago Defender*, February 12, 1937, 6; "Dawson Sees Victory as a Sign of Loyalty," *Chicago Defender*, November 14, 1942, 3.

63. W.E.B. DuBois, *The Autobiography of W.E.B. DuBois: A Soliloquy on Viewing My Life from the Last Decade of Its First Century* (New York: International Publishers, 1968), 125.

64. William L. Dawson, *Fisk Herald*, April 1908, 17, FUL; Saunders, 31; Richardson, *A History of Fisk University*, 59.

65. William wrote, "A careful study of the deeds of those men who so lived their lives here that their influence is felt long after they have passed away reveals the fact in every case these men had some object or purpose to which all else was secondary. In some cases it was country; in others, God, but in every instance they held their possessions, their comfort, and their lives as of little consequence as compared to the welfare of the thing which they considered first. Is it wonderful that these men accomplished something which made their influence felt through the ages? Is it wonderful that the man who was willing to lay his time, his talent and his life on the altar of his country's needs exerted an influence which worked toward the advancement of his

country even after he himself has passed away?" See William L. Dawson, *Fisk Herald,* April 1908, FUL.

66. DuBois, 112.

67. Saunders, 29.

68. *Fisk Herald,* November 1908, FUL; Deton J. Brooks Jr., "Fame Brings Dawson Chance to Help," *Chicago Defender,* April 3, 1943, 13; "Dawson Sees Victory as a Sign of Loyalty," *Chicago Defender,* November 14, 1942, 3.

69. Saunders, 29.

70. William wrote, "By laborious study we seek to master the intricacies of difficult mathematical problems; with patient endeavor do we seek to assimilate the knowledge and principles of ancient Greek and Roman writers; the late hours of night find us writing away on some brief or treatise in rhetoric. And our efforts along these lines are well-directed for the mastering these things goes a long distance indeed toward fitting us for life." See William L. Dawson, *Fisk Herald,* March 11, 1908, FUL.

71. William L. Dawson, *Fisk Herald,* March 11, 1908, FUL.

72. Richardson, *A History of Fisk University,* 17; Richardson, *Christian Reconstruction,* 125–26; Brazzell, 32.

73. Richardson, *A History of Fisk University,* 16.

74. Saunders, 31; Richardson, *A History of Fisk University,* 65.

75. Saunders, 29, 32.

76. DuBois, 109–13.

77. Ibid., 31; Deton J. Brooks Jr., "Fame Brings Dawson Chance to Help," *Chicago Defender,* April 3, 1943, 13.

78. Richardson, *A History of Fisk University,* 70.

79. Corneal Davis, interview by Doris Saunders, transcript, March 11, 1970, DSP-CGWL; Deton J. Brooks Jr., "Fame Brings Dawson Chance to Help," *Chicago Defender,* April 3, 1943, 13; *Fisk Herald,* March 12, 1908, FUL; Lovett, 241; "Index to Politicians: Carey," available at politicalgraveyard.com/bio/carey.html, retrieved October 18, 2006; Saunders, 38.

80. Lovett, 128; St. Clair Drake and Horace Cayton, *Black Metropolis: A Study of Negro Life in a Northern City,* rev. ed. (Chicago: University of Chicago Press, 1993), 39; "Daniel Hale Williams," available at www.blackinventor.com/pages/danielwilliams.html, retrieved October 18, 2006; "Daniel Hale Williams," available at www.pbs.org/wnet/aaworld/reference/articles/daniel_hale_williams.html, retrieved October 18, 2006.

81. Saunders, 34; Fred Wall, interview by Doris Saunders, March 29, 1970, DSP-CGWL.

82. Saunders, 34; Fred Wall, interview by Doris Saunders, March 29, 1970, DSP-CGWL.

83. Saunders, 34–35; Adam Cohen and Elizabeth Taylor, *American Pharaoh. Mayor Richard J. Daley: His Battle for Chicago and the Nation* (Boston: Little, Brown, 2000), 58; Deton J. Brooks Jr., "Fame Brings Dawson Chance to Help," *Chicago Defender,* April 3, 1943, 13.

84. Allan Spear, *Black Chicago: The Making of a Negro Ghetto, 1890–1920* (Chicago: University of Chicago Press, 1967), 158; Saunders, 34–35.

85. Branham, 377.

86. Adam Fairclough, *Better Day Coming: Blacks and Equality, 1890–2000* (New York: Penguin Books, 2001), 91; Gerald Astor, *The Right to Fight: A History of African Americans in the Military* (Cambridge, Mass.: Da Capo Press, 2001), 108; Gail Buckley, *American Patriots: The Story of Blacks in the Military from the Revolution to Desert Storm* (New York: Random House, 2001), 184; Jack D. Foner, *Blacks and the Military in American History: A New Perspective* (New York: Praeger, 1974), 112.

87. Dawson said of his war experience, "When World War I broke out, I was about draft age. I did not have to go, but I believed then, as I believe now that when the very existence of the country in which one claims the rights of citizenship is at stake it then becomes the duty of every citizen to protect and safeguard with his life if needs be, that country from outside destruction. . . . We suffered indignities off the battlefield more devastating to our souls than the injuries in the heart of battle were to our bodies. But I have learned some lessons. I came out with a deep conviction and pride for the loyalty of Negroes to each other if they understood the problems involved; that Negroes will follow and stand firmly back of a leadership that they trust and believe in; I had seen that proved when the price of standing was possible death; that men of good will and fair play are not limited to any race or locale. Though there were thousands of Negroes in the Armed Forces and millions back home, there was not one elected Negro representative in the National government to whom our boys could tell their troubles too. I came out of the Army with a deeper faith in God; a greater understanding of humanity; a firmer belief that under our constitution, a full and free citizenship can be attained for all citizens in this country. I returned to civilian life resolved to do everything in my power to remove some of the inequalities in Word War I." See Branham, 377.

88. St. Clair Drake and Horace Cayton, *Black Metropolis: A Study of Negro Life in a Northern City*, rev. ed. (Chicago: University of Chicago Press, 1993), 8, 53; James R. Grossman, *Chicago, Black Southerners, and the Great Migration* (Chicago: University of Chicago Press, 1989), 32.

89. Christopher Robert Reed, *"All the World Is Here!" The Black Presence at the White City* (Bloomington: Indiana University Press, 2000), 14; Drake and Cayton, 8–9.

90. Drake and Cayton, 177.

91. Ibid., 176; Allan H. Spear, *Black Chicago: The Making of a Negro Ghetto, 1890–1920* (Chicago: University of Chicago Press, 1967), 14, Map 1; Thomas Lee Philpott, *The Slum and the Ghetto: Immigrants, Blacks and Reformers in Chicago, 1880–1930* (Belmont, Calif.: Wadsworth, 1991), 131–33.

92. Spear, 20–25; Philpott, xx, 150, 152–57, 159, 162.

93. Drake and Cayton, 79, 184.

94. Reed, 83.

95. Spear, 57–58; Reed, 84.

96. Spear, 59–60; Harold F. Gosnell, *Negro Politicians: The Rise of Negro Politics in Chicago* (Chicago: University of Chicago Press, 1967), 26.

97. Wallace D. Best, *Passionately Human, No Less Divine: Religion and Culture in Black Chicago, 1915–1952* (Princeton, N.J.: Princeton University Press, 2005), 10.

98. Best, 131; Spear, 64–65.

99. Spear, 71; Reed, 89.

100. Drake and Cayton, 486–87, 525; Reed, 89; Spear, 75; Robert E. Weems Jr., *Black Business in the Black Metropolis: The Chicago Metropolitan Assurance Company* (Bloomington: Indiana University Press, 1996), xii.

101. Spear, 81–82; Ottley, 1–9, 11, 127.

102. Spear, 7.

103. Drake and Cayton, 344–46; John D. Buenker, "Edward F. Dunne: The Limits of Municipal Reform," in *The Mayors: The Chicago Political Tradition*, ed. Paul M. Green and Melvin G. Holli (Carbondale: Southern Illinois University Press, 1995), 33–34; Maureen A. Flanagan, "Fred A. Busse: A Silent Mayor in Turbulent Times," in *The Mayors*, ed. Green and Holli, 53–55.

104. Drake and Cayton, 343–45.

105. Spear, 77.

106. Drake and Cayton, 346–51; Spear, 120; Reed, 89.

107. Reed, 62–63; Drake and Cayton, 260–61; Spear, 150–51; Grossman, 129.

108. Saunders, 102; Corneal Davis, interview by Doris Saunders, transcript, March 11, 1970, DSP-CGWL; Julian Dawson, Northwestern University Alumni Biographical Files, A-NUL; Deton J. Brooks Jr., "Fame Brings Dawson Chance to Help," *Chicago Defender,* April 3, 1943, 13.

109. Saunders, 102; Corneal Davis, interview by Doris Saunders, transcript, March 11, 1970, DSP-CGWL; Julian Dawson, Northwestern University Alumni Biographical Files, A-NUL; Deton J. Brooks Jr., "Fame Brings Dawson Chance to Help," *Chicago Defender,* April 3, 1943, 13.

110. Given that Dawson's hand had been rendered unsuitable for the medical profession, it is curious that he could open a tailor shop. My research yielded no answer to that mystery. See Saunders, 34, 103; William L. Dawson, law school record, A-NUL; Deton J. Brooks Jr., "Fame Brings Dawson Chance to Help," *Chicago Defender,* April 3, 1943, 13; Fred Wall, interview by Doris Saunders, March 29, 1970, DSP-CGWL.

111. Buckley, 185; J. Foner, 110–12; Mark Ellis, "W.E.B. Du Bois and the Formation of Black Opinion in World War I: A Commentary on 'The Damnable Dilemma,'" *Journal of American History* 81 (1995): 1585.

112. Astor, 108; Buckley, 184; J. Foner 112; Mark Ellis, "'Closing Ranks' and 'Seeking Honors': W.E.B. Du Bois in World War I," *Journal of American History* 79 (1992): 98, 108–110, 113; Fairclough, 93; Astor, 108; Desmond King, *Separate and Unequal: Black Americans and the U.S. Federal Government* (New York: Oxford University Press, 1995), 28–30; Gerald W. Patton, *War and Race: The Black Officer in the American Military, 1915–1941* (Westport, Conn.: Greenwood Press), 88; Ellis, "Black Opinion," 1587.

113. Buckley, 166; Deton Brooks Jr., "Dawson Won Acclaim as Both Doctor and Soldier," *Chicago Defender,* April 13, 1944, 11.

114. J. Foner, 110–11.

115. Ibid., 112.

116. Ibid., 112.

117. Hal Chase, "Struggle for Equality: Fort Des Moines Training Camp for Colored Officers," *Phylon* 39 (1978): 298.

118. Astor, 109.

119. Chase, 298–99, 302–4, 309; J. Foner, 117; Morris J. MacGregor and Bernard C. Nalty, eds., *Blacks in the United States Armed Forces: Basic Documents.* Vol. 4: *Segregation Entrenched 1917–1940* (Wilmington, Del.: Scholarly Resources, 1977), 46; Ellis, "Closing Ranks," 100.

120. Chase, 305–6; MacGregor and Nalty, 95, 101–2.

121. MacGregor and Nalty, 103; Brooks, "Dawson Won Acclaim as Both Doctor and Soldier," 11; Saunders, 105; David W. Kellum, "Dawson Is New Chief of Old 8th," *Chicago Defender,* December 21, 1940, 1; Emett J. Scott, *Scott's Official History of the American Negro in the World War* (Chicago: Homewood Press, 1919), available at www.lib.byu.edu/estu/wwi/comment/Scott/SChA1ht, World War I Document Archive, the Harold B. Library, Brigham Young University, retrieved October 11, 2006; J. Foner, 118; Branham, 377.

122. MacGregor and Nalty, 103; Brooks, "Dawson Won Acclaim as Both Doctor and Soldier," 11; Saunders, 105; Kellum, "Dawson Is New Chief of Old 8th," 1; Emett J. Scott, *Scott's Official History of the American Negro in the World War* (Chicago: Homewood Press, 1919), available at www.lib.byu.edu/estu/wwi/comment/Scott/SChA1ht, World War I Document Archive, the Harold B. Library, Brigham Young University, retrieved October 11, 2006; J. Foner, 118.

123. Chase, 306; Buckley, 178.

124. Chase, 307.

125. Ibid., 308.

126. Ibid.

127. Ibid., 309.

128. Ibid., 297, 309; Scott, appendix, available at www.lib.byu.edu/estu/wwi/comment/Scott/SChA1ht, retrieved November 11, 2006; J. Foner, 118.

129. The conflict in Houston erupted on August 23rd when black soldiers went on a rampage killing five policemen and twelve civilians. Their violence came, though, after months of racial taunts, verbal abuse, and denial of access to the town's recreational facilities. Throughout their time in Houston the soldiers of the 24th, mostly from New York City, openly defied Jim Crow. Tensions rose to a crescendo, and on August 23 a black private named Edwards attempted to stop a policeman from harassing and assaulting a local black woman. The officer responded by beating and arresting Private Edwards, and when Corporal Charles Baltimore followed standard operating procedure in investigating Edwards's arrest, the police pistol-whipped and arrested him as well. Hearing rumors of an impending white attack, the soldiers of the 24th armed themselves and marched on the jail. In an exchange of gunfire, four policemen, twelve white civilians, and two black soldiers died. Following the affair the military arrested and court-martialed sixty-four soldiers for mutiny and murder. The military sentenced forty-two to life in jail, four received long prison terms, and five obtained acquittals. In a move worthy of any contemporary Southern court, the military summarily executed thirteen of the men with no review by the war department or the president. In subsequent trials twelve more men received sentences of life in prison and sixteen more received death sentences. After reviewing their cases, however, the president commuted ten of these to life in prison; the military executed the other ten men. In total, the military indicted one hundred eighteen men. Eight eluded the indictments by testifying against the others. Nineteen men lost their lives and sixty-three men faced life in prison. Upon further review in 1921, President Harding reduced their sentences and by 1924 most had been released. See Fairclough, 94–95; J. Foner, 113–15.

130. MacGregor and Nalty, 6, 8–11, 13–16.

131. Overall, during World War I, 403,308 blacks served, with 42,000 operating in combat situations. The overwhelming majority of black combat veterans, 37,000, came from the 92nd and the 93rd divisions. The 92nd Division contained primarily draftees and officers from Fort Des Moines, while the more highly decorated 93rd possessed more volunteers and veterans from various National Guard Regiments: the 369th from New York, the 370th from Illinois, the 371st (draftee) from South Carolina, and the 372nd with troops from Washington, D.C., Maryland, Massachusetts, and Ohio.

The 92nd Division contained the 183d Infantry Brigade, the 184th Infantry Brigade, the 167th Field Artillery Brigade, and divisional troops. The 183rd Brigade held the 365th Infantry Regiment, the 366th Infantry Regiment, and the 350th Machine Gun Battalion. The 184th Infantry Brigade held the 367th Infantry Regiment, the 368th Infantry Regiment, and the 351st Infantry Regiment. The 167th Field Artillery Brigade contained the 349th Field Artillery Regiment with 75-mm. guns, the 350th Field Artillery Regiment with 75-mm guns, the 351st Field Artillery Regiment with 155-mm howitzers, and the 317th Trench/Mortar Battery. The divisional troops included the 349th Machine Gun Battalion, the 325th Field Signal Battalion, and the 317th Engineer Regiment Headquarters troop. See Buckley, 166; J. Foner 116; Arthur E. Barbeau and Henri Florette, *The Unknown Soldiers: Black American Troops in World War I* (Philadelphia: Temple University Press, 1974), 151.

132. Astor, 109.

133. Saunders, 105; Scott, appendix, available at www.lib.byu.edu/estu/wwi/comment/Scott/SChA1ht, retrieved October 11, 2006; Kellum, "Dawson Is New Chief of Old 8th," 1; Brooks, "Dawson Won Acclaim as Both Doctor and Soldier," 11.

134. Astor, 111–12.

135. Patton, 83; J. Foner, 119.

136. Patton, 86–87; Buckley, 180.

137. Barbeau and Henri, 139. White officers' dedication to maintaining their sense of superiority in one such instance allowed black officers to stay in nicer quarters. White officers in one company in the 92nd Division refused the help of their black interpreter, Captain M. Virgil Boute, and without Boute the officers could not find their rooms. Consequently, Boute installed a group of black officers in them instead. See Saunders, 107.

138. Astor, 123; J. Foner, 121; Saunders, 107; Kellum, "Dawson is New Chief of Old 8th," 1; Barbeau and Henri, 139; Patton, 87.

139. Saunders, 107.

140. Astor, 115; Patton, 89; Buckley, 163–64.

141. Astor, 123; J. Foner, 122.

142. Buckley, 183; Barbeau and Henri, 144.

143. Astor, 115; Buckley, 164–65.

144. Patton, 87; Barbeau and Henri, 139–40, 154.

145. Scott, chap. 11, available at www.lib.byu.edu/estu/wwi/comment/Scott/SCh11.htm, retrieved October 11, 2006.

146. Patton, 93–94; Barbeau and Henri, 145; Macgregor and Nalty 154; Scott, chap. 11, available at www.lib.byu.edu/estu/wwi/comment/Scott/SCh11.htm, retrieved October 11, 2006.

147. "Trench Fever," available at www.firstworldwar.com/atoz/trenchfever.htm, retrieved November 2, 2007; "Trench Foot," available at www.spartacus.schoolnet.co.uk/FWWfoot.htm, retrieved November 2, 2007; Buckley, 169.

148. Barbeau and Henri, 145; Scott, chap. 11, available at www.lib.byu.edu/estu/wwi/comment/Scott/SCh11.htm, retrieved November 2, 2007; Patton, 93–94; MacGregor and Nalty, 154.

149. Brooks, "Dawson Won Acclaim as Both Doctor and Soldier," 11.

150. Saunders, 108; "House Cheers Plea of Negro Member. Southerners Join Applause When Dawson of Illinois Ends Segregation Plea," *The New York Times*, April 13, 1951, in WLDP-FUL.

151. Barbeau and Henri, 150; MacGregor and Nalty, 155.

152. Ibid., 151–55; Scott, chap. 11, available at www.lib.byu.edu/estu/wwi/comment/Scott/SCh11.htm, retrieved November 2, 2007; Buckley, 183.

153. Barbeau and Henri, 152–53.

154. Saunders, 108; Kellum, "Dawson Is New Chief of Old 8th," 1; Corneal Davis, interview by Horace Waggoner, transcript, 1979–1982, available at www.uis.edu/archives/memoirs/DAVISCORNEALvI.pdf, retrieved November 2, 2007. In reflecting upon the impact of the 368th's collapse in the Meuse Argonne offensive Arthur E. Barbeau and Florette Henri write in *The Unknown Soldiers*, "Of all the ironies that pepper the history of black troops in the First World War, this is the sharpest: that because of the weakness of a white officer, a weakness which for the sake of white supremacy had to be covered up, black soldiers and officers were made scapegoats, their reputation for character and ability so injured in the cover-up process that it has not yet completely healed." See Barbeau and Henri, 157.

155. Scott, chap. 20, available at www.lib.byu.edu/estu/wwi/comment/Scott/SCh20.htm, retrieved November 2, 2007; MacGregor and Nalty, 177–78.

156. Barbeau and Henri, 159–60.

157. Scott, chap. 20, available at www.lib.byu.edu/estu/wwi/comment/Scott/SCh20.htm, retrieved November 2, 2007; MacGregor and Nalty, 178–80; Saunders, 108. Brigadier General Malvern Hill Barnum described the attack as follows: "The attack was executed over a very difficult terrain. For a distance of about 10 km. in front of our lines the terrain was open, heavily wired with a downward slope. It was well registered

by the enemy artillery, as the numerous shell holes over its surface indicated. The Bois Fréhaut is a wood of about 1,500 meters square and breaks over the western half of the sector attacked, about 700 meters to the east of the Bois Voivrotte, a small wood about 600 meters square. Both of these woods were a mass of heavy German wire, much of it new. Their edges were protected by bands of heavy wire and *chevaux-de-frise*. Both of these woods were at the foot of and north of the ridge of which Eon hill, a hill 358 meters high, is the summit. From their southern slopes the ground rises slightly for a distance of about 700 meters, then falls again to a deep ravine traversing the Bois Fréhaut from east to west. It then rises again, culminating in La Cote Hill, a hill 1,500 meters north of the Bois Fréhaut, namely, Hill 260.8. This hill is heavily wooded on its summit, and was strongly held by infantry, machine guns, trench mortars, and light artillery. The southern slopes of this hill were protected by a small wood about 500 meters square about 200 meters north of the Bois Fréhaut and by the strongly fortified towns of Bouxières and Champey. These towns, together with the small wood in question, were heavily garrisoned by enemy infantry and machine guns. They formed together a dominating and strongly organized position, protected by heavy bands of wire. Numerous tank traps had been prepared south of this position. . . . The lines held by the Germans were unusually strong, being the result of four years of stabilization in that sector. The artillery was most active, as unquestionably during these years they had registered on every point of importance in the sector. Furthermore, their positions were the first line of defense of Metz. The troops occupying them were young efficient men not old soldiers from a rest sector." See Scott, chap. 20, available at www.lib.byu.edu/estu/wwi/comment/Scott/SCh20.htm, retrieved November 2, 2007.

158. Scott, chap. 20, available at www.lib.byu.edu/estu/wwi/comment/Scott/SCh20.htm, retrieved November 2, 2007; MacGregor and Nalty, 181–83.

159. Patton, 96; Buckley, 184.

160. MacGregor and Nalty, 182–83; Scott, chap. 20, available at www.lib.byu.edu/estu/wwi/comment/Scott/SCh20.htm, retrieved November 2, 2007; Saunders, 108.

161. Saunders, 110.

162. Branham, 377. Dawson was not alone in this sentiment. Two of his most important lieutenants and the two men responsible for finding a place for Dawson in the Democratic Party, Christopher Wimbish and Corneal Davis also felt this way. The three men knew each other during the war, and Davis actually served under Dawson. In an interview, Davis gave the impression that three men came up with this position together as they served in France. See Corneal Davis, interview by Horace Waggoner, transcript, 1979–1982, available at www.uis.edu/archives/memoirs/DAVISCORNEALvI.pdf, Illinois General Assembly Oral History Program, Brooken Library, University of Illinois at Springfield, Springfield, Ill, retrieved November 7, 2006.

2—Big Bill, the Ironmaster, and the Old Roman

1. Doris E. Saunders, "Black Politics and Chicago: The Bill Dawson Story," TS, DSP-CGWL, 126–27.

2. Charles Branham, "The Transformation of Black Political Leadership in Chicago, 1864–1942," Ph.D. diss., University of Chicago, 1981, 75.

3. Gail Buckley, *American Patriots: The Story of Blacks in the Military from the Revolution to Desert Storm* (New York: Random House, 2001), 223–24.

4. Christopher Robert Reed, "A Study of Black Politics and Protest in Depression-Decade Chicago: 1930–1939," Ph.D. diss., Kent State University, 1982, 10–11, 130, 192–93; Christopher Robert Reed, *The Chicago NAACP and the Rise of Black Professional Leadership, 1910–1966* (Bloomington: Indiana University Press, 1997), 49–51, 61–64;

Beth Tompkins Bates, *Pullman Porters and the Rise of Protest Politics in Black America, 1925–1945* (Chapel Hill: University of North Carolina Press, 2001), 57.

5. Allan H. Spear, *Black Chicago: The Making of a Negro Ghetto, 1890–1920* (Chicago: University of Chicago Press, 1967), 120; Reed, "Black Politics and Protest," 9.

6. St. Clair Drake and Horace Cayton, *Black Metropolis: A Study of Negro Life in a Northern City,* rev. ed. (Chicago: University of Chicago Press, 1993), 109; Spear, 119.

7. Spear, 77.

8. Ibid., 121; Drake and Cayton, 346.

9. Spear, 120.

10. Spear, 141; Drake and Cayton, 58; James Grossman, *Land of Hope: Chicago, Black Southerners, and the Great Migration* (Chicago: University of Chicago Press, 1989), 4, 34; Reed, *Chicago NAACP,* x; Lizabeth Cohen, *Making a New Deal: Industrial Workers in Chicago* (Cambridge: Cambridge University Press, 1990), 34; Gareth Canaan, "'Part of the Loaf:' Economic Conditions of Chicago's African-American Working Class During the 1920's," *Journal of Social History* 35 (2001), 153; Thomas Lee Philpott, *The Slum and the Ghetto: Immigrants, Blacks and Reformers, in Chicago, 1880–1930* (Belmont, Calif.: Wadsworth, 1991), 132; Roi Ottley, *The Lonely Warrior. The Life and Times of Robert S. Abbott* (Chicago: Henry Regnery, 1955), 159; William M. Tuttle Jr., *Race Riot: Chicago in the Red Summer of 1919* (New York: Atheneum Books, 1970), 84, 90–92; Adam Cohen and Elizabeth Taylor, *American Pharaoh. Mayor Richard J. Daley: His Battle for Chicago and the Nation* (Boston: Little, Brown, 2000), 31–32; Chicago Commission on Race Relations, *The Negro in Chicago: A Study of Race Relations and a Race Riot* (Chicago: University of Chicago Press, 1922), 79; Bates, 58.

11. Philpott, 131–12; Cohen, 21.

12. Spear, 120.

13. Branham, 202; Drake and Cayton, 344; Reed, *Chicago NAACP,* 63.

14. Drake and Cayton, 344; Corneal Davis, interview by Horace Waggoner, transcript, 1979–1982, available at www.uis.edu/archives/memoirs/DAVISCORNEALvI.pdf, Illinois General Assembly Oral History Program, Brooken Library, University of Illinois at Springfield, Springfield, Ill, retrieved November 7, 2006.

15. Branham, 202; Spear, 122–23.

16. Spear, 122–23.

17. Branham, 202.

18. Drake and Cayton, 350; Branham, 202.

19. Gerald Astor, *The Right to Fight: A History of African Americans in the Military* (Cambridge, Mass.: Da Capo Press, 1998), 125; Buckley, 223–24; Astor, 125.

20. Douglas Bukowski, "Big Bill Thompson: The 'Model' Politician," in *The Mayors: the Chicago Political Tradition,* ed. Paul M. Green and Melvin G. Holli (Carbondale: Southern Illinois University Press, 1995), 72; Douglas Bukowski, *Big Bill Thompson, Chicago, and the Politics of Image* (Urbana: University of Illinois Press, 1998), 95; Cohen, 29.

21. Reed, *Chicago NAACP,* 74; Drake and Cayton, 752.

22. Astor, 125.

23. Branham, 133.

24. Ibid., 234.

25. William L. Dawson law school record, A-NUL; *Northwestern University Bulletin, School of Law 1920–1921* 21 (1920): 15–17, A-NUL.

26. Hugh Gardner, "5 Chicago Lawyers Set Record; Four Amazing Careers Spring from One Office; Death Halts Fifth. Dawson, Mollison, Wilkins Moore Began as Partners," *Chicago Defender,* March 20, 1954, 1.

27. Saunders, 123–24.

28. Ibid., 124.

29. Ibid., 121–23.

30. Ibid, 124–25.

31. Ibid., 126.

32. Ibid., 126–27.

33. Branham, 234.

34. Milton Rakove, *Don't Make No Waves, Don't Back No Losers: An Insider's Analysis of the Daley Machine* (Bloomington: Indiana University Press, 1975), 118–23; Charles Bowen, interview by author, November 1, 1999, Chicago, tape recording, City Hall, Chicago, Illinois.

35. Branham., 234.

36. Ibid., 234.

37. Ibid., 234.

38. Branham, 202.

39. Ibid., 213–15, 219; Saunders, 136.

40. Saunders, 135.

41. Corneal Davis, interview by Horace Waggoner, IGAOHP-BL.

42. "Albert George is First Negro Judge Sitting in Record Court," *Daily Northwestern*, November 12, 1924, A-NUL.

43. Saunders, 135; "Senator A. H. Roberts Pushes His Fight for Renomination," *Chicago Defender*, March 24, 1934, 3.

44. Saunders, 137–38.

45. Ibid., 137–38.

46. Drake and Cayton, 350; Branham, 227–29.

47. Drake and Cayton, 350; Branham, 229–34; Saunders, 143–44; Corneal Davis, interview by Horace Waggoner, IGAOHP-BL.

48. Branham, 233; Corneal Davis, interview by Horace Waggoner, IGAOHP-BL.

49. Drake and Cayton, 366; Spear, 190.

50. Drake and Cayton, 366–67.

51. Corneal Davis, interview by Horace Waggoner, IGAOHP-BL.

52. John R. Schmidt, "William E. Dever: A Chicago Political Fable," in *The Mayors: the Chicago Political Tradition,* ed. Paul M. Green and Melvin G. Holli (Carbondale: Southern Illinois University Press, 1995), 84–87.

53. Corneal Davis, interview by Horace Waggoner, IGAOHP-BL; Schmidt, 87.

54. Bukowski, "Big Bill Thompson The 'Model' Politician," 75.

55. Cohen, 34; Phillpott, 199–200.

56. Canaan, 149–50; Cohen, 35.

57. Canaan, 150–53, 162; Cayton and Drake, 77.

58. Branham, 75.

59. Corneal Davis, interview by Horace Waggoner, IGAOHP-BL.

60. Saunders, 146–48; "Vote the America First Ticket," (Advertisement) *Chicago Defender*, March 7, 1928, 15.

61. Saunders, 148.

62. "Jam Armory to Hear Gov. Small Speak," *Chicago Defender,* March 17, 1928, 6; "Urges Support of Madden on Record as 'A Friend,'" *Chicago Defender,* March 31, 1928, 5; "Crow-Thompson Choices 'Best Yet' Says Watkins," *Chicago Defender,* March 7, 1928; "Madden Puts Howard Bill Thru House," *Chicago Defender,* March 7, 1928, 1.

63. William Grimshaw, *Bitter Fruit: Black Politics and the Chicago Political Machine, 1931–1991* (Chicago: University of Chicago Press, 1992), 75.

64. "Jam Armory to Hear Gov. Small Speak," *Chicago Defender,* March 17, 1928, 6; "Urges Support of Madden on Record as 'A Friend,'" *Chicago Defender,* March 31, 1928, 5; "Crow-Thompson Choices 'Best Yet' Says Watkins," *Chicago Defender,* March 7, 1928; "Madden Puts Howard Bill Thru House," *Chicago Defender,* March 7, 1928, 1.

65. Drake and Cayton, 375.

66. Corneal Davis interview by Horace Waggoner, IGAOHP-BL.

67. "Chicago Has A Hectic Election Day," *Chicago Defender*, March 14, 1928, 1.

68. Branham, 379; Grimshaw, 75.

69. Saunders, 150.

70. Ibid., 152–53; Corneal Davis interview by Horace Waggoner, IGAOHP-BL; Drake and Cayton, 367.

71. Drake and Cayton, 368.

72. "Rep. Oscar DePriest Praises Record of William L. Dawson," *Chicago Defender*, February 18, 1933, 12.

73. Branham, 380; Corneal Davis, interview by Doris Saunders, written notes, March 11, 1970, DSP-CGWL.

74. Saunders, n.p.

75. A. N. Fields, "'Vote for Dawson' Is Plea of DePriest in Second Ward," *Chicago Defender*, February 25, 1933, 3; "The Record and Achievement of a Faithful Servant," (advertisement) *Chicago Defender*, February 25, 1933, 5; A. N. Fields, "'Bill' Dawson Is New Member of City Council," *Chicago Defender*, March 3, 1933, 4.

76. Fields, "'Bill' Dawson Is New Member of City Council," 4.

3—"Second Ward for the Second Warders"

1. Doris E. Saunders, "Black Politics and Chicago: The Bill Dawson Story," TS, DSP-CGWL, n.p.

2. *Tenants' War Cry*, April 17, 1937, CBP-CHS.

3. "Dawson Sees Victory as Sign of Loyalty," *Chicago Defender*, November 14, 1942, 3.

4. Roger Biles, *Big City Boss in Depression and War: Mayor Edward J. Kelly of Chicago* (DeKalb: Northern Illinois University Press, 1984), 74–84.

5. For in-depth analyses of the new black activism of the period see both: Christopher Robert Reed, "A Study of Black Politics and Protest in Depression-Decade Chicago: 1930–1939," Ph.D. diss., Kent State University, 1982 (entire); and Beth Tompkins Bates, "A New Crowd Challenges the Agenda of the Old Guard in the NAACP, 1933–1941," *American Historical Review*, 102 (1997), 344–77.

6. Paul M. Green, "Anton Cermak: The Man and His Machine," in *The Mayors: The Chicago Political Tradition*, rev. ed., ed. Paul M. Green and Melvin G. Holli (Carbondale: Southern Illinois University Press, 1995), 102; Adam Cohen and Elizabeth Taylor, *American Pharaoh: Mayor Richard J. Daley: His Battle for Chicago and the Nation* (Boston: Little, Brown, 2000), 49.

7. Green, 104.

8. Green, 104; Dick Simpson, *Rogues, Rebels, and Rubber Stamps: The Politics of the Chicago City Council from 1863 to the Present* (Boulder, Colo.: Westview Press, 2002), 91; Alex Gottfried, *Boss Cermak of Chicago: A Study of Political Leadership* (Seattle: University of Washington Press, 1962), 241.

9. St. Clair Drake and Horace Cayton, *Black Metropolis: A Study of Negro Life in a Northern City*, rev. ed. (Chicago: University of Chicago Press, 1993), 352; Biles, 89–90; Len O' Connor, *Clout: Mayor Daley and His City* (Chicago: Henry Regnery, 1975), 38; Christopher Robert Reed, "A Study of Black Politics and Protest in Depression-Decade Chicago: 1930–1939," Ph.D. diss., Kent State University, 1982, 231; Mark H. Haller, "Policy Gambling, Entertainment, and the Emergence of Black Politics: Chicago from 1900–1940," *Journal of Social History* 24 (1991), 728.

10. Gottfried, 241; Biles, 21–22.

11. Reed, "Study of Black Politics and Protest," 56–57.

12. Bates, "A New Crowd," 341; Reed, "Study of Black Politics and Protest," 194; Martha Biondi, *To Stand and Fight: The Struggle for Civil Rights in Postwar New York City* (Cambridge, Mass.: Harvard University Press, 2003), 14, 16; James Ralph, *Northern Protest: Martin Luther King, Jr., Chicago, and the Civil Rights Movement* (Cambridge, Mass.: Harvard University Press, 1993), 2.

13. Reed, "Study of Black Politics and Protest," 324; Beth Tompkins Bates, *Pullman Porters and the Rise of Protest Politics in Black America, 1925–1945* (Chapel Hill: University of North Carolina Press, 2001), 112.

14. Reed, "Study of Black Politics and Protest," 81; Bates, *Pullman Porters,* 109–10.

15. Reed, "Study of Black Politics and Protest," 157–58, 165–67, 174–75; Bates, *Pullman Porters,* 111.

16. Gottfried, 210.

17. Corneal Davis, interview by Horace Waggoner, transcript, 1979–1982, available at www.uis.edu/archives/memoirs/DAVISCORNEALvI.pdf, Illinois General Assembly Oral History Program, Brooken Library, University of Illinois at Springfield, Springfield, Ill, retrieved November 7, 2006; Reed, 91.

18. Gottfried, 177–79; Biles, 15–19; Corneal Davis, interview by Horace Waggoner, IGAOHP-BL.

19. Corneal Davis, interview by Horace Waggoner, IGAOHP-BL; Doris E. Saunders, "Black Politics and Chicago: The Bill Dawson Story," TS, DSP-CGWL, n.p.

20. Biles, 90–94; "Race Students Attend Tilden High School Prom," *Chicago Defender,* June 22, 1935, 12; Reed, "Study of Black Politics and Protest," 216, 217.

21. Reed, "Study of Black Politics and Protest," 234–36, 237, 240.

22. Reed, "Study of Black Politics and Protest," 198, 220–21.

23. John A. Rogers to unknown recipient, March 6, 1910, AWMP-CHS; Arthur Mitchell, untitled newspaper editorial, circa 1910, n.p., AWMP-CHS; "West Alabama Normal Institute Burns Down," *Geiger Times,* March 11, 1911, AWMP-CHS; "Watertown Is Sorry: For the Destruction of Alabama Institution," n.t., n.p. November 14, 1911, AWMP-CHS; "Negro Institute Closes With Credit," n.t., circa 1912, AWMP-CHS.

24. Dennis Nordin, *The New Deal's Black Congressman: A Life of Arthur Wergs Mitchell* (Columbia: University of Missouri Press, 1997), 14–15, 23–27.

25. Nordin, 32–39.

26. Arthur Mitchell to John McDuffie, Washington, D.C., January 14, 1933, AWMP-CHS; Arthur Mitchell to Harry M. Fisher, Chicago, March 11, 1933, AWMP-CHS; Arthur Mitchell to Ed Kelly, Chicago, April 14, 1933, AWMP-CHS; Arthur Mitchell to John Foscoe, Washington, D.C., June 10, 1933, AWMP-CHS; John McDuffie to James A. Farley, Chicago, June 29, 1933, AWMP-CHS; John McDuffie to James A. Farley, Chicago, September 13, 1933, AWMP-CHS; Arthur Mitchell to Clark Foreman, Washington, D.C., October 14, 1933, AWMP-CHS; Arthur Mitchell to Joseph Tittinger, Chicago, January 12, 1934, AWMP-CHS.

27. Parke Brown, "Democrats May Give DePriest Negro as Rival," *Chicago Tribune,* May 16, 1934, n.p., AWMP-CHS; Earl Dickerson to Arthur Mitchell, Chicago, April 3, 1934, AWMP-CHS; Arthur Mitchell to Earl Dickerson, Chicago, August 8, 1934, AWMP-CHS; Richey V. Graham to Arthur Mitchell, Chicago, August 3, 1934, AWMP-CHS; "Democrats Pick Flynn as County Court Candidate," *Chicago Daily Tribune,* August 4, 1934, n.p., AWMP-CHS; H. Geo. Davenport, "Democrats Pick Mitchell," *Chicago World,* August 11, 1934, n.p., AWMP-CHS; H. Geo. Davenport, "Mitchell for Congress," *Chicago World,* August 11, 1934, AWMP-CHS.

28. "'Black Belt' Is Rallying to All Democratic Candidates," *Pittsburgh Courier,* circa 1934, n.p., AWMP-CHS; Reed, 245; "Chi Democratic Boom May Menace DePriest," *Pittsburgh Courier,* August 18, 1934, n.p., AWMP-CHS; *Chicago World,* February 10, 1934,

n.p., AWMP-CHS; "Democrats to Gain Strength 2nd Ward Votes," *Chicago World,* February 24, 1934, AWMP-CHS; Reed, "Study of Black Politics and Protest," 245.

29. "Democrats Name Atty. Mitchell for Congress," n.t., circa January 1934, n.p., AWMP-CHS; John McDuffie to Arthur Mitchell, Chicago, February 7, 1934, AWMP-CHS; John McDuffie to Ed Kelly, Chicago, March 6, 1934, AWMP-CHS; John McDuffie to Patrick Nash, Chicago, March 6, 1934, AWMP-CHS.

30. Arthur Mitchell to Kelly Miller, Washington, D.C., February 3, 1933, AWMP-CHS.

31. Charles N. Wheeler, "Democrats in Big Drive to Beat DePriest," *Herald Examiner,* September 6, 1934, n.p., AWMP-CHS; Arthur Mitchell to the United States Third Assistant Postmaster, Washington, D.C., September 25, 1934, AWMP-CHS; Paul R. Leach, "Two Alabamians Stage Fight for Congress Here," *Chicago Daily News,* October 20, 1934, n.p., AWMP-CHS; "DePriest Refuses to Meet Mitchell in Open Debate," *Chicago World,* October 20, 1934, n.p., AWMP-CHS; Arthur Mitchell to Oscar DePriest, Chicago, October 26, 1934, n.p., AWMP-CHS.

32. Parke Brown, "Democrats May Give DePriest Negro as Rival," *Chicago Tribune,* May 16, 1934, n.p., AWMP-CHS; Oscar DePriest to Arthur Mitchell, Chicago, October 5, 1934, AWMP-CHS; Nordin, 56–57.

33. P. Bernard Young to Arthur Mitchell, Washington, D.C., March 1, 1935, AWMP-CHS; Arthur Mitchell to P. Bernard Young, March 2, 1935, AWMP-CHS; "Mitchell Gets Washington 'Told' On Calling Him Plain Arthur," *Chicago Defender,* January 18, 1935, n.p., AWMP-CHS.

34. "Mitchell Gets Washington 'Told' On Calling Him Plain Arthur," *Chicago Defender,* January 18, 1935, n.p., AWMP-CHS.

35. "Smart Talk from Mr. Mitchell," *The Crisis,* February 1935, 48, AWMP-CHS.

36. "'From Farm to Congress'—The Story of Mitchell," *Pittsburgh Courier,* November 7, 1942, 1 and 15, AWMP-CHS.

37. "'From Farm to Congress'—The Story of Mitchell," *Pittsburgh Courier,* November 7, 1942, 1, 15, AWMP-CHS.

38. Susan Tolchin and Martin Tolchin, *To the Victor: Political Patronage From the Clubouse to the White House* (New York: Random Books, 1971), 18; Christopher Clapham, "Clientelism and the State," in *Private Patronage and Public Power: Political Clientelism in the Modern State,* ed. Christopher Clapham (New York: St. Martin Press, 1982), 4–5.

39. Desmond King, *Separate and Unequal: Black Americans and the U.S. Federal Government* (Oxford: Clarendon Press, 1993), 9.

40. See, for examples, Arthur Mitchell to Rachel Burton, Oklahoma City, February 21, 1935, AWMP-CHS; Arthur Mitchell to Martin Menafee, Denmark, S.C. February 21, 1935, AWMP-CHS; Arthur Mitchell to Earl Dickerson, Chicago, March 6, 1935, AWMP-CHS; Arthur Mitchell to Raymond McKeough, Washington, D.C., March 6, 1935, AWMP-CHS; Arthur Mitchell to Ulysses H. Harris, Richmond, Va., March 6, 1935, AWMP-CHS; Arthur Mitchell to Arrington Helm, Washington, D.C., March 6, 1935, AWMP-CHS; Arthur Mitchell to Arthur E. Myers, Chicago, March 27, 1935, AWMP-CHS; Arthur Mitchell to S. Edward Gilbert, Sioux City, Iowa, March 28, 1935, AWMP-CHS; Claude Holman to Smith D. Wilson, Chicago, April 1, 1935, AWMP-CHS; Arthur Mitchell to Virgil W. Hodges, Atlanta, April 2, 1935, AWMP-CHS; David Bond to Arthur Mitchell, Washington, D.C., April 6, 1936, AWMP-CHS; Arthur Mitchell to Thomas Echols, Chicago, March 1, 1935, AWMP-CHS; Arthur Mitchell to W.D. Britton, Chicago, March 1, 1935, AWMP-CHS; Arthur Mitchell to Garnie Tennon, Chicago, March 1, 1935, AWMP-CHS; "Use of Politics in Relief Jobs Bared By Letter," *Chicago Daily News,* November 17, 1939, 6, AWMP-CHS.

For sarcastic examples, see Arthur Mitchell to Bernice Clark, Chicago, March 21, 1939, AWMP-CHS; Arthur Mitchell to A. L. Lucas, Chicago, April 12, 1939, AWMP-CHS.

41. H.R. 5733 called for a five-member committee with at least three black members to (1) study black economic conditions; (2) study labor problems; (3) encourage thrift and industry among blacks; (4) promote blacks' general welfare in industry; (5) work on plans concerning the welfare of the negro race; (6) work on any problem relating to blacks submitted to the committee by "any officer of the United States Government, and report a suggested solution of any and all problems that may be presented to Commission by any officer of the United States, the governor or attorney general of any of the states, or labor department of any State in the" United States; (7) make recommendations to stabilize labor in the United States; (8) discourage "subversive doctrine and propaganda," (9) formulate a policy of mutual understanding between the races; and (10) report to the Congress through the President all of the acts of the commission. H.R. 5733, AWMP-CHS.

42. Ferdinand Barnett, Chicago, to Arthur Mitchell, Washington, D.C., February 26, 1935; William Alfred, Atlanta, to Arthur Mitchell, Washington, D.C., February 26, 1935, AWMP-CHS; E. L. Powell, Charleston, Virginia, to Arthur Mitchell, Washington, D.C., February 26, 1935, AWMP-CHS; Internal Staff Document, AWMP-CHS; Alain Locke, Washington, D.C., to Arthur Mitchell, Washington, D.C., March 11, 1935, AWMP-CHS.

43. William Pickens, n.t., July 24, 1935, CBP-CHS; "Congressman Mitchell Offers Vicious Bill," *The Guardian: Michigan's Progressive Weekly*, March 9, 1935, n.p., AWMP-CHS; A. N. Fields, "Mitchell 'Industrial Commission' Bill Would Set Race Back Declares Fields," March 9, 1935, n.p., AWMP-CHS; Arthur Mitchell, Washington, D.C., to Monroe Cook, Tuskegee, Ala., March 1, 1935, AWMP-CHS; Titus Alexander, Los Angeles to Arthur Mitchell, September 30, 1938, AWMP-CHS.

44. Titus Alexander, Los Angeles, to Arthur Mitchell, September 21, 1936, AWMP-CHS; Arthur Mitchell to Titus Alexander, Los Angeles, September 21, 1936, AWMP-CHS; Edward C. Eicher, Washington, Iowa, to Arthur Mitchell, September 22, 1936, AWMP-CHS; Orville G. Johnson, Lima, Ohio, to Arthur Mitchell, September 22, 1936, AWMP-CHS; James Farley to Titus Alexander, Los Angeles, September 26, 1936, AWMP-CHS; Arthur Mitchell to Sam Rayburn, New York, September 29, 1936, AWMP-CHS.

45. Arthur Mitchell to George McDonald, Newark, Ohio, September 21, 1936, AWMP-CHS; Arthur Mitchell, to Eugene V. Gavin, Youngstown, Ohio, September 21, 1936, AWMP-CHS; Arthur Mitchell to F. B. Ransom, Indianapolis, Ind., September 21, 1936, AWMP-CHS; Arthur Mitchell to C. B. Powell, New York, September 21, 1936, Arthur Mitchell, to Eugene V. Gavin, Youngstown, Ohio, September 21, 1936, AWMP-CHS; Arthur Mitchell to F. B. Ransom, Indianapolis, Ind., September 21, 1936, AWMP-CHS; Arthur Mitchell to Claude Parsons, Colconda, Ill., September 21, 1936, AWMP-CHS; Arthur Mitchell to Paul Paver, Chicago, September 21, 1936, AWMP-CHS.

46. James Farley to Bennet Champ, St. Louis, October 7, 1936, AWMP-CHS; Henry W. Dease, Des Moines, Iowa, to Arthur Mitchell, October 17, 1936, AWMP-CHS.

47. L. L. Rodgers, Cleveland Heights, Ohio, to James Farley, September 21, 1936, AWMP-CHS; Mary Dewson, New York, to Arthur Mitchell, October 13, 1936, AWMP-CHS; Arthur Mitchell to Edgar Brown, Washington, D.C., October 15, 1936, AWMP-CHS; Davis Lee, Topeka, Kans., to Arthur Mitchell, October 17, 1936, AWMP-CHS; R.J. Reynolds, Topeka, Kans., to Arthur Mitchell, October 21, 1936, AWMP-CHS.

48. Earl Brown, New York, to Arthur Mitchell, October 6, 1935, AWMP-CHS; Arthur Mitchell to James Farley, October 7, 1936, AWMP-CHS.

49. Arthur Mitchell to F. B. Ransom, Indianapolis, Ind., September 21, 1936, AWMP-CHS. Moreover, it is important to note that James Farley, the chairman of the Democratic National Committee, did not prioritize the retention of black support. See Daniel Scroop, *Mr. Democrat: Jim Farley, the New Deal & the Making of Modern American Politics* (Ann Harbor: University of Michigan Press, 2006).

50. Biles, 92–93; "Race Students Attend Tilden High School Prom," *Chicago Defender,* June 22, 1935, 12; Reed, "Study of Black Politics and Protest," 216.

51. "Winners in Council Race," *Chicago Defender,* March 2, 1935, 2; Biles, 94; Corneal Davis, interview by Horace Waggoner, IGAOHP-BL; Reed, "Study of Black Politics and Protest," 221.

52. Biles, 49–55; Corneal Davis, interview by Horace Waggoner, IGAOHP-BL.

53. Corneal Davis, interview by Horace Waggoner, IGAOHP-BL; Biles, 57.

54. "Anderson Picked to Run for Congress," *Chicago Defender,* February 8, 1936, 3; "Candidates Fave Voters in Most Bitter Primary Since 1928," *Chicago Defender,* April 18, 1936, 1; A. N. Fields, "DePriest, Mitchell Gird for Big Battle in November," *Chicago Defender,* April 25, 1936, 12; A. N. Fields, "Flareups In Wards Mark Early Vote," April 18, 1936, 1.

55. Arthur Mitchell to Davis Lee, Baltimore, April 4, 1936, AWMP-CHS; A. N. Fields, "Mitchell Beats DePriest as Nation Reelects Roosevelt," *Chicago Defender,* November 7, 1936, 1, 2.

56. Arthur Mitchell to Louis Anderson, Chicago, October 25, 1936, AWMP-CHS; Arthur Mitchell, Washington, D.C., to Corneal Davis, Chicago, September 13, 1940, AWMP-CHS; "G.O.P. Nominees Rap New Deal in Congress Fight," *Chicago Sunday Tribune,* September 27, 1936, n.p., AWMP-CHS. To emphasize his ability to work with others Mitchell solicited appraisals from several of his congressional colleagues, and published some of their responses in his campaign materials. See for examples: Thomas O'Malley to Arthur Mitchell, March 12, 1936, AWMP-CHS; William R. Thom to Arthur Mitchell, March 14, 1936, AWMP-CHS; John McCormack to Arthur Mitchell, March 16, 1936, AWMP-CHS; Virginia B. Jenckes to Arthur Mitchell, March 14, 1936, AWMP-CHS; P.H. Drewry to Arthur Mitchell, March 12, 1936, AWMP-CHS; Carter Heslep, "Southerners Indorse Negro Seeking House Re-Election," *Washington Daily News,* April 9, 1936, n.p., AWMP-CHS; "G.O.P. Nominees Rap New Deal in Congress Fight," *Chicago Sunday Tribune,* September 27, 1936, n.p., AWMP-CHS.

57. Oscar DePriest, "DePriest Asks Harmony for G.O.P. Success," *Chicago Defender,* May 2, 1936, 12; Christopher Wimbish, "Republicans Unite," May 9, 1936, AWMP-CHS; A. N. Fields, "Mitchell Beats DePriest as Nation Reelects Roosevelt," *Chicago Defender,* November 7, 1936, 1, 2; "DePriest and Mitchell a Comparison," *Second Ward News,* May 9, 1936, n.p., AWMP-CHS; "G.O.P. Nominees Rap New Deal in Congress Fight," *Chicago Sunday Tribune,* September 27, 1936, n.p., AWMP-CHS; "Says DePriest's Job is Vacant Yet," n.t., September 9, 1936, n.p., AWMP-CHS.

58. Arthur Mitchell to James Farley, October 14, 1936, AWMP-CHS; Arthur Mitchell to Edgar C. Brown, Washington, D.C., October 15, 1936, AWMP-CHS.

59. A. N. Fields, "Mitchell Beats DePriest as Nation Reelects Roosevelt," *Chicago Defender,* November 7, 1936, 1, 2.

60. Arnold R. Hirsch, *Making the Second Ghetto: Race ad Housing in Chicago, 1940–1960* (Cambridge: Cambridge University Press, 1983), 17–18; Branham, 381; Drake and Cayton, 204.

61. Branham, 384; Saunders, n.p.

62. Corneal Davis, interview by Horace Waggoner, IGAOHP-BL; Bill Booker, Chicago, to John H. Hamilton, Washington, D.C., May 12, 1938, CBP-CHS; M. Earl Sarden, interview by Christopher Manning, tape recording, July 30, 2002, recording in possession of the interviewer, Chicago; *Tenants' War Cry,* April 17, 1937, CBP-CHS; "Dawson Opens Campaign for Re-Election," *Chicago Defender,* January 28, 1939, 7; Branham, 384.

63. Bill Booker, Chicago, to John H. Hamilton, Washington, D.C., May 12, 1938, CBP-CHS; Branham, 384; Reed, "Study of Black Politics and Protest," 76.

64. Reed, "Study of Black Politics and Protest," 324–27; M. Earl Sarden, interview by Christopher Manning, tape recording, July 30, 2002, recording in possession of the interviewer, Chicago; "Theatre Hires Race Operator After Sunday Demonstration," *Chicago Defender,* September 24, 1938, 7.

65. Saunders, n.p.

66. Corneal Davis, interview by Doris Saunders, transcript, March 11, 1970, DSP-CGWL.

67. M. Earl Sarden, interview by Christopher Manning, tape recording, July 30, 2002, recording in possession of the interviewer, Chicago.

68. "Pick Candidates for Chicago Primaries," *Chicago Defender,* February 12, 1938, 19; David W. Kellum, "Dawson Beats DePriest and Anderson," *Chicago Defender,* April 23, 1938, 1.

69. Percy Wood, "Courtney Snubs State Fair Rally of Democrats," *Chicago Tribune,* August 19, 1936, 9; Percy Wood, "Democrats Put on Peace Front at Convention," *Chicago Tribune,* September 9, 1938, 1; C. C. Wimbish to Arthur Mitchell, October 17, 1938, AWMP-CHS; C. C. Wimbish to Arthur Mitchell, October 18, 1938, AWMP-CHS; Frederick P. Wall, Chicago, to Arthur Mitchell, October 8, 1938, AWMP-CHS.

70. Reed, "Study of Black Politics and Protest," 204–9.

71. Ibid.; "House, Senate Vote 'Yes' on Housing Bill," *Chicago Defender,* July 9, 1938, 4.

72. "Theater Hires Race Operator after Sunday Demonstration," *Chicago Defender,* September 24, 1938, 7.

73. "Near Riot Results When Police Try to Halt Theater Picketing," *Chicago Defender,* October 1, 1938, 2; "Labor League Wins Fight for Race Movie Operators," *Chicago Defender,* November 12, 1938, 22; Saunders, n.p.

74. "Chicago City Council Clears Way for Housing Project," *Chicago Defender,* November 12, 1938, 2.

75. Bates, 345; Reed, "Study of Black Politics and Protest," 210.

76. Wimbish to Arthur Mitchell, October 17, 1938, AWMP-CHS; C. C. Wimbish to Arthur Mitchell, October 18, 1938, AWMP-CHS; Frederick P. Wall, Chicago, to Arthur Mitchell, October 8, 1938, AWMP-CHS; Arthur Mitchell to Peter Brady, Chicago, October 24, 1938, Wimbish to Arthur Mitchell, October 17, 1938, AWMP-CHS; C. C. Wimbish to Arthur Mitchell, October 18, 1938, AWMP-CHS; Frederick P. Wall, Chicago, to Arthur Mitchell, October 8, 1938, AWMP-CHS; Mitchell Crusaders, "Congressman Mitchell Opens Fight on Jim Crow" (advertisement), AWMP-CHS; Arthur Mitchell to William L. Dawson, November 2, 1938, AWMP-CHS; "Drive Out Mitchell the Menace," AWMP-CHS; Branham, 388; Claude Barnett, Chicago, to Joseph W. Martin, Washington, D.C., June 18, 1938, CBP-CHS.

77. David W. Kellum, "Mitchell Beats Dawson for Congress," *Chicago Defender,* November 12, 1938, 1 and 2; Reed, "Study of Black Politics and Protest," 228, 240; *Statistics of the Congressional Election of November 8, 1939,* AWMP-CHS.

78. Corneal Davis, interview by Horace Waggoner, IGAOHP-BL.

79. Ibid.

80. "Nazi Advocacy of Roosevelt's Death Charged," *Chicago Daily Tribune,* May 27, 1938, 4; Adam Lapin, "Reports of Interracial Parties Shock Probers of Un-American Activities," *Chicago Defender,* September 3, 1938, 4; "Throwing Money Away," *Chicago Defender,* September 3, 1938, 16; "Dies Committee Gets $100,000 to Push Red Inquiry," *Chicago Daily Tribune,* February 10, 1939, 9; "Dies Will Quiz U.S. Officials on Red Affiliation; Will Ask Views About Communist League," *Chicago Daily Tribune,* September 12, 1939, 9; Willard Edwards, "Dies Demands Action," *Chicago Daily Tribune,* October 24, 1939, 4; William M. Brinkley, "What the Peoples Say," *Chicago Defender,* September 24, 1938, 16; "Dies' Activity Is Blasted by Howard Group; Students Call Committee's Report

on race schools 'Vague, Misleading,'" *Chicago Defender,* December 3, 1938, 4; "Ask Dies to Investigate Ku Klux Klan; Southern Negro Youth Congress Sends Communication," *Chicago Defender,* November 11, 1939, 6; "Denounce Dies Committee as Race Baiter," *Chicago Defender,* November 4, 1939, 2; "Dies Committee Probes Race Liberals in D.C.," *Chicago Defender,* November 4, 1939, 12; Willard Edwards, "House Extends Dies Quiz by 345 to 21 Vote," *Chicago Daily Tribune,* January 24, 1940, 1; Harold Smith, "Finan, Garrity Back Moynihan in 2nd District," *Chicago Daily Tribune,* October 13, 1940, SW1; Arthur Mitchell to A. P. Anthony, Chicago, February 25, 1939, AWMP-CHS.

81. Arthur Mitchell to A. P. Anthony, Chicago, February 25, 1939, AWMP-CHS; Harold Smith, "Each New Deal Roll Call Gets Mitchell's Aye!" *Chicago Tribune,* February 7, 1940, n.p., AWMP-CHS.

82. Walter White, New York, to Arthur Mitchell, April 3, 1939, AWMP-CHS; Arthur Mitchell, to Walter White, New York, April 3, 1939, AWMP-CHS; Arthur Mitchell to H. T. Allen, Winston-Salem, S.C., May 4, 1939, AWMP-CHS; Arthur Mitchell Press Release, April 12, 1939, AWMP-CHS.

83. "Along the Political Front," *Chicago Defender,* January 28, 1939, 7; Reed, "Study of Black Politics and Protest," 251–53; Earl Dickerson, Chicago, to Arthur Mitchell, Washington, D.C., March 1, 1939, AWMP-CHS; Arthur Mitchell, Washington, D.C., to Earl Dickerson, March 3, 1939, AWMP-CHS; Arthur Mitchell to James McClendon, Chicago, March 24, 1939, AWMP-CHS; Corneal Davis, interview by Horace Waggoner, IGAOHP-BL; Biles, 98; Robert J. Blakely, with Marcus Shepard, *Earl B. Dickerson: A Voice for Freedom and Equality* (Evanston, Ill.: Northwestern University Press, 2006), 68.

84. F. H. Brown, "Mark an X For Dawson He Deserves Your Vote," *Chicago Defender,* February 18, 1939, 2; "Dickerson Is Right Man for 2nd Ward," *Chicago Defender,* February 25, 1939, 10; "Dawson Opens Campaign for Re-Election," *Chicago Defender,* January 28, 1939; "Chicago Braves Rain to End Political War," *Chicago Defender,* March 4, 1939, 1; Reed, "Study of Black Politics and Protest," 251.

85. Corneal Davis, interview by Horace Waggoner, IGAOHP-BL.

86. Biles, 98.

87. Branham, 390; Biles, 180.

88. Branham, 393.

89. Blakely, 69.

90. Reed, "Study of Black Politics and Protest," 251; Joseph Tittinger, Chicago, to Arthur Mitchell, Washington, D.C., March 10, 1938, AWMP-CHS.

91. Blakely, 68; Saunders, n.p.

92. Truman K. Gibson Jr., with Steve Huntley, *Knocking Down Barriers: My Fight for Black America* (Evanston, Ill.: Northwestern University Press, 2005), 48.

93. William J. Grimshaw, *Bitter Fruit: Black Politics and the Chicago Political Machine, 1931–1991* (Chicago: University of Chicago Press, 1992), 77.

94. Branham, 393.

95. Saunders, n.p.

96. Corneal Davis, interview by Horace Waggoner, IGAOHP-BL.

97. James McClendon, Chicago, to Arthur Mitchell, Washington, D.C., March 22, 1939, AWMP-CHS; "Intra-Party Squabble Beats Republican Vets," *Chicago Defender,* April 15, 1939, 11; Christopher Wimbish to Arthur Mitchell, October 17, 1938, AWMP-CHS; Christopher Wimbish to Arthur Mitchell, October 18, 1938, AWMP-CHS.

98. "Intra-Party Squabble Beats Republican Vets," *Chicago Defender,* April 15, 1939, 11; James McClendon, Chicago, to Arthur Mitchell, Washington, D.C., April 5, 1939, AWMP-CHS; Grimshaw, 77; Reed, "Study of Black Politics and Protest," 254.

99. Biles, 98; Corneal Davis, interview by Horace Waggoner, IGAOHP-BL.

100. Earl Dickerson to Arthur Mitchell, Washington, D.C., March 1, 1939, AWMP-CHS; Arthur Mitchell, Washington, D.C., to Earl Dickerson, Chicago, March 3,

1939, AWMP-CHS; Arthur Mitchell, Washington, D.C., to Joseph Tittinger, Chicago, March 17, 1939, AWMP-CHS; Arthur Mitchell, Washington, D.C., to Earl Dickerson, Chicago, March 27, 1939, AWMP-CHS; Earl Dickerson, Chicago, to Arthur Mitchell, March 28, 1939, AWMP-CHS.

101. Biles, 97; Thomas J. Price, Chicago, to Arthur Mitchell, Washington, D.C., May 27, 1939, AWMP-CHS; Arthur Mitchell, Washington, D.C., to Thomas J. Price, Chicago, May 29, 1939, AWMP-CHS; Arthur Mitchell, Washington, D.C., to Pat Nash, Chicago, June 27, 1939, AWMP-CHS; Arthur Mitchell, Washington, D.C., Joseph Tittinger, Chicago, June 27, 1939, AWMP-CHS; Arthur Mitchell to 2nd Ward Precinct Captains, August 25, 1939, AWMP-CHS.

102. Reed, 259, 262; "Mayor 'Killing' 1940 Ticket 6,500 'Boo' Dawson Ward Captains Join Demonstration," *The 2nd Ward Political News*, December 21, 1939, 1, AWMP-CHS; Perry C. Thompson, Chicago, to James Farley, February 7, 1940, AWMP-CHS.

103. Blakely, xvi, 34–36.

104. "Aldermen Hear About Housing on South Side," *Chicago Defender*, July 15, 1939, 24; "Dickerson Asks More U.S. Homes for Chicagoans," *Chicago Defender*, March 2, 1940, 11.

105. Biondi, 5–6, 9–10.

106. "South Side School Probe Asked of City," *Chicago Defender*, June 3, 1939, 7; "WPA Strikers Caught in Middle as Government Action Threatens Jobs," *Chicago Defender*, July 15, 1939, 2; Willard Edwards, "Beat Roosevelt; Slash WPA: House Clips 150 Millions Off Bill, Then Passes It," *Chicago Daily Tribune (1872–1963)*, January 14, 1939, www.proquest.com/, retrieved July 31, 2008; "Asks Council to Assist in WPA Protest," *Chicago Defender*, July 22, 1939, 4; Hollis A. Woods, "Say Job Discrimination Causes Races Problems," *Chicago Defender*, June 1, 1940, 8; John H. Johnson, "Dickerson Wins First Skirmish for Race at Traction Ordinance Hearing," *Chicago Defender*, January 25, 1941, 7; "The Program of Alderman Dickerson," *Chicago Defender*, November 4, 1939, 14.

107. Johnson, "Dickerson Wins First Skirmish for Race at Traction Ordinance Hearing," 7; Diana Briggs, "Citizens Storm City Hall to Hear Dickerson Champion Traction Jobs," *Chicago Defender*, February 15, 1941, 12; "The Program of Alderman Dickerson," *Chicago Defender*, November 4, 1941, 14.

108. "Colorado Column," n.t, February 24, 1940, n.p., AWMP-CHS.

109. Lewis A.H. Caldwell, "Lewis A.H. Caldwell's Commentary," *Chicago Daily Defender*, December 3, 1958, A8.

110. Biles, 99.

111. Joseph Tittinger, Chicago, to Arthur Mitchell, Washington, D.C., November 11, 1939, AWMP-CHS; Arthur Mitchell, Washington, D.C., to James McClendon, Chicago, December 30, 1939, AWMP-CHS; Arthur Mitchell, Washington, D.C, to Harrison Young, Chicago, December 30, 1939.

112. Branham, 411.

113. M. Earl Sarden, interview by Christopher Manning.

114. Corneal Davis, interview by Horace Waggoner, IGAOHP-BL.

115. Charles N. Wheeler, "2nd Ward Gets a New Boss of Patronage," *Chicago Daily News*, November 14, 1939, n.p., AWMP-CHS; "Dickerson for Congress Group Is Organized," *Chicago Bee*, February 11, 1940, n.p. AWMP-CHS; "Colorado Column," n.t, February 24, 1940, n.p., AWMP-CHS; Earl B. Dickerson, "The Race and the 1940 Election," *Chicago Defender*, January 27, 1940, 13.

116. "Jourdain Speaks to Fraters," *Pittsburgh Courier*, February 17, 1940, n.p., AWMP-CHS; "Legislators Renominated; Torrence Wins," *Chicago Defender*, April 20, 1940, 7, AWMP-CHS.

117. Arthur Mitchell, Washington, D.C., to Corneal Davis, Chicago, September

19, 1940, AWMP-CHS; Arthur Mitchell, Washington, D.C., to William Dawson, Chicago, September 19, 1940, AWMP-CHS.

118. Nordin, 117.

119. Arthur Mitchell, Washington, D.C., to J. E. Mitchell, St. Louis, August 28, 1940, AWMP-CHS; "Developments in Politics," *Louisville Leader*, August 31, 1940, AWMP-CHS; Arthur Mitchell, Washington, D.C., to J. L. Marshall, East St. Louis, Ill., September 6, 1940, n.p., AWMP-CHS; "Internal War Hits Democrats," *Washington Afro-American*, September 7, 1940, n.p., AWMP-CHS; Joseph P. Coles, Detroit, to Arthur Mitchell, September 7, 1940, AWMP-CHS; Luke Tiller, Detroit, to Arthur Mitchell, Washington, D.C., September 7, 1940, AWMP-CHS; Luther C. Keith, Detroit to Arthur Mitchell, Washington, D.C., September 7, 1940, AWMP-CHS; Louis R. Taylor, Detroit, to Arthur Mitchell, Washington, D.C., September 8, 1940, AWMP-CHS; Arthur Mitchell, Washington, D.C., to Joseph P. Coles, Detroit, September 13, 1940, AWMP-CHS.

120. Arthur Mitchell, Washington, D.C, to Ed Kelly, Chicago, February 14, 1940, AWMP-CHS; "Negroes Still for Roosevelt," *St. Louis Argus*, February 9, 1940, n.p., AWMP-CHS; St. Clair Drake and Horace Cayton, *Black Metropolis: A Study of Negro Life in a Northern City*, rev. ed. (Chicago: University of Chicago Press, 1993), 355; "Developments in Politics," *Louisville Leader*, August 31, 1940, n.p., AWMP-CHS.

121. "Developments in Politics," *Louisville Leader*, August 31, 1940, n.p., AWMP-CHS; "Bishop Wright Here for Democratic Conference," *Chicago Defender*, September 28, 1940, 2.

122. C. Cecil Craigne, "Race Democrats Bolt Thompkins; Set Up Opposing Organization," *Chicago Defender*, July 27, 1940, 5; "Internal War Hits Democrats," *Washington Afro-American*, September 7, 1940, n.p., AWMP-CHS.

123. Grimshaw, 79; Blakely, 86.

124. "These Candidates Emerged Victorious in Primary Election," *Chicago Defender*, April 25, 1942, 13.

125. Grimshaw, 79.

126. Blakely, 87.

127. Earl Dickerson campaign flyer, BBP-CGWL.

128. Earl Dickerson campaign flyer, BBP-CGWL.

129. *People's Voice*, April 11, 1942, 3, BBP-CGWL.

130. *The Voice*, March 14, 1942, 1, Ben Burns Papers, BBP-CGWL.

131. *The Voice*, March 14, 1942, 1, BBP-CGWL.

132. Truman Gibson Jr., interview by author, February 25, 2000, tape recording, Chicago; Grimshaw, 79.

133. Saunders, DSP-CGWL, n.p.

134. *The Voice*, March 14, 1942, 1, BBP-CGWL; *The Voice*, March 21, 1942, 4, BBP-CGWL; *Chicago Defender*, October 17, 1942, 3, BBP-CGWL.

135. Clayton, 56.

136. Associated Negro Press, "Dawson Elected to House Seat Vacated by Mitchell," *Atlanta Daily World*, November 10, 1942, n.p., AWMP-CHS; William Dawson, Chicago, to Arthur Mitchell, Washington, D.C., November 7, 1942, AWMP-CHS; Arthur Mitchell, Washington, D.C., to William Dawson, Chicago, November 16, 1942, AWMP-CHS.

4—A New Era in the Political Life of the Nation

1. Gunnar Myrdal, *An American Dilemma: The Negro Problem and Modern American Democracy* (New York: Harper & Brothers, 1944), 505.

2. Nancy Weiss, *Farewell to the Party of Lincoln: Black Politics in the Age of FDR* (Princeton, N.J.: Princeton University Press, 1983), xiii, 3–7, 120–36, 299–300; Desmond

King, *Separate and Unequal: Black Americans and the US Federal Government* (Oxford: Clarendon Press, 1995), 7; St. Clair Drake and Horace Cayton, *Black Metropolis: A Study of Negro Life in a Northern City, 4th ed.* (Chicago: University of Chicago Press, 1993), 369; Harvard Sitkoff, *A New Deal for Blacks: The Emergence of Civil Rights as a National Issue.* Vol. 1: *The Depression Decade* (New York: Oxford University Press, 1978), 18–19, 139–69, 331–33, 335.

3. Weiss, xiii, 3–7, 120–36; Desmond King, *Separate and Unequal: Black Americans and the US Federal Government* (Oxford: Clarendon Press, 1995), 7; St. Clair Drake and Horace Cayton, *Black Metropolis: A Study of Negro Life in a Northern City, 4th ed.* (Chicago: University of Chicago Press, 1993), 369; Sitkoff, 18–19, 139–69, 331–33.

In the political biographies of Democratic presidential candidates Franklin Roosevelt, Harry Truman, Adlai Stevenson, and John F. Kennedy, for example, scholars cover party tensions over race issues in great detail. However, the party's black leaders, William Dawson, Adam Clayton Powell Jr., and Charles Diggs are rarely factored into the conversation. See, for example: *Roosevelt: The Party Leader* by Sean J. Savage, *Man of the People: A Life of Harry S. Truman* by Alonzo L. Hamby, *Harry S. Truman: A Life* by Robert H. Ferrell, *Adlai Stevenson and American Politics: The Odyssey of a Cold War Liberal* by Jeff Broadwater, *Adlai Stevenson: His Life and Legacy* by Porter McKeever, *Prophet in Politics: Henry Wallace and the War Years, 1940–1965* by Edward L. and Frederick H. Schapsmeier, and *John F. Kennedy and the Second Reconstruction* by Carl M. Brauer. Except for Donald R. McCoy's and Richard T. Reuten's *Quest and Response: Minority Rights and the Truman Administration*, civil rights scholars have not done much better. In *Freedom Bound*, Robert Weistbrot, for instance, pays little attention to black efforts to affect Democratic racial policy until he discusses the Mississippi Freedom Democratic Party's effort to challenge the regular Mississippi delegation in 1964.

4. Harvey, a former social worker and fireman, won the primary, and Dickerson actually came in third behind the Republican candidate despite his well-known and widely respected protest leadership.

Charles Branham, "The Transformation of Black Political Leadership in Chicago, 1864–1942," Ph.D. diss., University of Chicago, 1981, 444; Roger Biles, *Big City Boss in Depression and War: Mayor Edward J. Kelly of Chicago* (DeKalb: Northern Illinois University, 1984), 101; "Runoffs Set for Aldermen on South Side," *Chicago Defender*, March 6, 1943, 4; "Everybody Goes When the Wagon Comes," *Chicago Defender*, April 17, 1943, 21.

5. Though aware of the importance of being the nation's only black congressman, Dawson did not intend to let himself become too comfortable in Washington, D.C. He did not bring his family, and he did not purchase or rent a home. Instead, he stayed with his mother-in-law and sister-in-law. He generally refrained from taking part in social activities with Washington's black elite, preferring to stay at home with a mystery novel and good jazz record. Mrs. Brown encouraged him, though, to accept an invitation by the Mu-So-Lit Club for their regular poker game, and Dawson finally gave in. The next morning Mrs. Brown asked her son-in-law how he did, and, unsmiling, he replied "Not too bad." All along Dawson had begged off from the invitations saying that the stakes were too high. Now Mrs. Brown feared he had lost saying, "Oh, Bill I shouldn't have let you go!" "But you did," he replied as he put a roll of bills on the table and suggested that she go shopping. The Mu-So-Lits invited him once more thinking Dawson had a case of beginner's luck, but Mrs. Brown got another shopping trip out of it. The invitations stopped after that. Little did the Mu-So-Lits know that Dawson and the other soldiers played poker to wile away many hours in the trenches of France.

Nellie certainly wished to make more of a life in Washington, D.C. It was her home after all, and she had not taken well to Chicago. As she put it, "the ignorance and the lack of culture and refinement were too much." Years before her husband became a congressman, Nellie would beg him to make a career in Washington. But, Nellie said, he did not feel that he had a future there and that Chicago "was where he could do the job he had to do." Staying in Chicago frayed Nellie's nerves, but her husband was cold and unsympathetic, telling her, "Nell, your father and mother shielded you too much. You're not fitted to cope with reality." See Doris E. Saunders, "Black Politics and Chicago: The Bill Dawson Story," TS, DSP-CGWL, n.p., 127.

6. Saunders, n.a.; John McCormack to Arthur Mitchell, March 16, 1936, AWMP-CHS.

7. Christopher Robert Reed, *The Chicago NAACP and the Rise of Black Professional Leadership, 1910–1966* (Bloomington: Indiana University Press, 1997), 187.

8. Edward Clayton, *The Negro Politician* (Chicago: Johnson Publishing, 1964), 56.

9. Walter Christmas, *Negroes in Public Affairs*, vol. 1 (Yonkers, N.Y.: Educational Heritage, 1966), 104; U.S. Congress, *Congressional Record: Proceedings and Debates of the 78th Congress First Session*, vol. 89, part 4 *May 14, 1943 to June 14, 1943* (Washington, D.C.: Government Printing Office, 1943), 4843–44, 4853, 4889; U.S. Congress, *Congressional Record Proceedings and Debates of the 79th Congress First Session*, vol. 91, part 1, *January 3, 1945 to February 23, 1945* (pp. 1–1402) (Washington, D.C.: Government Printing Office, 1945), 18; U.S. Congress, *Congressional Record Proceedings and Debates of the 79th Congress First Session Index*, vol. 91, part 7, *September 11, 1945 to October 18, 1945* (pp. 8467–9822) (Washington, D.C.: Government Printing Office, 1945), 9463; U.S. Congress, *Congressional Record Proceedings and Debates of the 79th Congress First Session*, vol. 91, part 6, *July 2, 1945 to September 10, 1945* (pp. 7105–8466) (Washington, D.C.: Government Printing Office, 1945), 7484; "Dawson in Washington," *The Voice*, February 6, 1943, 1, WLDP-FUL; Katherine Shryver, to William L. Dawson, February 12, 1946, WLDP-FUL: Isabelle Graham, "William L. Dawson, Democrat, Incumbent, 60; Seeking Third Term," *CS*, October 29, 1946, n.p., WLDP-FUL; "Poll-Tax Filibusters Win Fresh Stall on Bill. Hearing on Constitutionality Is Recessed Until Next Week," *PM*, October 27, 1953, n.p., WLDP-FUL; Transcript of a speech given by William L. Dawson before the United States House of Representatives, May 26, 1944, WLDP-FUL; Brenda Gayle Plummer, *Rising Wind: Black Americans and U.S. Foreign Affairs, 1935–1960* (Chapel Hill: University of North Carolina Press, 1996), 178–18; Penny Von Eschen, *Race against Empire: Black Americans and Anticolonialism, 1937–1957* (Ithaca, N.Y.: Cornell University Press, 1997), 5, 85–95, 120; *Chicago Defender*, February 25, 1950, 1, 3; U.S. Congress, *Congressional Record Proceedings and Debates of the 79th Congress First Session*, vol. 91, part 7, *July 2, 1945 to September 10, 1945* (pp. 7105–8466) (Washington, D.C.: Government Printing Office, 1945), 7484; Transcript of a speech given by William L. Dawson before the U.S. House of Representatives, May 26, 1944, WLDP-FUL; Venice T. Spraggs, "New Life Given FEP by House Appropriation," *Chicago Defender*, June 14, 1945, 4; William L. Dawson, Washington, D.C., to Harry S Truman, June 6, 1945, WLDP-FUL; McCoy and Reutten, 23–25; Ruchames, 138.

10. U.S. Congress, *Congressional Record: Proceedings and Debates of the 78th Congress First Session*, vol 89, Part 4, *May 14, 1943 to June 14, 1943* (Washington, D.C.: Government Printing Office, 1943), 700–702; Lloyd Stanwick, "DAWSON DOES IT!—Defeats Dies Committee in Effort to Oust Pickens," *The Voice*, February 13, 1945, 1, WLDP-FUL; "Dawson Defends Pickens in First House Address," *Chicago Defender*, February 13, 1943; Transcript of a speech, entitled "A Case for William Pickens a Plea for Democracy for an Underprivileged People," given by William L. Dawson before the House of Representatives, February 8, 1943, WLDP-FUL; Venice T. Spraggs, "William (Bill) Dawson's Rise—Democracy on the March," *Chicago Defender*, January 8, 1949, WLDP-FUL.

11. Phineas Indritz, letter to the American Veterans Committee, March 25, 1958, WLDP-FUL; U.S. Congress, *Congressional Record Proceedings and Debates of the 78th Congress Second Session*, vol. 90, part 2, *February 9, 1944 to March 21, 1944* (pp. 1445–2870) (Washington, D.C.: Government Printing Office, 1944), 2703; U.S.

Congress, *Congressional Record Proceedings and Debates of the 79th Congress First Session Index*, vol. 91, part 14 *January 3, 1945 to December 21, 1945* (Washington, D.C.: Government Printing Office, 1945), 900, 941; "Congressman Dawson's Bill Seeks Causes of Racial Tensions," *Chicago Defender*, March 25, 1944, 1.

12. Branham, 444.

13. David Robertson, *Sly and Able: A Political Biography of James F. Byrnes* (New York: W.W. Norton, 1994), 349; "Dawson Talks to Roosevelt on Demo. Plank. Chicago Congressman Goes to White House for Conference," *Chicago Defender*, July 15, 1944, 1 and 2; "Wallace Rips Poll Tax! Race Issue Ties Up Demos," *Chicago Defender*, July 22, 1944, 1 and 2.

14. Sean J. Savage, *Roosevelt: The Party Leader, 1932–1945* (Lexington: University Press of Kentucky, 1991), 175–97; Harold Gosnell, *Truman's Crises: A Political Biography of Harry S Truman* (Westport, Conn.: Greenwood Press, 1980), 179; Robertson, 4.

15. Harold Gosnell, *Truman's Crises: A Political Biography of Harry S. Truman*. (Westport, Conn.: Greenwood Press, 1980), 180; St. Clair Drake and Horace R. Cayton, *Black Metropolis: A Study of Negro Life in a Northern City*, rev. ed. (Chicago: University of Chicago Press, 1993), 359; "Dawson Talks to Roosevelt on Demo. Plank. Chicago Congressman Goes to White House for Conference," *Chicago Defender*, July 15, 1944, 1 and 2; Robertson, 355.

16. Savage, 179; Edward L. Schapsmeier and Frederick H. Schapsmeier, *Prophet in Politics: Henry A. Wallace and the War Years, 1940–1965* (Ames, Iowa: Iowa State University Press, 1970), 102; Gosnell, 180.

17. Gosnell, 100, 103–5.

18. Robertson, 4–5, 300–18.

19. Ibid., 6–7, 333, 335; "To Oppose U.S. Bench for Sen. James Byrnes," *Chicago Defender*, February 1, 1941, 4; John Hope Franklin and Alfred A. Moss, *From Slavery to Freedom: A History of African Americans*, 7th ed. (New York: McGraw-Hill, 1994), 437.

20. Savage, 181–82; Drake and Cayton, 333, 353–54.

21. Sitkoff, 84; Weiss, 27–28, 180–81.

22. "Democratic Leaders Urge 4th Term for Roosevelt," *Chicago Defender*, April 3, 1944, 1 and 3.

23. "Democratic Leaders Urge 4th Term for Roosevelt," *Chicago Defender*, April 3, 1944, 1 and 3.

24. Fred Atwater, "GOP Platform Makes Bid for Negro Vote," *Chicago Defender*, July 1, 1944, 1; Bob Armstrong, New York, to Stephen Early, September 28, 1944, WLDP-FUL.

25. Robertson, 349.

26. Robertson, 350; "Dawson Talks to Roosevelt on Demo. Plank. Chicago Congressman Goes to White House for Conference," *Chicago Defender*, July 15, 1944, 1 and 2; "Wallace Rips Poll Tax! Race Issue Ties Up Demos," *Chicago Defender*, July 22, 1944, 1 and 2.

27. George F. Wilson and J. Berger, eds., *Official Report of the Proceedings of the Democratic National Convention, held at Chicago, Illinois, July 19th to July 21st, inclusive, 1944, resulting in the re-nomination of Franklin D. Roosevelt of New York For President and the nomination of Harry S Truman of Missouri For Vice-President* (Chicago: Publicity Division of the Democratic National Committee, 1944), 14 and 15.

28. "Wallace Rips Poll Tax! Race Issue Ties Up Demos," *Chicago Defender*, July 22, 1944, 1 and 2.

29. The pledges they wanted included (1) a permanent FEPC; (2) abolition of the poll tax; (3) antisegregation legislation; (4) correction of black mistreatment in the armed forces; and (5) open Democratic primaries. See "Wallace Rips Poll Tax! Race Issue Ties Up Demos," *Chicago Defender*, July 22, 1944, 1 and 2.

30. "Democrats Hear Negro Wishes from NAACP Head," *The Black Dispatch,* July 29, 1944, 1, WLDP-FUL; "Wallace Rips Poll Tax! Race Issue Ties Up Demos," *Chicago Defender,* July 22, 1944, 1 and 2.

31. Wilson and Berger, 94; Louis Martin, "Dawson Opened the Door for Black Politicians," *Chicago Daily Defender,* October 14, 1970, 3, WLDP-FUL.

32. Richard Durham, "Democrats Face a Bolt By Negro Voters," *Chicago Defender,* July 29, 1944, 1 and 4.

33. "Wallace Rips Poll Tax! Race Issue Ties Up Demos," *Chicago Defender,* July 22, 1944, 1 and 2.

34. Robertson, 350; "Dawson Talks to Roosevelt on Demo. Plank. Chicago Congressman Goes to White House for Conference," *Chicago Defender,* July 15, 1944, 1 and 2; Schapsmeier and Schapsmeier, 106.

35. Wilson and Berger, 79.

36. Schapsmeier and Schapsmeier, 106.

37. "Wallace Rips Poll Tax! Race Issue Ties Up Demos," *Chicago Defender,* July 22, 1944, 1 and 2.

38. Schapsmeier and Schapsmeier, 106; Wilson and Berger, 193.

39. Robertson, 349–53, 355, 357.

40. Ibid., 355.

41. Doris E. Saunders, "The Day Dawson Saved America from a Racist President," *Ebony,* July 1, 1972, 42–48.

42. Robertson, 355; Saunders, "The Day Dawson Saved America," 49.

43. Robertson, 591.

44. "Wallace Rips Poll Tax! Race Issue Ties Up Demos," *Chicago Defender,* July 22, 1944, 1 and 2; Biles, 130

45. Robertson, 360; Fred Atwater, "Dixie Beats Wallace; Truman Seeks Votes: Winning Smile for Backers," *The Chicago Defender* (National Edition), July 29, 1944; www.proquest.com/, retrieved January 27, 2008.

46. Robertson, 359.

47. *Jackson Advocate,* April 1, 1950, 2, WLDP-FUL; Phineas Indritz, letter to the American Veterans Committee, March 25, 1958, Dawson Papers, WLDP-FUL; "Dawson to Direct Political Campaign," paper unknown, circa 1944, CBP-CHS; *Chicago Defender,* September 12, 1944, 1.

48. Bob Armstrong, New York, to Stephen Early, September 28, 1944, WLDP-FUL; Louis Martin, "Dawson Opened the Door for Black Politicians," *Chicago Daily Defender,* WLDP-FUL; "Dawson to Direct Political Campaign," paper unknown, circa 1944, CBP-CHS.

49. Fred Atwater, "GOP Platform Makes Bid for Negro Vote," *Chicago Defender,* July 1, 1944, 1.

50. Richard Durham, "FDR against Jim Crow–Dawson," *Chicago Defender,* August 19, 1944, 1 and 4.

51. John D'Emilio, *Lost Prophet: The Life and Times of Bayard Rustin* (Chicago: University of Chicago Press, 2003), 144.

52. Joe W. Trotter and Earl Lewis, eds., *African Americans in the Industrial Age: A Documentary History, 1915–1945* (Boston: Northeastern University Press, 1996), 250–51; Louis Ruchames, *Race, Jobs, and Politics: The Story of the FEPC* (New York: Columbia University Press, 1953), 12–23; Trotter and Lewis, 251.

53. Trotter and Lewis, 250–51; Plummer, 85; George H. Roeder, *The Censored War: American Visual Experiences During World War II* (New Haven, Conn.: Yale University Press, 1993), 47; Christopher Robert Reed, *The Chicago NAACP and the Rise of Professional Black Leadership, 1910–1966* (Bloomington: Indiana University Press, 1997), 118.

54. Reed, *The Chicago NAACP,* 118.

55. Robert J. Blakely, *Earl B. Dickerson: A Voice for Freedom and Equality* (Evanston, Ill.: Northwestern University Press, 2006), 116–22; "Fair Employment Practice Committee Calls on President," *Chicago Defender,* September 13, 1941, 13; "F.D. Orders U.S. to Stop Job Discrimination; All Government Branches Told to Forget Color of Workers' Skin," *Chicago Defender,* September 13, 1941, 13.

56. "Gas Company Opens Its Doors to Negroes," *Chicago Defender,* December 18, 1943, 12; "Score Green for Defeat of FEPC Bill in Senate," *Chicago Defender,* May 26, 1945, 18; "Illinois FEP Bill May Pass," *Chicago Defender,* June 16, 1945, 13; "Vote on State Job Bill Shows GOP Opposition," *Chicago Defender,* June 23, 1945, 5; "Silent Vote Kills Illinois FEPC," *Chicago Defender,* July 7, 1945, 6.

57. Congress, *Congressional Record Proceedings and Debates of the 78th Congress Second Session,* vol. 90, part 1, *January 10, 1944 to February 8, 1944* (pp. 3–1444), 368; Reed, 118; Richard Durham, *Chicago Defender,* November 10, 1945, 1.

58. *Chicago Defender,* February 13, 1942, 1; "Urges Negro OCD Training in Florida," *Chicago Defender,* August 29, 1942, 4; "Calls U.S. Draft Laws Impractical for South," *Chicago Defender,* September 5, 1942, 15; "Save White Man, Draft Negro—Dixie Solon," *Chicago Defender,* September 26, 1942, 5; "Anti-Negro Agitation," *Chicago Defender,* December 12, 1942, 14; Harry McAlpin, "Draft to Take 600,000 In '43," *Chicago Defender,* March 20, 1943, 1; "This Is News! Dixie Solon Flays Race Discrimination," *Chicago Defender,* November 27, 1943, 1; John LeFlore, "Draft Boards Breaking Up Families in Dixie as Boards Induct All Available Negroes," *Chicago Defender,* December 18, 1943, 3; Truman Gibson Jr., interview by author, February 25, 2000, tape recording, Chicago.

59. Truman Gibson Jr., interview by author, February 25, 2000, tape recording, Chicago.

60. "Truman Gibson Gets Medal of Merit Award," *Chicago Defender,* September 22, 1945, 1, 3.

61. "A. Philip Randolph," *Chicago Defender,* February 8, 1941, 14; A. Philip Randolph, "The Randolph Plan," *Chicago Defender,* March 15, 1941, 14; "Other Papers Say," *Chicago Defender,* April 12, 1941, 14.

62. Deton Brooks Jr., "Stimson's Removal Is Demanded By Dawson," *Chicago Defender,* March 4, 1944, 1, 4; Steve Huntley, *Knocking Down Barriers: My Fight for Black America* (Evanston, Ill.: Northwestern University Press, 2005), 129–37.

63. Congress, *Congressional Record Proceedings and Debates of the 78th Congress Second Session,* vol. 90, part 2, *February 9, 1944 to March 21, 1944* (pp. 1445–2870) (Washington, D.C.: Government Printing Office, 1944), 2703.

64. "Congressman Dawson's Bill Seeks Causes of Racial Tensions," *Chicago Defender,* March 25, 1944, 1.

65. Phineas Indritz, letter to the American Veterans Committee, March 25, 1958, WLDP-FUL.

66. U.S. Congress, *Congressional Record Proceedings and Debates of the 79th Congress First Session Index,* vol. 91, part 14 *January 3, 1945 to December 21, 1945* (Washington, D.C.: Government Printing Office, 1945), 900, 941.

67. Richard Durham, "FDR against Jim Crow–Dawson," *Chicago Defender,* August 19, 1944, 1 and 4.

68. Ruchames, 101–6; Drake and Cayton, 359.

69. Drake and Clayton, 359.

70. Schapsmeier and Schapsmeier, 115; "Wallace Gets Warm Welcome at Chicago FDR Rally," *Chicago Defender,* November 4, 1944, 13; Edwina Harleston, "Wallace Gets Wild Welcome at Chicago Rally," *Chicago Defender,* November 4, 1944, 1.

71. Grimshaw, 68; Drake and Cayton, 360.

72. Arnold R. Hirsch, *Making the Second Ghetto: Race and Housing in Chicago 1940–1960* (Cambridge: Cambridge University Press, 1983), 20–26.

73. Biles, 135, 158.

74. "Airport Homes," *Chicago Defender*, November 30, 1946, 14; "Mayor Assures Vet Protection," *Chicago Defender*, 5; Hirsch, 219.

75. Hirsch, 219–20; Biles, 135, 146–47; J. S. Fuerst, *When Public Housing Was Paradise: Building Community in Chicago* (Urbana: University of Illinois Press, 2005), 134; William Grimshaw, *Bitter Fruit: Black Politics and the Chicago Political Machine, 1931–1991* (Chicago: University of Chicago Press, 1992), 58–59, 82–85.

76. Louis Martin, "Chicago's $64 MILLION Question," *Chicago Defender*, May 14, 1948, 1; Grimshaw, 58–59, 82–85; Hirsch, "Martin H. Kennelly," 140.

77. "The Struggle for Existence," *Chicago Defender*, April 26, 1941, 14; "Cab Driver Loses $2,000 Damage Suit," *Chicago Defender*, November 25, 1939, 12; Complaint for injunction in *Bertel W. Diagre, et al vs Carter Harrison Collector of Internal Revenue Service*, November 1, 1942, WLDP-FUL; Unspecified legal document, March 4, 1943, WLDP-FUL; IRS legal document, May 6, 1942, WLDP-FUL.

78. "Begin to Tighten Control on Taxis," *Chicago Defender*, March 29, 1947, 5; "Continue Fight over Taxi Nuisance Case," *Chicago Defender*, February 28, 1948, 3; "Round-Up," *Chicago Defender*, September 3, 1949, 5; Felton Bridgewater, "People Want the Jitneys," *Chicago Defender*, December 24, 1950, 12; M. J. Ramsey, "Keep Those Jitneys!" *Chicago Defender*, September 2, 1950, 6; Aaron Price and Laura Jordan, "Dangers in Slums," *Chicago Defender*, November 4, 1950, 6; Calloway Ferguson, "He's for the Jitneys," *Chicago Defender*, January 20, 1951, 6; Helen Miller, "Stop Whitewashing," *Chicago Defender*, January 27, 1951; James Spears, "Let Jitneys Alone," *Chicago Defender*, March 10, 1950, 6; "Groups Seek End of Illegal Jitney Cabs," *Chicago Defender*, April 7, 1951, 3.

79. Hirsch, 130.

80. Ibid., 101–2, 111–13.

81. Ibid., 113.

82. Ibid., 115–25.

83. Fay, "Fay Says," *Chicago Defender*, February 26, 1949, 14; Albert Barnett, "More Housing Projects, Few Individual Homes," *Chicago Defender*, March 5, 1949, 7; "Dr. J. B. Martin Raps Defeat of Housing Bill," *Chicago Defender*, March 12, 1949, 2.

84. See, for example, Arnold Hirsch's extensive examination of the early development of public housing: *Making the Second Ghetto*. Hirsch's generally excellent work is unsure of how to characterize Dawson's reactions to slum removal. On the one hand, Hirsch recognizes the extreme disagreement within Chicago's black community regarding the merits of slum removal and public housing. He also indicates that a Dawson-led effort to block the process "in all probability, would have been futile." Nevertheless, he frequently scores Dawson for not leading a movement against slum renewal. Given these contradictory assessments, Hirsch should have provided an example of a protest movement that could have succeeded in the circumstances at hand. Hirsch, 128, 130, 133, 150–51.

85. Walter Christmas, *Negroes in Public Affairs*, vol. 1 (Yonkers, N.Y.: Educational Heritage, 1966), 104; U.S. Congress, *Congressional Record: Proceedings and Debates of the 78th Congress First Session*, vol. 89, part 4, *May 14, 1943 to June 14, 1943* (Washington, D.C.: Government Printing Office, 1943), 4,843–4,844, 4,853, 4,889; U.S. Congress, *Congressional Record Proceedings and Debates of the 79th Congress First Session*, vol. 91, part 1, *January 3, 1945 to February 23, 1945* (pp. 1–1402) (Washington, D.C.: Government Printing Office, 1945), 18; U.S. Congress, *Congressional Record Proceedings and Debates of the 79th Congress First Session Index*, vol. 91, part 7, *September 11, 1945 to October 18, 1945* (pp. 8,467–9,822) (Washington, D.C.: Government Printing Office, 1945), 9,463; U.S. Congress, *Congressional Record Proceedings and Debates of the 79th Congress First Session*, vol. 91, part 6, *July 2, 1945 to September 10, 1945* (pp. 7,105–8,466) (Washington, D.C.:

Government Printing Office, 1945), 7,484; "Dawson in Washington," *The Voice,* February 6, 1943, 1, WLDP-FUL; Katherine Shryver to William L. Dawson, February 12, 1946, WLDP-FUL; Isabelle Graham, "William L. Dawson, Democrat, Incumbent, 60; Seeking Third Term," *CS,* October 29, 1946, n.p., WLDP-FUL; Ruchames, 90, 93–96; Transcript of a speech given by William L. Dawson before the U.S. House of Representatives, May 26, 1944, WLDP-FUL; *Chicago Defender,* February 25, 1950, 1, 3; U.S. Congress, *Congressional Record Proceedings and Debates of the 79th Congress First Session,* vol. 91, part 7, *July 2, 1945 to September 10, 1945* (pp. 7,105–8,466) (Washington, D.C.: Government Printing Office, 1945), 7,484; Transcript of a speech given by William L. Dawson before the U.S. House of Representatives, May 26, 1944, WLDP-FUL; Venice T. Spraggs, "New Life Given FEP by House Appropriation," *Chicago Defender,* June 14, 1945, 4; William L. Dawson, Washington, D.C., to Harry S Truman, June 6, 1945, WLDP-FUL; Donald R. McCoy and Richard T. Reuten, *Quest and Response: Minority Rights and the Truman Administration* (Lawrence: University Press of Kansas, 1973), 23–25; Ruchames, 138; Congress, *Congressional Record Proceedings and Debates of the 78th Congress Second Session,* vol. 90, part 1, *January 10, 1944 to February 8, 1944* (pp. 3–1444), 368; Reed, 118; Richard Durham, *Chicago Defender,* November 10, 1945, 1.

86. "Gas Company Opens Its Doors to Negroes," *Chicago Defender,* December 18, 1943, 12; "Score Green for Defeat of FEPC Bill in Senate," *Chicago Defender,* May 26, 1945, 18; "Illinois FEP Bill May Pass," *Chicago Defender,* June 16, 1945, 13; "Vote on State Job Bill Shows GOP Opposition," *Chicago Defender,* June 23, 1945, 5; "Silent Vote Kills Illinois FEPC," *Chicago Defender,* July 7, 1945, 6; William H. Harefield, "From Our Readers," *Chicago Defender,* March 23, 1974, 10.

87. Hirsch, 248–49; "Housing Issue Stirs Ruckus at City Hall," *Chicago Defender,* March 4, 1950, 3; Albert Barnett, "Chicago Takes Lead in Building Low Cost Homes," *Chicago Defender,* March 18, 1950, 7; "Hunt for Homes on in Chicago," *Chicago Defender,* October 10, 1950, 11; "Council Unit Approves Mackleman," *Daily Defender,* September 17, 1950, 2.

88. *Chicago Defender,* October 12, 1946, 1.

89. "Vote For Your Rights, an Editorial," *The Chicago Defender* (National Edition), October 19, 1946, 1 www.proquest.com/, retrieved February 19, 2008.

90. A cartoon next to the article drove home the uncertainty surrounding black votes. A GOP elephant wearing a king's attire and holding a piece of paper with the words "liberalism or reaction?" looks questioningly at a sphinx-like statue labeled the "Unpredictable black vote." Referring to the shifts in black voting habits, the elephant exclaims, "Things ain't what they used to be!" Meanwhile the elephant does not seem to notice a dagger labeled 1948 hanging over its head. Nor does he see a scroungy, but hopeful-looking, white man, labeled "the solid south," lurking in the background. The cartoon backed up Sengstacke's argument in the article, which indicated black support not for the Democratic Party, but for the New Deal, regardless of the party that kept it going. See John Sengstacke, *Chicago Defender,* January 1, 1947, 18.

91. McCoy and Reuten, 98; Roy Wilkins, *Standing Fast* (New York: Viking Press, 1982), 200.

92. Drake and Cayton, 359; McCoy and Reuten, 15–19.

93. Harvard Sitkoff, "Harry Truman and the Election of 1948, The Coming of Age of Civil Rights in American Politics," *Journal of Southern History* 37 (November 1971): 615–16.

94. McCoy and Reuten, 47–52.

95. Sitkoff, 269; Hamby, 366, 447; Ferrel, 268–69.

96. McCoy and Reuten, 92.

97. Plummer, 182.

98. Schapsmeier and Schapsmeier, 117; Hamby, 434; McCoy and Reuten, 98–99.

99. Hamby, 435; McCoy and Reuten, 99.

100. McCoy and Reuten, 100.

101. Hamby, 435; McCoy and Reuten, 99–102.

102. McCoy and Reuten, 123.

103. Hamby, 445.

104. The Humphrey-Biemiller-Murray plank asked Congress to help the President bring about "(1) the right of full and equal political participation; (2) the right to equal opportunity of employment; (3) the right of security of person; and (4) the right of equal treatment in the service and defense of our nation." See Brown, 535.

105. Ibid., 178–94.

106. Ibid., 535.

107. Ibid., 210.

108. "Southern Rebels Beaten Twice in Rights Fight," *Chicago Defender,* July 17, 1948, 1 and 2.

109. "Southern Rebels Beaten Twice in Rights Fight," *Chicago Defender,* July 17, 1948, 1 and 2.

110. McCoy and Reuten, 127; "Southern Rebels Beaten Twice in Rights Fight," *Chicago Defender,* July 17, 1948, 1 and 2.

111. Ferrel, 274.

112. McCoy and Reuten, 128, 138–39; Ferrel, 273–74.

113. McCoy and Reuten, 140.

114. *Chicago Defender,* March 25, 1950, 1, WLDP-FUL; *Daily News,* March 23, 1950, 4, WLDP-FUL.

115. American Bar Association, "William Henry Hastie (1904–1976)," available at www.abanet.org/publiced/bh_hastie.html, retrieved December 30, 2006; William Hastie, Interview by Jerry N. Hess, March 1, 1977, Transcript, Oral History Project, Truman Library, Independence, Mo.; McCoy and Reuten, 140.

116. Martha Biondi, *To Stand and Fight: The Struggle for Civil Rights in Postwar New York City* (Cambridge, Mass.: Harvard University Press, 2003), 144; Corneal Davis, interview by Horace Waggoner, IGAOHP-BL; John Sengstacke, "Let's Put Up or Shut Up," *Chicago Defender,* July 17, 1948, 1; Louis Martin, *Chicago Defender,* August 7, 1948, 1; "Leaders to Help Raise Funds for Demo Campaign," *Chicago Defender,* July 24, 1948, 1; Louis Martin, "Million Dollar Truman Fund," *Chicago Defender,* August 7, 1948, 1.

117. Louis Martin, *Chicago Defender,* August 7, 1948, 1; R. O'Hara Lanier, Houston, Texas, to William L. Dawson, September 3, 1948, TP-TL.

118. "Leaders to Help Raise Funds for Demo Campaign," *Chicago Defender,* July 24, 1948, 1; "Set $50,000 Chicago Goal for Truman," *Chicago Defender,* September 11, 1948, 7; "Man Donates $1,000, Woman $5 to Truman," *Chicago Defender,* August 21, 1948; "1948—Honor Roll—1948. *Defender* Cites 17 Citizens, 9 Groups on 1948 Honor Roll," *Chicago Defender,* January 8, 1949, 1.

119. Ferrel, 268.

120. Hamby, 464–65; Ferrel, 282–83.

121. Edward Clayton, *The Negro Politician* (Chicago: Johnson Publishing, 1964), 76; McCoy and Reuten, 144.

122. David W. Kellum, *Chicago Defender,* November 6, 1948, 1.

123. Corneal Davis, interview by Horace Waggoner, IGAOHP-BL; Harry S Truman, Washington, D.C., to William L. Dawson, November 9, 1948, WLDP-FUL; *Daily News,* March 23, 1950, 4, WLDP-FUL.

124. Harry S Truman, Washington, D.C., to Corneal Davis, Chicago, October 28, 1950, TP-TL.

125. Harry S Truman, Washington, D.C., to William L. Dawson, July 28, 1952, WLDP-FUL.

126. Corneal Davis, interview by Horace Waggoner, IGAOHP-BL; Harry S Truman, Washington, D.C., to William L. Dawson, September 24, 1952, WLDP-FUL.

127. William L. Dawson, Washington, D.C., to Harry S Truman, May 8, 1970, WLDP-FUL; Donald S. Dawson, Washington, D.C., to William L. Dawson, January 17, 1953, WLDP-FUL.

128. Alice Dunnigan, *Philadelphia Tribune*, January 8, 1949, n.p., WLDP-FUL; *Daily News*, March 23, 1950, 4, WLDP-FUL; *Chicago Defender*, January 8, 1949, n.p., WLDP-FUL; James D. Ewing, *Daily Commercial*, January 29, 1949, n.p., Dawson Papers, WLDP-FUL.

129. Walter Christmas, *Negroes in Public Affairs*, vol. 1 (Yonkers, N.Y.: Educations Heritage, 1966), 104; "Wipe Out Race and Creed Barriers for Truman Inaugural Events," *Chicago Defender*, December 4, 1948, 2.

130. King, 3, 12–16; Wil Haygood, *King of the Cats: The Life and Times of Adam Clayton Powell, Jr.* (Boston: Houghton-Mifflin, 1993), 116; Emilio, 143.

131. Phineas Indritz, to the American Veterans Committee, March 25, 1958, WLDP-FUL.

132. James D. Ewing, *Daily Commercial*, January 29, 1949, n.p., WLDP-FUL; *Daily News*, March 23, 1950, 4, WLDP-FUL; John Sengstacke, *Chicago Defender*, January 29, 1949, 6.

133. King, 3–4, 24.

134. The so-called rule of three, for instance, stipulated that a government office could select one person from the top three applicants without giving any justification; if an applicant, however, made it to the top tier for the same job on three occasions without being chosen, that applicant could no longer apply for the job. The rule maintained the appearance of equal opportunity by showing that qualified blacks had made it to the top tier of many selection processes. In practice though, the rule of three kept blacks out of the civil service. Blacks who ranked high in the hiring process felt encouraged to try again should the position be open in the future, but three failures prohibited them from reapplying. See King, 55–56, 108.

135. Venice T. Spraggs, "Dawson Fights Winning Battle for Equal Rights: Illinois Democrat Foremost Champion of Negro Cause," *Chicago Defender*, November 2, 1946, 1, 2; "Third of Chicago Jobs to Dawson," *Chicago Defender*, December 11, 1948, 1; Louis Lautier, "The Capital Spotlight," paper unidentifiable, n.p., WLDP-FUL; Al Sweeney, "Rambling Reporter," *Washington Afro-American*, March 4, 1950, n.p., WLDP-FUL; Roi Ottley, "Truman's New Black Cabinet. Politics Replaces Idealism as Dawson Takes over and Installs Loyal Democrats," *Ebony*, August 1, 1949, 15.

136. A. N. Fields, "Dawson Pledges Anew His Fight for Rights," *Chicago Defender*, October 30, 1948, 1 and 2; Clayton, 84.

137. Susan Tolchin and Martin Tolchin, *To the Victor: Political Patronage From the Clubhouse to the White House* (New York: Random Books, 1971), 18.

138. Christopher Clapham, "Clientelism and the State," in *Private Patronage and Public Power: Political Clientelism in the Modern State*, ed. Christopher Clapham (New York: St. Martin Press, 1982), 4–5.

139. Desmond King, *Separate and Unequal: Black Americans and the U.S. Federal Government* (Oxford: Clarendon Press, 1993), 9.

140. Percy P. Cruezot, New Orleans, to William L. Dawson, August 22, 1950, WLDP-FUL; E. Vincent Suitt, Buffalo, N.Y., to William L. Dawson, April 25, 1952, WLDP-FUL.

141. Victor R. Daly, Washington, D.C., to William L. Dawson, June 2, 1952, WLDP-FUL.

142. Walter White, to William L. Dawson, April 3, 1950, Dawson Papers, File 13, Box 2, Archives, Fisk University Library, Fisk University, Nashville, Tenn.; Louis Martin, to William L. Dawson, WLDP-FUL.

143. Jean M. Capers, Cleveland, Ohio, to William L. Dawson, January 24, 1952, WLDP-FUL.

144. Clayton, 84.

145. Charles Branham, "The Transformation of Black Political Leadership in Chicago, 1864–1942," Ph.D. diss., University of Chicago, 1981, 120, 263.

146. Walter White, *Chicago Defender*, February 2, 1946, 17; Albert Anderson, "Strengthen Dawson's Power in Making Political Appointments," *Gary American*, March 31, 1950, 7, WLDP-FUL; Roi Ottley, "Truman's New Black Cabinet. Politics Replaces Idealism as Dawson Takes Over and Installs Loyal Democrats," *Ebony*, August 1, 1949, 15.

147. This transition is similar to the one Charles Branham documents in *The Transformation of Black Political Leadership in Chicago, 1864–1942*, where he contends that one of the first hard-fought contests in Chicago between black Republican and black Democratic candidates for aldermen marked a turning point in the professionalization of black politics at the local level, for neither of the candidates could run solely on race based appeals. See Branham, 120.

148. It is important to note that the initial appeals for help from those who sent Dawson letters of thanks are not contained within his files. This omission means that the Dawson papers do not keep close tabs on all of the individuals whom Dawson aided from start to finish, and it is most likely that there were more people who received appointments through Dawson's efforts than is indicated by the dozen or so letters of thanks in his papers.

See, for example, Helen Bell, to William L. Dawson, August 28, 1949, WLDP-FUL; M.J. Sleet, to William L. Dawson, January 10, 1951, WLDP-FUL; Hortense and Milton Young, Louisville, Ky., to William L. Dawson, September 27, 1964, WLDP-FUL; Grace Marshall Osten, Washington, D.C., to William L. Dawson, December 23, 1947, WLDP-FUL; Mrs. Ruth Beverly Whitson, Arlington, Va., to William L. Dawson, October 27, 1962, WLDP-FUL; William C. Hall, to William L. Dawson, May 18, 1949, WLDP-FUL; Robert Boyle, to William L. Dawson, April 11, 1949, Dawson File, TP-TL; Robert Boyle, to William L. Dawson, March 2, 1950, Dawson File, TP-TL; Robert Boyle, to William L. Dawson, March 17, 1950, Dawson File, TP-TL.

149. "Jurists Honor Herman Moore, Federal Judge," *Chicago Defender*, May 26, 1945, 8; Venice T. Spraggs, "Irvin C. Mollison Named to Federal Court Bench," *Chicago Defender*, October 13, 1945, 1; "President Congratulates New U.S. Judge," *Chicago Defender*, October 13, 1945, 10; "Chicagoans Witness Historic Ceremony," *Chicago Defender*, November 10, 1945, 7; Earl Conrad, "Mollinson Sworn In as First Federal Judge," November 10, 1945, 1; Harry Keane, "Dawson's Record Shows Great Value to Race," *Chicago Defender*, October 2, 1948, 1, 3; Al Sweeney, "Rambling Reporter," *Washington Afro-American*, March 4, 1950, n.p., WLDP-FUL; *Washington Post*, May 12, 1950, n.p., WLDP-FUL; Helen Laville and Scott Lucas, "The American Way: Edith Sampson, the NAACP, and African American Identity in the Cold War," *Diplomatic History* 20 (Fall 1996): 572; Herman Moore, to William L. Dawson, June 25, 1952, WLDP-FUL; "In His Rise, He Has Taken Others with Him," *Chicago Defender*, November 4, 1950, 25; Truman Gibson Jr., interview by author, February 25, 2000, tape recording, Chicago.

150. Walter Christmas, *Negroes in Public Affairs*, vol. 1 (Yonkers, N.Y.: Educational Heritage, 1966), 104; Phineas Indritz, to the American Veterans Committee, March 25, 1958, WLDP-FUL; Clayton, 84; "Dawson Levels Blast at Foes in Campaign Talk," *Chicago Defender*, October 10, 1956, 3.

151. Weiss, 234; John Hope Franklin and Alfred A. Moss Jr., *From Slavery to Freedom: A History of African Americans*, 7th ed. (New York: McGraw-Hill, 1994), 356, 465; McCoy and Reuten, 158; Waldo E. Martin, *Brown v. Board of Education: A Brief History with Documents* (Boston: Bedford Books, 1998), 21; John Dittmer, *Local People: The Struggle for Civil Rights in Mississippi* (Urbana: University of Illinois Press, 1994), 25; Charles D. Hadley, "The Transformation of the Role of Black Ministers and Black Political

Organizations in Louisiana Politics," in *Blacks in Southern Politics,* ed. Laurence W. More-land, Robert P. Steed, and Tod A. Baker (New York: Praeger, 1987), 133–34, 136; McCoy and Reuten, 156. Also see McCoy and Reuten, chap. 5.

152. "Virginia Negroes Are Urged to Concentrate on Politics by Dawson Speech Here," *Richmond Times Dispatch,* March 21, 1949, 2, WLDP-FUL; *Richmond Afro-American,* December 18, 1948, n.p., WLDP-FUL.

153. Ibid.

154. Speech given by William L. Dawson before the graduating class of University of Virginia University, Charlottesville, June 2, 1953, WLDP-CHS.

155. "Virginia Negroes Are Urged to Concentrate on Politics By Dawson Speech Here," *Richmond Times Dispatch,* March 21, 1949, 2, WLDP-FUL.

156. "Congressman Tells Negroes to 'Get Smart, Not Mad,'" *Cleveland Plain Dealer,* September 26, 1949, 24, WLDP-FUL.

157. "Dawson Thrills 800 Dallasites," *Texas Edition of the Call,* May 4, 1951, 1, WLDP-FUL; "Dawson Thrills 800 Dallasites," *Dallas Express,* May 5, 1951, 1, WLDP-FUL.

In 1953 he gave a similar message to the graduating class of University of Virginia that anyone who allowed their votes to be bought had sold their most sacred birthright for a mere "mess of potage." Then the defeatists, appeasers, and disfranchisers swoop in crying, "Politics is dirty!" Yet this argument did not excuse anyone from the political process, Dawson claimed, because complaining about political corruption only furthered blacks' political isolation. Any institution could become corrupt when controlled by the wrong people. See Speech given by William L. Dawson before the graduating class of University of Virginia, Charlottesville, June 2, 1953, WLDP-CHS.

158. "Dawson Thrills 800 Dallasites," *Texas Edition of the Call,* May 4, 1951, 1, WLDP-FUL; "Dawson Thrills 800 Dallasites," *Dallas Express,* May 5, 1951, 1, WLDP-FUL.

159. Clayton, 84.

160. Clayton, 84; Speech given before the North Carolina Regional Council of Negro Leadership, May 2, 1953, WLDP-FUL; "Virginia Negroes Are Urged to Concentrate on Politics by Dawson in Speech Here," *Richmond Times-Dispatch,* March 21, 1949, 2, WLDP-FUL; "Mississippi Regional Council of Negro Leadership Reveals New Approach to Problems of Negro Life in the State: Cong. Dawson Cites Value of Voting and Political Participation at the State and Local Levels," *Jackson Advocate,* May 10, 1952, 1, WLDP-FUL.

161. Dittmer, 19, 31–34.

162. "Mississippi Regional Council of Negro Leadership Reveals New Approach to Problems of Negro Life in the State. Cong. Dawson Cites Value of Voting and Political Participation at the State and Local Levels," *Jackson Advocate,* May 10, 1952, 1, WLDP-FUL.

163. Charles Payne, *I've Got the Light of Freedom* (Berkeley: University of California Press, 1995), 123–24, 174; Robert Weisbrot, *Freedom Bound: A History of America's Civil Rights Movement* (New York: Penguin Books, 1991), 53–54.

5—A Dream Deferred

1. John Sengstacke, "Kennedy Predicts Split of North-South Democrats," *Chicago Defender,* November 10, 1957, 1.

2. Mattie Colon Smith, "The Political Door," *Chicago Defender,* May 5, 1962, 2.

3. Desmond King, *Separate and Unequal: Black Americans and the US Federal Government* (Oxford: Clarendon Press, 1995), 26.

4. Exclusive or major committees were those committees whose work was so

central to the running of the government that their members could not be members of any other committee. These committees included: Ways and Means, Appropriations, and Rules. Dan Rostenkowski, interview by author, January 5, 2000, tape recording, Chicago; King, 24.

5. "Dawson Slated for Key Chairmanship in Congress," *Chicago Defender,* November 13, 1948, 1; "Even South May Back Dawson!" *Chicago Defender,* November 20, 1948, 6; "Dawson's New Post," *Chicago Defender,* December 25, 1948, 6; James Free, *The New York Times,* March 12, 1956, n.p., WLDP-FUL; Louis Lautier, *Journal and Guide,* October 7, 1950, 10, WLDP-FUL; Venice Spraggs, "William Bill Dawson's Rise—Democracy on the March," *Chicago Defender,* January 8, 1949, 13; Transcript of a speech given by John McCormack before the U.S. House of Representatives, March 22, 1956, WLDP-FUL.

6. Harry Ploski and Roscoe C. Brown, *Negro Almanac* (New York: Bell Weather, 1967), 468; U.S. Congress, *Congressional Record Proceedings and Debates of the 87th Congress,* vol. 107, part 4, *March 16, 1961, to April 6, 1961* (pp. 4095–5510), (Washington, D.C.: Government Printing Office, 1961), 4,923; Louis Lautier, *Journal and Guide,* October 7, 1950, 10, WLDP-FUL; *Chicago Defender,* October 27, 1951, 1; "National Grapevine," *Chicago Defender,* August 3, 1957, 2; U.S. Congress, *Congressional Record Proceedings and Debates of the 87th Congress,* vol. 107, part 4, *March 16, 1961, to April 6, 1961* (pp. 4,095–5,510) (Washington, D.C.: Government Printing Office, 1961), 4,923; Walter Christmas, *Negroes in Public Affairs,* vol. 1 (Yonkers, N.Y.: Educational Heritage, 1966), 105; U.S. Congress, *Congressional Record Proceedings and Debates of the 91st Congress Second Session,* vol. 116, part 29, *November 24, 1970, to December 3, 1970* (pp. 38,593–39,928) (Washington, D.C.: Government Printing Office, 1970), 39, 395.

7. Lucius J. Barker and Mack H. Jones, *African Americans and the American Political System,* 3rd ed. (Englewood Cliffs, N.J.: Prentice Hall, 1994), 251.

8. Dan Rostenkowski, interview by author, January 5, 2000, tape recording, Chicago; Sydney Yates, interview by author, January 12, 2000, notes, via telephone call to Washington, D.C.

9. I could find only two pieces of evidence pointing to any civil rights accomplishments by the committee. Indritz writes that in 1957 Dawson issued a CGO investigative report "concerning the reservoir projects of the Department of the Army and the Department of the Interior, in which he stressed the importance of including a non-discrimination clause in all leases, licenses and concession agreements for public recreational use of federal lands." Responding to Dawson's report the U.S. Bureau of Land Management, the Army Corps of Engineers, and the U.S. Bureau of Land Reclamation all issued departmental directives to enact nondiscrimination clauses in their respective jurisdictions. Phineas Indritz, letter to the American Veterans Committee, March 25, 1958, WLDP-FUL.

10. In discussing the upcoming presidential election *Defender* reporter, Richard Durham, asked blacks to consider their voting power carefully as the "the Negro vote will be a balance of power in 1944 and will cast the deciding ballot." The *Defender* also published election outcomes, which traced black support for Dewey and Roosevelt, in major black centers like Detroit and Philadelphia. See *Chicago Defender* (undated) WLDP-FUL; *Chicago Defender,* September 9, 1944, WLDP-FUL; *Chicago Defender,* September 16, 1944, WLDP-FUL; *Chicago Defender,* September 23, 1944, WLDP-FUL; *Jackson Advocate,* April 1, 1950, 1, WLDP-FUL; Louis Lautier article, Archives, WLDP-FUL; Richard Durham, *Chicago Defender,* August 19, 1944; *Jackson Advocate,* April 1, 1950, 2, WLDP-FUL; Phineas Indritz, letter to the American Veterans Committee, March 25, 1958, WLDP-FUL.

11. *Chicago Defender,* 1950, Archives, WLDP-FUL.

12. Osburn Zuber, *Birmingham Post,* WLDP-FUL; Al Sweeney, *Washington Afro-American,* March 4, 1950, WLDP-FUL.

13. *Chicago Daily Tribune,* February 23, 1950, pt. 4, 10, WLDP-FUL; Joseph Hearst, *Washington Times Herald,* February 23, 1950, n.p., WLDP-FUL; *Chicago Defender,* February 25, 1950, 1 and 5, WLDP-FUL; *Chicago Defender,* March 4, 1950, 6, WLDP-FUL; *Pittsburgh Courier,* March 4, 1950, n.p., WLDP-FUL; *Washington Afro-American,* February 28, 1950, 1, WLDP-FUL; Al Sweeney, *Washington Afro-American,* March 4, 1950, n.p., WLDP-FUL; James L. Hicks, *Washington Afro-American,* April 4, 1950, n.p., WLDP-FUL.

14. "Promises vs. Performance," *Chicago Defender,* March 4, 1950, n.p., WLDP-FUL.

15. *Chicago Defender,* ca. 1950, n.p., WLDP-FUL; *Chicago Defender,* ca. 1950, n.p., WLDP-FUL; John O'Donnell, *Washington Daily News,* March 7, 1950, 4 WLDP-FUL; *Washington Daily News,* March 10, 1950, 34, WLDP-FUL; *Chicago Defender,* March 23, 1950, 4; Henry Richardson, to William L. Dawson, 3, March 31, 1950, WLDP-FUL; William Boyle, Washington, D.C., to William L. Dawson, March 20, 1950, WLDP-FUL; *Chicago Defender,* March 25, 1950, 1, WLDP-FUL; Albert Anderson, *Gary American,* March 31, 1950, 7, WLDP-FUL; *Jackson Advocate,* April 1, 1950, 1, WLDP-FUL; Almena Lomax, *Los Angeles Tribune,* March 25, 1950, n.p., WLDP-FUL; Almena Lomax, *Los Angeles Tribune,* March 25, 1950, n.p.,WLDP-FUL.

16. King, 138.

17. "House Cheers Plea of Negro Member. Southerners Join Applause When Dawson of Illinois Ends Segregation Plaint," *The New York Times,* April 13, 1951, n.p., WLDP-FUL.

18. Phineas Indritz agreed, writing that Dawson's "speech of April 13, 1951 in the 82nd Congress is largely credited with defeating the segregation provision, sponsored by Congressman Winstead of Mississippi and Barden of North Carolina . . . under which segregation would have been required in the Armed forces." Likewise, William Clay, who would join the black Congressional delegation in 1969, wrote, "Dawson was primarily responsible for the defeat of the Winstead Amendment in the House." See James Free, *Champaign-Urbana Courier,* March 16, 1956, 25, WLDP-FUL; Phineas Indritz, letter to the American Veterans Committee, March 25, 1958, WLDP-FUL; Clay, 77.

19. U.S. Congress, *Congressional Record Proceedings and Debates of the 82nd Congress First Session,* vol. 97, part 5, *May 28, 1951 to June 27, 1951* (pp. 5,855–7,296) (Washington, D.C.: Government Printing Office, 1951), 6,192, 6,194, 6,197, 6,199.

20. Ibid., 6196.

21. Speech on the floor of the House against a bill to create a Booker T. Washington hospital, June 6, 1951, WLDP-FUL.

22. U.S. Congress, *Congressional Record Proceedings and Debates of the 82nd Congress First Session,* vol. 97, part 5, *May 28, 1951 to June 27, 1951* (pp. 5855–7296) (Washington, D.C.: Government Printing Office, 1951), 6,197.

23. Ibid., 6,197.

24. Ibid., 6,201.

25. Ibid., 6,194, 6,195, 6,199.

26. Dawson remained a vice-chairman until his death in 1970. He clearly convinced white Democrats of his value as vice-chairman. In 1960, for instance, Mrs. Emily Douglas, wife of Democratic Senator Paul Douglas, told a mass meeting of Chicago precinct captains that Dawson was the "greatest vice-chairman in the history of the Democratic National Committee" for carrying on the battle for civil rights in Washington. See *Chicago Defender,* April 2, 1960, 1 and 2.

27. "They Could Win the Election," *Washington Afro-American,* April 17, 1950, n.p., WLDP-FUL.

28. Porter McKeever, *Adlai Stevenson: His Life and Legacy* (New York: William Morrow, 1989), 173–86, 201.

29. *Chicago Defender,* July 26, 1952, 1, WLDP-FUL; Roy Grimes, *San Antonio Press,* May 28, 1952, 1, WLDP-FUL; William J. Bray and Venice T. Spraggs, eds., *Official Report of the Proceedings of the Democratic National Convention, Chicago, Illinois, July 21 to July 26, Inclusive, 1952, resulting in the nomination of Adlai E. Stevenson of Illinois for President and the nomination of John J. Sparkman of Alabama for President* (Chicago: M. Kallis, 1952), 54–76, 139; *Chicago Defender,* July 26, 1952, 1, WLDP-FUL; Speech given by William L. Dawson at the 1952 Democratic National Convention, 1952, WLDP-FUL; Bray and Spraggs, 95.

30. Specifically, the plan called for "(1) the right to equal opportunity for employment; (2) the right to security of persons; and (3) the right to full and equal participation in the Nation's political life, free from arbitrary restraints." The platform also pledged Democrats to "favor legislation to perfect existing civil rights statutes and to strengthen the administrative machinery for the protection of civil rights." See Bray and Spraggs, 275; McCoy and Reuten, 323–25.

31. Harry S Truman, Washington, D.C., to William L. Dawson, July 28, 1952, WLDP-FUL; McCoy and Reuten, 323.

32. McKeever, 221.

33. Louis E. Martin, "Dope and Data," *Chicago Defender,* December 10, 1955, 9.

34. "Herman Exposes Sparkman's Record," *New Jersey Herald News,* October 11, 1952, 3, WLDP-FUL; *New Jersey Herald News,* October 11, 1952, 1, WLDP-FUL; *Chicago Defender Second Front,* October 18, 1952, 1, WLDP-FUL.

35. "Herman Exposes Sparkman's Record," *New Jersey Herald News,* October 11, 1952, 3, WLDP-FUL.

36. *New Jersey Herald News,* October 11, 1952, 1, WLDP-FUL.

37. *Chicago Defender Second Front,* October 18, 1952, 1, WLDP-FUL.

38. McCoy and Reuten, 323.

39. Charles Hamilton, *Adam Clayton Powell, Jr.: The Political Biography of an American Dilemma* (New York: Atheneum, 1991), 197–98; Haygood, 168–72.

40. Carter Jewel, "Stevenson's Richmond Address Wins Friends of Both Races," *Black Dispatch,* October 4, 1952, WLDP-FUL; John H. Sengstacke, "Race Bars Fall as Adlai Swings Through South," *Chicago Defender,* October 18, 1952, 2 WLDP-FUL; *Chicago Defender,* October 11, 1952, 1, WLDP-FUL; *Chicago Defender,* October 18, 1952, 1, WLDP-FUL; *Chicago Defender,* October 25, 1952, 1, WLDP-FUL; *Chicago Defender Second Front,* October 18, 1952, 1; *Chicago Defender,* October 25, 1952, 1, WLDP-FUL; *Washington Afro-American,* September 23, 1952, 3, WLDP-FUL; "Gen. Ike Forms Alliance With Boss of Dixiecrats," *Chicago Defender,* October 11, 1952, 1, WLDP-FUL; *Chicago Defender,* October 18, 1952, 8.

41. "Leaders Map Out Drive for Adlai," *Chicago Defender,* October 11, 1952, 1.

42. Broadwater, 128; McKeever, 262.

43. *Chicago Defender,* November 8, 1952, 1 and 2; Broadwater, 128–29; McKeever, 262; McCoy and Reuten, 160.

44. Haygood, 251; Charles Bowen, interview by author, November 1, 1999, tape recording, City Hall, Chicago.

45. *Chicago Defender,* November 8, 1952, 1 and 2.

46. Kennelly served as Chicago's mayor from 1947–1955.

47. St. Clair Drake and Horace Cayton, *Black Metropolis: A Study of Negro Life in a Northern City, 4th ed.* (Chicago: University of Chicago Press, 1993), 470–72, 480–81, 486; Mark H. Haller, "Policy Gambling, Entertainment, and the Emergence of Black Politics: Chicago from 1900–1940," *Journal of Social History* 24 (1991): 720.

48. Robert E. Weems Jr., *Black Business in the Black Metropolis: The Chicago Metropolitan Assurance Company* (Bloomington: Indiana University Press, 1996), xii; Haller, 722–23.

49. Weems, xii, 62; Drake and Cayton, 487; Haller, 730–31.

50. Drake and Cayton, 481–82; Haller, 724–25.

51. Grimshaw, 59, 84; James Doherty, "Rep. Dawson Has 2d Ward in the Palm of His Hand," *Chicago Sunday Tribune,* May 1, 1960, WLDP-FUL.

52. Roger Biles, *Big City Boss in Depression and War: Mayor Edward J. Kelly of Chicago* (DeKalb: Northern Illinois University Press, 1984), 90; Christopher Robert Reed, "A Study of Black Politics and Protest in Depression-Decade Chicago: 1930–1939," Ph.D. diss., Kent State University, 19; Haller, 734.

53. Grimshaw, 82; Drake and Cayton, 481; "West Side Hoods Muscling in on S. Side Policy Racket. Syndicate Demands 20% Cut of Operators' Profits or Else," Newspaper unidentifiable, ca. 1952, n.p., WLDP-FUL.

54. In an interview, both Ward Committeeman Terry Gabinski and Congressman Dan Rostenkowski commented that Kennelly attacked policy on the South Side to avoid tackling gambling in Chicago's white communities. Both Gabinski and Rostenkowski recollected that gambling was commonplace during their childhoods in the 1940s and 1950s. They even joked about how local storeowners took bets, and there was little indication that such activity was frowned upon. See Dan Rostenkowski, interview by author, January 5, 2000, tape recording, Chicago.

55. Louis Martin, "Chicago's $64 MILLION Question," *Chicago Defender,* May 14, 1948, 1; Grimshaw, 58–59, 82–85; Hirsch, "Martin H. Kennelly," 140–41; Clayton, 82–83.

56. Grimshaw, 58–59, 82–85.

57. Hirsch, 54, 55; Hirsch, "Martin H. Kennelly," 138.

58. L. F. Palmer, "Family Prisoner of Mob Two Weeks," *Chicago Defender,* August 22, 1953, 4; "It's Hate Mob vs. Cops, Not Race vs. Race in Trumbull Park," *Chicago Defender,* August 22, 1953, 7; Albert Barnett, "How 'Plan Five' Quelled the Riot in Trumbull Park," *Chicago Defender,* September 12, 1953, 9.

59. "Says Future of Trumbull Up to Mayor, "Urge Mayor To Halt Riot or Resign," *Chicago Defender,* September 18, 1954, 1; "Dawson Not a Candidate, But Key Man in Election," *Chicago Defender,* February 12, 1955, 1.

60. Corneal Davis, interview by Horace Waggoner, transcript, 1979–1982, available at www.uis.edu/archives/memoirs/DAVISCORNEALvI.pdf, Illinois General Assembly Oral History Program, Brooken Library, University of Illinois at Springfield, Springfield, Ill, retrieved November 7, 2006; Stone, 179; Charles Bowen, interview by author, November 1, 1999, tape recording, City Hall, Chicago; *Chicago Daily News,* February 1, 1955, Harsch Collection, Carter Woodson Library, Chicago; James Doherty, *Chicago Sunday Tribune,* May 1, 1960, 3, WLDP-FUL; *Chicago Sun-Times,* February 9, 1955, 5, WLDP-FUL; Wilson, 81.

61. Dan Rostenkowski, interview by author, January 5, 2000, tape recording, Chicago; Grimshaw, 90–92; Corneal Davis, interview by Horace Waggoner; Lemann, 89; Roger Biles, *Richard J. Daley: Politics, Race, and the Governing of Chicago* (DeKalb: Northern Illinois University Press, 1995), 92; Leon Despres, interview by author, January 21, 2000, tape recording, Chicago.

62. McKeever, 363.

63. Waldo E. Martin Jr., *Brown v. Board of Education: A Brief History with Documents* (Boston: Bedford/St. Martins, 1998), 33–36; Frances Wilhoit, *The Politics of Massive Resistance* (New York: George Braziller, 1973), 28–34, 49, 87–88, 111–15; Robert Weisbrot, *Freedom Bound: A History of America's Civil Rights Movement* (New York: Penguin, 1991), 12.

64. Broadwater, 157; McKeever, 364.

65. *Chicago Defender,* November 11, 1955, 11; Louis E. Martin, "Dope and Data," *Chicago Defender,* December 10, 1955, 9.

66. Diggs' sense of legislative responsibility to the poor whites and blacks in his district was quite evident during a public celebration of his victory when Diggs announced, "Joyous as the occasion is and important as it is to our race we must [not] forget for one moment that I am here to represent all of the people of my district."

See U.S. Congress, *Congressional Record Proceedings and Debates of the 84th Congress Second Session*, vol. 102, part 10, *July 17, 1956 to July 24, 1956* (pp. 12981–14322) (Washington, D.C.: United States Government Printing Office, 1956), 13181; Carol M. Swain, *Black Faces, Black Interests: The Representation of African Americans in Congress* (Cambridge, Mass.: Harvard University Press, 1997), 49; U.S. Congress, *Congressional Record Proceedings and Debates of the 84th Congress, First Session Index*, vol. 101, part 11, *January 5, 1955 to August 2, 1955* (Washington, D.C.: United States Government Printing Office, 1955), 162, 797, 834.

67. *Chicago Daily Defender*, March 3, 1956, 17; Michael Killian, "2,000 Led By Mayor Daley Attend Rep. Dawson's Funeral," *Chicago Tribune*, November 13, 1970.

68. *Chicago Defender*, March 31, 1956, 10.

69. Weisbrot, 12; Robert Frederick Burke, *Eisenhower and Black Civil Rights* (Knoxville: University of Tennessee Press, 1984), 23–43, 65–69, 109–27, 206–7.

70. Frances Wilhoit, *The Politics of Massive Resistance* (New York: George Braziller, 1973), 12, 28–34, 49, 54, 87–88, 105–7, 111–15, 207; Weisbrot, 12.

71. Ethel Payne, *Chicago Daily Defender*, August 6, 1956, 6.

72. *Chicago Daily Defender*, August 6, 1956, 2; William Theis, *Chicago Daily Defender*, August 6, 1956, 2.

73. William Theis, *Chicago Daily Defender*, August 6, 1956, 6.

74. *Chicago Defender*, July 7, 1956, 1; U.S. Congress, *Congressional Record Proceedings and Debates of the 84th Congress*, vol. 102, part 9, *July 2, 1956 to July 16, 1956* (pp. 11,515–12,980) (Washington, D.C.: Government Printing Office, 1956), 11,757.

75. Clarence Mitchell, *Chicago Defender*, July 14, 1956, 1, 2; "National Grapevine," *Chicago Defender*, July 14, 1956, 2.

An effect of the mischaracterization of the Powell Amendment fight is that Dawson's opposition to the Powell Amendment has been used in tandem with his involvement in the Regular Democratic Organization as evidence for a lack of civil rights zeal. For example, in 1968 Chuck Stone, in his book *Black Political Power*, called Dawson an "establishment nigger," as evidenced by his opposition to the Powell Amendment and his interaction with the Daley machine. Nearly thirty years later, Robert Singh writes in *The Congressional Black Caucus*: "Dawson achieved the dual political distinction of becoming the first black to gain real institutional influence in Congress and of becoming a significant figure in the national Democratic Party because of his machine's influence. He nonetheless declined to act as a national spokesperson for blacks and, though he lobbied for individual black appointments, his civil rights record was singularly undistinguished. Placidly accepting the discriminatory procedures then regulating the use of Congressional facilities, Dawson rarely raised issues of a racial nature. Moreover, he opposed the Powell Amendment, which sought to ban federal aid to segregated schools." It does not appear, however, that either of these scholars spent much time investigating Dawson's legislative record, nor the history of the Powell amendment itself. See Chuck Stone, *Black Political Power in America* (New York: Dell, 1968), 179; Robert Singh, *The Congressional Black Caucus: Racial Politics in the U. S. Congress* (Thousand Oaks, Cal.: Sage Publications, 1997), 46.

76. Darlene Clark Hine, Elsa Barkley Brown, and Rosalyn Terborg-Penn, eds., *Black Women in America: An Historical Encyclopedia* (Bloomington: Indiana University Press, 1993), 33, 1019; Haygood, 117, 128; *Chicago Defender*, February 21, 1948, 1; E.D. Talley, *New York Age*, February 24, 1951, n.p., CBP-CHS; William L. Dawson, Chicago, to Gordon B. Hancock, Kans., August 26, 1952, WLDP-FUL; James Free, *Champaign-Urbana Courier*, March 16, 1956, 25, WLDP-FUL; *Chicago Defender*, June 7, 1955, 1.

77. U.S. Congress, *Congressional Record Proceedings and Debates of the 84th Congress*, vol. 102, part 9, *July 2, 1956 to July 16, 1956* (pp. 11515–12980) (Washington, D.C.: Government Printing Office, 1956), 11,880–11,883; Carol M. Swain, *Black Interests, Black Faces: The Representation of African Americans in Congress* (Cambridge, Mass.: Harvard University Press, 1995), 35.

78. Robert Frederick Burke, *Eisenhower and Black Civil Rights* (Knoxville: University of Tennessee Press, 1984), 16.

79. Swain, 34–36.

80. Haygood, 208.

81. Swain, 35; Congressional Quarterly Service, *Congress and the Nation 1945–1964: A Review of Government and Politics in the Postwar Years* (Washington, D.C.: Congressional Quarterly Service, 1965), 739.

82. Speech given by William L. Dawson before the U.S. House of Representatives, Washington, D.C., July 3, 1956, WLDP-FUL.

83. U.S. Congress, *Congressional Record Proceedings and Debates of the 84th Congress Second Session*, vol. 102, part 10, *July 17, 1956 to July 24, 1956* (pp. 1,298–14,322) (Washington, D.C.: Government Printing Office, 1956), 13,741; Swain, 35.

84. The Powell Amendment evidently never received the wholehearted support of liberal Congressmen and amendments resembling it divided the expanding black Congressional delegation into the late 1950s and early 1960s. In 1957 Diggs argued that a Powell-style amendment to an education bill was a "distraction," and attempts to add Powell amendments to various other education bills in 1960, and 1963 also split the growing black congressional delegation. Moreover, the black press never gave such amendments the same urgency as they had in 1956, and, by 1960, the NAACP actually opposed a Powell Amendment. See U.S. Congress, *Congressional Record Proceedings and Debates of the 86th Congress Second Session*, vol. 106, part 9, *May 26, 1960 to June 13, 1960* (pp. 11,137–12,496) (Washington, D.C.: Government Printing Office, 1960), 11,296; U.S. Congress, *Congressional Record Proceedings and Debates of the 88th Congress First Session*, vol. 109, part 11, *August 5, 1963 to August 20, 1963* (pp. 14,059–15,506) (Washington, D.C.: Government Printing Office, 1963), 14,258–14,260, 14,333; U.S. Congress, *Congressional Record Proceedings and Debates of the 85th Congress First Session*, vol. 103, part, 9 *July 11, 1957 to July 25, 1957* (pp. 1,307–12,784) (Washington, D.C.: Government Printing Office, 1957), 12,483–12,737; U.S. Congress, *Congressional Record Proceedings and Debates of the 84th Congress Second Session*, vol. 102, part 10, *July 17, 1956 to July 24, 1956* (pp. 1,298–14,322) (Washington, D.C.: Government Printing Office, 1956), 13,741.

85. *Chicago Daily Defender,* August 6, 1956, 4; *Chicago Daily Defender,* August 13, 1956, 2; *Chicago Daily Defender,* August 13, 1956, 5; *Chicago Daily Defender,* August 13, 1956, 8; Ethel Payne, *Chicago Daily Defender,* August 14, 1956, 3; Ethel Payne, *Chicago Daily Defender,* August 6, 1956, 2.

86. Congressman Sam J. Ervin, North Carolina, to William L. Dawson, September 13, 1956, WLDP-FUL.

87. Ethel Payne, *Chicago Daily Defender,* August 6, 1956, 2; *Chicago Daily Defender,* August 6, 1956, 3; *Chicago Daily Defender,* August 13, 1956, 8.

88. The controversy had an odd effect on two of Illinois's most powerful leaders. Apparently, Senator Paul Douglas, also a member of the Resolution Committee, announced that he would not fight for a strong civil rights plank for the sake of party unity. The Democrat's behavior, he claimed, was more important than promises. This statement prompted a harsh, somewhat surprising reaction from Chicago's Mayor Richard M. Daley at the Resolutions Committee meeting. Even though the committee was not scheduled to discuss civil rights that day, Daley told Douglas that the parties "should mean what they say and say what they mean." Although he made few efforts

to promote racial equality in Chicago, Daley wanted a civil rights plank that would explicitly support *Brown*. See *Chicago Daily Defender*, August 8, 1956, 1.

89. *Chicago Daily Defender*, August 8, 1956, 3; *Chicago Daily Defender*, August 11, 1956, 2.

90. Ethel L. Payne, *Chicago Daily Defender*, August 15, 1956, 2.

91. Ruth Aull and Daniel M. Ogden, eds., *Official Report of the Proceedings of the Democratic National Convention, Chicago, Illinois, August 13 through August 17, 1956, Resulting in the Re-Nomination of Adlai E. Stevenson of Illinois for President and the Nomination of Estes Kefauver of Tennessee for Vice-President* (Chicago: Democratic National Convention, 1956), 323–36.

92. Ethel L. Payne, *Chicago Daily Defender*, August 20, 1956, 8.

93. According to Corneal Davis, Abner then started an effort to undercut Dawson's 1956 reelection campaign. He also began organizing UAW workers to oppose Dawson throughout the First Congressional District. Dawson responded by starting an "anti-Abner" squad in the NAACP that eventually resulted in Abner's removal from the presidency of the local branch. See Ethel L. Payne, *Chicago Daily Defender*, August 16, 1956, 3; "Negro Group Raps Dawson on Civil Rights Stand," *Chicago Daily Tribune*, August 31, 1956, WLDP-FUL; Lee Blackwell, *Chicago Daily Defender*, September 4, 1956, 8; Corneal Davis interview by Doris Saunders, transcript, March 11, 1970, DSP-CGWL.

94. "Political Grapevine," *Chicago Defender*, October 13, 1956, 1; "Political Grapevine," *Chicago Defender*, October 20, 1956, 2; Ethel L. Payne, *Chicago Daily Defender*, August 21, 1956, 3.

95. Haygood, 218–19; Hamilton, 272–73; "Denies Tax Troubles Caused Powell's Shift," *Chicago Daily Defender*, October 15, 1956, 4.

96. *Chicago Daily Defender*, October 10, 1956, 10.

97. Robert Nixon, *Chicago Daily Defender*, October 1, 1956, 5; Alfred Duckett, *Chicago Defender*, October 20, 1956, 1 and 2.

98. *Chicago Daily Defender*, October 18, 1956, 3; *Chicago Daily Defender*, November 1, 1956, 3; Robert Howard, *Chicago Tribune*, October 21, 1956, pt. 3, 6, BBP-CGWL; J. F. Estes, Memphis, Tenn., to William L. Dawson, September 12, 1956, WLDP-FUL; Broadwater, 172.

99. McKeever, 378–79; Ethel L. Payne, November 8, 1956, 3; John Sengstacke, *Chicago Defender*, November 10, 1957, 1.

100. Ethel L. Payne, n.t., *Chicago Defender*, November 8, 1956, 3; John Sengstacke, n.t., *Chicago Defender*, November 10, 1956, 1.

101. John Sengstacke, *Chicago Defender*, November 10, 1957, 1.

102. Lewis A. H. Caldwell, *Daily Defender*, September 4, 1958, 8A.

103. Leon Despres, interview by author, January 21, 2000, tape recording, Chicago; Green, 104.

104. Leon Despres, interview by author, January 21, 2000, tape recording, Chicago.

105. Nicholas Lemann, *The Promised Land: The Great Black Migration and How It Changed America* (New York: Vintage Books, 1991), 95.

106. Leon Despres, interview by author, January 21, 2000, tape recording, Chicago; Biles, 93.

107. I use the term "so-called" for it is apparent that the appellation "Dawson alderman" did not reflect the reality of the Mayor Daley's control over the city's black city council members.

108. "Open Occupancy Bill to Be Debated," *Chicago Defender*, March 17, 1958, 4; "Ald. Despres' Housing Resolution," *Chicago Defender*, March 29, 1958, 10; "Chicago Fight for Fair Housing Gets Big Boost," *Chicago Defender*, April 5, 1958, 9.

109. Greg Harris, "The Greg Harris Notebook," *Daily Defender*, December 16, 1958, A8; Ted Coleman, "All Negro Aldermen Back Open Occupancy," *Daily Defender*, June 30, 1960, A3; "City Council Approves Study of Housing Bias," *Chicago Daily Defender*, November 28, 1960, 7; "Despres Rips City on Open Occupancy," *Chicago Defender*, March 23, 1961; Mattie Colon Smith, "The Political Door," *Chicago Defender*, May 5, 1962, 2; Leon Despres, interview by author, January 21, 2000, tape recording, Chicago.

110. "Mississippi Regional Council of Negro Leadership Reveals New Approach to Problems of Negro Life in the State. Cong. Dawson Cites Value of Voting and Political Participation at the State and Local Levels," *Jackson Advocate*, May 10, 1952, 1, WLDP-FUL; John Dittmer, *Local People: The Struggle for Civil Rights in Mississippi* (Urbana: University of Illinois Press, 1994), 32–33.

111. "Protest Mississippi Shame," *Chicago Defender*, September 10, 1955, 1; "Howard Sees Light Sentence," *Chicago Defender*, September 17, 1955, 5; "10,000 Across Nation Protest Till Lynching," *Chicago Defender*, October 8, 1955, 4.

112. "Mrs. Bradley Bares Dawson Aid. Says Ike Ignored Pleas for Help," *Chicago Defender*, October 22, 1956, 3; Ethel Payne, "Dawson Tells Reason for Aiding Till's Mother," *Daily Defender*, October 30, 1956, 2; "Aid in Dawson Case Just Human Thing to Do—Dawson," *Daily Defender*, October 31, 1956, 5.

113. Ethel Payne, "Mrs. Bradley Bares Dawson Aid. Says Ike Ignored Pleas for Help," *Chicago Defender*, October 22, 1956, 3.

114. Adam Green, *Selling the Race: Culture, Community, and Black Chicago, 1940–1955* (Chicago: University of Chicago Press, 2007), 191, 198–99, 208–9; Weisbrot, 94.

115. "Howard Out to Unseat Dawson," *Chicago Defender*, October 11, 1958, 1; "1,400 Hear Howard Rip Mississippi 'Hell Hole,'" *Chicago Defender*, February 11, 1956, 3; "Howard Urges Troops in Dixie," *Daily Defender*, February 22, 1956, 5; "Dr. Howard to Talk in Milwaukee," *Chicago Defender*, April 7, 1956, 10; "Howard Here For Rights Talk," *Daily Defender*, May 24, 1956, 4; "UPWA Bids Ike to Aid Bus Boycotters," *Chicago Defender*, June 30, 1956, 5; "Dr. Howard's Wife, Tots Leave Miss.," *Chicago Defender*, December 17, 1955, 1; Albert G. Barnett, "Howard Joins Ida Mae Scott Surgical Staff," *Chicago Defender*, January 19, 1957, 8; "Howard Calls for Change to Correct Racial Ills," *Chicago Defender*, February 15, 1958, 3; Greg Harris, "The Political Pot," *Daily Defender*, October 29, 1958, 9; Louis Martin, "Off the Cuff," *Daily Defender*, April 3, 1958, A8; Greg Harris, "The Political Pot," *Daily Defender*, October 27, 1958, A6.

6—"Where Is the Invisible Man?"

1. Simeon Booker, "Nation Mourns Dawson's Death as Capital Flag Flies at Half-Mast," *Jet*, November 26, 1970, 20–27.

2. Dionne Danns, *Something Better for Our Children: Black Organizing in Chicago Public Schools, 1963–1971* (New York: Routledge, 2003), 61–62.

3. William L. Dawson, to John F. Kennedy, August 23, 1958, WLDP-FUL; "Sen. Kennedy Honored for Record on Civil Rights," *Chicago Defender*, November 8, 1958, 3; Walter White, "Asks Readers to Send Telegrams of Thanks to Senators Who Fought Hard for Cloture," January 24, 1953, 11; "Urges Democrats Not to 'Weasel' on Civil Rights," *Chicago Defender*, February 18, 1956; "Senator Douglass to Speak at Fete Honoring Kennedy," *Chicago Defender*, October 11, 1958, 15.

4. See, for examples, "Sen. Kennedy and the School Bill," *Chicago Defender*, March 2, 1957, 6; "Sen. Kennedy Takes Exception," *Chicago Defender*, April 6, 1957, 11; "Mansfield Denies Deal on Rights," *Chicago Defender*, June 25, 1957, 9; "Powell Says Dems to Desert Negro, Labor," *Chicago Defender*, July 1, 1957, 5; Ethel L. Payne, "Kennedy

Defends His Votes on Rights Bill in Senate," *Chicago Defender,* July 20, 1957, 12; "The Issue—First Class Citizenship," *Chicago Defender,* September 7, 1957, 10.

5. Weisbrot, 44; Taylor Branch, *Parting the Waters: America in the King Years, 1954–1963* (New York: Simon & Schuster, 1988), 323.

6. Corneal Davis, interview by Horace Waggoner, transcript, 1979–1982, available at www.uis.edu/archives/memoirs/DAVISCORNEALvI.pdf, Illinois General Assembly Oral History Program, Brooken Library, University of Illinois at Springfield, Springfield, Ill., retrieved November 7, 2006; Charles Bowen, interview by author, November 1, 1999, tape recording, City Hall, Chicago.

7. Davis remembered the conversation between himself and Dawson as follows:

Owson: "You want to help them Kennedy's?"
Davis: "Well they asked me to help them."
Dawson: "Lyndon Johnson is going to beat him. You know that. Johnson has the money behind him. But if you want to help him, Kennedy, you won't be embarrassing me."
Davis: "They came to see me."
Dawson: "They did?"
Davis: "Yes. They want you with them."
Dawson: "If you want to go on with them that's all right with me. I wouldn't tell you not to go with them."
Davis: "Well won't it be embarrassing to you?" [LBJ had helped WD get the vice-chairmanship]
Dawson: "No, it won't embarrass me. I'll still be the vice-chairman of the Democratic National Committee. . . . If you want to do it, go ahead and do it."
Davis: "I want to do it."

Corneal Davis, interview by Horace Waggoner, transcript, 1979–1982, available at www.uis.edu/archives/memoirs/DAVISCORNEALvI.pdf, Illinois General Assembly Oral History Program, Brooken Library, University of Illinois at Springfield, Springfield, Ill., retrieved November 7, 2006; Charles Bowen, interview by author, November 1, 1999, tape recording, City Hall, Chicago.

8. Brauer, 30–31; Weisbrot, 45; Branch, 305; Robert G. Spivak, "Watch on the Potomac," *Daily Defender,* March 31, 1960, A12; "Study Kennedy Wisconsin Win," *Daily Defender,* April 7, 1960, A2; "W. Va., Neb. Voting Boosts Kennedy," *Daily Defender,* May 12, 1960, 10.

9. Branch, 306.

10. *Chicago Defender,* September 7, 1960, 1 and 2.

11. Brauer, 31–33; Weisbrot, 45–46; Branch, 319.

12. Brauer, 31–33; Weisbrot, 45–46; Branch, 319.

13. Illinois Congressman Dan Rostenkowski, an important member of the Daley organization, said in an interview that Dawson submitted Johnson's nomination due to Daley's behind the scenes machinations. Kennedy spoke to Daley about the potential problems of having Johnson on the ticket, particularly Johnson's relationship to labor leaders. Daley felt these concerns were overblown and suggested that, if Johnson called Dawson, Dawson would be glad to make the nomination speech. Dan Rostenkowski, interview by author, January 5, 2000, tape recording, Chicago.

14. Speech by William L. Dawson nominating Lyndon B. Johnson for the Democratic vice-presidential nomination, WLDP-FUL; "Text of Dawson's Speech for VP Nominee Johnson," *Daily Defender,* July 19, 1960, A4.

15. We do have some indication of the speech's success in a letter from one of Dawson's associates, attorney Henry Richardson Jr., of Indianapolis. While Richardson expressed reserve regarding Johnson's work on the Civil Rights Bill of 1957, a bill

that many observers believed Johnson gutted to gain its passage, he felt that Dawson's nomination speech helped Johnson to reach "new heights of admiration in the hearts of minorities." Moreover, Richardson wrote, "this opinion is shared by my friends and your admirers Dr. Benjamin Mays, President of Morehouse College, and Ralph McGill, publisher and editor of [the] 'Atlanta Constitution'." Henry Richardson Jr., Indianapolis, Ind., to William L. Dawson, September 12, 1960, WLDP-FUL.

16. Brauer, 35; Branch, 318.

17. *Chicago Defender*, July 16, 1960, 2; Brauer, 35–36; Branch, 319.

18. *Chicago Defender*, July 16, 1960, 1 and 2.

19. Kenneth C. Field, "Dawson's Power Is Success Key," *Daily Defender*, July 19, 1960, A4.

20. Congressman Chester Bowles (Conn.) to WLDP-FUL.

21. "Hail Demo Plank As Step Forward," *Chicago Defender*, July 23, 1960, 1 and 2.

22. Branch, 321 and 375.

23. Ibid., 44; Dan Rostenkowski, interview by author, January 5, 2000, tape recording, Chicago.

24. Branch, 342.

25. Reverend Paul E. Turner, Chicago, to William L. Dawson, October 10, 1960, WLDP-FUL; Henry Richardson Jr., Indianapolis, Ind., to William L. Dawson, September 12, 1960, WLDP-FUL.

26. Charles Bowen, interview by author, November 1, 1999, Chicago, tape recording, City Hall, Chicago, Illinois; "All Dawson Had To Say Was For Them To Be There and & 10,000 Were There," *The Voice*, October 21, 1960, 1, WLDP-FUL.

27. Clayton, 76, 106.

28. Brauer, 45; Branch, 342.

29. *The Courier*, October 29, 1960, n.p., WLDP-FUL; *Chicago Defender*, October 1, 1960, 6.

30. *The Courier*, October 8, 1960, n.p., WLDP-FUL; *Chicago Defender*, October 21, 1960, 5, 7, 19; *Chicago Defender*, November 4, 1960, 2, 3, 4, 17; *Chicago Defender*, October 11, 1960, 5.

31. *The Courier*, October 29, 1960, 8, n.p., File 5, Box 17, WLDP-FUL.

32. Brauer, 41; Weisbrot, 46.

33. Brauer, 48–51.

34. Clayton, 41.

35. Weisbrot, 48.

36. *Chicago Defender*, November 18, 1960, 1.

37. Branch, 374.

38. Carol Kilpatrick, *Washington Post*, December 16, 1960, 1, WLDP-FUL; Chalmers Roberts, *Washington Post*, December 14, 1960, 17, WLDP-FUL; *Chicago Defender*, December 23, 1960, 1.

39. *Long Island Daily Press*, December 16, 1960, n.p., WLDP-FUL; "Rumor Dawson for Cabinet Post," *Chicago Daily Defender*, November 14, 1960, 1.

40. Bolin V. Bland, Chicago, to William L. Dawson, December 21, 1960, WLDP-FUL; Chalmers Roberts, *Washington Post*, December 14, 1960, 17, WLDP-FUL.

41. Carol Kilpatrick, "Freeman Is Appointed Agriculture Secretary," *Washington Post*, December 16, 1960, 1, WLDP-FUL; "Dawson Rejects Cabinet Job," *Chicago Defender*, December 23, 1960, 1.

42. Blanche Dawson Roney, to William L. Dawson, February 23, 1961, WLDP-FUL.

43. A. L. Dua, Washington, D.C., to William L. Dawson, WLDP-FUL; Allene Drain, N.C., to William L. Dawson, December 16, 1960, WLDP-FUL; Cecil E. Newman, St. Paul, Minn., to William L. Dawson, December 12, 1960, WLDP-FUL; H. T. Medford,

to William L. Dawson, December 23, 1960, WLDP-FUL; Ira Combs, to William L. Dawson, December 31, 1960, WLDP-FUL; Rudolph Chambers, Denver, Colo., to William L. Dawson, January 1, 1960, WLDP-FUL.

44. Weisbrot, 49.

45. The federal government's movement into the public housing arena with the Federal Housing Acts of 1949 and 1954, based in large part on the Chicago model, only reinforced the pattern begun with the Lake Meadows project discussed in chap. 6. See J. S. Fuerst, *When Public Housing Was Paradise* (Urbana: University of Illinois Press, 2005), 197; Sudhir Alladi Venkatesh, *American Project: The Rise and Fall of a Modern Ghetto* (Cambridge, Mass.: Harvard University Press, 2001), ix–x; Arnold R. Hirsch, *Making the Second Ghetto: Race and Housing in Chicago, 1940–1960* (Cambridge: Cambridge University Press, 1983), 15, 271.

46. Venkatesh, 17–18.

47. Ernestine Cofield, "27,000 'Blessed in Unity' Living in Robert Taylor Homes," *Chicago Defender,* March 2, 1963, 11; Venkatesh, 13, 18, 30–36; Fuerst, 69, 146, 145, 196, 205–9.

48. Ernestine Cofield, "27,000 'Blessed in Unity' Living in Robert Taylor Homes," *Chicago Defender,* March 2, 1963, 11; Venkatesh, 13, 18, 30–36; Fuerst, 69, 146, 145, 196, 205–9.

49. Fuerst, 116.

50. Ibid., 46.

51. Charles Bowen, interview by author, November 1, 1999, tape recording, City Hall, Chicago.

52. Rakove, 118–23.

53. Ibid., 123.

54. Mary Patillo-McCoy, *Black Picket Fences: Privilege and Peril Among the Black Middle Class* (Chicago: University of Chicago Press, 1999), 24–27.

55. James R. Ralph Jr., *Northern Protest: Martin Luther King, Jr., Chicago and the Civil Rights Movement* (Cambridge, Mass.: Harvard University Press, 1993), 14.

56. Ralph, 16–20; "Double Shift Death Does Not Satisfy, Says Counsel," *Chicago Daily Defender,* October 2, 1961, 9; "Raise $1,049 In School Bias Fight," *Chicago Daily Defender,* November 8, 1961, 1; Audrey T. Weaver, "Board of Education Fires McCosh Teacher," *Chicago Daily Defender,* November 9, 1961, 1; "Fuqua Calls Chicago Schools Not Only Separate But Unequal During TV Show," *Chicago Daily Defender,* December 4, 1961, 8; "The 'Truth Squad' Mothers," *Chicago Daily Defender,* May 22, 1962, 11.

57. Ralph, 15–16; "Double Shift Death Does Not Satisfy, Says Counsel," *Chicago Daily Defender,* October 2, 1961, 9.

58. Kenneth C. Field, "Daley, Council 'Rubber Stamps' Dawson Charges," *Chicago Daily Defender,* April 25, 1962, 1; "Dawson, Daley Talk; Reopen Nominations," *Chicago Daily Defender,* April 26, 1962, 1.

59. Danns, 36, 40.

60. Ralph, 84; Leon Despres, interview by author, January 21, 2000, tape recording, Chicago.

61. Kenneth C. Field, "Daley, Council 'Rubber Stamps' Dawson Charges," *Chicago Daily Defender,* April 25, 1962, 1.

62. Ralph, 9; "Coordinating Council of Community Organizations," *Encyclopedia of Chicago History,* ed. James Grossman, www.encyclopedia.chicagohistory.org/pages/221.html, retrieved May 16, 2008.

63. Robert Dallek, *Flawed Giant: Lyndon Johnson and His Times, 1961–1973* (New York: Oxford University Press, 1998), 11.

64. Speech before the U.S. House of Representatives to present civil rights to Speaker John McCormack, October 18, 1963, WLDP-FUL.

65. Ted Coleman and Jerry Goldberg, "New 'Rights' Group a Phony?" *Chicago Daily Defender,* January 27, 1964, A3; Chuck Stone, "A Stone's Throw; Politicians and Civil Rights: Who's Going to Be 'Mr. Big'?" *Chicago Daily Defender,* January 27, 1964, 4; Ted Coleman, "Chicago Boycott 'On,' Says CCCO," *Chicago Daily Defender,* February 4, 1964, A3; Ted Coleman, "Hope Boycott Flops, Says Ald. Campbell," *Chicago Daily Defender,* February 5, 1964, A2; Rep. William H. Robinson, "Calls Jan. 23 Chicago's Day of Infamy on Civil Rights," *Chicago Defender,* February 8, 1964, 9; Jerry Goldberg, "Those Aldermen Are Getting Us (And Themselves) All Mixed Up," *Chicago Defender,* February 8, 1964, 3; Ted Coleman, "Daley Lauds ATEPIP Anti-Boycott Move," *Chicago Daily Defender,* February 11, 1964, A3; "Picket Ald. Campbell in School Boycott Ban," *Chicago Daily Defender,* February 17, 1964, 5; "Daley and Willis Pitted Against Negroes in Show of Strength; 2 Rallies Held," *Chicago Daily Defender,* February 24, 1964, A1; "Students Picket S. Side Aldermen," *Chicago Daily Defender,* February 24, 1964, A3; "CCCO May Move Into Politics Against School Boycott Foes," *Chicago Daily Defender,* March 2, 1964, 6.

66. Ralph, 81; Abie Miller, "Civil Worker Says the New Unit Is Insult to the People," *Chicago Defender,* September 18, 1965, 11; Abie Miller, "Raby's Change of Heart Queried," *Chicago Defender,* October 2, 1965, 11.

67. Danns, 39, 40, 64.

68. Ralph, 17–37, 42–171; Lemann, 23.

69. Danns, 61, 62, and 66.

70. Ralph, 83.

71. Press release from the office of William L. Dawson, September 11, 1964, WLDP-FUL; Jerome M. Sachs, *The Voice,* September 18, 1964, 3, WLDP-FUL.

72. Arthur Siddon, *Chicago Tribune,* June 20, 1967, n.p., WLDP-FUL; *New Crusade,* June 24, 1967, n.p., WLDP-FUL.

73. Press release from the office of William L. Dawson, ca. 1969, WLDP-FUL; Unknown newspaper, ca. 1969, n.p., WLDP-FUL; Congress, *Congressional Record Proceedings and Debates of the 90th Congress First Session,* vol. 113, part 7 *April 5, 1967, to April 14, 1967* (pp. 8,333–9,702), (Washington, D.C.: Government Printing Office, 1967), 9,089.

74. Danns, 61, 62, and 66.

75. Madelene Chafin, "Yes, Virginia, There Is a Congressman Dawson and He Knows Ben Willis Exists," *Chicago Daily Defender,* January 8, 1964, A5.

76. "'Willisism' To Go, Say Candidates," *Chicago Daily Defender,* February 4, 1964, 3.

77. "Rayner to Run Against Dawson," *The Chicago Defender,* January 25, 1964, 1.

78. "IVI Supporting Rayner in Bid Against Dawson," *Chicago Daily Defender,* April 8, 1964, 1; "Meredith Throws Support Behind Rayner," *Chicago Defender,* April 4, 1964, 1; Ted Coleman, "Nearly A Million Votes Possible in Chi. Today," *Chicago Daily Defender,* April 14, 1964, 3.

79. Danns, 2, 61, 62, 67, 70.

80. "Students Picket as Dawson Holds Rally," *Chicago Daily Defender,* April 1, 1964, 22.

81. M. Wilson Lewis, "Fight in Street at Dawson Rally," *Chicago Daily Defender,* April 13, 1964, 1.

82. "Landry, SNCC Set to Picket Rep. Dawson," *Chicago Daily Defender,* April 9, 1964, 3; M. Wilson Lewis, "Fight in Street at Dawson Rally," *Chicago Daily Defender,* April 13, 1964.

83. "Landry, SNCC Set to Picket Rep. Dawson," *Chicago Daily Defender,* April 9, 1964, 3; "Dawson Losing Voters, Chas. Skyles Charges," March 17, 1964, 2.

84. Lee Blackwell, "Dawson Hailed at Big Banquet," *Chicago Daily Defender,* September 15, 1964, 4.

85. "Dawson Asks Unity As Campaign Gets Started," *Chicago Daily Defender,* April 6, 1964, 4; "Ministers From Unit to Re-Elect Dawson," *Chicago Daily Defender,* April 8, 1964, 4; The Sixth Ward, "Just Who Is Bishop Ford," http://thesixthward.blogspot. com/2008/01/just-who-is-bishop-ford.html, retrieved May 15, 2008; CBS2Chicago. com, "Bishop Ford Honored at DuSable Museum," CBS 2 Chicago, http://cbs2chicago. com/local/bishop.ford.honored.2.623852.html, retrieved May 15, 2008.

86. "Rev. Bodie Pledges Support to Dawson," *Chicago Defender,* April 13, 1964, 4.

87. "Rayner Backers Ask Atty. Gen to Guard Polls," *Chicago Daily Defender,* April 13, 1964, A2; C. C. Nugent Jr., "Where Was the Revolt During the Recent Primary," *Chicago Defender,* May 2, 1964, 9; "Dawson Wins! Still the Boss," *Chicago Defender,* April 15, 1964, 1; I. Wright, "Sorry Rayner Lost; But Gives Advice," *Chicago Defender,* April 25, 1964, 9; Chuck Stone, "A Stone's Throw," *Chicago Daily Defender,* April 15, 1964, 2.

88. Chuck Stone, "A Stone's Throw," *Chicago Daily Defender,* April 15, 1964, 2.

89. "Rev. Daniel Challenges Rep. Dawson to Debate," *Chicago Daily Defender,* October 14, 1964, 2; "Dawson Swept back in Office," *Chicago Daily Defender,* November 4, 1964, 2.

90. Weisbrot, 68–73, 76–85; Aldon Morris, *Origins of the Civil Rights Movement: Black Communities Organizing for Change* (New York: Free Press, 1984), 250–74; U.S. Congress, *Congressional Record Proceedings and Debates of the 88th Congress Second Session,* vol. 110, part 2 *January 30, 1964 to February 10, 1964* (pp. 1,391–2,840) (Washington, D.C.: Government Printing Office, 1964), 2,731–2,732; Speech before the House Committee on Rules in support of H.R. 7152, January 23, 1964, WLDP-FUL.

91. Weisbrot, 88–92.

92. Congressional Quarterly Service, *Congress and the Nation 1945–1964: A Review of Government and Politics in the Postwar Years* (Washington, D.C.: Congressional Quarterly Service, 1965), 1,635–1,636.

93. Congressional Quarterly Service, *Congress and the Nation.* Vol. 2: *1965–1968: A Review of Government and Politics* (Washington, D.C.: Congressional Quarterly Service, 1969), 905; U.S. Congress, *Congressional Record Proceedings and Debates of the 89th Congress First Session,* vol. 111, part 18, *September 14, 1965 to September 23, 1965* (pp. 23,627–25,022) (Washington, D.C.: Government Printing Office, 1965), 24,281; John Dittmer, *Local People: the Struggle for Civil Rights in Mississippi* (Urbana: University of Illinois Press, 1994), 351; Charles M. Payne, *I've Got the Light of Freedom: The Organizing Tradition and the Mississippi Freedom Struggle* (Berkeley: University of California Press, 1995), 322.

94. Speech before the House of Representatives in support of the Civil Rights Bill of 1968, March 1, 1968, WLDP-FUL.

95. U.S. Congress, *Congressional Record Proceedings and Debates of the 89th Congress First Session,* vol. 111, part 19, *September 24, 1965 to October 7, 1965* (pp. 25,023–26,2378) (Washington, D.C.: Government Printing Office, 1965), 25,373–25,374; Christopher, 191–92.

96. These issues included abolishing the death penalty, guaranteeing productive employment, terminating the House Committee on Un-American Activities, adding an Equal Rights Amendment for men and women to the Constitution, and lowering the voting age to 18. Indeed the *Congressional Record* shows that black representatives tended to propose very similar legislation in these areas. Clearly this growing unity of purpose would factor into the development of the Congressional Black Caucus led by Diggs in 1970.

97. "President Endorses Rep. William L. Dawson," *The Voice,* March 3, 1964, 8, WLDP-FUL; John W. McCormack, to William L. Dawson, October 6, 1964, WLDP-FUL; Orville Freeman, to William L. Dawson, October 14, 1964, WLDP-FUL; Press release from the office of William L. Dawson, April 16, 1968, WLDP-FUL; William L. Dawson,

to Lawrence O'Brien, September 7, 1965, WLDP-FUL; Press release from the office of William L. Dawson, August 10, 1965, WLDP-FUL.

98. William L. Dawson, Washington, D.C., to Richard M. Nixon, Washington, D.C., June 30, 1969, WLDP-FUL; Ethel L. Payne, "Dawson Tells Why He Nixed Black Paper," n.t., September 29, 1969, 2, DSP-CGWL; Larry Bryant, "'Black Eight' Rap Nixon's Domestic Policy," n.t., November 11, 1969, n.p., WLDP-FUL; N.A., "Cong. Dawson Hits HEW in Letter to President," n.t., June 10, 1969, n.p., DSP-CGWL.

Conclusion—"Times Are Different Now"

1. Joseph L. Turner, "'I'll Run for Congress' Says Sen. Chew," *Chicago Daily Defender,* May 26, 1969, 1.

2. Olive M. Diggs, "From Our Readers: A Political Professional," *Chicago Daily Defender,* November 17, 1970, 13.

3. Dawson easily won every election in the 1960s. See Sheryl Fitzgerald and Betty Johnson, "Dawson Assured of Re-Election," *Chicago Defender,* December 6, 1968, 2, DSP-GGWL.

4. The only indication in Dawson's files prior to 1957 of any kind of sickness or illness was a single get well note in 1951 when Dawson spent some time in the National Naval Medical Center in Bethesda, Maryland. Sylvester O' Neal, Chicago, to William L. Dawson, Washington, D.C., May 21, 1951, WLDP-FUL.

For sources pointing to Dawson's increasing illnesses and hospital stays see Frank Weitzel, Washington, D.C., to William L. Dawson, Washington, D.C., May 18, 1957, WLDP-FUL; Ernest Rather and the Chicago Committee of One Hundred, Chicago, to William L. Dawson, Washington, D.C., May 18, 1957; A.T. Thomas to William L. Dawson, Washington, D.C., May 18, 1957, WLDP-FUL; Charlie (last name unidentified), Washington, D.C., to William L. Dawson, Washington, D.C., May 18, 1957, WLDP-FUL; Mr. and Mrs. James Carter, Chicago, to William L. Dawson, Washington, D.C., May 19, 1957, WLDP-FUL.

5. How exactly Woods became part of the organization is unclear. Chuck Bowen, Dawson's top precinct captain in the mid-1950s, indicated that Woods had been one of few blacks associated with the Arkansas's segregationist governor, Orval Faubus. When civil rights demonstrations elevated racial tensions in Arkansas, Faubus could no longer keep an African American on his staff while maintaining his image as a defender of white supremacy, and he asked Dawson if he could take Woods on. Woods gave a different story. He claimed that he merely intended to visit Chicago in April 1957 and he headed to Dawson's office because he had heard him give a speech back in Arkansas. Dawson, said Woods, suggested that he stay in Chicago to become involved in politics and he offered him a position as an assistant precinct captain. Of the two stories, Bowen's seems more likely. We know, for instance, that Dawson maintained relationships even with segregationist Democrats like Faubus, and it is unlikely that Dawson would welcome a non-Chicagoan as an assistant precinct captain based on a single visit.

Charles Bowen, interview by author, November 1, 1999, Chicago, tape recording, City Hall, Chicago; Faith C. Christmas, "Woods States His Case as a 2d Ward Hopeful," *Chicago Defender,* January 8, 1969, n.p., DSP-CGWL; Drew Pearson, *Washington Post,* May 14, 1950, WLDP-FUL; Ethel L. Payne, "Is Dawson Aide, Woods, Bounced or Not," *Chicago Daily Defender,* March 18, 1969, 1; James Free, *Champaign—Urbana Courier,* March 16, 1956, 25, WLDP-FUL; Louis Lautier, "Rep. Dawson-From Georgia Bootblack to Congressman," *Journal and Guide,* October 7, 1950, 10, WLDP-FUL; "Sidney

Sanders McMath (1949–1953)," available at www.oldstatehouse.com/exhibits/virtual/ governors/from_the_forties_to_faubus/mcmath.asp, A Multimedia Museum of Arkansas History, People, and Culture, Old State House Museum, Little Rock, AR, retrieved March 17, 2007; Mike Royko, "Woods Pays a Visit," *Chicago Daily News,* February 27, 1969, n.p., DSP-CGWL; Jay McMullen, "2d Ward Aldermanic Choice: Black Militant or Dawson Aide," *Chicago Daily News,* February 26, 1969, n.p., DSP-CGWL.

6. Faith C. Christmas, "Woods States His Case as a 2d Ward Hopeful," *Chicago Defender,* January 8, 1969, n.p., DSP-CGWL; Charles Bowen, interview by author, November 1, 1999, Chicago, tape recording, City Hall, Chicago.

7. Mike Royko, "Woods Pays a Visit," *Chicago Daily News,* February 27, 1969, n.p., DSP-CGWL.

8. Jay McMullen, "2d Ward Aldermanic Choice: Black Militant or Dawson Aide," *Chicago Daily News,* February 26, 1969, n.p., DSP-CGWL; N.A., "Chicago Voters Tilt Mayor Daley's Machine," *Commonweal,* April 25, 1969, n.p., DSP-CGWL; Basil Talbott Jr. and Sam Washington, "Cousins, Rayner Hail Hubbard: 'Now There Are Three of Us," *Chicago Sun-Times,* March 12, 1969, n.p., DSP-CGWL.

9. "Democrats Brand Dawson Illness Rumor as Politics," *Chicago Daily-Defender,* October 29, 1962, 2, WLDP-FUL; Robert Gruenberg, Chicago, to William L. Dawson, October 30, 1962, WLDP-FUL; William H. McDowell, to William L. Dawson, Washington, D.C., February 23, 1963, WLDP-FUL; Sheryl Fitzgerald and Betty Johnson, "Dawson Assured of Re-Election," *Chicago Defender,* December 6, 1968, 2, DSP-GGWL; "Black Voters Reject Three Independents," *Chicago Daily Defender,* June 12, 1968, 3, DSP-CGWL; Ethel L. Payne, "Dawson Tells Why He Nixed Black Paper," *Chicago Defender,* September 29, 1969, 2, DSP-CGWL.

10. Jay McMullen, "2d Ward Aldermanic Choice: Black Militant or Dawson Aide," *Chicago Daily News,* February 26, 1969, n.p., DSP-CGWL; Mike Royko, "Woods Pays a Visit," *Chicago Daily News,* February 27, 1969, n.p., DSP-CGWL; Mike Royko, "Endorsements of Woods Hokey," *Chicago Daily News,* February 18, 1969, n.p., DSP-CGWL; N.A., "Seeks Aldermanic Post," *Chicago Tribune,* January 5, 1969, n.p., DSP-CGWL; Faith C. Christmas, "Woods States His Case as a 2d Ward Hopeful," *Chicago Defender,* January 8, 1969, n.p., DSP-CGWL; N.A., *Chicago Sun-Times,* "Woods Gets There First," n.p., January 1, 1969, DSP-CGWL.

11. Edmund J. Rooney, "Dawson Rival Shot in Campaign Office," *Washington Post,* April 6, 1966, n.p., WLDP-FUL; "Few Surprises in Quiet Primary Voting," *Chicago Daily Defender,* June 15, 1966, 5; "Here Are Our Aldermanic Preferences," *Chicago Daily Defender,* February 27, 1967, 11; Doris E. Saunders, "Negroes a Cinch to Win 8 Races, Maybe 9," *Chicago Daily Defender,* January 12, 1967, 4; Doris E. Saunders, "Confetti," *Chicago Daily Defender,* January 26, 1967, 12; Basil Talbott Jr., "Dawson's Regulars Challenged Anew by Hubbard in the 2d Ward," *Chicago Sun-Times,* July 4, 1969, n.p. DSP-CGWL.

12. "IVI Backing Hubbard, Stevens, Singer in March 11 Elections," *Chicago Daily Defender,* January 29, 1969, 10; "3 Aldermen May Back Hubbard," *Chicago Daily Defender,* February 8, 1969, 3.

13. "Hubbard Won't Quit 2d Ward Race, Aid Tells Black IVI," *Chicago Daily Defender,* February 4, 1969, 1; Faith C. Christmas, "New Breed Group Backs Woods for Second Ward Aldermancy," January 11, 1969, 1.

14. Mike Royko, "Endorsements of Woods Hokey," *Chicago Daily News,* February 18, 1969, n.p., DSP-CGWL; Mike Royko, "Woods Pays a Visit," *Chicago Daily News,* February 27, 1969, n.p., DSP-CGWL; "Hubbard No Underdog, Defeats Machine," *Chicago Daily Defender,* March 12, 1969, 1.

15. Vernon Jarrett, "Fred Hubbard's Actual Crime," *Chicago Tribune,* January 10,

1973 18; "Chicago Voters Tilt Mayor Daley's Machine," *Commonweal*, April 25, 1969, n.p., DSP-CGWL.

16. Basil Talbott Jr. and Sam Washington, "Cousins, Rayner Hail Hubbard: 'Now There Are Three of Us,'" *Chicago Sun-Times*, March 12, 1969, n.p., DSP-CGWL.

17. Harry Golden Jr., "Daley: Dawson Fate up to Slatemakers," *Chicago Sun-Times*, November 5, 1969, 40, DSP-CGWL; Harry Golden Jr., "Asks Daley's OK on Metcalfe bid for Dawson Seat," *Chicago Sun-Times*, November 4, 1969, 3; "Rayner Officially Enters Race for Rep. Dawson's Seat," *Chicago Sun-Times*, December 10, 1969, 10; Pierre Guilmant, "Rayner Will Run Against Dawson," *Chicago Daily Defender*, August 12, 1969, 4, DSP-CGWL.

18. "William L. Dawson Decides He Won't Run for Reelection," *Washington Afro-American*, n.p., November 25, 1969, WLDP-FUL; John H. Sengstacke, "Dawson Will Not Run!" *Chicago Daily Defender*, November 17, 1969, 1.

19. *Chicago Defender*, November 11, 1970, 3; Ellen Hoffman, *Washington Post*, November 10, 1970, B6; "Dawson Rites Set Thursday," *Chicago Daily Defender*, November 10, 1970, 1; "Flags in D.C. Flown Half-Mast," *Chicago Daily Defender*, November 10, 1970, 6; "LBJ, Daley Laud Dawson," *Chicago Daily Defender*, November 10, 1970, 4; "William L. Dawson: The Man," *Chicago Daily Defender*, November 10, 1970, 6; "U.S. House Vet Dawson Dies at 84," *Chicago Tribune*, November 10, 1970, A10.

20. "Flags in D.C. Flown Half-Mast," *Chicago Daily Defender*, November 10, 1970, 6; Maron B. Campfield, "Top Leaders at Dawson Rites," *Chicago Daily Defender*, November 12, 1970, 1.

21. Steven Pratt, "Dawson's Pals of Old File by Bier," *Chicago Tribune*, November 12, 1970, C16; Michael Killian, "2,000 Led By Mayor Daley Attend Rep. Dawson's Funeral," *Chicago Tribune*, November 13, 1970.

22. Warner Saunders, "William Dawson: A Really Great Man in His Time," *Chicago Defender*, December 8, 1970, 8.

23. Diane M. Pinderhughes, *Race and Ethnicity in Chicago Politics: A Reexamination of Pluralist Theory* (Urbana: University of Illinois Press, 1987), 58, 239; Patrick D. Joyce, "A Reversal of Fortunes: Black Empowerment, Political Machines, and City Jobs in New York City and Chicago," *Urban Affairs Journal* 32 (1997), 299; Charles Branham, "The Transformation of Black Political Leadership in Chicago, 1864–1942," Ph.D. diss., University of Chicago, 1981, iii, 444.

24. Earl Dickerson, I contend, saw the same series of events as Dawson, but he essentially sought political office as a means of obtaining a platform to address civil rights issues and largely ignored the political considerations necessary to retain office.

25. Nancy Weiss, *Farewell to the Party of Lincoln: Black Politics in the Age of FDR* (Princeton, N.J.: Princeton University Press, 1983), xiii, 120–36; Desmond King, *Separate and Unequal: Black Americans and the US Federal Government* (Oxford: Clarendon Press, 1995), 7; St. Clair Drake and Horace Cayton, *Black Metropolis: A Study of Negro Life in a Northern City*, 4th ed. (Chicago: University of Chicago Press, 1993), 369; Harvard Sitkoff, *A New Deal for Blacks: The Emergence of Civil Rights as a National Issue*. Vol. 1: *The Depression Decade* (New York: Oxford University Press, 1978), 18–19, 139–69, 331–33.

26. Charles Bowen, interview by Christopher Manning, tape recording, November 1, 1999, recording in possession of the interviewer, Chicago; M. Earl Sarden, interview by Christopher Manning, tape recording, July 30, 2002, recording in possession of the interviewer, Chicago; Corneal Davis, interview by Horace Waggoner, IGAOHP-BL.

27. Harry Keane, "Dawson's Record Shows Great Value to Race," *Chicago Defender*, October 2, 1948, 1, 3; "Dawson Aide Voted Vice-Chairman," paper unidentifiable, n.p., WLDP-FUL; Richard J. Daley campaign posters, circa 1959, WLDP-FUL; "In His Rise, He Has Taken Others With Him," *Chicago Defender*, October 4, 1950, 25; Edward Clayton,

The Negro Politician (Chicago: Johnson Publishing, 1964), 74; Nicholas Lemann, *The Promised Land: The Great Black Migration and How It Changed America* (New York: Vintage Books, 1991), 75; "In His Rise, He Has Taken Others With Him," *Chicago Defender,* November 4, 1950, 25; Branham, 444; Patrick D. Joyce, 299.

Though they may disagree on the length of time Dawson held sway over black politics in Chicago and on the length of time Dawson exercised influence over the entire Regular Organization, historians and political scientists, such as James Wilson and William Grimshaw, agree that William Dawson created the most powerful black political machine in Chicago history. For examples see Clayton, *The Negro Politician;* William J. Grimshaw, *Bitter Fruit: Black Politics and the Chicago Machine, 1931–1909;* Nicholas Lemann, *The Promised Land: The Great Black Migration and How it Changed America;* Christopher Robert Reed, *The Chicago NAACP and the Rise of Black Professional Leadership, 1910–1966;* Chuck Stone, *Black Political Power in America;* James Q. Wilson, *Negro Politics the Search for Leadership.*

28. Pinderhughes, xvii–xix, 199.

29. William J. Grimshaw, *Bitter Fruit: Black Politics and the Chicago Machine, 1931–1991* (Chicago: University of Chicago Press, 1992) 94; Pinderhughes, 241.

30. His colleagues Adam Clayton Powell and Charles Diggs submitted even more civil rights bills, 76 and 53 respectively. Yet these higher numbers made little difference, for no black representative's civil rights bills made it out of committee during the period in question. My examination of the *Congressional Record* indicates that over the entire period examined (1942–1968) the black delegation—William Dawson, Adam Clayton Powell, Charles Diggs, Augustus Hawkins, Robert Nix, and John Conyers—proposed a total of 202 civil rights bills; none of which passed its initial committee assignment.

31. In *The Congressional Black Caucus: Racial Politics in the U.S. Congress,* Robert Singh makes the following argument regarding black Congressmen in the postwar era: "One-party dependence and majority black districts limited the coalitional potential of black legislators, and securing policy advances for blacks remained dependent on the building of broad-based legislative coalitions for which black members possessed few resources."

32. The real battle for these bills occurred in the Senate, where Johnson had to maneuver to prevent Southern filibusters of his legislation. Consequently, although he welcomd support from the black delegation, it does not appear to have been necessary.

See Weisbrot, 88–92; Congressional Quarterly Service, *Congress and the Nation 1945–1964: A Review of Government and Politics in the Postwar Years* (Washington, D.C.: Congressional Quarterly Service, 1965), 1635–36.

33. There were several other moments when Dawson's blackness rendered him second rate in the eyes of white, and sometimes black, politicians. When Dawson ran against Congressman Madden, for example, the Thompson Republican organization did not take his campaign seriously, and Oscar DePriest questioned the legitimacy of an black American in a position of such esteem. In *Big City Boss In Depression and War: Mayor Edward J. Kelly of Chicago,* Roger Biles noted that Mayor Kelly did not envision Dawson as a man to "whom he could entrust the administration of the party's interests in the black community: he initially chose Dawson for a very specific purpose, to take control of one troublesome ward."

34. Chew said, "Congressman Dawson was the first man who inspired me into politics. I have sat and talked to him long hours at a time and the advice he gave me back in those early years is responsible for me being an elected official today." See Richard Slusser, November 11, 1970, WLDP-FUL.See also Dempsey Travis, *Harold The People's Mayor: An Authorized Biography of Mayor Harold Washington* (Chicago: Urban Research Press, 1989), 70.

35. In an interview with Doris Saunders, Metcalfe said that Dawson "has been an inspiration . . . [he] brought to the American public a new image of the black man. He was instrumental when redistricting occurred. I saw him wage a fight to get a black committeeman. He forced the County Central Committee. It was not easy. Then the fight that he waged which was much harder was to get the white man out. He had to lay his own committeemanship on the line." See Ralph Metcalfe, interview by Doris Saunders, transcript, February 25, 1970, DSP-CGWL.

See also Pinderhughes, 240; Grimshaw, 136–37, 148, 221.

36. Travis, 10, 12, 47–51, 60–71.

37. Clayton, 74.

38. Ethel L. Payne, "Dawson: Master Quiet Politician," *Chicago Daily Defender,* November 14, 1970, 2, WLDP-FUL.

SELECTED BIBLIOGRAPHY

Interviews

William Levi Dawson. Interview by Nathaniel C. Standifer, date n.a. Video tape recording. Retrieved October 6, 2006, from www.umich.edu/~afroammu/standifer/dawson.html, Nathaniel C. Standifer Video Archive of Oral History: Black American Musicians, African American Music Collection, University of Michigan, Ann Harbor, Mich.

Despres, Leon. Interview by Christopher Manning, January 21, 2000. Audio recording in possession of the author, Chicago.

Bowen, Charles. Interview by Christopher Manning, November 1, 1999. Audio recording in possession of the author, Chicago.

Davis, Corneal. Interview by Doris Saunders, March 11, 1970. Transcript in Doris Saunders Papers, Vivian G. Harsh Research Collection, Carter G. Woodson Library, Chicago.

Davis, Corneal. Interview by Horace Waggoner, 1979–1982. Transcript. Retrieved November 7, 2006, from www.uis.edu/archives/memoirs/DAVISCORNEALvI.pdf and www.uis.edu/archives/memoirs/DAVISCORNEALvII.pdf, Illinois General Assembly Oral History Program, Brooken Library, University of Illinois at Springfield, Springfield, Illinois.

Gibson, Truman Jr. Interview by Christopher Manning, February 25, 2000. Audio recording in possession of the author, Chicago.

Rostenkowski, Dan. Interview by Christopher Manning, January 5, 2000. Audio recording in possession of the author, Chicago.

Sarden, M. Earl. Interview by Christopher Manning, July 30, 2002. Audio recording in possession of the author, Chicago.

Wall, Fred. Interview by Doris Saunders, March 29, 1970. Transcript in Doris Saunders Papers, Vivian G. Harsh Research Collection, Carter G. Woodson Library, Chicago.

Archives and Paper Collections

Barnett, Claude Papers. Chicago Historical Society, Chicago.

Burns, Ben Papers. Vivian G. Harsh Research Collection. Carter G. Woodson Library, Chicago.

Dawson, William L. Papers. Archives, Fisk University Library. Fisk University, Nashville, Tenn.

Civil Unrest in Camilla, Georgia, 1868. Digital Library of Georgia. Retrieved October 2, 2006, from http://dlg.galileo.usg.edu/camilla/

DePriest, Oscar Papers. Chicago Historical Society, Chicago.

Mitchell, Arthur Papers. Chicago Historical Society, Chicago.

1910 Census Soundex. Rare Books Collection. Genealogy and Special Collections Room, Dougherty County Public Library, Albany, Ga.

Saunders, Doris E. Papers. Vivian G. Harsh Research Collection, Carter G. Woodson Library, Chicago.

Truman, Harry S. Papers. Truman Library and Museum, Independence, Mo.

Wimbish, Christopher C. Papers. Chicago Historical Society, Chicago.

Works Cited

"2005 Republican Freedom Calendar." Retrieved May 15, 2006, from http://policy. house.gov/2005_calendar/sep.cfm.

Allen, James, Hilton Als, John Lewis, and Leon F. Litwack. *Without Sanctuary: Lynching Photography in America*. Santa Fe, N.M.: Twin Palms Publishers, 2005.

Anderson, James D. *The Education of Blacks in the South, 1860–1935*. Chapel Hill: University of North Carolina Press, 1988.

Anderson, Jervis. *A. Philip Randolph: A Biographical Portrait*. Berkeley: University of California Press, 1986.

Astor, Gerald. *The Right to Fight: A History of African Americans in the Military*. Cambridge, Mass.: Da Capo Press, 2001.

Aull, Ruth, and Daniel M. Ogden, eds. *Official Report of the Proceedings of the Democratic National Convention, Chicago, Illinois, August 13 through August 17, 1956, Resulting in the Re-Nomination of Adlai E. Stevenson of Illinois for President and the Nomination of Estes Kefauver of Tennessee for Vice-President*. Chicago: Democratic National Convention, 1956.

Bacon, Mary Ellen. *Albany on the Flint: Indians to Industry, 1836–1936*. Albany: Albany Town Committee of the Colonial Dames of America in the State of Georgia, 1970.

Barbeau, Arthur E., and Florette Henri. *The Unknown Soldiers: Black American Troops in World War I*. Philadelphia: Temple University Press, 1974.

Barker, Lucius J., and Mack H. Jones. *African Americans and the American Political System*, 3rd ed. Englewood Cliffs, N.J.: Prentice Hall, 1994.

Bartley, Numan V. *The Creation of Modern Georgia*, 2nd ed. Athens: University of Georgia Press, 1990.

Bates, Beth Tompkins. "A New Crowd Challenges the Agenda of the Old Guard in the NAACP, 1933–1941." *American Historical Review* 102 (1997): 340–77.

———. *Pullman Porters and the Rise of Protest Politics in Black America, 1925–1945*. Chapel Hill: University of North Carolina Press, 2001.

Best, Wallace D. *Passionately Human, No Less Divine: Religion and Culture in Black Chicago, 1915–1952*. Princeton, N.J.: Princeton University Press, 2005.

Biles, Roger. *Big City Boss in Depression and War: Mayor Edward J. Kelly of Chicago*. DeKalb: Northern Illinois University Press, 1984.

———. *Richard J. Daley: Politics, Race, and the Governing of Chicago*. DeKalb: Northern Illinois University Press, 1995.

———. "Edward Kelly: New Deal Machine Builder." In *The Mayors: The Chicago Political Tradition*, ed. Paul M. Green and Melvin G. Holli. Carbondale: Southern Illinois University Press, 1995.

Biondi, Martha. *To Stand and Fight: The Struggle for Civil Rights in Postwar New York City*. Cambridge, Mass.: Harvard University Press, 2003.

"Black History Month a Medical Perspective." Retrieved October 6, 2006, from www. mclibrary.duke.edu/hmc/exhibits/blkhist/.

Blakely, Robert J., with Marcus Shepard. *Earl B. Dickerson: A Voice for Freedom and Equality*. Evanston, Ill.: Northwestern University Press, 2006.

Branch, Taylor. *Parting the Waters: America in the King Years, 1954–1963*. New York: Simon & Schuster, 1988.

———. *Pillar of Fire: America in the King Years, 1963–65*. New York: Simon & Schuster, 1998.

Branham, Charles. "The Transformation of Black Political Leadership in Chicago, 1864–1942." Ph.D. dissertation, University of Chicago, 1981.

Brauer, Carl M. *John F. Kennedy and the Second Reconstruction*. New York: Columbia University Press, 1977.

Bray, William J., and Venice T. Spraggs, eds., *Official Report of the Proceedings of the Democratic National Convention, Chicago, Illinois, July 21 to July 26, Inclusive, 1952, resulting in the nomination of Adlai E. Stevenson of Illinois for President and the nomination of John J. Sparkman of Alabama for Vice President.* Chicago: M. Kallis, 1952.

Brazzell, Johnetta Cross. "Brick Without Straw: Missionary-Sponored Higher Education in the Post-Emancipation Era." *Journal of Higher Education,* 63 (1992): 26–49.

Brown, Aaron. *The Negro in Albany.* Albany, Georgia: Np, 1945. Rare Books Collection, Genealogy and Special Collections Room, Dougherty County Public Library, Albany, Ga.

Brown, Edgar C. ed. *Democracy At Work, Being The Official Report of the Democratic National Convention, Philadelphia, Pennsylvania, July 12 to July 14, inclusive, 1948, Resulting in the Nomination of Harry S. Truman of Missouri For President and Alben W. Barkley of Kentucky For Vice-President.* Philadelphia: Local Democratic Council of Pennsylvania, 1948.

Brundage, W. Fitzhugh. *Lynching in the New South: Georgia and Virginia, 1880–1930.* Urbana: University of Illinois Press, 1993.

Buckley, Gail. *American Patriots: The Story of Blacks in the Military from the Revolution to Desert Storm.* New York: Random House, 2001.

Buenker, John D. "Edward F. Dunne: The Limits of Municipal Reform." In *The Mayors: The Chicago Political Tradition,* rev. ed., ed. Paul M. Green and Melvin G. Holli. Carbondale: Southern Illinois University Press, 1995.

Bullock, Henry Allen. *A History of Negro Education in the South: From 1619 to the Present.* Cambridge, Mass.: Harvard University Press, 1967.

Burke, Robert Frederick. *Eisenhower and Black Civil Rights.* Knoxville: University of Tennessee Press, 1984.

Butchart, Ronald E. "Mission Matters; Mount Holyoke, Oberlin, and the Schooling of Southern Blacks." *History of Education Quarterly* 42 (2002): 1–17.

———. "'Outthinking and Outflanking the Owners of the World': A Historiography of the African American Struggle for Education." *History of Education Quarterly* 28 (1998): 333–66.

———. "Remapping Racial Boundaries: Teachers as Border Police and Boundary Transgressors in Post-Emancipation Black Education, USA, 1861–1971." *Pedagogia Historica* 43 (2007): 61–78.

Canaan, Gareth. "'Part of the Loaf': Economic Conditions of Chicago's African-American Working Class During the 1920's." *Journal of Social History* 35 (fall 2001): 147–68.

Carlyle, Ramsey B. "History of Albany State College." Ph.D. dissertation, Florida State University, 1973.

Carmichael, Stokely, and Charles V. Hamilton. *Black Power: The Politics of Liberation in America.* New York: Vintage Books, 1967.

Cartwright, Joseph H. *The Triumph of Jim Crow: Tennessee Race Relations in the 1880s.* Knoxville: University of Tennessee Press, 1976.

"Bishop Ford Honored at DuSable Museum." Retrieved May 16, 2008, from http://cbs2chicago.com/local/bishop.ford.honored.2.623852. CBS 2 Chicago.

Chase, Hal. "Struggle for Equality: Fort Des Moines Training Camp for Colored Officers." *Phylon* 39 (1978): 297–310.

"Chicago Beach Hotel." Retrieved October 16, 2006, from patsabin.com/illinois/chicagobeach.html. Old Chicago History and Architecture in Vintage Postcards.

"Chicago Beach Hotel, c. 1903." Retrieved October 10, 2006, from www.encyclopedia.chicagohistory.org/pages/10935.html.

Chicago Commission on Race Relations. *The Negro in Chicago: A Study of Race Relations and a Race Riot.* Chicago: University of Chicago Press, 1922.

Christmas, Walter. *Negroes in Public Affairs.* Yonkers, N.Y.: Educational Heritage, 1966.

Christopher, Maurine. *America's Black Congressmen.* New York: Thomas Y. Crowell, 1971.

Cimbala, Paul A. "A Black Colony in Dougherty County: The Freedman's Bureau and the Failure of Reconstruction in Southwest Georgia." *Journal of Southwest Georgia History* 4 (1986): 72–89.

———. "Reconstruction's Allies: The Relationship of the Freedmen's Bureau and Georgia Freedmen." In *The Freedmen's Bureau and Reconstruction,* ed. Paul A. Cimbala and Randall M. Miller. New York: Fordham University Press, 1999.

———. *Under the Guardianship of the Nation: The Freedmen's Bureau and the Reconstruction of Georgia, 1865–1879.* Athens: University of Georgia Press, 1997.

Clapham, Christopher. "Clientelism and the State." In *Private Patronage and Public Power: Political Clientelism in the Modern State,* ed. Christopher Clapham. New York: St. Martin's Press, 1982.

Clay, William L. *Just Permanent Interests: Black Americans in Congress, 1870–1991.* New York: Amistad Press, 1992.

Clayton, Edward T. *The Negro Politician.* Chicago: Johnson Publishing, 1964.

Cobb, James C. *The Most Southern Place on Earth: The Mississippi Delta and the Roots of Regional Identity.* New York: Oxford University Press, 1992.

Cohen, Adam, and Elizabeth Taylor. *American Pharaoh. Mayor Richard J. Daley: His Battle for Chicago and the Nation.* Boston: Little, Brown, 2000.

Cohen, Lizabeth. *Making a New Deal: Industrial Workers in Chicago, 1919–1939.* New York: Cambridge University Press, 1990.

Congressional Quarterly Service. *Congress and the Nation, 1945–1964: A Review of Government and Politics in the Postwar Years.* Washington, D.C.: Congressional Quarterly Service, 1965.

———. *Congress and the Nation. Volume II 1965–1968: A Review of Government and Politics.* Washington, D.C.: Congressional Quarterly Service, 1969.

"Coordinating Council of Community Organizations." Retrieved May 16, 2008, from www.encyclopedia.chicagohistory.org/pages/221.html.

County Government of Dougherty County, Ga. *Albany and Dougherty County, Georgia: A Descriptive and Illustrated Pamphlet Issued Under the Auspices of the City and Council Authorities.* Albany, Ga.: H. T. McIntosh & J. A. Davis, Jr., 1904.

Cuoto, Richard A. "Race Relations and Tennessee Centennials." In *Trial and Triumph: Essays in Tennessee's African-American History,* ed. Caroll Van West, 244–63. Knoxville: University of Tennessee Press, 2002.

"Daniel Hale Williams." Retrieved October 18, 2006, from www.blackinventor.com/pages/danielwilliams.html.

"Daniel Hale Williams." Retrieved October 18, 2006, from www.pbs.org/wnet/aaworld/reference/articles/daniel_hale_williams.html.

Danns, Dionne. *Something Better for Our Children: Black Organizing in Chicago Public Schools, 1963–1971.* New York: Routledge, 2003.

Darnell Hunt. "A Different World." Retrieved October 10, 2006, from www.museum.tv/archives/etv/D/htmlD/differentwor/differentwor.html.

D'Emilio, John. *Lost Prophet: The Life and Times of Bayard Rustin.* Chicago: University of Chicago Press, 2003.

Dickerson, Dennis C. *Militant Mediator: Whitney M. Young, Jr.* Lexington: University Press of Kentucky, 1998.

Dittmer, John. *Local People: The Struggle for Civil Rights in Mississippi.* Urbana: University of Illinois Press, 1994.

———. *Black Georgia in the Progressive Era, 1900–1920.* Urbana: University of Illinois Press, 1977.

Drake, St. Clair, and Horace Cayton. *Black Metropolis: A Study of Negro Life in a Northern City,* rev. ed. Chicago: University of Chicago Press, 1993.

Drago, Edmund L. *Black Politicians and Reconstruction in Georgia*. Baton Rouge: Louisiana State University Press, 1982.

DuBois, W.E.B. *Souls of Black Folk*. 1903. Reprint, New York: Vintage, 1990.

Ellis, Mark. "'Closing Ranks' and 'Seeking Honors': W.E.B. DuBois in World War I." *Journal of American History* 79 (1992): 96–124.

———. "W.E.B. DuBois and the Formation of Black Public Opinion in World War I: A Commentary on 'The Damnable Dilemma.'" *Journal of American History* 81 (1995): 1584–90.

Eschen, Penny Von. *Race Against Empire: Black Americans and Anticolonialism, 1937–1957*. Ithaca, N.Y.: Cornell University Press, 1997.

Fair, John D. "Nelson Tift: A Connecticut Yankee in King Cotton's Court." *Georgia Historical Quarterly* 88 (2004): 338–74.

Fairclough, Adam. *Better Day Coming: Blacks and Equality, 1890–2000*. New York: Penguin Books, 2001.

Ferrel, Robert H. *Harry S. Truman: A Life*. Columbia: University of Missouri Press, 1994.

Fitzgerald, Michael. *The Union League Movement in the Deep South*. Baton Rouge: Louisiana State University Press, 1989.

Flanagan, Maureen A. "Fred A. Busse: A Silent Mayor in Turbulent Times." In *The Mayors: The Chicago Political Tradition*, rev. ed., ed. Paul M. Green and Melvin G. Holli. Carbondale: Southern Illinois University Press, 1995.

Flynn, Charles L, Jr. *White Land, Black Labor: Caste and Class in Late Nineteenth Century Georgia*. Baton Rouge: Louisiana State University Press, 1983.

Foner, Eric. *Reconstruction America's Unfinished Revolution, 1863–1877*. New York: Harper & Row, 1988.

Foner, Jack D. *Blacks and the Military in American History: A New Perspective*. New York: Praeger, 1974.

Formwalt, Lee W. "The Origins of African-American Politics in Southwest Georgia: A Case Study of Black Political Organization During Presidential Reconstruction, 1865–1867." *Journal of Negro History* 77 (1992): 211–22.

———. "Petitioning for Protection: A Black View of Reconstruction at the Local Level." *Georgia Historical Quarterly* 73 (1989): 302–22.

———. "Planter Persistence in Southwestern Georgia, 1850–1870." *Journal of Southwest Georgia History* 2 (1984): 40–58.

Franklin, John Hope, and Alfred A. Moss. *From Slavery to Freedom: A History of African Americans*. New York: McGraw-Hill, 1994.

Fuerst, J.S. *When Public Housing Was Paradise*. Urbana: University of Illinois Press, 2005.

"Georgia Constitution of 1868," Georgia Info, Carl Vinson Institute of Government, University of Georgia. Retrieved October 6, 2006, from www.cviog.uga.edu/Projects/gainfo/con1868.html.

Gosnell, Harold F. *Negro Politicians: The Rise of Negro Politics in Chicago*. Chicago: University of Chicago Press, 1967.

———. *Truman's Crises: A Political Biography of Harry S. Truman*. Westport, Conn.: Greenwood Press, 1980.

Granger, Bill, and Lori Granger. *Lords of the Last Machine: The Story of Chicago Politics*. New York: Random House, 1987.

Grant, Donald L. *The Way it Was in the South: The Black Experience in Georgia*. New York: Birch Lane Press, 1993.

Green, Adam. *Selling the Race: Culture, Community, and Black Chicago, 1940–1955*. Chicago: University of Chicago Press, 2007.

Green, Paul M. "Anton Cermak: The Man and His Machine." In *The Mayors: The Chicago Political Tradition*, rev. ed., ed. Paul M. Green and Melvin G. Holli. Carbondale: Southern Illinois University Press, 1995.

———. "Irish Chicago: The Multiethnic Road to Success." In *Ethnic Chicago*, ed. Peter d' A. Jones and Melvin Holli. Grand Rapids, Mich.: William B. Eerdmans, 1981.

Gottfried, Alex. *Boss Cermak of Chicago: A Study of Political Leadership*. Seattle: University of Washington Press, 1962.

Grimshaw, William. *Bitter Fruit: Black Politics and the Chicago Political Machine, 1931–1991*. Chicago: University of Chicago Press, 1992.

Grossman, James. *Land of Hope: Chicago, Black Southerners, and the Great Migration*. Chicago: University of Chicago Press, 1989.

Hadley, Charles D. "The Transformation of the Role of Black Ministers and Black Political Organizations in Louisiana Politics." In *Blacks in Southern Politics*, ed. Laurence W. Moreland, Robert P. Steed, and Tod A. Baker. New York: Praeger, 1987.

Haller, Mark H. "Policy Gambling, Entertainment, and the Emergence of Black Politics: Chicago from 1900–1940." *Journal of Social History* 24 (1991): 719–39.

Hamby, Alonzo. *Man of the People. A Life of Harry S. Truman*. New York: Oxford University Press, 1995.

Hamilton, Charles V. *Adam Clayton Powell, Jr.: The Political Biography of an American Dilemma*. New York: Atheneum, 1991.

Hahn, Steven. *The Roots of Southern Populism: Yeoman Farmers and the Transformation of the Georgia Upcountry, 1850–1890*. New York: Oxford University Press, 1983.

Haygood, Wil. *King of Cats: The Life and Times of Adam Clayton Powell, Jr.* Boston: Houghton-Mifflin, 1993.

Hine, Darlene Clark, Elsa Barkley Brown, and Rosalyn Terbog-Penn, eds. *Black Women in America: An Historical Encyclopedia*. Bloomington: Indiana University Press, 1993.

Hirsch, Arnold R. "The Cook County Democratic Organization and the Dilemma of Race, 1931–1987." In *Snowbelt Cities: Metropolitan Politics in the Northwest and Midwest Since World War II*, ed. Richard M. Bernard. Bloomington: Indiana University Press, 1990.

———. *Making the Second Ghetto: Race and Housing in Chicago, 1940–1960*. New York: Cambridge University Press, 1983.

"Index to Politicians: Carey." Retrieved April 15, 2007, from politicalgraveyard.com/bio/carey.html.

Inglot, Tomasz, and John P. Pelissero. "Ethnic Political Power in a Machine City. Chicago's Poles at Rainbow's End." *Urban Affairs Quarterly* 28 (June 1993): 526–43.

Joyce, Patrick D. "A Reversal of Fortunes. Black Empowerment, Political Machines, and City Jobs in New York City and Chicago." *Urban Affairs Review* 32 (January 1997): 291–318.

Kantowicz, Edward R. "Carter H. Harrison II: The Politics of Balance." In *The Mayors: The Chicago Political Tradition*, ed. Paul M. Green and Melvin G. Holli. Carbondale: Southern Illinois University Press, 1995.

Kennedy, William Howland. *Chicago Jazz: A Cultural History, 1904–1930*. New York: Oxford University Press, 1993.

King, Desmond. *Separate and Unequal: Black Americans and the U.S. Federal Government*. Oxford: Oxford University Press, 1995.

Kravitz, Walter, ed. *American Congressional Dictionary*, 2nd ed. Washington, D.C.: Congressional Quarterly Press, 1997.

Kyriakoudes, Louis M. *The Social Origins of the Urban South: Race, Gender, and Migration in Nashville and Middle Tennessee, 1890–1930*. Chapel Hill: University of North Carolina Press, 2003.

Lammon, Lester C. *Black Tennesseans, 1900–1903*. Knoxville: University of Tennessee Press, 1977.

Lawson, Steven F. *In Pursuit of Power: Southern Blacks and Electoral Politics, 1965–1982.* New York: Columbia University Press, 1985.

Laville, Helen, and Scott Lucas. "The American Way: Edith Sampson, the NAACP, and African American Identity in the Cold War." *Diplomatic History* 20 (fall 1996): 565–90.

Lemann, Nicholas. *The Promised Land: The Great Black Migration and How It Changed America.* New York: Vintage Books, 1991.

Lovett, Bobby L. *The African-American History of Nashville, Tennessee, 1780–1930.* Fayetteville: University of Arkansas Press, 1999.

MacGregor, Morris J., and Bernard C. Nalty, eds. *Blacks in the United States Armed Forces. Basic Documents.* Vol. IV: *Segregation Entrenched 1917–1940.* Wilmington, Del.: Scholarly Resources, 1977.

Martin, Waldo E., Jr. *Brown v. Board of Education: A Brief History with Documents.* Boston: St. Martin's Press, 1998.

McCoy, Donald R., and Richard T. Reuten. *Quest and Response: Minority Rights and the Truman Administration.* Lawrence: University Press of Kansas, 1973.

McKeever, Porter. *Adlai Stevenson: His Life and Legacy.* New York: William Morrow, 1989.

McMillen, Neil R. *Dark Journey: Black Mississippians in the Age of Jim Crow.* Urbana: University of Illinois Press, 1990.

Morris, Aldon. *Origins of the Civil Rights Movement: Black Communities Organizing for Change.* New York: Free Press, 1984.

Myrdal, Gunnar. *An American Dilemma: The Negro Problem and Modern American Democracy.* New York: Harper & Brothers, 1944.

National Association for the Advancement of Colored People [NAACP]. *Thirty Years of Lynching in the United State, 1889–1918.* New York: Negro Universities Press, 1969.

Nordin, Dennis S. *The New Deal's Black Congressman: A Life of Arthur Wergs Mitchell.* Columbia: University of Missouri Press, 1997.

O'Connor, Len. *Clout: Mayor Daley and His City.* Chicago: Henry Regnery, 1975.

Ottley, Roi. *The Lonely Warrior: The Life and Times of Robert S. Abbott.* Chicago: Henry Regnery, 1955.

Payne, Charles M. *I've Got the Light of Freedom: The Organizing Tradition and the Mississippi Freedom Struggle.* Berkeley: University of California Press, 1995.

Pfeffer, Paula F. *A. Philip Randolph, Pioneer of the Civil Rights Movement.* Baton Rouge: Louisiana State University Press, 1990.

Philpott, Thomas Lee. *The Slum and the Ghetto: Immigrants, Blacks and Reformers in Chicago, 1880–1930.* Belmont, Calif.: Wadsworth, 1991.

Pinderhughes, Diane M. *Race and Ethnicity in Chicago Politics: A Reexamination of Pluralist Theory.* Urbana: University of Illinois Press, 1987.

Ploski, Harry, and Roscoe C. Brown. *Negro Almanac.* New York: Bell Weather, 1967.

Plummer, Brenda Gayle. *Rising Wind: Black Americans and U.S. Foreign Affairs, 1935–1960.* Chapel Hill: University of North Carolina Press, 1996.

Rakove, Milton. *Don't Make No Waves, Don't Back No Losers: An Insider's Analysis of the Daley Machine.* Bloomington: Indiana University Press, 1975.

Ralph, James R., Jr. *Northern Protest: Martin Luther King, Jr., Chicago, and the Civil Rights Movement.* Cambridge, Mass.: Harvard University Press, 1993.

Ramsey, Carlyle B. "History of Albany State College, 1903–1965." Ph.D. dissertation, University of Michigan, 1973.

Reed, Christopher Robert. *"All the World Is Here! The Black Presence at the White City.* Bloomington: Indiana University Press, 2000.

———. *The Chicago NAACP and the Rise of Black Professional Leadership, 1910–1966.* Bloomington: Indiana University Press, 1997.

————. "A Study of Black Politics and Protest in Depression-Decade Chicago, 1930–1939." Ph.D. dissertation, Kent State University, 1982.

Reeves, Andree E. *Congressional Committee Chairmen: Three Who Made an Evolution.* Lexington: University Press of Kentucky, 1993.

Richardson, Joe M. *Christian Reconstruction: The American Missionary Association and Southern Blacks, 1861–1890.* Athens: University of Georgia Press, 1986.

Robertson, David. *Sly and Able: A Political Biography of James F. Byrnes.* New York: W.W. Norton, 1994.

Roeder, George H. *The Censored War: American Visual Experiences During World War II.* New Haven, Conn.: Yale University Press, 1993.

Rogers, William Warren. "A Reconstruction Referendum in Southwest Georgia: Richard Whiteley Versus Gideon Wright in 1872." *Journal of Southwest Georgia History* 12 (2000): 1–17.

Rosengarten, Theodore. *All God's Dangers: The Life of Nate Shaw,* 2nd ed. New York: Vintage Books, 1989.

Ruchames, Louis. *Race, Jobs, and Politics: The Story of the FEPC.* Westport, Conn: Westport Universities Press, 1953.

Saunders, Doris E. "Black Politics and Chicago: The Bill Dawson Story." TS, Doris Saunders Papers, Vivian G. Harsh Research Collection, Carter G. Woodson Library, Chicago.

Savage, Sean J. *Roosevelt: The Party Leader, 1932–1945.* Lexington: University Press of Kentucky, 1991.

Schapsmeier, Edward L., and Frederick H. Schapsmeier. *Prophet in Politics: Henry A. Wallace and the War Years, 1940–1965.* Ames: Iowa State University Press, 1971.

Schmidt, John R. "William E. Dever: A Chicago Political Fable." In *The Mayors: The Chicago Political Tradition,* ed. Paul M. Green and Melvin G. Holli. Carbondale: Southern Illinois University Press, 1995.

Scott, Emett J. *Scott's Official History of the American Negro in the World War.* Chicago: Homewood Press, 1919. Available at www.lib.byu.edu/estu/wwi/comment/Scott/ScottTC.htm#contents. World War I Document Archive, Harold B. Library, Brigham Young University.

Simpson, Dick. *Rogues, Rebels, and Rubber Stamps: The Politics of the Chicago City Council from 1863 to the Present.* Boulder, Colo.: Westview Press, 2002.

Singh, Robert. *The Congressional Black Caucus: Racial Politics in the U.S. Congress.* Thousand Oaks, Calif.: Sage, 1988.

Sitkoff, Harvard. *A New Deal for Blacks: The Emergence of Civil Rights as a National Issue. Volume 1: The Depression Decade.* New York: Oxford University Press, 1978.

————. "Harry Truman and the Election of 1948, The Coming of Age of Civil Rights in American Politics." *Journal of Southern History* 37 (1971): 597–616.

"Just Who is Bishop Ford." Retrieved May 17, 2008, from http://thesixthward.blogspot.com/.

Soule, Sarah A. "Populism and Black Lynching in Georgia, 1890–1900." *Social Forces,* 71 (1992): 431–449.

Spear, Allan H. *Black Chicago: The Making of a Negro Ghetto, 1890–1920.* Chicago: University of Chicago Press, 1967.

Stern, Mark. "The Democratic Presidency and Voting Rights in the Second Reconstruction." In *Blacks in Southern Politics,* ed. Lawrence W. Moreland, Robert P. Steed, and Tod A. Bake. New York: Praeger, 1986.

Stone, Chuck. *Black Political Power in America.* New York: Dell, 1968.

Sugrue, Thomas J. "Crabgrass-Roots Politics: Race, Rights, and the Reaction Against Liberalism in the Urban north, 1940–1964." *Journal of American History* 82 (1995): 551–78.

Swain, Carol M. *Black Faces, Black Interests: The Representation of African Americans in Congress*. Cambridge, Mass.: Harvard University Press, 1997.

Tolchin, Susan, and Martin Tolchin. *To the Victor: Political Patronage From the Clubhouse to the White House*. New York: Random, 1971.

Travis, Dempsey J. *"Harold" The People's Mayor: An Authorized Biography of Mayor Harold Washington*. Chicago: Urban Research Press, 1989.

Trotter Joe W., and Earl Lewis, eds. *African-Americans in the Industrial Age: A Documentary History, 1915–1945*. Boston: Northeastern University Press, 1996.

Tuttle, William M., Jr. *Race Riot: Chicago in the Red Summer of 1919*. New York: Atheneum Books, 1970.

U.S. Congress. *Congressional Record: Proceedings and Debates*. 78th–84th Congresses. Vols. 89–116. Washington, D.C.: Government Printing Office, 1943–1967.

———. *Congressional Record Proceedings and Debates*. 79th, 84th, 85th, 86th Congresses. Index Vols. 101, 103, 104, 105, 107. Washington, D.C.:U.S. Government Printing Office, 1945. 1955, 1957, 1959, 1961.

Weems, Robert E., Jr. *Black Business in the Black Metropolis: The Chicago Metropolitan Assurance Company*. Bloomington: Indiana University Press, 1996.

Weisbrot, Robert. *Freedom Bound: A History of America's Civil Rights Movement*. New York: Penguin, 1991.

Weiss, Nancy. *Farewell to the Party of Lincoln: Black Politics in the Age of FDR*. Princeton, N.J.: Princeton University Press, 1983.

Wells, Ida B. *Selected Works of Ida B. Wells*. Compiled by Trudier Harris. New York: Oxford University Press, 1991.

White, Walter. *Rope and Faggot: A Biography of Judge Lynch*. Notre Dame, Ind.: University of Notre Dame Press, 2001.

Wilhoit, Frances. *The Politics of Massive Resistance*. New York: George Braziller, 1973.

Wilkins, Roy. *Standing Fast*. New York: Viking Press, 1982.

Wilson, George F., and J. Berger, eds. *Official Report of the Proceedings of the Democratic National Convention, held at Chicago, Illinois, July 19th to July 21st, inclusive, 1944, resulting in the re-nomination of Franklin D. Roosevelt of New York For President and the nomination of Harry S. Truman of Missouri For Vice-President*. Chicago: Publicity Division of the Democratic National Committee, 1944.

Wilson, James Q. *Negro Politics: The Search for Leadership*. New York: Free Press, 1960.

Wright, Richard. *American Hunger*. New York: Harper & Row, 1944.

Wynne, Lewis Nicholas and Milly St. Julien Vappie. "The Camilla Race Riot and the Failure of Reconstruction in Georgia." *Journal of South Georgia History* 16 (2004): 31–50.

INDEX

1st Congressional District Business and Professional Men's Club, 154
2nd Ward Advisory Council, 86
8th Illinois Infantry, 30
24th Infantry Battalion, 31
35th Division, 35
92nd Division, 31-35
93rd Division, 31
365th Regiment, 32-36
368th Division, 34-35
1919 Chicago Race Riot, 53–54
1949 National School Lunch Act, 132
1956 Federal Aid to Education Bill, 131

Abbot, Robert S., 27
Abner, Willoughby, 134
A Different World, 19
Airport Homes Riots, 105
Alabama Normal and Industrial Institute, 71
Albany Bible and Manual Institute, 17
Albany, Georgia, 12, 14–15, 18–19, 23–24, 36
Albany Normal, 16, 19–20
Albright, Joseph F., 96
Allen, George, 96
Allied Civic Clubs, 79
AME Church and Social Settlement, 26
America First Coalition, 63
American Federation of Labor, 86
American Missionary Association, 16, 19, 20
American Veterans Committee, 103
Americans for Democratic Action, 109–10, 131
Anderson, James, 19
Anderson, Louis, 28, 37, 62–65, 69, 72, 75, 76, 79, 80, 164, 167–68
Anderson, Marian, 82
Army Air Corps, 29
Army Corp of Engineers, 29
Army Field Artillery, 29
Arvey, Jacob M., 110
Assembly To End Prejudice, Injustice, and Poverty, 152, 155

Atlanta University, 18, 20–21

Bailey, Cleve, 132
Baker, Newton (Secretary of War), 30
Balance of Power, 108
Ballou, Charles C. (Major General), 30–31
Barnett, Ferdinand, 51–52, 57
Barnett, William, 83
Battle, John H., 133
Belafonte, Harry, 146
Berry, Edwin, 151
Best, Wallace, 26
Bethune, Mary McCleod, 104, 112
Bibb, Joseph, 69
Biemiller, Andrew, 109-110
Binga Bank, 26
Binga, Jesse, 26
"Birth of a Nation," 70
Black Cabinet, 112, 116
Black Dispatch, 125
Black Eight, 159
Black Independent Voters of Illinois, 161
Black, Timmuel, 155
Blackwell, Lee, 134
Blighted Areas Redevelopment and Relocation Act of 1947, 106
Bliss, Tasker (Major General), 31
Bodie, Louis, 156
Booker, Simeon, 7
Bourbonne-les-bains, Champagne-Ardenne, France, 33
Boston Riot, 17
Bowles, Chester, 143–44
Bowen, Chuck, 149, 150
Boyle, Robert, 121
Bullard, Robert (General), 35
Bunche, Ralph, 103
Bundesen, Herman, 76,
Butchart, Ronald E., 20
Bradley, Mamie, 138
Brest, Breton, France, 32
Brotherhood of Sleeping Car Porters, 69
Brown, Edgar G., 65, 85, 98
Brown, Thomas Jacob, 55–56

Brown vs. Topeka Board of Education, 129, 130–33, 135, 137, 139
Bruce, Herbert, 96, 125
Bullock, Henry, 20
Byrnes, James F., 94, 96–99, 167

Campbell, Kenneth, 152, 162
Capers, Jean Murrel, 115
Carey, Archibald, 26, 63,
Carey, Archibald, Jr., 107, 162
Carey's family, 24, 28
Carver, George Washington, 123–24
Cayton, Horace, 103
Celler, Emmanuel, 123, 133
Central Committee of College Negro Men, 30
Cermak, Anton, 67–69
Champaign-Urbana Courier, 122
Chatham-Avalon Council, 151
Chew, Charles, 6, 160, 168
Chicago Bee, 103
Chicago Citizens Committee of 1,000, 102
Chicago Conference to Fulfill These Rights, 153
Chicago Daily Herald, 78
Chicago Daily News, 147, 162
Chicago Defender, 27; *Defender* Vote Crusade, 107; Great Northern Drive, 51
Chicago Freedom Movement, 10, 68, 140, 152–53
Chicago Friends of the Student Nonviolent Coordinating Committee, 155
Chicago Housing Authority, 105–6, 148
Chicago Kent College of Law, 28
Chicago Real Estate Board, 79
Chicago Teachers College, 153–54
Chicago Title and Trust Company, 106
Chicago Tribune, 154
Chicago Transit Authority, 86
Chicago Urban League, 69, 80, 151
Chicago Whip, 69
Cicero, IL (race rioting), 125
Citizens School Committee, 151
Civil Rights Act of 1964, 157
Civil Rights Section (Kennedy Campaign), 144, 146
Civil War, 14, 27, 32, 110, 116
Clayton, Edward, 6
Cleveland Gazette, 103

Cole, Nat King, 146
Commonweal, 161
Communist Party USA (CPUSA), 69
Congress of Industrial Organizations, 90
Consolidated Tenants Association, 66, 77, 78, 80
Cook County Democratic Central Committee, 68
Cook County Physicians Association, 80
Coordinating Committee of Community Organizations, 151–52
Cooper, Richard, 151
Cosby, William, 19
Council of Negro Organizations, 80
Courtney, Thomas J., 79, 82
Cousins, William, Jr., 161
The Crisis, 73
Crosser, Robert, 115
Crummell, Alexander, 55
Cunningham, Emmett S., 96

Dallas Council of Negro Women, 117
Daley, Richard J., 5–6, 8, 10–11, 48, 119, 129, 136–37, 139, 144, 148, 149, 151–53, 156, 160–62, 165–66, 168
Daniel, Wilbur, 157
Daughters of the American Revolution, 82
Davis, Charles, 151
Davis, Corneal, 5, 9, 38, 58–60, 63-64, 67, 71, 76, 79–85, 87–88, 90–91, 101, 107, 112, 141, 160, 163–64, 168
Davis, John P., 111
Dawson, Barbara, 48
Dawson, Blanche, 18
Dawson, Janie, 16, 24, 28
Dawson, Julian Levi, 13, 16–18, 23–24, 28, 30–32, 34, 163
Dawson, Lee, 16
Dawson, Levi, I, 13
Dawson, Levi, II, 12–13, 15–18, 24, 163
Dawson, Nellie (nee Brown), 54–56, 65
Dawson, Rebecca, 12–13, 15–18, 163
Dawson, Wallace, 16, 94
Dawson, William Levi: 1944 Democratic Convention, 96–100; 1948 Democratic Convention, 109–10; 1952 Democratic Convention, 124–25; 1956 Democratic Convention, 133; 1960 Democratic Convention, 142–44; Community Development, 77–80; Congressio-

nal Civil Rights Legislation, 94, 96, 101–3, 152, 158; Dawson Plan for Education, 153; Dawson School of Business Management, 154, 162; Democratic National Committee, 5, 100, 103, 111, 119–21, 141, 167; House Committee on Government Operations, 5, 119, 120–21, 158 168; Housing (Chicago), 104–7; Military desegregation, 100, 101–2; OUTREACH Employment Program, 154; Patronage, 114–16; Postmaster General nomination, 147
Dawson, William Levi, 13
Depression, The, 68
DePriest, Oscar, 4, 9, 28, 37, 50, 52–54, 56, 57, 59, 61–62, 64–65, 69, 71, 72, 76–77, 79, 91, 164, 167–68
Despres, Leon, 129, 136–37, 161
DeValera, Eamon, 53
Dever, Paul, 132
Dever, Willaim E., 62
Dewey, Thomas, 96, 100, 104, 108, 109, 112, 125
Diagre, Bertel T., 152
Dickerson, Earl, 30–33, 60, 75, 82-85, 87–88, 93, 101
Dies Committee, 81, 94
Diggs, Charles, 130, 132–34, 144, 163, 166
Diggs, Olive, 160
Dittmer, John, 117
Dixiecrats. *See* States Rights Party
Dodson, Hattie Freeman, 134
"Don't Spend You Money Where You Can't Work Campaign," 69, 78
Double V Campaign, 100, 102
Dougherty County, Georgia, 14, 24
Douglass, Helen Gahagan, 45, 113
Drake, St. Clair, 103
Draft Dickerson for Congress Committee, 89
DuBois, W.E.B., 15, 20–21, 23, 26–27, 29
Dunbar, Paul Lawrence, 16, 21
Dunne, Edward, 62

Early, Stephen, 95
Eckstine, Billy, 146
Economic Opportunity Act, 154
Eisenhower, Dwight D., 125–26, 129–31, 134–36, 146
Elser, Max (Major), 35

Eleanor Roosevelt Club, 87
Equal Employment Opportunities Commission, 148
Executive Order 8802, 101

Fahy Committee (President's Committee on Civil Rights), 103, 108
Fair Employment Practices Committee, 95–96, 104, 109, 111, 121, 125
Farley, James, 71, 75
Faucett, Crystal Byrd, 96
Federal Housing Authority, 148
Fernwood Park Homes Riots, 128
Fields, A.N., 65
Field, Kenneth C., 151
First Great Migration, 51, 82
Fisk Herald, 21, 22–23, 30
Fisk University, 12, 18–24, 163
Ford, Henry Louis, 156
Fort Des Moines, 30–32
Fort Meade, Kansas, 32
Fort Riley, Kansas, 32
Frapelle, Vosges, France, 34
Free, James, 122
Freedman's Bureau, 14
Fuqua, Carl, 151

Gahagan, Helen, 45, 113
Gaines, Harris B., 63
Gaines, William, 90
Garvey, Marcus, 53
George, Albert B., 57–58
Georgia Equal Rights Association, 14
Gibson, Truman, Jr., 39, 83, 101–2
Gibson, Truman, Sr., 161–62
Gill, Joe, 128
Gill, Patsy, 13, 15–18
Grace Church, 28
Great Society, 11, 153, 156; Aid to Families With Dependent Children, 158; Social Security Act of 1967, 158
Gregg Memorial Church, 145
Gregory, Dick, 155–56
Greene, Percy, 112
Griffen Family (Chicago), 23

Hamill, Pete, 6
Hampton Institute, 20
Hannegan, Robert, 95-96, 98, 100
Harewood, Richard, 79

Harriman, Averell, 132
Harrison, Carter, II, 51, 62
Harvard University, 24, 163
Harvey, William, 93, 101, 107, 151, 161
Hastie, William, 40, 111, 116
Havenner, Franck, 122
Hayes, Brooks, 124
Hedgeman, Anna Arnold, 112, 116
Hoffman, Clare, 120
Holley, John Winthrop, 17, 18
Hollifield, Chet, 162
Holman, Claude, 119, 137, 152, 166
Hoover, Herbert, 71, 95
Horne, Lena, 146
Horner, Henry, 75, 76, 79, 80
Houston, Charles, 32,
Houston Riot, 31
Houston, William, 112
Howard, Donald and Betty, 128
Howard, T.R.M., 3, 137–39, 155
Howard University, 64, 111, 123
Howell, Brenetta, 154
Hubbard, Fred, 161, 162
Humphrey, Hubert, 109–10, 141, 142

Illinois Bell, 78
Illinois Commerce Commission, 106
Illinois Institute of Technology, 106
Independent Voters of Illinois, 155
Indritz, Phineas, 103
Institutional AME Church and Social
    Settlement, 26

Jackson Advocate, 3–4, 112
Jackson, Dan, 59–60, 63, 65
Jackson, Jesse, 161
Jackson, Mahalia, 3, 146, 163
Jackson, Maynard, 98
Jackson, Robert R., 28, 65, 70, 75–76, 86
Jarecki, Edmund, 79
Javits, Jacob, 123
Jefferson, Joseph, 77–78, 80
Jenkins, Charles, 101
Jitney Cabs, 7, 105–6, 126
Johnson, Lyndon, 133, 141–43,
    145–47, 157–58, 163, 166
Johnson, John "Mushmouth," 26
Johnson, John (Johnson Publishing),
    161–62
Jones, J. Raymond, 112
Junction City, Kansas, 32

Kelly, Edward (Mayor), 70, 75–77,
    79–80, 82–85, 87, 95-98, 105,
    127–28, 165
Keating, Kenneth, 123
Kendrick, Judge, 13
Kennedy, John F., 11, 119, 136,
    140–48, 152, 160, 166
Kennedy, Robert, 143–44, 156
Kennelly, Martin, 7, 93, 105–7, 119,
    126–29, 137, 165
Kent College of Law, 28
King, Corretta Scott, 146
King, Martin Luther, Jr., 42, 142–43,
    152–53
King, Martin Luther, Sr., 141
King, William E., 57, 63, 65, 72, 76,
    79, 80–83, 88, 90,
Klein, Arthur G., 94
Ku Klux Klan, 130

Lake Meadows Project, 106–7, 126
Landry, Lawrence, 155–56
Lane, Frayser T., 80
Lanier, R. O'Hara, 112
Lawless, T.K., 161
Leadership Conference on Civil
    Rights, 130
Leuder, Arthur C., 62
Lincoln, Abraham, 5, 81, 104
Lipscomb, Eugene "Big Daddy," 146
Louis, Joe, 70
Lucas, Scott, 113
Ludlow, Louis, 94

MacNeal, A.C., 69
MacNeal, T.D., 146
Madden, Martin, 3, 57–59, 60–61,
    63–64
Marbache offensive, 36
Marcantonio, Vito, 94, 150
March on Washington Movement,
    100, 111
Marine Corps, 29
Marshall Fields, 106
Martin, Louis, 6, 129, 138, 144, 146
Massiah, J.B., 26
Masaryk, Thomas, 53
McCormack, John, 93, 120, 132
McGrath, Howard, 111, 113, 121
Meharry Medical School, 21, 24, 123
Meredith, James, 155

Metcalfe, Ralph, 7, 146, 151, 153, 162, 168
Metropolitan Housing Committee, 106
Meuse Argonne Offensive, 35, 36
Michael Reese Hospital, 106
Michigan Chronicle, 103
Migration of the Talented Tenth, 25
Military Desegregation, 102–3
Miller, Kelly, 72
Mississippi Freedom Democratic Party, 3, 8, 157
Mitchell, Arthur, 70–77, 79–81, 85, 87–88, 90, 93
Mollinson, Irvin, 54, 116
Moon, Henry Lee, 8, 108
Moore, Herman, 54, 116
Morris, Edward H., 57
Morton, Thruston B., 147
Motion Pictures Operators' Union, 80
Moss, John, 133
Mothers on the Move Against Slums, 149
Moton, Robert Russa, 31
Mound Bayou, Misissippi, 3, 136
Multer, Abraham, 123
Murray, Esther, 109–10
Myrdal, Gunnar, 92

Nash, Pat, 68, 70, 79, 85, 87
National Alliance for Postal Workers, 58
National Association for the Advancement of Colored People, 6, 8, 30, 74, 82, 98, 100–1, 108, 110, 115, 122, 124, 130–32, 134
NAACP (Chicago Branch), 69, 100, 151
National Citizens Committee for the Reelection of President Truman, 111–12
National Colored Democrats Association, 88
National Council for a Permanent FEPC, 112
National Council of Negro Democrats, 88
National Defense Act of 1916, 29
National Guard, 29
National Medical Association, 26
National Negro Business League, 17, 26
National Negro Campaign, 98
National Negro Council, 102
National Recovery Act, 79
Negro American Labor Council, 155

Negro Industrial Relations Commission, 74
Negro Labor Relations League, 3, 78, 80
New Breed, 161
New Deal, 5, 10, 66, 70, 72–73, 80–82, 85, 87–88, 92, 96, 98, 100, 153, 163–64
New Jersey Times Herald, 125
New York Age, 103
New York Life Insurance Company, 106
New York Times, 122
Nixon, Richard M., 144–46, 159
Norris, B.F. (Major), 35
Northwestern University, 24, 28, 54
Norton, Mary T., 94

O'Brien, Thomas, 155
Office of War Mobilization, 95
Ohio 9th Infantry, 30
Old Settlers (Chicago), 25–26
Olivet Baptist Church, 28
O'Mahoney, Joseph, 133
Operation Breadbasket, 162

Parker, William, 69
Party Building, 4, 9, 10, 112, 119–20, 139, 140, 158, 160, 166, 167
Patronage, 114–16
Payne, Aaron, 57, 65
Payne, Ethel, 168
People's Movement, 61, 91
People's Voice, 89
Pershing, John J. (General), 35
Phalanx Club, 58
Philadelphia Afro-American, 103
Pickens, William, 74, 94, 179
Pickney, Joseph, 125
Pittsburgh Courier, 95, 100, 102
Policy Gambling, 7, 26–27, 126–28
Populist Movement, 14, 16
Powell, Adam Clayton, Jr., 86, 104, 122–23, 125, 131–35, 142–43, 166
Prattis, P.L., 146
Progressive Democrats, 98
Progressive Party, 108, 110
Protest at the Polls, 155
Provident Hospital, 24
Pullman Company, 26, 28

Raby, Albert, 155
Rainey, Julian, 75, 88

Randolph, A. Philip, 100, 102, 125, 142
Rankin, John E., 123, 124
Ransom, Reverdy, 95
Rayburn, Sam, 120, 134
Rayner, A.A. Sammy, 155–56, 161–62
Reconstruction (Congressional), 14, 33
Redding, Jack, 121
Reeves, Frank, 144
Regional Council of Negro Leadership, 3, 5, 117, 137
Restrictive Covenants, 26
Reuther, Walter, 133
Robert Taylor Homes, 148, 149
Roberts, Aldebert H., 58, 60, 63
Roberts, Chalmers, 147
Roosevelt, Eleanor, 103, 126, 133
Roosevelt, Franklin Delano, 66, 69, 72, 94, 96–99, 101, 103–4, 111, 116, 126, 145–46
Rostenkowski, Daniel, 121
Royko, Mike, 162
Russel, Richard, 142
Rustin, Bayard, 143

Saint Nazaire, Breton, France, 32
Sampson, Edith, 46, 116
Sarden, M. Earl (Reverend), 79
Saunders, Doris Evans, 36
Saunders, Warner, 7, 8, 163
Scott, C.A., 112
Scott, Emmett J., 36
Scribner, Dora, 23
Selective Service Act of 1917, 29
Sengstacke, John, 45, 107, 111–13, 161
Serritella, Daniel A., 59, 65
Shriver, Sargent, 141, 144
Simmons, Roscoe Conkling, 79, 81
Skyles, Charles M., 156
Small Business Administration, 154
Small, Len (Governor), 57, 59
Smith, T.V., 80
Smith vs. Allwright, 116
Sneed, Mike, 68, 70, 81
Social Service Roundtable, 80
Southern Christian Leadership Conference, 152
Southern Manifesto, 130
Southside Gardens Project, 79–80, 106
Sparkman, John, 124–25

Spraggs, Venice, 112
Springarn, Stephen, 111
St. Louis Argus, 103
Stamps, James, 20–21, 23
States Rights Party, 110–11, 125
Stevenson, Adlai, 11, 120, 124–26, 129, 130, 132–36, 142
Stimson, Henry, 102
Stone, Chuck, 7, 156
Streetcar Riots, 69
Sullivan, Roger, 61
Swift, George B., 52
Syndicate, The, 127–28

Talented-Tenth, 27
Talmadge, Eugene, 73
The Tenants' War Cry, 66
Thompson, William Hale, 53, 57, 59–61, 63–64, 67–69, 75–76; America's First Coalition, 63
Tift, Nelson, 14–15
Till, Emmett, 129, 134, 138
Tittinger, Joseph, 68, 70–73, 75–77, 79, 81–83, 85, 87, 91
To Secure These Rights, 108
Townsend, Willard, 88, 90
Trotter, William Monroe, 17
Truman, Harry S., 41, 98, 103, 108–14, 120, 124, 126, 132–33, 135, 145, 163
Turner, Paul E., 145
Tuskegee Institute, 31, 71

Union League Movement, 14
United Nations, 108
United States Department of Education, 153
Universal Military Training and Service Act, 122
Universal Negro Improvement Association, 53
University of Mississippi, 155

Vann, Robert L., 95
Vardaman, (Senator) James K., 30
Veterans' Administration, 123
Virginia Civil rights Organization, 116
Virgin Islands, 115–16, 121
Virgin Islands Corporation, 115
The Voice, 89

Voting Rights Act of 1965, 157
Wabash YMCA, 77–78
Wagner, Clarence, 129
Walcott, Jersey Joe, 146
Wall, Fred, 66, 78
Wallace, Henry, 94–95, 97–99, 103–4, 108, 110, 126, 167
Walton, Lester, 95
Warren, Earl, 109
Washington, Booker T., 17, 23, 26–27, 71, 123, 127
Washington, Harold, 168
Washington, S. Timothy, 79
Washington Afro-American, 103, 124
Washington Post, 147
Wells, Ida B., 26, 56, 63
White Citizens Councils, 130
White, Walter, 82, 98, 106, 112, 124–25
Whitman, Alden, 7
Wilberforce University, 21
Williams, Daniel Hale, 24, 26
Willis, Benjamin, 150–51, 154

Wilkie, Wendell, 88
Wilkins, Roy, 6, 130–32
Wilson, James Q., 7, 11, 30
Wimbish, Christopher, 5, 9, 30–31, 38, 63, 67, 70–71, 76, 79, 80–91, 93, 101, 107, 160, 163–64
Winstead, William, 122
Winstead Amendment, 122, 166
Wofford, Harris, 143–44, 146
Wood, Elizabeth, 105
Woods, Lawrence, 145, 160–62
Woodson, Carter G., 55, 95
World War I, 3, 8, 9, 12, 24, 28–36, 86, 163
World War II, 97, 101
Works Progress Administration, 77, 86
Wright, Edward, 4, 9, 28, 50, 52–53, 56–61, 63, 66, 90, 164, 167–68
Wright, R.R., 88

Young Mens' Christian Association (YMCA), 117
Young Womens' Christian Association (YWCA), 112